URBAN
AND
METROPOLITAN
ECONOMICS

URBAN AND METROPOLITAN ECONOMICS

John M. Levy

Virginia Polytechnic Institute and State University

With contributions by

James Bohland
W. David Conn
John W. Dickey
John R. Gist

Virginia Polytechnic Institute and State University

McGRAW-HILL BOOK COMPANY

New York   St. Louis   San Francisco   Auckland   Bogotá
Hamburg   Johannesburg   London   Madrid   Mexico   Montreal   New Delhi
Panama   Paris   São Paulo   Singapore   Sydney   Tokyo   Toronto

This book was set in Times Roman by Santype-Byrd.
The editors were Patricia A. Mitchell and Peggy Rehberger;
the production supervisor was Diane Renda.
The drawings were done by Burmar.
The cover was designed by Rafael Hernandez.
Halliday Lithograph Corporation was printer and binder.

URBAN AND METROPOLITAN ECONOMICS

2 3 4 5 6 7 8 9 0 HALHAL 8 9 8 7 6

ISBN 0-07-037455-4

Library of Congress Cataloging in Publication Data

Levy, John M.
    Urban and metropolitan economics.

    Includes bibliographical references and index.
    1. Urban economics. 2. Metropolitan areas—
Economic aspects. 3. Urbanization. I. Title.
HT321.L47 1985   330.9173'2   84-12603
ISBN 0-07-037455-4

To Bernard, Lucie,
Morris, Myrril,
and Rachel

CONTENTS

PART 2 PROBLEMS, POLICIES, AND PROSPECTS

PART 3   THE URBAN FUTURE

PREFACE

This is a text on the economics of cities and metropolitan areas. It is intended both for introductory and intermediate level undergraduate courses and for graduate urban economics courses taught in departments of urban planning, urban affairs, or public administration.

The level of treatment is such that a student with a modest background in economics should have no trouble following the discussion. Some more technical material on welfare economics, on the algebra of the export base model and its relationship to Keynesian models, and on the mathematics of input-output models is covered in the appendices. The instructor may decide to integrate these materials into the course or may easily take a more general and conceptual approach and bypass them.

The book is divided into two main sections followed by a wrap-up chapter. The first four chapters present a general view of urbanization and the urban economy. Specifically, Chapters 1 and 2 provide a general theory of urbanization and a description of the U.S. experience. Chapter 3 presents a description of the urban land-use pattern, developed in part from more general concepts such as the Ricardian theory of rent, which are explained in detail in the preceding chapters. Chapter 4, which is really the core chapter of the book, presents a detailed discussion of formal models of the urban economy.

Chapters 5 through 12 cover various subject areas. Chapter 5 on local economic development programs follows logically from the discussion of models in Chapter 4. After that, however, the sequence in which the subject area chapters are arranged is necessarily somewhat arbitrary. It can easily be rearranged to suit instructor or student preference.

Chapter 13, a discussion of the urban future, integrates and reviews much of the material covered earlier in the course. However, it might be taken up after Chapter 4. At that point the student will have the conceptual and historical background to understand the chapter and to think about some of the issues it raises.

The book presents much theory that is traditional in urban economics texts. As do most texts on the subject, it makes many linkages between urban economics and microeconomics. The reader who is versed in microeconomic theory will encounter numerous familiar figures and concepts. In fact, several topics have been included partly because they give students an opportunity to use microeconomic concepts they have presumably encountered in other courses. However, I do not take the view, as do a number of authors, that urban economics is simply a subfield of microeconomics. Rather, I regard it as a valid field in its own right though, admittedly, it owes a great debt to and makes much use of microeconomics. The book is written from that viewpoint.

This book differs from the traditional urban economics text in several ways. Throughout the text there is a consistent attempt to tie fact and theory to the practice of urban planning and urban governance. My experience in teaching both graduates and undergraduates is that students exhibit much interest in how things really work and in the practical uses of theory. I have therefore striven to satisfy that curiosity as much as possible. For example, the chapter on models of the urban economy describes traditional models in detail. However, it also contains considerable material on the uses of models, the data requirements of various types of models, and the pros and cons of different types of models. It provides the sort of material that students employed a few years from now in fields such as urban planning, municipal government, or community development will find useful.

Economic development programs are of interest to thousands of communities. The student headed for a career in planning, urban affairs, or public affairs is likely to have some professional involvement with the subject at one time or another. However, the topic is neglected in most urban economics texts. This book provides a detailed discussion of the subject in Chapter 5. The chapter covers several theoretical questions like the economic efficiency or inefficiency of subsidization and the "people versus places" issue. It also discusses the realities of intermunicipal economic competition and describes a number of commonly used development financing techniques.

Chapter 8 on public intervention in housing markets contains a far more detailed discussion of land-use controls than is customarily found in urban economics books. Given their near universal use in urban areas, I believe they deserve serious treatment in a book that addresses itself to public policy. Again, there is a blend of theoretical and practical questions. Thus, there is a discussion of externalities, of the optimality or suboptimality of controls, and of the effects of controls on land values and the pattern of land use. There is also a discussion of the practical, political, and legal realities of land-use controls. For example, the chapter describes fiscal and other motivations behind the use of land-use controls by suburban communities, and examines some of the strategies and tactics used by such communities.

Urban rent controls, a topic generally covered lightly or not at all in urban economics texts, is discussed in detail. The subject, a live issue in many municipalities, provides a good opportunity for the application of microeconomic theory to urban housing markets. Beyond the theory, however, Chapter 8 looks at the mechanisms used and at the empirical evidence of the effects of controls.

There is more emphasis on financial matters in this book than in most urban economics texts. For example, Chapter 7, includes a detailed discussion of topics such as mortgage lending, the tax treatment of owner occupied housing, the effects of leverage and inflation, and changes in housing finance in the early 1980s.

The financial emphasis is another attempt to make the text a realistic description of how things actually work. My experience has been that many students, even those who have had a number of economics courses, know little about how things are paid for. Yet they recognize the importance of the question and find it interesting.

Finally, the reader will note that one thread running through the entire book is the significance of technological change. All urban economics texts give at least some consideration to the effects of changes in technology on transportation and communications costs. In my view, however, the subject tends to be somewhat underemphasized. Perhaps this is because it does not fit easily into traditional models. However, it is central to our understanding of our present situation and to our thoughts about the urban future. I have therefore sought to give it the weight it deserves.

It is not possible to remember everyone to whom one becomes indebted in the preparation of a book of this sort. However, I would like to take note of a few individuals. Four of my colleagues at Virginia Tech, James Bohland, David Conn, John Dickey, and John Gist, took time out of crowded schedules to write guest chapters that strengthen the book by bringing in their considerable expertise in their particular fields.

Going back further, I owe some intellectual debt to several faculty members at New York University, specifically Dick Netzer in public finance, Emanuel Tobier in urban economics, and Ralph Kaminsky in microeconomics and public policy. At the same time that I was a part time graduate student at NYU, I was employed full time in various aspects of planning research and economic development for the Westchester County Planning Department in New York. During that time I had the chance to integrate theory and practice and to observe a little of how the world really works. In that connection, I am indebted to my former boss, the very able commissioner of that agency, Peter Eschweiler, and to the chairman of the Westchester County Planning Board, Dr. William Cassella.

Drafts of the book were reviewed for McGraw-Hill by Jerome Dasso, University of Oregon; Richard Fritz, University of Central Florida; Gerald McDougall, Wichita State University; David McKee, Kent State University; and Hugh Nourse, University of Georgia. I am indebted to them for their comments and support.

Finally, I would like to express my thanks to Professor Roger Riefler of the University of Nebraska who reviewed the entire manuscript at both the preliminary and the final draft stages. Numerous points in the text bear the imprint of his careful and perceptive review in regard to general direction, manner of presentation, and technical detail. One could not ask for a more competent and fair-minded reviewer than Professor Riefler. I might also note that writing a text is something of an exercise in deferred gratification, and one's morale can flag along the way. Professor Riefler's words of encouragement en route were much appreciated.

John M. Levy

PART **ONE**

URBANIZATION
AND THE URBAN ECONOMY

CHAPTER 1

URBAN GROWTH

In the mid-1970s demographers received the first inkling of a historic change in U.S. population patterns. For the first time in over a century the number of Americans moving out of metropolitan areas exceeded the number moving into them.[1] This change in net migration, confirmed when the results of the 1980 census became available, marks a turning point in a long and remarkable history of urbanization. In the period from 1800 to 1980 the urban population of the United States increased by a factor of roughly 500. The percent of the population living in urban areas rose from 6 percent to 70 percent. The population of the nation's largest metropolitan area rose from under 100,000 to about 17.5 million.

Within the history of U.S. urbanization we see three major phases: (1) a period in which urban areas grew both more populous and more densely developed; (2) a period in which urban populations continued to grow but in which densities at the center fell sharply; and, within the last decade, (3) a period in which the historic pattern of rural to urban migration has been reversed and in which the largest metropolitan areas, taken as a group, have ceased entirely to grow. At the turn of the century population, economic activities, and wealth were pouring into urban areas and reformers saw their major goal as being that of enabling people and jobs to move outward and so reduce the overwhelming congestion of the city. Urban Development Action Grants and Enterprise Zones designed to draw economic activities into central cities would have seemed like total madness to a turn-of-the-century urban reformer like Jacob Riis. Today planners and others concerned

---

[1] Even though net migration (moves in minus moves out) became negative in the early 1970s, substantial metropolitan growth continued to occur on the basis of natural increase (births minus deaths).

with the central city wonder how to stop the flight of jobs and people to suburbia or out of the metropolitan area entirely.

If we are to understand something about where we are, how we got here, and where we might be headed we must take a look backward. No purely economic interpretation will tell the whole story of urbanization, for there are many noneconomic reasons for the building of cities. The walls of ancient towns and the cathedrals of medieval cities suggest that at times safety and faith have been reasons for urbanization. Given that we humans need each other's company, there are, obviously, social and psychological forces behind urbanization. But much of the force behind urbanization has been economic and much can be explained in economic terms. Let us look at some of these forces and the history of the urbanization to which they have led.

THE LOGIC OF URBANIZATION

One way to begin is to consider a contrary-to-fact situation. What circumstances would have to prevail for it to be reasonable to expect that population would be distributed more or less homogeneously over the earth's surface? Let us assume a general line of argument articulated by Mills.[2]

1 Homogeneity of land. All parcels of land are, for practical purposes, identical except in their location. All differences of fertility, slope, natural resources, climate, etc., are eliminated.

2 Constant returns to scale prevail in all productive activities.

3 All labor is homogeneous and infinitely divisible. That is, all workers have the same skills, and there is no minimum amount of labor that may be hired.

4 The existence of economic man. People's behavior is rational and motivated by self-interest. We assume there is an abstraction called total utility which is made up of the utility that one's income can purchase minus the disutility of having to earn that income. We also assume that people will seek to maximize total utility.

Under the above assumptions there is no reason to believe that population will not be spread evenly. The assumptions about homogeneity of land, homogeneity of labor, and constant returns to scale suggest that there will be no grouping of people or productive facilities for purposes of production. The existence of a large factory, for example, is really testimony to the fact that production processes have increasing rather than constant returns to scale. If one worker could produce as much automobile working alone as by working in concert with 10,000 others, then we would not have automobile factories. The making of automobiles would be a cottage industry, just as the weaving of cloth once was. In point of fact, there are enormous economies of scale; therefore, we do have automobile factories.

What has been said about production could as well be said about extractive industries. We would not have large groups of people gathered in one place to engage in coal mining, for example, because our assumptions about the homoge-

[2] Edwin S. Mills, *Studies in the Structure of the Urban Economy*, Johns Hopkins, Baltimore, 1972, chap. 1.

neity of land and the lack of increasing returns to scale void the economic advantage for such concentrations. Nor would there be any need to locate coal mining where the coal miners live because we have assumed homogeneity of labor.

Under our assumptions regarding homogeneity of land, divisibility of labor, and lack of economies of scale any one individual would be able to produce any item or service as efficiently as any other. Thus there would be no need for specialization of labor. Without specialization of labor there would be no need for exchange. Thus markets as we know them would not exist.

In brief, then, we have pictured a world in which there is no reason to believe that concentration of population or economic activity will occur. In fact, we can further argue that if concentration did begin to occur, rising land costs in the gaining area and falling costs in the losing area would generate forces that would tend to restore the initial distribution.

The reader might ask at this point whether the simple desire to minimize transportation costs might not cause concentration. The answer, if we are to follow our reasoning rigidly and allow no other motivations than economic, is no. Or, perhaps more cautiously, not necessarily. For given all the other assumptions and ruling out all noneconomic motivations like the company of one's fellow human beings, we have shown no motivation to travel.

As soon as we relax any of the assumptions in the model, reasons for concentration become apparent. If we no longer postulate that land is homogeneous, then concentration for reasons having to do with the characteristics of land will appear. Coal miners will concentrate in some places and residents of beachfront condominiums in other places—all because of the heterogeneity of land.

If we relax the assumption about the homogeneity of labor, then certain types of activity may concentrate in areas where the right type of labor is available. Here, of course, we note that causality may run in both directions.

When we eliminate the assumption about constant returns to scale and replace it with the admission that increasing returns to scale exist, we have then made the case for specialization and the concentration of employment. Granting the obvious—that transportation to work takes time and money—the concentration of employment implies concentration of population.

In brief, as soon as we relax any of the four assumptions we have tacitly admitted that for any given area what is consumed may not be identical with what is produced. This implies the need for the movement of goods or workers, which in turn establishes the importance of transportation costs as a factor in location. Then, by noting that the clustering of activities will reduce transportation requirements, we can see that relaxing any of the four assumptions enables us to account for the grouping of population and economic activity.

THE ADVANTAGES OF SIZE

Those who have studied urbanization often place great weight on the question of economies of scale and a closely related idea, economies of agglomeration. We discuss these two ideas in the following paragraphs.

Economies of Scale

Economies of scale exist when increases in the scale, or size, of an operation produce more than proportionate increases in output. For example, if doubling all of the factors that go into the making of a product yields a more than twofold increase in output, then economies of scale exist in that size range. Another way to state the matter is that if costs per unit of land, labor, and capital remain constant, the marginal costs of production will fall as output rises. In other words, the increase in total costs in expanding production from n units to $n + 1$ units will be less than the increase in total costs that was experienced in expanding production from $n - 1$ units to n units.[3]

Historically, manufacturing has been a great creator of urban concentrations because of its major economies of scale. If large plants achieve lower unit costs than small plants, then competition will generally cause production to take place in a limited number of large plants. The large labor forces associated with large production facilities contribute to the development of large cities and large metropolitan areas.

To a great extent, the growth of cities in the western world has been a function of the growth of manufacturing. It is no coincidence that the spectacular growth of urban populations in the western world coincided with the industrial revolution. Table 1-1 shows that the rapid increase in the percentage of the U.S. population living in urban areas begins about 1840. This corresponds fairly closely to the real beginnings of industrialization in the United States—the period which the economic historian W. W. Rostow calls the "stage of economic takeoff."[4] Table 1-2 shows the growth of manufacturing in the same period.

Of course, economies of scale are not limited to manufacturing. The specialization of labor and the ability to spread capital costs across a larger operation create substantial economies of scale in other activities—in many aspects of transportation and goods handling, for instance. The department store and the shopping center are testimony to the existence of economies of scale in retailing. These may include savings on administrative costs, purchasing, advertising, and shared infrastructure like parking facilities, security, and the like. There are also some economies of scale in many service activities, for example, in education. In principle, it is no more difficult to give a lecture to 100 people than to 10. Similarly, it is presumably not that much more work to put on a play of equal quality before a large audience than before a small one. If one defines providing adequate library service as offering the patron a choice among a given number of titles, there are obvious economies of scale to be realized here. And so on.

Economies of Agglomeration

We have just noted the existence of economies of scale in manufacturing and other operations. Comparable economies may apply to urban places themselves.

---

[3] See any standard introductory text on economics for further discussion of economies of scale—for example, *Economics* by Paul Samuelson or *Economics* by Campbell McConnell.

[4] Walt Whitman Rostow, *The Stages of Economic Growth*, Cambridge University Press, Cambridge, England, 1971, p. 38.

TABLE 1-1
THE URBANIZATION OF THE UNITED STATES

Year	Total population (in thousands)	Urban population (in thousands)	Urban population as a percentage of total population
1800	5,297	322	6.1
1810	7,224	525	7.3
1820	9,618	693	7.2
1830	12,901	1,127	8.7
1840	17,120	1,845	10.8
1850	23,261	3,544	15.2
1860	31,513	6,217	19.7
1870	39,905	9,902	24.8
1880	50,262	14,130	28.1
1890	63,056	22,106	35.1
1900	76,094	30,160	39.6
1910	92,407	41,999	45.5
1920	106,461	54,158	50.9
1930	123,077	68,955	56.0
1940	131,954	74,424	56.4
1950	151,684	96,468	63.6
1960	179,323	125,269	69.9
1970	203,235	149,325	73.5
1980	226,505	166,965	73.7

Source: U. S. Bureau of the Census, *Statistical History of the United States*, and *U. S. Census of the Population*, 1960, 1970, and 1980.

These place-related—as distinct from industry-related—economies of scale are generally termed *agglomeration economies.*

Any economic activity must draw something from its environment. The firm, no matter how large, is dependent upon the economic and social infrastructure just as a plant is dependent upon the soil in which its roots are embedded. If firms cluster they can share a common infrastructure and reduce infrastructure costs by

TABLE 1-2
THE CHANGING COMPOSITION OF EMPLOYMENT
(In Thousands)

Year	Total employment	Agriculture	Manufacturing	Trade	Other
1800	1,900	1,400	—	—	100
1860	11,110	5,880	1,530	890	1,667
1880	17,390	8,920	3,290	1,930	3,122
1900	26,858	11,680	5,468	2,502	7,208
1920	38,224	10,702	10,702	4,012	12,720
1940	41,952	9,575	10,985	6,750	14,642
1950	52,382	7,160	15,241	9,386	20,595
1960	59,691	5,458	16,796	11,391	26,046
1970	78,627	3,566	20,737	14,996	39,327
1980	97,270	3,470	21,593	19,727	52,480

Note: Figures from 1800 to 1940 represent "gainful workers" regardless of whether they were actually employed.
Source: U.S. Bureau of the Census, *Historical Statistics of the United States, Colonial Times to 1957*, and *Statistical Abstract of the United States*, 1970, 1980.

spreading them over a large number of units. The infrastructure is supplied in part by government and in part by other firms. For example, roads and sewage disposal facilities are generally supplied by the public sector. Shared transportation facilities like railroad terminals and harbor facilities may be supplied publicly or privately. Since labor force quality is affected by education, the educational system of the area must be regarded as a major infrastructure component. To the extent that any commercial enterprise uses factors of production supplied by other firms, the rest of the business community constitutes part of the infrastructure. The labor force accumulated by the presence of many firms is in itself a shared resource. When the firm seeks to hire it draws from a pool of labor whose presence is largely due to other firms and public sector activity and whose skills have been partly acquired while working for other employers.

For a great many services that the firm requires, the cost of providing them internally is higher than the cost of purchasing them from specialized vendors. The corporate headquarters, for example, may require legal services, financial services, advertising and public relations services, and management consulting services, all of which are more efficiently furnished by firms specializing in these activities than by the corporation itself. Thus corporate headquarters are likely to be located in an area where these services can be found. In effect, a corporate headquarters shares its infrastructure with other firms, including competitors, and achieves an economy of scale in doing so. If there were no economies of scale in the provision of the factors of production, the firm could produce them itself as cheaply as it could buy them and the agglomeration economies would not exist. It is no coincidence that Manhattan, which still contains the largest concentration of corporate headquarters in the United States, also contains the nation's largest concentration of advertising and public relations firms, firms specializing in corporation law, etc.

The Industrial Complex   Localization economies, those economies which are external to the individual firm but internal to the industry, are a particular case of agglomeration economies. They go far in explaining why certain cities become specialized in particular industries. Very often, firms in the same industry can reduce their unit costs by grouping together. For example, by sharing a common labor pool each firm is able to benefit from skills and techniques workers have learned working for its competitors. To the extent that firms in the industry use various subcontractors, grouping may reduce costs. For if servicing a large number of firms enables a subcontractor to achieve economies of scale, then the firms themselves are likely to capture some of those economies in the form of lower supply prices (factor costs). Thus, even though firms may be in intense competition with each other, it may still be advantageous for them to group together.

The clustering of automobile manufacturers in Detroit and steel manufacturers in Pittsburgh originates in part from these localization economies. So, too, does the concentration of clothing manufacturers—an intensely competitive group—in New York's garment district. California's "Silicon Valley" is another example of localization economies. In this case the critical shared resource is a highly skilled and specialized labor force. The emerging genetic engineering industry appears to be grouping itself in several complexes near major universities or research institutes: one in and around Boston, another in the San Francisco Bay area, a third in the Rockville-Bethesda area in Maryland, and a fourth in the Denver area.[5] The firms are small and there may not be great economies of scale to be achieved within individual firms. There do not appear to be any particular physical resources that these firms need to share. But they do share a very skilled, very specialized, and highly educated labor force and a body of knowledge possessed by that labor force. The firm that isolates itself from these complexes might well have difficulty recruiting adequately trained personnel and staying current in this rapidly changing "high-tech" field.

SOME PRINCIPLES OF SIZE AND DENSITY

We have stated that the existence of economies of scale and agglomeration in the production of goods or services, coupled with the fact that transportation has time and monetary costs, can account for concentrations of population. Let us advance a few simple propositions. All of them are *ceteris paribus* (abbreviated *cet. par.*) statements. The qualifying phrase "all other things being equal" implicitly follows each one.

1 *The higher the transportation costs, the more densely population and activity will be clustered around central points.* The argument behind this proposition has two parts: (1) lower costs of transportation associated with more central locations will be capitalized in higher land costs, and (2) higher land costs will be reflected in greater densities of development. The first of these two points is a very old idea. It goes back at least as far as the early nineteenth century. Writing in an age when agriculture was the predominant economic activity, the English economist David Ricardo used the rents on agricultural land as his example.[6] Figure 1-1 illustrates Ricardo's argument.

Assume that in a given region there is a central point to which all agricultural products are delivered prior to sale, that the surrounding land is homogeneous in character, and that transportation costs per mile are the same in all directions. Assume also that farmers rent the land they till from a separate class of owners. The cost of producing a wagonload of produce is $160 (for labor, seed, normal return on investment, etc.), and it can be sold at the market for $200. Transportation costs $1 per mile per wagonload. At a distance of 40 miles from the market land rent would be zero, for at any positive rent farming will yield a net loss. At a distance of 39 miles, the farmer would be willing to pay up to $1 for the land required to produce one wagonload of produce; at 38 miles, $2; and so on until land rents reach $40 per acre at the center. Were the cost of transportation to be reduced to, say, 10 cents per mile, then land rents would not fall to zero until a distance of 400 miles rather than 40 miles, and the rent gradient would be only

---

[5] Survey by author, presented in "Economic and Social Factors Influencing Future Industrial Land Use in the U.S." at International Workshop on Technological Change and Urban Form, Waterloo, Ontario, July 1983. Publication forthcoming.

[6] This is only a small part of Ricardian rent theory. Ricardo also argued that differences in fertility of land were, in effect, capitalized in differences in rent. For a brief summary of early theories of land rent see William Alonso, *Location and Land Use*, Harvard University Press, Cambridge, 1964.

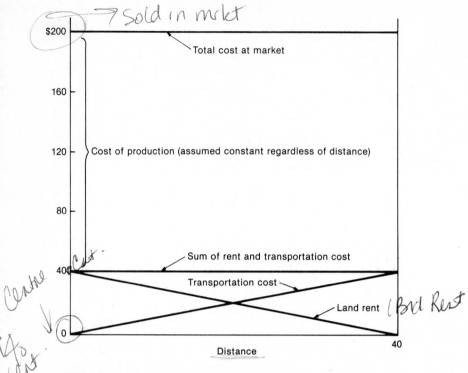

[handwritten annotations on figure: "→ Sold in mrkt", "Centre", "$ to rent", "Cost", "(Brd Rent"]

FIGURE 1-1
The Ricardian theory of land rent. In this example it is assumed that the cost of production for a wagonload of produce is $160, the transportation cost is $1 per mile, and the selling price at market is $200. Land rent falls from $40 at market to $0 at a distance of 40 miles, while transportation costs move oppositely. As shown, the sum of the land rent and the transportation costs is constant. The model assumes that all produce will be delivered to a central marketplace, a homogeneous transportation surface, constant production costs at all points, homogeneity of land, and a competitive market in land rental.

one-tenth as steep. Were there no costs associated with transportation, the gradient would disappear and land close in would rent for no more than distant land.

Once we grant that a land-rent or land-price gradient will exist, differences in density of development follow from it. If land is a factor in the production of any good or service (housing, manufacturing, recreation, etc.), then the higher its price the less it will be used in proportion to other factors. This is simply to say that land will be used to the point at which its marginal revenue product equals its cost, and the higher its cost the sooner that point will be reached. Thus if land costs several thousand dollars per acre it might be combined with the other factors of residential construction at the rate of, say, one dwelling unit per acre to produce low-density single-family housing. If it costs several hundred thousand dollars per acre it may be combined with the other factors of housing construction at the rate of 1/100 of an acre per dwelling unit to produce high-rise apartments.

We need not adhere to the rigid assumptions of the Ricardo illustration to be convinced that proximity will be capitalized in higher land prices or higher land rents. And, in fact, in large metropolitan areas such as Washington, D.C., or New York City the per acre price of land does range from some millions per acre at the most central points to thousands or hundreds at the periphery. If construction costs alone are considered, there are diseconomies of scale in building high-rises (space lost to elevator shafts, heavier structural members to bear the weight of additional stories, etc.). Quite evidently, then, there is a positive relationship between the cost of land and the height of buildings as evidenced in the downtown area of almost every major city. Land varies in quality (slope, soil characteristics, etc.), in accessibility to transportation facilities, in closeness to various subcenters, and in proximity to other land uses that may impose positive or negative externalities. Thus the land-price surface will be far more complex than the continuous gradient discussed before. But the essential idea of the capitalization of transportation cost savings in land prices remains intact.

2 *The greater the population of an urbanized place, the higher densities will be at any given distance from the center.* The greater value of a more central location arises from the savings in transportation costs. If the difference in land values between points is the capitalized travel cost differential, then—all other things being equal—the greater the number of travelers the higher should be the maximum point of the land-price gradient. The higher land prices, on the basis of the argument developed under the preceding point, should lead to higher densities.

3 *The more pronounced and widespread the economies of scale in the production of goods and the provision of services, the more uneven the distribution of population and employment is likely to be.* This is equivalent to saying that as economies of scale increase, the number of locations at which the activity in question will be found will decrease. Figure 1-2 illustrates the argument. For plants A, B, and C the unit costs of production are represented by vertical lines. The total cost of delivering the product at a given point is the cost of production plus the cost of transportation. The latter increases with distance and so is shown as an upward sloping line. The points at which the lines intersect are the competition frontiers; each plant has a cost advantage inside its own frontier and a cost disadvantage outside its own frontier.[7] In a competitive situation the market will be divided among the three plants at the frontiers, as shown in Figure 1-2(*a*).

Assume that the production of the product is characterized by economies of scale and that plant A is able to expand, take advantage of these economies, and reduce its unit costs. Figure 1-2(*b*) shows this situation; plant B has been eliminated from the market and the competition frontier between plants A and C is relatively distant from A and close to C.

Assume that A expands a second time, achieving further economies of scale and thus a further reduction of unit costs. This situation is shown in Figure 1-2(c); plant A is able to undersell plant C at any point and capture the entire market. Thus, given a particular structure of transportation costs, the more prone the

---

[7] For further discussion of competition frontiers see William Alonso, "Location Theory," reprinted in *Regional Analysis*, L. Needleman (ed), Penguin, London, 1968.

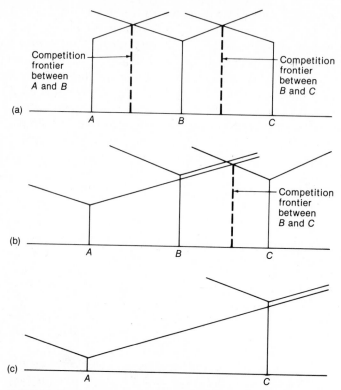

FIGURE 1-2
Economies of scale and the number of producers. The vertical lines indicate production costs per unit, and the sloping lines indicate transportation costs rising with the distance from the point of production. (*a*) Unit production costs are the same for all three plants, with the result that the competition frontiers are equidistant between firms. (*b*) Plant A has achieved economies of scale that permit it to undersell plant B at any location. The only remaining competition frontier lies between A and C. (*c*) Plant B is gone, and plant A has lowered its unit costs again and can now undersell plant C at any location.

product to economies of scale, the fewer will be the locations at which it is produced.

If we postulate continuously declining marginal costs and zero transportation costs, then all production of any product in question should occur at a single point. If the effect of economies of scale is overwhelming in regard to transportation costs (of both materials to the site and products to customers), we might also expect all production to occur at a single point. And while it is hard to name any industry for which this is literally true, there are a number of industries for which it is approached very closely—airliners and diesel locomotives, for example.

4 *The more pronounced the economies of agglomeration, the fewer will be the number of urban centers for a given population and land area.* The argument for this point is essentially the same as for the preceding point. If economies of agglomeration are great, large places will be able to extend their dominance a greater distance than small places. This is analogous to the previous argument that if economies of scale in production are large, they will make up for more transportation costs and hence extend the competition frontier further than if they were small. The slowing of the growth of the largest metropolitan areas in the mid- and late twentieth century, a point discussed in more detail in the next chapter, may be due in part to the effects of modern communications and transportation technology, which have diminished the agglomeration advantages of very large places.

The Urban Hierarchy

The concept of economies of scale also leads to another concept—that of the urban hierarchy. Economies of scale exist in virtually every enterprise up to some point. Even in an activity that can be done as efficiently by a single person as by many people, economies of scale exist out to the point where the volume of production is sufficient to occupy one person full-time. This suggests that for virtually any activity there exists some minimal market size for lowest-unit-cost operation. For any operation marginal costs—and hence average costs—fall until some finite scale of activity is reached. If this is so, it is reasonable to believe that there will be a tendency for activities of a more specialized nature to collect in places where markets are larger. For example, a town with a population of 5000 may have several attorneys who handle wills, divorces, and real estate closings. It is unlikely to have attorneys who handle corporate law, for it is unlikely that the town market can keep even one such attorney occupied full-time. It is still less likely that such a town would contain a patent attorney or an attorney who specializes in international or maritime law. Thus even if all of these types of law involved no economies of scale—an unlikely circumstance in view of the amount of specialized knowledge involved—the more specialized the practice was, the more that type of practice would be concentrated in large places.

Generalizing the above argument, the smallest place will contain a very limited range of services. These will be ones used by a large proportion of the population and in which great economies of scale do not prevail. Thus even a small population will generate enough activity to make the provision of service practical. As place size grows the range of services contained within it will grow. In general, all of those activities contained in smaller places will be present, as well as some activities which are not present in smaller places. Thus the very specialization of economic activity suggests the evolution of variety of size in urban places. Obviously, there are other causes as well. But even on the flat, featureless plain beloved by location theorists, the concepts of economy of scale and specialization of activity are sufficient to make the case for the concept of urban hierarchy. To state it very briefly, if a product or service achieves most of its economies of scale at a relatively small level of operation and if it is purchased by a significantly large percentage of the business or residential population, we would expect it to be more or less ubiquitously distributed. If the reverse is true, we would expect it to be found only in higher centers. There will always be exceptions based on historic accident, the location of particular natural resources, climatic or topographic considerations, etc. But, on balance, this proposition will be true more often than not.[8]

The concept of urban hierarchy casts a certain amount of doubt on the usefulness of the concept of optimal city size (see Chapter 10). Even if there is a city size which is optimal for delivering a given package of services at minimum per capita cost, the logic behind the concept of urban hierarchy suggests that a range of city sizes must exist for a system of cities to produce maximum output from a given set of factors.

Diseconomies of Scale and Agglomeration

So far, we have identified a group of powerful forces tending to create both large agglomerations of people and economic activities and high densities within these agglomerations. Can we identify countervailing forces that limit the total size or the maximum densities of urban places in them? To push the matter to an extreme point, what prevents the entire urban population of the United States from being concentrated in a single vast urban complex of, say, 175 million people—an agglomeration containing roughly ten times the population of the New York metropolitan area? Obviously there are some matters of taste and psychology here. Many would find it oppressive, aliening, and confining. Most people have some feeling for the natural world and would find themselves unhappy at being as separated from it as such an agglomeration would suggest. But we can also point to other clear-cut economic forces that limit the urban size and density.

Location of Raw Materials   Turning to the first point, we note that even though the percent of the population employed in agriculture and extractive industries has been declining over time, it is still substantial. In many instances it makes sense for productive processes to be near raw materials. In a situation in which raw materials from one place are processed and made into a product that is sold at another point, processing will most likely be done either where materials are extracted or where the finished product is to be sold. An intermediate location is less likely because it necessarily implies another set of *terminal*, or loading and unloading, costs.

The terms *weight losing* and *weight gaining* are frequently used in this connection. They refer to the weight of the final product compared to the raw materials which go into it. The making of steel for example, is a weight-losing process. Several tons of ore and coke are used to make one ton of steel. If the cost of production itself is the same at various locations, then the costs of transportation will determine the point at which production does occur. For weight-losing processes these will generally be lowest if production is located close to the source of raw materials. In point of fact, most production processes which begin with extractive industry or agricultural products are weight-losing. Thus the distribution of agriculturally productive land, forested areas, and mineral resources has a powerful effect on the distribution of urban populations. In the case of two raw materials originating in different places and a single market for the

---

[8] For a detailed discussion of the concept of urban hierarchy see Peter Haggett, Andrew Cliff, and Allen Frey, *Locational Analysis in Human Geography*, Wiley, New York, 1977.

finished product, the situation is somewhat more complicated. But, in general, if the process is weight-losing, transportation costs will tend to pull the process toward the source of the raw materials.

Congestion Costs In a large place the most noticeable diseconomy of scale is likely to be congestion. Casual strollers on the streets of New York City's garment district may realize that they are moving faster than the trucks in the street. The garment manufacturer pays for this slowness with increased shipping costs. One consultant, writing on the future of the Manhattan office-space market a few years ago, noted that in many parts of the nation normal business hours are 8 to 5 but in New York they are 9 to 5, a difference which he described as a "concession" to the typically long commutes of Manhattan office workers. The shorter workday is a diseconomy of agglomeration, which employers experience as a higher unit labor cost and perceive as a drawback to that location when they consider questions of expansion or relocation.

For reasons discussed earlier, at any given distance from the center land prices are likely to be higher in a large metropolitan area than a small one. High land prices will be reflected in both increased housing costs and smaller amounts of land per housing unit. The same consultant's report mentioned the cost of housing in the New York suburbs as a disadvantage of a Manhattan location because of the higher salaries necessary to induce professional and managerial workers in non-New York locations to move to New York.

The Cost of Public Services Another diseconomy is to be found in the area of public services. As discussed in detail in Chapter 9, there appears to be a U-shaped cost curve when per capita costs are plotted on the vertical axis and population on the horizontal axis. The U shape is simply a graphical expression of the fact that up to some point economies of scale predominate, but past that point diseconomies of scale predominate. At least two reasons for the appearance of diseconomies of scale can readily be found:

1 Some services will cost more per capita in a large area than in a small area.
2 Some services that are not necessary in small places will be necessary in large places.

As an example, consider the disposal of solid waste. In a small place, solid waste may be trucked several miles and deposited in a landfill operation on relatively cheap land. In a larger place refuse may have to be trucked several times as far and disposed of in a landfill operation on more expensive land. Or, in a larger place, the landfill option may not be feasible, and some more expensive form of disposal such as incineration or long-distance rail haul may be required. A small place may be able to dispose of its sewage with only primary treatment, while a larger place with a large volume to dispose of may need secondary or tertiary treatment at several times the per unit cost.

Some services that are required in larger places are not needed in smaller places. For example, professional fire protection is a must in a densely developed area but less dense areas often get by quite well with a volunteer company. In a less dense or smaller place the parking problem may be adequately dealt with by meters and white lines on the ground, whereas in a larger place parking structures at construction costs of, say, $5000 per vehicle are needed.[9] A much more complete system of public transportation is needed in larger places. Virtually every public transportation system in the United States runs at a deficit (see Chapter 9). At least part of that deficit is covered by municipal funds, a fact which the firm and the resident sense through their tax bills.

In brief, then, we can readily see a number of diseconomies that attach both to size and to density. These counterbalance those agglomerating forces noted earlier, with the actual size and density of urban areas resulting from these conflicting forces. The situation is made more complex by the very durability of the built environment. Thus the distribution of urban development may reflect these forces as they operated in the past, not as they now are. In fact, much of distress of urban places is a result of this lack of correspondence, a matter to which we shall return at a number of points.

THE LOCATION OF CITIES

In any study of the forces behind urbanization we should briefly consider the question of where major urban agglomerations form. A glance at a map of the United States—or Europe, for that matter—would reveal that most of the great cities of the world have developed at transshipment points. These are points at which a change in the mode of transportation occurs and thus goods must be unloaded and then reloaded. Most of the great cities of the eastern United States—New York, Boston, Philadelphia—are port cities. For the most part the great inland cities are located either on major navigable rivers—St. Louis, New Orleans—or on the Great Lakes—Chicago, Detroit, Cleveland, Buffalo. In the western states the situation is repeated with San Francisco, Oakland, Los Angeles, and Seattle—all port cities. Among inland cities that are not on rivers or lakes the origin or the predominance of the city can sometimes be traced to a time in its history when it was a major transshipment point—for instance, a point at which a railroad ended.

Why is it that being a transshipment point so often gives a city a significant growth advantage? The most important reason pertains to costs, as illustrated in Figure 1-3. Assume, for example, that raw materials produced or assembled at point A are ultimately to appear as finished products at point C and that they must go, whether in finished or raw form, through point B. Perhaps they travel from A to B by rail and from B to C by ship. Somewhere, either at A or at C or at some point in between, the raw materials must be processed into the finished product. The minimum possible transportation costs will be composed of the following:

1 Loading at A
2 Transportation from A to B
3 Unloading at B (from the first mode)
4 Loading at B (to the second mode)
5 Transportation from B to C
6 Unloading at C

[9] This is a typical cost for 1980. See *Means Cost System*, R. S. Means, Duxbury, Mass, 1980.

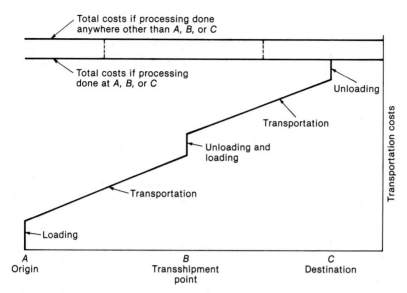

FIGURE 1-3
Transportation costs and transshipment points. This figure shows transportation costs, including terminal costs through a transshipment point. If processing is done anywhere en route other than at A, B, or C, an additional set of unloading and loading costs are incurred. These additional costs are represented by the broken lines between the two horizontal lines at the top of the figure. *[Adapted from W. Alonso, in J. Friedman and W. Alonso (eds.),* Regional Development and Planning: A Reader, *MIT Press, Cambridge, 1964.]*

This assumes that processing will be done at either A, B, or C. If processing is done anywhere else, say, at some point between A and B, then another set of loading and unloading costs must be incurred. If we know nothing of the product we cannot say where it will be processed. But it is highly likely that it will be processed at either A, B, or C.

Let us now assume that there are a number of originating points (A^1, A^2, etc.) and, similarly, a number of destinations (C^1, C^2, etc.) but that there is only one transshipment point (B). If for any combination of raw materials and product there is an equal probability that processing will be done at the origin, the transshipment point, or the destination, then on a purely probabilistic basis more processing will be done at B than at any other point.

For example, because of its location at the eastern end of Lake Erie it was natural for Buffalo to become a major grain transshipment point. Grain produced at numerous points in the midwest was shipped by water to Buffalo and then shipped by other modes to various points east. Because grain had to be unloaded at Buffalo it made sense for processing to be done there. Thus geography made the city a transshipment point and indirectly led to the development of a major milling and processing industry as well.

The foregoing is sufficient by itself to demonstrate that transshipment points will be the sites of many of a nation's or area's major cities. But the matter can be pursued slightly further. If a port or transshipment point processes more of a particular raw material than competing places, it has more opportunity to exploit economies of scale and gain a cost advantage over other places. This will increase the probability of its getting further processing business, thus setting in motion a cumulative, or positive-feedback, process that will accentuate the original advantage until the port becomes predominant in that activity.

Finally, if an area is a transshipment point this in itself implies jobs and revenues coming from the very acts of cargo handling. The additional economic mass that the cargo-handling activity gives to the local economy may produce economies of agglomeration, which manifest themselves in lower costs and increased competitiveness over a wide range of activities. The buying power coming from the earnings of dock workers, railroad employees, shipping executives, etc., may help to build up a larger and more varied retail establishment, which will draw customers from other towns or cities. The larger retailing establishment may then stimulate the development of a larger wholesaling sector, enabling the city to gain an edge over competing cities in this regard. The legal activity connected with shipping contracts and maritime law may build the size and expertise of the city's law firms, which then enables them to compete more successfully for legal business quite unrelated to shipping and transportation. The argument could be extended *ad infinitum*.

THE URBANIZATION OF AMERICA IN THE NINETEENTH CENTURY

Having established some general explanation for the existence and growth of cities, let us turn to the urbanization of the United States. We will discuss nineteenth-century trends here and pursue twentieth-century events in the following chapter. One of the striking developments of the nineteenth century was the massive urbanization. The urban population of the United States went from about 300,000 in 1800 to about 30 million in 1900—a hundredfold increase. In 1800 about 6 percent of the U.S. population lived in urban areas. By 1900 the figure had risen to almost 40 percent. In the course of an entire century the urban population grew at a compounded annual rate of almost 5 percent, compared to a compounded rate of 2.4 percent for total population.

Not only did the number of urban areas increase greatly, but the population of individual places increased enormously. In 1800, New York City, the nation's largest city, contained under 100,000 inhabitants. By 1900 it contained about 3.4 million. Population densities also increased spectacularly. Manhattan Island, the most densely populated political subdivision of the country then, as now, contained slightly over 2 million people on roughly 22 square miles, a density of over 90,000 per square mile. In the Lower East Side (the most congested part of the city) population densities in some wards rose as high as half a million people per square mile.[10] Such a density is hard to visualize. If the State of Connecticut were populated at such a density it would contain roughly the present population of the world.

---

[10] Adna Weber, *The Growth of Cities in the 19th Century*, 1899, Columbia University Press, New York, 1965, p. 460.

Obviously the forces behind urbanization were enormous, and they bear some looking into if we are to understand why we have arrived at our present state and where we are likely to be going. The process of overwhelming significance in the urbanization of America, as well as the urbanization of Europe, was the industrial revolution. It began in England, where much of its early technology was developed and where the capital and the economic and political freedom necessary for its beginning existed. Technology diffused more slowly then than now, and the next country in which it appeared was France, about half a century later. It made its appearance shortly thereafter in the United States, and throughout the remainder of the century it appeared in one European country after another. The economic historian W. W. Rostow breaks economic growth up into a number of stages and defines that stage at which industrialization is clearly and irreversibly underway as the stage of "economic takeoff." He dates this stage for a number of countries as indicated below:

Nation	Stage of "Economic Takeoff"
United Kingdom	1780–1800
France	1830–1860
Belgium	1830–1860
United States	1840–1860
Germany	1850–1870
Sweden	1870–1890
Russia	1890–1910

Although every country's history with regard to industrialization and its effects is somewhat different, some common elements are present. One profound effect is simply population growth. Most of the countries of western and central Europe entered the industrial revolution in a condition of slow growth, with fairly high birthrates counterbalanced by fairly high death rates. Increases in food supply and improved living conditions cut death rates, while fertility remained high for several generations. The result was a long period in which natural increase (births minus deaths) was rapid. In most cases population more than doubled in the course of the century. Thus population increased more in one century than it did from the beginning of the human race to the year 1800. In the case of virtually all European countries the increases took place in spite of net outmigration (moves in minus moves out) to the new world.

A second effect was the mechanization of agriculture, which reduced the amount of labor needed to produce a given amount of food. This falling percentage, combined with large absolute increases in population, produced an even more rapid increase in the actual or potential urban population.

A third effect was the introduction into the economy of large amounts of manufacturing activity characterized by significant economies of scale. The weaver working at home was replaced by the textile mill employing hundreds or even thousands of workers; the blacksmith was replaced by the foundry; the self-employed, home-based tailor was replaced by the massed labor force of a garment factory; and so on. As economies of scale produced productive processes involving thousands of employees, the need for administration rose, and the growth of factories was followed by the growth of massive administrative and clerical staffs. The increased flow of goods in turn also led to the need for massive retailing establishments. Thus the department store is as much the product of industrial technology as the factory itself. All of these developments have in common the creation of points at which mass labor forces, whether of laborers or mechanics, bookkeepers or sales clerks, are required—a phenomenon that had never been seen before on a comparable scale.

Virtually every country in Europe experienced a massive growth in urban population in the nineteenth century. In general growth was more rapid in those countries in which industrialization had proceeded farthest. Both the total population and the density of urban areas rose.

In the United States the phenomenon was similar, though there were a few key differences. As the country was settled new urban areas were created, whereas in Europe virtually all urban population growth was absorbed in existing urban centers. A second difference was that in the United States population growth was much more rapid, and hence the number of people to be urbanized was much greater. The difference in population growth was due partly to more rapid natural increase in the United States and partly to net inmigration.[11] Immigration was fostered by the mechanization of European agriculture and the population growth associated with the industrial revolution. It was greatly facilitated by improvements in transportation made possible by the mechanical technology of the industrial revolution. Up to about 1840 all immigrants to the United States from Europe arrived by sailing ship. The trip was relatively expensive and took a month or more—an ordeal not to be contemplated lightly. Most of the service was from northern Europe, the destination of most United States exports. Ships sailed from the United States carrying argricultural and forest products and returned carrying manufactured goods and immigrants. For most of the population of southern Europe immigration to the United States was not an option. With the beginning of transatlantic service by steamer in the mid-nineteenth century the potential for immigration to the United States increased tremendously. The costs and time of passage fell sharply, increasing the flow of immigrants from northern Europe and at the same time opening up the United States to immigration from southern Europe. Both the changing composition and the increased volume of the immigrant population in the second half of the nineteenth century reflect this change in transportation technology.[12]

The primary forces behind urbanization of the United States in the nineteenth

---

[11] The U.S. rate of natural increase in the nineteenth century is among the highest ever recorded for any nation. See Simon Kuznets, *Modern Economic Growth*, Yale University Press, New Haven, 1966. Immigration averaged about 200,000 per year across the nineteenth century, with very large rate increases in the midcentury and the largest absolute figures reached at the end of the century. See the section on immigration and naturalization in the *Statistical Abstract of the United States* for annual and decade figures.

[12] For a discussion of this point, as well a general history of the immigration of various groups, see Thomas Sowell, *Ethnic America*, Basic Books, New York, 1981.

century can be summed up as follows:

1 Rapid population growth, resulting from high rates of natural increase and massive immigration

2 Development of production, distribution, and administrative processes requiring mass labor forces

3 Increased mechanization of agriculture, resulting in the freeing of labor for nonagricultural pursuits

Granted that the forces described were bound to produce a period of rapid urbanization, let us quickly look at some of the factors shaping that urbanization. These forces are primarily technological, for technology shapes the structure of costs and in a competitive economy costs will determine in large measure what can and cannot be done.

Technology and Urban Form in the Nineteenth Century

At the beginning of the nineteenth century water transportation was cheap and overland transportation was expensive. A sailing vessel carrying several hundred tons of freight, crewed by two or three dozen men and traveling 100 miles per day might produce approximately 1000 ton-miles per crew member per day.[13] By contrast, a man with a wagon and a team of horses might produce a dozen or so ton-miles in a day. The obvious effect of this disparity in costs was to concentrate urban development at points with water access and to cause activities within the urban area to cluster very closely about waterfronts. The great age of canal building in the United States—roughly 1800 to 1830—was an attempt to obtain the cost advantages of water transport in inland areas. The canal-building era ended abruptly with the development of railroad technology. From then on there were two cheap modes for the transportation of freight—rail and water—and one expensive mode—horse and wagon.

Thus the economic force behind and clustering of productive activity at sites having rail or water access was enormous. An ideal location was the sort that prevailed in lower Manhattan. On the west side of the island were piers and wharves, while several blocks to the east were railroad tracks leading to upstate New York and from there westward. The space between was a favored area for the location of manufacturing and wholesaling. Goods or raw materials could be shipped from, say, Chicago to London making all but a few hundred yards of the trip by low-cost modes.

At the same time that the economics of freight transportation tended to pile up activity at railroads and waterfronts, the economics of human transportation tended to produce huge concentrations of housing in close proximity to workplaces. The overwhelming majority of workers walked to work. Thus the transportation technology of the time and the economic forces that it dictated

---

[13] As an example, in 1816 the cost of shipping corn overland to Philadelphia for a distance of 136 miles was equal to its market price. This cost was about 10 times that for shipment by canal boat a few years later, which, in turn, was substantially higher than the cost of shipment by coastal sailing vessel. See Alan Pred, *City Systems in Advanced Economies*, Wiley, New York, 1977, p. 66.

tended to produce a city center with dense concentration of industry, surrounded by high-density residential development.

> The residence of the worker in New York City and other large industrial cities in the United States in 1850 was frequently the "railroad flat," a walk-up structure that was generally five to seven stories high, 25 feet wide and 75 feet long on a 25 by 100 foot lot. Constructed solidly in rows across entire block faces, these units had four apartments on each floor surrounding a central common staircase. The rooms in these apartments were constructed in tandem, with just one room in each apartment provided with a window or two for light and air. No sanitary facilities or water supply were provided for in these structures. The small rear yard contained a multiseat outhouse and often a well, resulting in deplorable conditions of sanitation and public health.[14]

Thus on a plot of land roughly 2500 square feet in area (about 1/17 of an acre) might stand a structure with 20 or more apartments housing a population of 100 or more. Adjacent to it with no separation at all might be another such structure. As urban growth continued, the more open and gracious pattern of development of the preindustrial age was overwhelmed by the economic and demographic pressures of the nineteenth century.

The Beginnings of Decentralization and Suburbanization

Until about 1880 it is hard to see any forces seriously opposing the increasing concentration of people in cities and the increase in the density of urban development. But about this time the picture became somewhat more mixed. On the one hand the basic forces behind increasing size—growth of manufacturing and immigration from Europe—continued unabated. To add to these effects, two new technologies, both favoring higher densities, appeared shortly after the American Civil War. These were steel-frame construction and the elevator. Respectively, they made the skyscraper physically and economically possible. Thus the ability to crowd workers into central areas was increased. However, decentralizing technologies began to appear at the same time. Again, shortly after the Civil War the horse-drawn trolley appeared. It was hardly a major technological leap. However, because the vehicle ran on tracks rather than on dirt or cobblestoned streets, somewhat higher speeds and longer commuting distances were possible. In the 1880s electric power transmission and electric motor technology made the electric streetcar possible. Capable of several times the speed of a horse-drawn trolley and less costly to operate, it was a tremendous force for the decentralizing of population. It at least doubled practical commuting radii and promoted the first major wave of suburbanization. The title of a book by Warner, *Streetcar Suburbs*, expresses the effect quite directly.[15] Figure 1-4 shows the expansion of the urban area and the star-shaped pattern of development promoted by the streetcar.

The effect cannot be captured by statistics of city population for two reasons. In many cases, the suburbanizing effect took place within the city boundaries. For

---

[14] Frank S. So et al. (eds.), *The Practice of Local Government Planning*, International City Managers Association, Washington, D.C. 1979. p. 27.
[15] Sam Bass Warner, *Street Car Suburbs: A Process of Growth in Boston*, Atheneum, New York, 1968.

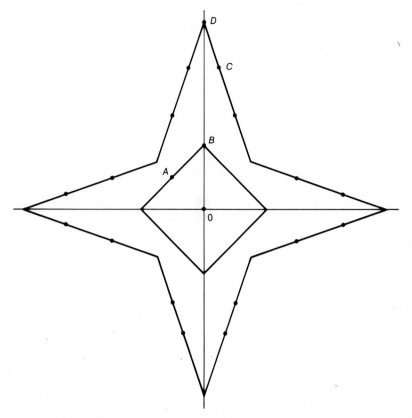

FIGURE 1-4
The streetcar and the star-shaped pattern of development. Assume a city with a square grid pattern and a center at 0. Maximum acceptable commuting time is 1 hour and point B is a 1-hour walk (at 3 mph) from 0. The diamond shape represents the outer limits of the "walking city." Note that point A is the same time away from the center as point B even though the straight-line distance is shorter. This is because the pedestrian must travel along the rectangular grid pattern. Assume that streetcar service at an average speed of 9 mph is now instituted along the east-west and north-south streets that pass through point 0. Point D is now 1 hour away from the city center. So, too, is point C, for the resident at C can walk one block west in the same time as the streetcar travels three blocks south to meet him. By the same reasoning all points on the star can be shown to be 1 hour from point 0. The figure thus illustrates the expansion of the city and the change of shape produced by the streetcar.

example, in the city of Brooklyn (now one of the five boroughs of New York City) the 1880 population was 590,000, making it a city of substantial size even by present standards. But in the more peripheral parts of the city population densities were extremely low and much of the land was in agricultural use. Thus even though the extension of streetcar lines promoted suburbanization, it was all captured by the city. The second factor is annexation. In the nineteenth century many cities grew by annexation of peripheral lands. In general, annexation tends to proceed until there is enough population and political structure in outlying areas to resist it. If the lands outside the city limits are relatively empty of these, the city may capture suburbanizing populations before they have had a chance to offer effective resistance to annexation. Thus, again, the suburbanizing process will be undetectable if one looks only at municipal statistics.

The Urban Density Gradient

To estimate when deconcentration began statistics on a much finer grain are required, and these are hard to come by for most cities if one goes back more than several decades. Some evidence, however, is available for a few places in the form of estimates of urban population density gradients going back as far as 1880 (see Box 1-1 on density gradient). The manner in which they were done takes some explanation. A number of empirical studies have shown that population densities in urban areas tend to fall exponentially from the center to the outskirts. That is, the percentage change in density per mile from the center out seems to be relatively constant for a given area at a given time. Thus the absolute change with each mile decreases and density gradients like those shown in Box 1-1 result. The gradient itself represents the rate at which density falls with distance. It is a relative, not an absolute, measure. Thus by looking at the gradient for the same

---

BOX 1-1

DENSITY GRADIENTS

Figure 1-5 shows population densities for Milwaukee calculated from Mills's data as shown in Table 1-3. The difference between the 1880 and 1920 gradients may not be immediately apparent, since the lines lie roughly parallel for most of their length. But note that at the center the calculated 1920 density is about half again as high as the 1880 figure, while at a distance of 4 miles, it is about 6 times as great. By 1963 central densities had fallen to substantially lower levels than in previous years, while a few miles out they were a large multiple of earlier densities. The calculations are made using the equation

$$D(u) = De^{-\mu\lambda}$$

where D = density at the center
u = distance from the center
e = natural logarithm
λ = density gradient

As an example, for the 1963 density at a distance of 5 miles

$D(u) = 31,123 \times 2.71828^{-(5 \times .27)}$
$= 31,123 \times 1/2.71829^{1.35}$
$= 8,068$

Although population densities are shown as rising all the way to the center of the region, in fact they actually decline very close to the center as commercial development crowds out residential uses.

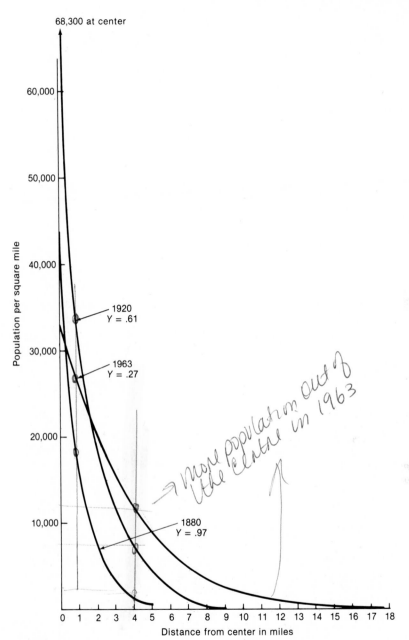

FIGURE 1-5
The changing population density gradient of Milwaukee, 1880–1963.

city or metropolitan area over time it is possible to determine whether population is becoming more or less concentrated, regardless of changes in total population and the rise or fall of the absolute density at the center.

Mills has summarized work on a very limited number of metropolitan areas,

TABLE 1-3
URBAN DENSITY GRADIENTS FOR FOUR METROPOLITAN AREAS

| | Metropolitan area | | | | Average density |
Year	Baltimore	Milwaukee	Philadelphia	Rochester	gradient
1880	1.82	.97	.30	1.78	1.22
1890	1.08	.92	.28	1.83	1.06
1900	1.05	.90	.28	1.59	.96
1910	.93	.78	.28	1.20	.80
1920	.70	.61	.25	1.18	.69
1930	.64	.56	.37	.96	.63
1940	.60	.51	.36	.88	.59
1948	.48	.47	.31	.73	.50
1963	.33	.27	.23	.40	.31

Source: Edwin S. Mills, *Studies in the Structure of the Urban Economy*, Johns Hopkins, Baltimore, 1972, pp. 48–49.

which, in four cases, goes back as far as 1880.[16] In general, the gradients have been developed from census data for the central cities and surrounding minor civil divisions (MCDs). Using what is essentially point data to infer a continuous gradient is justified by the uniformities discussed above. The smaller the gradient the more gradual the population decline. Thus a decreasing gradient over time means a flattening and spreading of the metropolitan area's population distribution. Mills's data are shown in Table 1-3. As can readily be seen there appears to be a deconcentrating trend as far back as the data goes. The number of cases is very small and the historical data are no doubt less than perfect; thus one should not leap to firm conclusions. However, there is in the data a very strong suggestion that a decentralizing population trend was in evidence in the late nineteenth century. This in turn suggests that the automobile, though it unquestionably accelerated the deconcentration of American cities, was neither the original nor the sole cause of such deconcentration. The data Mills cites say nothing about the deconcentration of economic activity, for the data to make such statements is simply not available. Because there was no technological advance in the carrying of freight comparable to the improvement the streetcar achieved in the carrying of people, it seems reasonable to believe that the decrease in the gradient of economic activity was smaller. But even here some decentralization appeared as manufacturing moved out from urban centers along the rail lines leading into those centers. As Adna Weber noted in 1899:

> Attention has been called to another encouraging tendency favoring suburban growth, namely, the transference of manufacturing industries to the suburbs. The local advantages of a suburban town have been pointed out; they include not only a great saving in rent and insurance, but economy in the handling and storing of goods. All carting is avoided by having a switching [railroad siding] run directly into the factory; saving to machinery is effected by placing it all on solid foundations on the first floor; and plenty of space is at hand for the storing of fuel and materials, so these may be bought when the market offers the most favorable terms. . . . A similar tendency is noticeable in Europe

---

[16] Mills, op. cit., chap. 3. Mills notes that the apparent anomaly of Philadelphia in the 1920 to 1930 period is probably the result of difficulties in the data owing to the large number of municipalities involved and frequent changes in municipal boundary lines.

. . . although Manchester, Leeds and Lyons are still the chief centers of trade in cotton, woolen and silk goods, they no longer produce any great part of these stuffs.[17]

One can speculate that if the automobile and the motor truck had not been invented, much of the dispersal of population would still have occurred via streetcars and rapid transit. However, it is possible that downtowns would be much healthier economically than they are today, for there might have been much less dispersion of economic activity.

The potential of rapid transit for reducing urban population densities was widely appreciated in the late nineteenth century, and those who deplored the overwhelming congestion of nineteenth-century cities placed great faith and hope in rapid transit as an agency of reform. The goal of enabling workers and their families to live outside the congestion of the city in a place where they would have access to sunlight, nature, and clean air inspired considerable idealism. One might contrast the following quote to today's preoccupation with helping central places retain population and jobs.

> But if society wishes to minimize the evils of concentration of population, it must abandon the hope of accomplishing great things by such palliatives as model tenements (which, if located in the city, often serve merely to prevent factories from moving to the suburbs), building laws, inspection of buildings, and the various other ameliorations already discussed. Four goals are of fundamental importance: (1) a shorter working day, which will permit the workingman to live at a distance from the factory; (2) associations for promoting the ownership of suburban homes by workingmen; (3) cheap transit; (4) rapid transit. The importance of the two latter policies has been urged in so eloquent words by Dr. Cooley that they deserve quotation: "Humanity demands that men should have sunlight, fresh air, the sight of grass and trees. It demands these things for the man himself, and it demands them still more urgently for his wife and children. No child has a fair chance in the world who is condemned to grow up in the dirt and confinement, the dreariness, ugliness and vice of the poorer quarters of a great city. It is impossible to think with patience of any future condition of things in which such a childhood shall fall to the lot of any large part of the human race. Whatever struggles manhood must endure, childhood should have room and opportunity for healthy moral and physical growth. Fair play and the welfare of the human race alike demand it. There is, then, a permanent conflict between the needs of industry and the needs of humanity. Industry says men must aggregate. Humanity says they must not, or if they must, let it be only during working hours and let the necessity not extend to their wives and children. *It is the office of the city railways to reconcile these conflicting requirements.*"[18]

At the end of the nineteenth century we see rapid growth of the urban populations, with most growth occurring within cities themselves rather than in their surrounding political subdivisions. The rates of urban population increase are far beyond those which could be sustained by natural increase—37 percent from 1890 to 1900 and 39 percent from 1900 to 1910—so massive in-migration is evident. Both European immigration, averaging 370,000 per year from 1890 to 1900 and 880,000 per year from 1900 to 1910, and in-migration from rural areas supplied the major share of the growth.

Systematic employment data by location is simply not available for that time period, but all evidence points to the overwhelming concentration of manufac-

---

[17] Weber, op. cit., p. 473.
[18] Weber, ibid., p. 207.

turing activity in major cities. In fact, not only was manufacturing heavily concentrated in cities as such, but in the later part of the nineteenth century it was becoming increasingly concentrated in larger cities. Clearly, economies of scale and agglomeration outweighed the corresponding diseconomies. To quote Weber again:

> The statistics of manufactures furnished by the United States government are not altogether trustworthy, but they at least show that in the period of 1860–90 the movement was a centralizing one, toward the larger cities. In 1860 the annual production of manufactures per capita was $60 for the United States as a whole, $193.50 for ten cities having a population of 50,000 or more, $424 for ten cities under 50,000, and $44 for the rural districts. Thus the per capita production was at that time largest in the smaller cities. In 1890, however, the per capita product of manufactures was $455 in the 28 great cities, $355 in the 137 cities of 20,000–100,000 population, and $58 for the remainder of the country. The superiority of the smaller cities in 1860 had in 1890 given way to that of the great.[19]

The inverse relationship between city size and city growth, a phenomenon which shows up later in the twentieth century, was absent. If anything, size and growth rate appeared positively related at this time.

A NOTE ON THIRD-WORLD URBANIZATION

The picture presented here for the United States and, indirectly, for the rest of the industrialized world is one of urbanization stemming from the consequences of the industrial revolution. That picture is strengthened in Chapter 4, in which a variety of models of the urban economy are presented. All of them suggest, in one way or another, that a major factor in determining which metropolitan areas grow and how rapidly they grow is their ability to sell products or services outside their own borders. In a sense the models, like Keynesian macroeconomic models, are demand-driven. The city or metropolis grows because the demand for what it produces grows.

The reader may wonder whether this industrial revolution-originated demand-driven model is the only way that urbanization can or will occur. A look at many third-world cities would suggest that urban growth can come about from an entirely different set of causes. A brief discussion is presented here for the perspective it may yield. Rapid urban growth is much newer to the third world than to the western world, and the fact is that most economists are westerners. For these reasons it is a much less understood phenomenon and the few paragraphs which follow are hardly definitive.

Perhaps the first thing we note about third-world urbanization is that cities with huge populations appear in countries that are no further into the industrial revolution than England was in, say, 1800 or the United States in 1860. Mexico City, for example, has a population of over 10 million, putting it in the size range of New York or London. Yet Mexico has just started on the road to industrialization, with a per capita gross national product (GNP) about one-eighth that of the United States. Nor can its size in any way be explained on the basis of international trade, for it is an inland city. The Calcutta metropolitan area has a

[19] Weber, ibid., p. 208.

greater population than the Chicago metropolitan area, yet if India has entered Rostow's stage of economic takeoff it has been within the last decade or so. India's per capita GNP, a very rough indicator of the nation's entry into the realm of industrial nations, is about 1/50 that of the United States (though such statistics probably underestimate the per capita GNPs of nations with large numbers of households more or less outside the money economy). The Karachi, Pakistan, metropolitan area has roughly the same population as the Detroit metropolitan area. Examples of the point abound.

How can we account for a city or metropolitan area with a population numbered in the millions evolving in a preindustrial or just-industrializing economy? Since the third world is not a single place, and since it may contain as large differences within itself as there are between many third-world and western nations, it is likely that no single explanation is possible. Let us simply note some relevant considerations.

First, in nineteenth-century Europe rates of natural increase edged up into the 1 to 1.5 percent a year range during the industrial revolution, while at the same time population pressure was eased by emigration. In nineteenth-century America population grew at an annual average of 2.4 percent across the century. Population pressure on urban areas was eased however, by the existence of an expanding frontier until close to the end of the century. Population growth rates of 2 to 2.5 percent a year are common in many third-world countries either prior to or in the earlier stages of industrialization without the safety valves of emigration or virgin lands. The population pressure on urban areas may thus be far larger than it was in the west. In third-world countries with high rural population densities, the marginal productivity of agricultural labor may be very low (an illustration of the law of diminishing returns), so even very marginal sorts of employment in urban areas offer a better return. These marginal activities may be possible in part because of a trickle-down effect from the higher incomes of those employed in government or the emerging industrial and commercial sectors. According to Roberts in *Cities of Peasants*, a title which itself captures some of the reality:

> Marginal employment is likely to concentrate in the large cities of each underdeveloped country. Earning opportunities are greater in these centers given the concentration of high income earners. Also, access to educational and to welfare facilities and proximity to the centers of government make possible a greater range of strategies for survival. In contrast, demographic pressure on inadequate land resources, diminishing opportunities for craft work and relative isolation make rural areas less attractive places for survival.[20]

In some third-world countries we observe the "primate-city" phenomenon. In this, a main city—almost inevitably the capital city—is disproportionately larger than any other city, a violation of the rank-size rule.[21] One reason for primacy

---

[20] Bryan R. Roberts, *Cities of Peasants: The Political Economy of Urbanization in the Third World*, E. Arnold, London, 1978, p. 161.

[21] The rank-size rule is an empirical generalization that seems to hold for a number of countries, even though no adequate explanation has been offered for it. According to the rule the population of the second largest metropolitan area will be roughly one-half that of the largest, the population of the third largest metropolitan area one-third that of the largest, and so on. In the case of primacy, the population of the largest metropolitan area is far greater than the rule would suggest. The rule was first enunciated by Zipf. See G. K. Zipf, *National Unity and Disunity*, Principia Press, Bloomington, Ind., 1941.

may be international trade: If international trade is important in the economic life of the country and if most of it goes through a single port, primacy may pertain. It is likely to be seen in former colonies or in countries where investment has oriented the development of the transportation system to a single port. It has been suggested that the very large size of Buenos Aires is in part due to this sort of investment pattern, mainly by the British in the nineteenth century. But international trade cannot entirely explain primacy, as demonstrated by the case of Mexico City.

The role of government may be another factor in primacy. In many third-world countries, both of the right and the left, the government sector is relatively larger than it was in nineteenth-century Europe and plays a far larger role in the management of the economy. If government is heavily concentrated in a single city the trickle-down or multiplier effects of that concentration may produce a kind of urban hypertrophy.

Redistributionist economic policies may play some role in producing massive urban populations. In the western world redistributionist policies generally followed industrialization. Today's "welfare capitalism" came after a more Darwinian sort of capitalism. Thus hope of receiving the benefits of redistributionist public policy was not a cause of rural to urban migration in nineteenth-century Europe or America, but it may be in some twentieth-century third-world nations.

Perhaps there are also other explanations. The American farmer of, say, 1860 had a higher living standard than the average Indian peasant of 1980. But he didn't have a $5 Japanese-made transistor radio telling him daily about the attractions of the world beyond his farm. Thus there may be forces behind third-world urbanization which cannot be fully measured in terms of marginal rates of return or comparative utility functions—but which are still real and powerful.

CHAPTER 2

SUBURBANIZATION
AND DECENTRALIZATION

In the preceding chapter we examined the forces behind both urban growth and increased urban density. As the twentieth century wore on the pattern began to change. Urban areas continued to grow in size but growth was concentrated in peripheral areas. In central areas growth slowed, and in many cases there were absolute losses of population and employment. In recent years growth and metropolitan-area size seem to be inversely related and a number of the largest metropolitan areas have essentially ceased to grow. In the last decade the historic pattern of net migration from rural to urban areas reversed; more people migrated from metropolitan to nonmetropolitan areas than moved in the other direction. Clearly, there have been powerful dispersing and deconcentrating forces at work. These forces and their results form the subject of this chapter. Because trends within a given urban area take place within a regional setting it is necessary to know something of regional trends as well. Thus a certain amount of material on regional population and economic trends is included.

THE AGE OF SUBURBANIZATION

The particular technological event that portended great changes in the physical form of the city and the relationship of the city to the ring of communities around it was the invention of the automobile and the truck. The first prototypes appeared in the 1890s, and the numbers of automobiles increased slowly, reaching about 5 million in 1915. At this time assembly line production of Ford's Model T began, the output of cars went up sharply, and prices fell dramatically. By 1930 there were about 25 million autos in the United States, roughly one for every five people. The decentralizing work done by the streetcar—and in a few larger municipalities like New York, Boston, and Chicago, by subway and elevated train—was greatly accelerated. The trolley and the interurban railroad car disappeared from the American scene with amazing speed as the auto, with its greater flexibility of route and time and the attractions of privacy, captured their markets. The automobile made possible not only the continued linear growth begun by streetcars and rapid transit but also the filling in of the spaces between the spokes of earlier streetcar suburbanization.

The truck, of course, had a similar decentralizing effect on industry, or at least on light industry. Whereas the suburbanization of industry had once been physically limited to movement out along rail lines, industry was now freed to go anywhere within the metropolitan area that topography, land-use controls, and availability of land and utilities would permit. Figure 2-1 pictures rail versus truck transportation costs in a schematic way. The cost per ton-mile for truck transportation is higher than for rail, but terminal costs (those costs which must be incurred for handling before the product can begin to move) are higher for rail. Thus, out to the crossover point truck transportation is cheaper. The crossover point will vary by the type of commodity and particular considerations like the characteristics of the road network. However, as a general figure, most texts on transportation show the crossover point at about 150 miles from the origin. Therefore, within even the largest metropolitan area truck transportation will be cheaper than rail transportation for most goods.

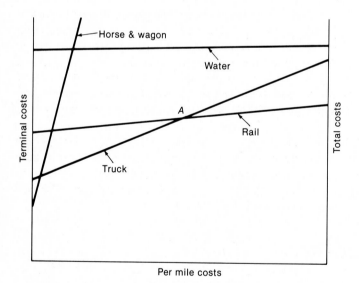

FIGURE 2-1

Terminal and per mile costs of various modes (not to scale). The cost characteristics of various modes have much to do with the form of metropolitan areas, as discussed in the text. Per mile costs here are shown as linear, but in general they do decline somewhat with distance. The crossover point (point A) between truck and rail is generally given as about 150 miles, though this varies greatly with the types of goods being shipped.

From about 1920 on a process of suburbanization, within the larger process of metropolitan-area growth, became evident. The very rapid pace of suburbanization established in the 1920s slowed somewhat in the 1930s for several reasons. One was the slowing of national population growth resulting from the immigration quotas established in the mid-1920s. A second was the contraction of employment during the Great Depression. Thus the rural to urban migration promoted by the economic opportunities offered in the cities was greatly diminished. The reader will note that during the 1930s the rural to urban population ratio of the United States remained virtually unchanged for the first time in over 100 years. But even in this decade of economic decline suburban growth outpaced central-city growth when measured in percentage terms. World War II stopped the clock on the suburbanization of population and economic activity for at least two reasons. First, except for housing for war workers and military personnel, residential construction came to an almost complete halt. Second, the production of civilian automobiles was stopped for about 4 years and simultaneously gasoline was rationed. In retrospect it is clear that the period from 1930 to 1945 encompassing the Great Depression and World War II represented a halt in a long-term historical process. In 1946 the suburbanization process resumed. Suburban housing was built at a rapid pace, driven by the unsatisfied demand stemming from years of slow construction, and facilitated by low-interest, long-term mortgages, federal mortgage guarantees, rapid economic growth, and steadily rising real per capita income. The favorable federal tax treatment of owner-occupied housing was also undoubtedly a factor (see Chapter 7). Sharply climbing rates of automobile ownership and cheap gasoline provided the mobility needed for suburbanization.

Although the decentralizing trends within metropolitan areas had been over-whelmingly clear since World War II (and actually in progress for several decades preceding), metropolitan-area populations continued to grow both in absolute numbers and as a percentage of total population. In the aggregate, metropolitan areas were recipients of net in-migration while nonmetropolitan areas experienced net out-migration. Many of the basic forces that had produced metropolitan growth in earlier years continued to operate. Agricultural productivity rose so much that the agricultural labor force not only continued declining as a percent of total employment but, from the 1940s on, declined precipitously in absolute numbers as well. Population growth was rapid until the nation made the transition from the postwar baby boom to the "baby bust" in the mid-to-late 1960s.[1] Though manufacturing employment topped out in absolute numbers and steadily declined as a percentage of total employment, its place was taken by the increase in business and personal services. Economies of scale and agglomeration seemed to virtually guarantee continued growth of metropolitan areas. In the 1960s urban economists spoke of the "urban size ratchet."[2] It was believed that once an urban area grew past a certain size—half a million was a commonly quoted figure—further growth was virtually certain on the basis of scale and agglomeration

[1] The baby boom is generally considered to have begun in the late 1940s and to have ended in the mid-1960s. Its peak year, measured in absolute numbers of births, was 1957. For a time series on births see U.S. Bureau of the Census, *Statistical Abstract of the United States*, 1981, Table 83, p. 58.

[2] See Wilbur Thompson, *Preface to Urban Economics*, Johns Hopkins, Baltimore, 1965.

TABLE 2-1
POPULATION IN SMSAS, 1900–1980 (in millions)

Year*	Total U.S.	Total SMSA	Central city	Ring§	SMSA as percentage of total	Central city as percentage of SMSA
1900	76.0	24.1	16.0	8.1	31.7	66.4
1910	92.0	34.5	22.9	11.6	37.5	66.4
1920	105.7	46.1	30.5	15.6	43.6	66.2
1930	122.8	61.0	39.0	22.0	49.7	63.9
1940	131.7	67.1	41.5	25.6	50.9	61.8
1950†	151.3	84.9	49.7	35.2	56.1	58.5
1960	179.3	112.9	58.0	54.9	63.0	51.4
1970	203.2	139.4	63.8	75.6	68.6	45.8
1970‡	203.2	153.9	67.9	85.8	75.7	44.1
1980	226.5	169.4	67.9	101.5	74.8	40.1

* Figures for 1900 through 1940 are estimates based upon 1950 SMSA boundaries.
† Alaska and Hawaii included from 1950 on.
‡ Two sets of 1970 figures are shown. The upper set is that actually recorded after the 1970 census. The lower set is 1970 population applied to SMSA boundaries as they existed in 1980. Thus comparison of the second set of 1970 figures with 1980 figures shows change within the same set of boundaries.
§ The term *ring* means all of the SMSA other than the central city.
Source: For 1940 and earlier, Donald J. Bogue, *Population Growth in Standard Metropolitan Areas, 1900–1950,* Housing and Home Finance Agency, Washington, D.C., 1953, pp. 11 and 13. For 1950 through 1980, U.S. Bureau of the Census, "SMSA and Standard Consolidated Statistical Areas".

economies. Today, the urban size ratchet seems consigned to the intellectual scrap heap. But looking at the evidence available in 1965 it was quite convincing. In fact, the only metropolitan area that had ever violated this rule was Pittsburgh, a situation which appeared to be explainable in terms of the area's heavy dependence upon steel manufacture, not a growth industry in the postwar world.

The Slowing of Central-City Growth

Table 2-1 shows the rapid growth of standard metropolitan statistical area (SMSA) populations and the relatively slow growth of central-city populations within SMSAs in the postwar years. To a considerable extent Table 2-1 actually understates the suburbanizing trend. In each census the number of areas meeting Bureau of the Census criteria for SMSA status increased. Thus a substantial percentage of central-city growth results merely from the addition of new central cities. For example, if we use 1970 SMSA definitions, according to Table 2-1 central cities gained 4.1 million people from 1970 to 1980. However, if we apply 1980 SMSA boundaries to the 1970 population figure, thus using the same set of central cities for both censuses, we see that there was no central-city population gain.

The slowing of growth and the loss of population for many of the larger cities in the postwar period is evident in Table 2-2. For many of the larger cities the year of maximum population is two or three decades back and the decade of maximum growth still further back. There are several larger cities which still show rapid growth to the present time. In general these are cities in the west or south that are in rapidly growing regions and that have relatively low population densities,

BOX 2-1

WHAT IS A STANDARD METROPOLITAN STATISTICAL AREA?

Standard metropolitan statistical areas (SMSAs) are areas designated by the Office of Management and the Budget. The criteria for designation, as of January 1980, were:

(a) One city with 50,000 or more inhabitants, or
(b) A Census Bureau-defined urbanized area of at least 50,000 inhabitants and a total SMSA population of at least 100,000 (75,000 in New England).

The standards provide that the SMSA include as "central county(ies)" the county in which the central city is located, and adjacent counties, if any, with at least 50 percent of their population in the urbanized area. Additional "outlying counties" are included if they meet specified requirements of commuting to the central counties and of metropolitan character (such as population density and percent urban). In New England the SMSA's are defined in terms of cities and towns rather than counties.

Source: U.S. Bureau of the Census, *Statistical Abstract of the United States,* 1981, p. 917.

suggesting that much of the suburban growth within the metropolitan area can still take place within the city boundaries. In the northeast and north-central regions, where the regional economy has been stagnating and where cities are generally characterized by an older, denser, pre-automobile pattern of development, population shrinkage has occurred. As the data in Table 2-2 indicates, the

TABLE 2-2
POPULATION TRENDS IN THE 15 LARGEST US CENTRAL CITIES

City	Population (in thousands) 1970	1980	Percent change, 1970–1980	Year ending decade of maximum absolute population growth	Percent change, 1940–1980
New York	7,895	7,071	−10.4	1910	−5.2
Chicago	3,367	3,005	−10.8	1930	−11.5
Los Angeles	2,816	2,967	5.5	1930	97.2
Philadelphia	1,947	1,688	−13.4	1920	−12.6
Houston	1,233	1,594	29.2	1980	314.0
Detroit	1,511	1,203	−20.5	1930	−25.9
Dallas	844	904	7.1	1960	206.4
San Diego	697	876	25.5	1960	313.5
Baltimore	906	787	−13.1	1950	−8.4
San Antonio	654	785	20.1	1960	209.0
Phoenix	582	765	35.2	1960	1,076.9
Indianapolis*	734	701	−4.9	1970	81.1
San Francisco	716	670	−5.1	1950	6.9
Memphis	624	646	3.6	1970	120.4
Washington, D.C.	757	638	−15.7	1940	−3.8

* Data distorted by annexation.
Source: U.S. Bureau of the Census, *Census of the Population,* various years.

shrinkage has been quite substantial in many cities. In general, the percentage loss of population is greater in the larger cities. Along the eastern seaboard, shrinkage in a few cities, notably New York, has been substantially reduced by immigration from abroad. In percentage terms the biggest population losses often occurred in large inland cities. From 1970 to 1980 Cleveland lost 23.6 percent of its population; Buffalo, 22.7; Cincinnati, 15.0; Detroit, 20.5; and St. Louis, 27.2 percent.

The Role of Net Migration The growth-rate differences between city, suburb, and nonmetropolitan area, as well as those between regions, are primarily the result of differences in net migration. These differences are shown in Table 2-3. The massive in-migration to suburban areas is a continuation of past trends, although the rate has accelerated. The net in-migration to nonmetropolitan areas is a new phenomenon, which apparently began in the early 1970s. The figures are only for internal migration; when immigration to the United States is considered as well, all the net-migration figures are moved in a positive direction. The fact that central-city populations did not decline in spite of the startlingly large net out-migration is due to the combined effects of natural increase and immigration.

The Changing Racial Composition of Central Cities The racial change in central cities in the 1970s is important for what it reveals of recent events and for what it implies about the future. Although central-city population remained constant, the white population in central cities shrank by 6.1 million. Given the countervailing effect of natural increase and immigration from abroad, this means the net white out-migration was actually at least twice as large. Black populations in central cities grew by about 1.8 million. This increase was entirely on the basis of natural increase, since blacks also showed net out-migration from central cities during the decade, though at a much smaller rate than whites. The difference between the shrinkage of the white population and the growth of the black population was made up by a very large increase in the other-nonwhite population of central cities. This growth is at least partly due to a large amount of immigration from Asia during the 1970s, but it may also be due to changes in the way race is recorded by the census or changes in the pattern of response to census questions. Some of the other-nonwhite growth may thus be a statistical artifact, with people who were counted as either white or black in 1970 being counted as other-nonwhite in 1980.

TABLE 2-3
INTERNAL MIGRATION, 1970–1980
(In Thousands)*

Place	In-migrants	Out-migrants	Net migration
Central cities	12,878	26,242	−13,364
Suburbs	26,360	15,936	10,428
Nonmetropolitan areas	14,058	11,120	2,938

* Figures may not add due to rounding.
Source: U.S. Bureau of the Census, *Current Population Reports*, ser. P-20, no. 368.

TABLE 2-4
RACE AND RESIDENCE IN METROPOLITAN AREAS
(In Millions)*

	1960†	1970	1970‡	1980
SMSA population	119.6	139.4	153.7	169.4
White	105.8	120.6	133.6	138.0
Black	12.7	16.8	17.9	21.5
Central-city population	59.9	63.8	67.9	67.9
White	49.4	49.4	53.1	47.0
Black	9.9	13.1	13.5	15.3
Suburban ring	59.6	75.6	85.8	101.5
White	56.4	71.1	80.5	91.0
Black	2.9	3.6	4.3	6.2

Source: U.S. Bureau of the Census, Census of the Population, 1960, 1970; Census of Population and Housing, 1980.
* Black and white figures do not add to totals due to omission of other-nonwhite data.
† Figures based on 1970 SMSA boundaries so as to make direct comparison possible between 1960 and 1970.
‡ Figures based on 1980 SMSA boundaries so as to make direct comparison possible between 1970 and 1980 figures.

Table 2-4 shows the changing racial composition of metropolitan areas from 1960 to 1980. Note that although the white population increased by roughly 32 million, all of that increase was in the suburbs. In fact, the white population of central cities actually fell by over 2 million. Conversely, the black population rose by almost 9 million, but over 5 million of that increase was in central cities.

The Suburbanization of Employment   Data on the location of employment is not as good as that on population, so we cannot speak with quite such certainty about the suburbanization of employment. However, from what data we do have, it appears that from the end of World War II on the suburbanization of economic activity has proceeded about as rapidly as the suburbanization of population. Mills's data in Table 2-5 show decentralizing trends by major industrial category in the early postwar period.

The figures shown in Table 2-5 are simply pure numbers and may seem hard to

TABLE 2-5
DENSITY GRADIENTS FOR 18 SMSAS, 1948–1963

	1948	1963
Population	.58	.38
Manufacturing	.68	.42
Retailing	.88	.44
Services	.97	.53
Wholesaling	1.00	.56

Source: Edwin S. Mills, Studies in the Structure of the Urban Economy, Johns Hopkins, Baltimore, 1972, p. 42.

interpret. The reader can attach some meaning to them by examining the data and the explanation in Box 2-2 on decentralization of population and income. Recall from Chapter 1 that the smaller the figure the less rapidly the density declines in percentage terms as one moves out from the center of the region. If the figure declines over time this means that the region's density profile has flattened. This is to say, densities at the center have fallen relative to densities farther out. As a quick indication of what the gradients mean consider a metropolitan area divided

---

BOX 2-2

THE DECENTRALIZATION OF POPULATION AND INCOME IN THE NEW YORK REGION

Because of its size New York cannot always be considered typical of metropolitan areas generally. However, its long history and the availability of historical data by county make it useful for illustrating the long-term pattern of deconcentration observed in most metropolitan areas. Note that the population of the core (Manhattan) peaked about 70 years ago and has declined by over 1 million people since then. The inner-ring counties reached their peak population about 1970, but as the figure indicates, growth in the several preceding decades was slow. The inner-ring population is now back at 1930s levels. Middle-ring growth also peaked about 1970 but had been proceeding much more rapidly up to that point. In the outer ring growth continues, even though regional population is falling.

The table at the bottom of the facing page shows the increasing income gap between the city and the suburbs with the passage of time and the process of decentralization. Note both the higher absolute income levels in the suburban counties and also the generally more rapid rate of increase. For example, the lowest percentage rate of increase is recorded for the Bronx in the inner ring and the highest for Rockland County in the outer ring. In 1949 Rockland and the Bronx had virtually identical median family incomes. Thirty years later, Rockland's was 98 percent higher.

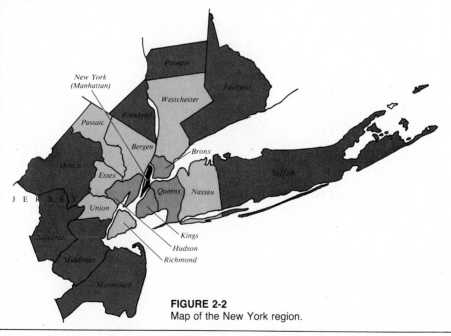

FIGURE 2-2
Map of the New York region.

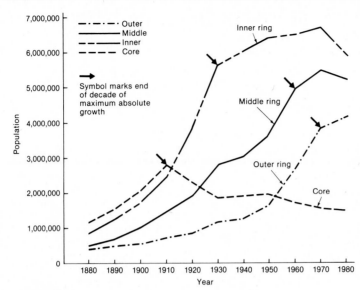

FIGURE 2-3
Population change in the New York region, 1880–1980.

MEDIAN FAMILY INCOME, 1949–1979

County	1949	1959	1969	1979	Ratio of 1979 income to 1949 income
Core					
Manhattan	$3,073	$5,338	$8,983	$16,326	5.31
Inner ring					
Bronx	$3,612	$5,830	$8,308	$14,292	3.96
Hudson	3,484	6,151	9,698	17,659	5.07
Kings	3,447	5,816	8,859	14,664	4.25
Queens	4,121	7,176	11,555	20,506	4.98
Middle ring					
Bergen	$4,277	$7,978	$13,579	$27,517	6.43
Essex	3,769	6,651	10,685	19,931	5.29
Nassau	4,524	8,515	14,632	28,444	6.29
Passaic	3,675	6,432	10,933	21,011	5.72
Richmond	3,845	6,836	11,894	23,842	6.20
Union	4,312	7,746	12,593	25,266	5.86
Westchester	4,353	8,052	13,784	27,278	6.27
Outer ring					
Fairfield	$3,664	$7,371	$13,086	$26,598	7.26
Middlesex	3,725	7,054	11,982	25,603	6.87
Monmouth	3,324	6,413	11,635	24,526	7.38
Morris	3,758	7,696	13,421	29,283	7.79
Putnam	3,339	6,539	11,996	26,305	7.88
Rockland	3,554	7,472	13,753	28,243	7.95
Somerset	3,667	7,484	13,433	29,172	7.96
Suffolk	3,411	6,795	12,084	24,194	7.09

Source: U.S. Bureau of the Census. *Census of the Population,* various years.

TABLE 2-6

SUBURBAN EMPLOYMENT AS A PERCENT OF TOTAL EMPLOYMENT IN EIGHT SMSAS, 1970–1977

	1970	1977		1970	1977
Baltimore			Philadelphia		
Total employment	39.3	53.2	Total employment	48.8	59.5
Manufacturing	47.4	55.4	Manufacturing	54.5	65.6
Wholesale trade	24.6	48.9	Wholesale trade	39.7	59.6
Retail trade	46.9	65.0	Retail trade	55.9	66.7
F.I.R.E.	21.3	39.5	F.I.R.E.	31.0	45.5
Services	29.2	46.2	Services	42.7	52.4
Business services	20.2	54.5	Business services	38.2	51.6
Health services	21.3	39.3	Health services	46.1	51.6
Denver			St. Louis		
Total employment	33.3	47.1	Total employment	51.6	65.2
Manufacturing	45.8	54.5	Manufacturing	53.9	61.3
Wholesale trade	13.1	31.2	Wholesale trade	34.7	58.7
Retail trade	42.6	58.5	Retail trade	63.4	77.8
F.I.R.E.	17.0	32.9	F.I.R.E.	42.7	54.1
Services	30.3	41.4	Services	45.5	64.8
Business services	24.7	38.7	Business services	29.5	62.0
Health services	35.3	42.6	Health services	52.0	66.3
New Orleans			San Francisco		
Total employment	27.0	41.8	Total employment	58.9	61.1
Manufacturing	40.9	51.6	Manufacturing	71.9	76.5
Wholesale trade	20.7	45.8	Wholesale trade	51.5	68.3
Retail trade	34.1	50.4	Retail trade	68.3	74.0
F.I.R.E.	10.5	28.7	F.I.R.E.	33.7	37.6
Services	17.8	32.1	Services	54.0	57.8
Business services	19.6	30.6	Business services	46.8	54.1
Health services	22.1	36.3	Health services	66.3	66.1
New York			Washington, D.C.		
Total employment	45.1	52.3	Total employment	54.1	65.6
Manufacturing	55.5	62.1	Manufacturing	57.6	68.0
Wholesale trade	40.5	53.7	Wholesale trade	53.6	74.3
Retail trade	53.4	61.4	Retail trade	65.7	77.4
F.I.R.E.	25.2	31.3	F.I.R.E.	47.7	57.7
Services	38.0	45.3	Services	43.4	54.7
Business services	32.0	41.8	Business services	51.9	67.9
Health services	47.0	52.3	Health services	54.6	60.5

Source: Peter Muller, *Contemporary Suburban America*, Prentice-Hall, 1981, p. 132. Reprinted by permission.

into concentric 1-mile rings. If the gradient is .58, the figure for population at the beginning of the time period, each move from an outer ring to an inner ring, indicates a population density increase of 79 percent. On the other hand, if the gradient is .38, as at the end of the time period, the increase from outer ring to inner ring is 46 percent. There is a compounding effect to the process described. For example, a move inward of four rings with a gradient of .58 would increase the density by $(1.79)^4$, or a factor of 10.3. For a gradient of .38 the increase would be $(1.45)^4$, or a factor of 4.5. This is a rather substantial change in the form of metropolitan areas. The time period Mills used presumably catches much of the peripheral movement that was blocked by the Depression and the war years, but even so it is still a very impressive change in a 15-year period.

If anything, the peripheral movement of employment may have accelerated since Mills gathered his data. Muller studied eight SMSAs in the 1970s, with the results shown in Table 2-6.

The reader will note that the losses of business activity seem to be across the board. There may be some categories, particularly business services, in which there are activities which the city is not losing. However, at this level of aggregation, there does not appear to be any major category of activity upon which the central city has an unshakeable grip.

The Suburbanization of Income   In most metropolitan areas there exists an income gradient, with personal income rising as distance from the center increases. Average income is higher in the suburban ring than at the center, and the disparity has been increasing with the passage of time. In general, the disparity is greater for large metropolitan areas than for small ones. These facts are illustrated in Table 2-7.

To an extent that is large but hard to measure, the figures understate the city-suburban income dichotomy. Within most cities there are some areas which are in fact suburban—low density with a predominance of owner-occupied housing stock. Similarly, within what we have been calling the suburbs but what the Bureau of the Census more accurately refers to as "balance of SMSA" are many urban areas. If one were to disaggregate (break into finer subdivisions) most "suburbs," the urban-suburban differences would again appear.

Studies of the incomes of in-migrants and out-migrants to central cities support the above view. When the migration of individuals to and from central cities is analyzed, it is seen that those who migrate in have lower incomes than those who migrate out. This is true both of families and of unrelated individuals. The

TABLE 2-7
MEDIAN FAMILY INCOME BY PLACE OF RESIDENCE

	1959	1969	1979
Central city	$5,940	$9,507	$18,046
Suburban ring	$6,707	$11,411	$22,934
Central city as % of suburban, all SMSAs	89	83	79
SMSAs with population over 1 million			71
SMSAs with population under 1 million			81

Source: U.S. Bureau of the Census, *The City-Suburb Income Gap,* CDS 80-1, and *Current Population Survey,* ser. P-60, no. 129.

migration studies suggest that Americans are treating urban residence as an "inferior good."[3]

The income loss to central cities is twofold. First, in general more affluent households are replaced by less affluent households. Second, the number of households leaving is greater than the number of households entering. According to calculations by Sternlieb, central cities between 1970 and 1977 lost an annual average of $9.3 billion in income (measured in 1976 dollars). The effect is cumulative.[4] Adjusting for inflation and extending it to 1980 it appears likely that incomes earned by central city residents (in 1980 dollars) were at least $100 billion lower than they would have been had there been no migration since 1970.

Why does the income differential exist and why does it appear to be growing in both absolute and relative terms? Various explanations can be afforded, some elegant and some simple. A mathematical explanation based on the work of Alonso is offered in Chapter 3. A simpler and perhaps more commonsensical explanation based on work by Downs is offered in Chapter 7.

Nonmetropolitan Growth   In the 1970s the historic pattern of net migration from nonmetropolitan to metropolitan areas was reversed. For the first time in over a century—or possibly for the first time in the nation's history—the net flow of migrants was from metropolitan to nonmetropolitan areas.

The growth of nonmetropolitan population startled many demographers and observers of the urban scene. Net out-migration from nonmetropolitan areas was a fact of American life for so many decades that its reversal was almost universally unanticipated. One might be tempted to think it had to do with some "return to soil," but this is anything but the case. Farm employment declined by about 800,000 from 1970 to 1980, and farm population by about 2.5 million. Nor does it appear that the growth in nonmetropolitan population is simply a phenomenon peripheral to large metropolitan areas—a situation in which the fact of suburbanization simply outran the redefinition of SMSA boundaries. Rather, it appears in all census regions and seems to apply to nonmetropolitan areas that are both close to and remote from SMSAs.

Nonmetropolitan growth is a largely white phenomenon. In fact, the growth of black nonmetropolitan population from 1970 to 1980 is so slow (about 6 percent) as to strongly indicate that nonmetropolitan areas are still exhibiting black out-migration. Again, considering the pattern of migration and what we know about the disparity between black and white income, it could be argued that nonmetropolitan location is becoming or has become a "superior good." According to Kasarda:

> Until the mid-1960s, most nonmetropolitan counties were viewed as the areas left behind. For nearly 100 years, the industrialization of the U.S. economy had generated

---

[3] The term *inferior good* does not have a pejorative or judgmental meaning. It simply refers to a good, the absolute consumption of which falls as income rises.

[4] Testimony by George Sternlieb in "Is the Urban Crisis Over?" *Report by the Subcommittee on Fiscal and Intergovernmental Policy*, Joint Economic Committee, 95th Congress of the United States, March 20, 1979.

concentrative migration to metropolitan areas. So large was the migration of nonmetropolitan residents to the metropolitan centers through the 1950s that, despite higher rural birth rates, national population increase became largely synonymous with metropolitan growth.

However, by the early 1970s the net migration to metropolitan areas had reversed, and reversed significantly. Between 1970 and 1978, more than 2.7 million more people moved out of metropolitan areas than moved into them. Whereas one-sixth of all metropolitan areas lost population, three-fourths of all nonmetropolitan counties gained population. What makes this turnaround all the more striking is that it has been apparent in all major census regions and in relatively remote counties nonadjacent to metropolitan areas, as well as those adjacent. Moreover, among the nonmetropolitan counties, there is an inverse association between the size of the largest urban places within the county and its net migration. Fuguitt and Voss (1979) have shown that those nonmetropolitan counties with no incorporated places larger than 2,500 experienced the largest annual net migration between 1970 and 1975. The next largest net migration was found for those nonmetropolitan counties whose largest urban place was between 2,500 and 10,000 and net migration gains were the least in those nonmetropolitan counties containing an incorporated place greater than 10,000. Furthermore, in all these counties the rural, unincorporated areas grew much faster than the incorporated towns, and the incorporated towns themselves exhibited an inverse growth rate with their size.[5]

A definitive statement on the changing pattern of income distribution as between central city, ring, and nonmetropolitan residents will have to await the complete publication of detailed 1980 census income statistics. But on the basis of fragmentary evidence, it seems clear that the results will show that in percentage as well as absolute terms ring incomes will have grown faster than central-city incomes. It is also very likely to show nonmetropolitan incomes passing central-city incomes and quite possibly growing at a faster percentage rate than ring incomes.

A NOTE ON EUROPEAN EXPERIENCE

The experience of European countries with regard to the loss of jobs and population from central cities and from larger metropolitan areas is instructive for the United States in that it constitutes something of a controlled experiment. In the United States much has been made of race and tax policy in regard to the movement of population and employment within metropolitan areas. It has been suggested that the antagonism between the races, a legacy which goes back to the institution of slavery, has been a powerful factor in driving both population and jobs out of central places. It has also been argued that the U.S. tax system, with its very favorable treatment of home ownership (see Chapter 7), has been a powerful and perhaps misguided suburbanizing force.

If these were the primary causes of urban decline in America, one might expect to see a radically different situation in European countries, where these factors are more or less absent. In fact, however, the European situation seems to bear

---

[5] John D. Kasarda, "The Implications of Contemporary Redistribution Trends for National Urban Policy," *Social Science Quarterly*, vol. 61, nos. 3 and 4, December 1980, p. 380.

significant resemblance to the American situation. Writing about Great Britain, Hall and Metcalf note:

> The declining metropolis is not a phenomenon confined to the United States. Population and employment are falling in many European conurbations, particularly in the inner cores of these urban areas.
>
> The population of the biggest British urban agglomerations, or conurbations, is declining steadily. Between 1961 and 1974 their total population fell by 7 percent. In contrast, the population of the rest of Britain rose by 14 percent. The overall population fall reverses the trend of the century and a half preceding 1950, much as in the United States.
>
> In each conurbation the central city now accounts for a smaller proportion of the total conurbation population than it did twenty years ago. Thus, the overall population decline experienced by the conurbations is caused disproportionately by the fall in the population in cores. Second, the decline in conurbation populations is part of a suburbanization process which has been in operation for some time. Conurbations and other urban areas with populations over 250,000 have tended to experience falling populations since 1961, while the smaller urban and suburban areas on the fringes of the larger town and conurbations have increased their populations.[6]

The decline in central-city manufacturing employment in Britain has paralleled the U.S. experience. Between 1961 and 1971 Hall and Metcalf note the following changes.

CHANGES IN MANUFACTURING
EMPLOYMENT IN MAJOR URBAN
CONURBATIONS, GREAT BRITAIN, 1961–1971

Greater London	−25
Central Clydeside	−18
Merseyside	−9
South East Lancashire	−20
Tyneside	−7
West Midlands	−10
West Yorkshire	−16
Rest of Britain	+11

Between 1961 and 1974 Greater London lost almost half a million, or one-third of its manufacturing jobs. During 1966–74 alone, the loss was 383,000. This decline was seven times the national average. The decline in manufacturing in Greater London differs from that in other metropolitan areas, where a large part of the decline can be traced to one or a few dominant industries in the local industrial structure. In contrast, London has many industries which have grown nationally, but even these have declined steeply in London. Had London industries followed the national pattern, manufacturing employment would have grown between 1961 and 1971 by some 13,000 rather than declining by 335,000.[7]

---

[6] Peter Hall and David Metcalf, "The Declining Metropolis: Patterns, Problems and Policies in Britain and Mainland Europe," in Charles E. Leven (ed.), *The Mature Metropolis*, Lexington, Boston, 1978, pp. 65–68.

[7] Ibid., p. 70.

From 1961 to 1971 urban cores in Great Britain lost 2.8 percent of their population, while population in the urbanized portion of metropolitan rings grew by 17.2 percent and the nonurbanized portions by 9.8 percent.

In much of western Europe the pattern seems to be the same. Hall and Metcalf note that the city of Paris lost 300,000 residents between 1968 and 1975, while the suburban ring gained 900,000. Comparable trends are reported for Scandinavia and the Low Countries.

REGIONAL TRENDS

Although the focus of this book is the city and the metropolitan area, much of what happens with the metropolitan area can only be understood in the regional context. New York is losing population and Dallas is gaining population. Were we to look only at the city or the metropolitan area for the disparity, we would come up with only partial answers, for the latter is in a growing region and the former is in a region whose growth has just about stopped. In a growing region the demand for the goods and services produced by a city will grow. Thus employment and, indirectly, population growth within the city will be stimulated. If regional population grows then the number of people who might migrate to the city will grow. If we assume a constant probability that any one individual in the area will migrate to the city, then the larger the population from which such individuals are drawn, the larger will be the amount of in-migration. Thus the problems of the older cities in the northeast and north-central regions—that aging industrial region that Wilbur Thompson has referred to as the American Ruhr—are in part a regional rather than a specifically urban problem.

Migration and Population Growth

Table 2-8 shows regional population change from 1940 to 1980. To some extent the trends simply represent the historic diffusion of population that has been going on almost since the beginning of the country. But we should note some recent trends, particularly the virtual cessation of population growth in the northeast, the marked slowing of growth in the north-central region, and the accelerating growth in the south. We might also note that southern growth, which was formerly heavily concentrated in the Atlantic coast states, is now more evenly distributed, with major growth also occurring in the east and west south-central regions as well.

The prime factor in the difference in growth rate is net migration. Table 2-9 shows net migration for the 1940 to 1980 period.

A number of trends should be noted. First is the consistent pattern of net migration into the western United States throughout the 40-year time period. A look at state level data would reveal that a single state, California, accounted for a large share of net migration into the entire region—63 percent from 1960 to 1970 and 38 percent in the 1970s. Net migration into the west was overwhelmingly white. Two factors would appear to account for the relatively small amount of black migration. One is the distance from major concentrations of black population. The other is the absence of large black populations in the west at the start of

TABLE 2-8
REGIONAL POPULATION CHANGE, 1940–1980
(In Thousands)

Region*	1940	1950	1960	1970	1980	1970–1980
Northeast	35,977	39,478	44,678	49,061	49,139	.2
New England	8,437	9,314	10,509	11,848	12,348	4.2
Mid-Atlantic	27,539	30,164	34,168	37,213	36,788	−1.1
North-Central	40,143	44,461	51,619	56,589	58,854	4.0
East North-Central	26,626	30,399	36,225	40,262	41,670	3.5
West North-Central	13,517	14,061	15,394	16,327	17,184	5.2
South	41,666	47,197	54,973	62,812	75,349	20.0
South Atlantic	17,823	21,182	25,972	30,678	36,943	20.4
East South-Central	10,778	11,477	12,050	12,808	14,663	14.5
West South-Central	13,065	14,538	16,951	19,326	23,743	22.9
West	14,379	20,190	28,053	34,838	43,165	23.9
Mountain	4,150	5,075	6,855	8,289	11,368	37.1
Pacific	10,229	15,115	21,198	26,549	31,797	19.8

* The above regions are standard Bureau of the Census groupings, as follows: *New England:* Maine, New Hampshire, Vermont, Massachusetts, Rhode Island, Connecticut; *Mid-Atlantic:* New York, New Jersey, Pennsylvania; *East North-Central:* Ohio, Indiana, Illinois, Michigan, Wisconsin; *West North-Central:* Minnesota, Iowa, Missouri, North Dakota, South Dakota, Nebraska, Kansas; *South Atlantic:* Delaware, Maryland, District of Columbia, Virginia, West Virginia, North Carolina, South Carolina, Georgia, Florida; *East South-Central:* Kentucky, Tennessee, Alabama, Mississippi; *West South-Central:* Arkansas, Louisiana, Oklahoma, Texas; *Mountain:* Montana, Idaho, Wyoming, Colorado, New Mexico, Arizona, Utah, Nevada; *Pacific:* Washington, Oregon, California, Alaska, Hawaii.
Source: U.S. Bureau of the Census, *Census of the Population,* 1940, 1950, 1960, 1970, 1980.

the time period. Migrations of minority or, perhaps, all groups appear to be heavily influenced by where earlier migrants have gone.

A second trend to be noted is the consistent but accelerating net out-migration of white population from the northeast and north-central states. The figures

TABLE 2-9
NET MIGRATION BY REGION AND RACE, 1940–1975
(In Thousands)

Region	1940–1950 White	1940–1950 Nonwhite	1950–1960 White	1950–1960 Nonwhite	1960–1970 White	1960–1970 Black*
Northeast	−173	+483	−206	+541	−519	+612
North-Central	−948	+632	−679	+558	−1,272	+382
South	−583	−1,597	+52	−1,457	+1,806	−1,380
West	+3,181	+323	+3,518	332	+2,269	302

	1970–1975 White	1970–1975 Black	1975–1980 White and other nonwhite	1975–1980 Black
Northeast	−916	87	−608	−48
North-Central	−968	−18	−1,226	7
South	2,395	44	+2,522	293
West	1,112	120	+2,929	−85

Note: Net migration is moves in minus moves out. Because of immigration to the United States the algebraic sum for all regions in any time period is positive. Were only internal migration counted the algebraic sum would be zero.
Source: U.S. Bureau of the Census, *Current Population Reports,* ser. P. 20, no. 285 and earlier.

considerably understate the out-migration of residents of the region because immigration from Europe decreases the net outflow. Note also that during the period up to about 1970 the northeast and north-central states received heavy in-migrations of blacks.

The southern pattern changes considerably over the time period. At the start the south experienced net out-migration of both blacks and whites, though the number for the former was much larger. In the 1950s net out-migration of whites ceased, while the net out-migration of blacks continued at a rapid pace. In the 1960s the south began to receive massive white in-migration, while black out-migration continued. The corresponding figures for the northeast and north-central regions suggest a process of massive population exchange, with the south exchanging its own black population for an in-migrating white population from the northeast and north-central regions. In the 1970s the net out-migration of blacks from the south appeared to have ended, and the south began receiving a small black net in-migration. At the same time the rate of white in-migration to the south increased drastically, with the south receiving more than twice as much net-migration from 1970 to 1980 as it had in the previous decade. Table 2-9 suggests that, if anything, net migration into the south accelerated slightly in the second half of the decade.

Regional Shifts in Employment

Employment in the United States grew very rapidly during the 1970s, with the nation adding almost 20 million jobs. As can be seen from Table 2-10, employment growth was quite uneven when viewed on a regional basis.

Of the 19.6 million nonagricultural jobs the United States added during the

TABLE 2-10
NONAGRICULTURAL EMPLOYMENT BY REGION, 1970–1980
(In Thousands)

Region	Total		% Change	Manufacturing		% Change
	1970	1980		1970	1980	
Northeast	18,660	20,486	9.8	5,611	5,085	−9.4
New England	4,549	5,474	20.3	1,450	1,523	5.0
Mid-Atlantic	14,111	15,012	6.3	4,161	3,562	−14.4
North-Central	19,953	23,730	18.9	6,265	6,094	−2.7
East North-Central	14,594	16,827	15.3	5,042	4,715	−6.5
West North-Central	5,359	6,903	28.8	1,223	1,379	12.8
South	20,379	29,071	42.7	5,126	6,068	18.4
South Atlantic	10,572	14,625	38.3	2,679	3,042	13.5
East South-Central	3,825	5,133	34.2	1,228	1,364	11.1
West South-Central	5,982	9,313	55.7	1,219	1,662	36.3
West	11,787	17,544	58.8	2,377	3,124	31.4
Pacific	29,124	13,059	43.1	2,014	2,560	27.1
Mountain	2,663	4,485	68.4	363	564	55.4
United States total	70,920	90,564	27.6	19,379	20,371	4.7

Source: U.S. Department of Labor, Bureau of Labor Statistics, *Employment and Earnings,* 1970, 1980.

decade, about 14 million were in the south and the west. Employment in the north and east grew by 14.5 percent, while employment in the south and west grew by 44.9 percent. The north and east lost a total of 697,000 manufacturing jobs, while the south and west gained almost 1.7 million manufacturing jobs. While one should be cautious in generalizing, it may well be that the movement of a given number of jobs in manufacturing is more significant than the same number in another category of work, simply because manufacturing is more likely to be export sector activity and thus have a higher employment multiplier attached to it. (The multiplier concept is discussed in detail in Chapter 4.)

FORCES BEHIND SUBURBANIZATION AND DECENTRALIZATION

In the previous chapter we noted that the growth of urban populations in the nineteenth century was closely related to the industrial revolution and the mechanization of agriculture. We also noted that the very high population and employment densities that characterized many nineteenth-century cities were largely a function of the transportation technology.

The Effects of Technology

The more recent changes in urban form also have roots in technology, and a brief digression on the subject will help to set the stage for the discussion that follows. In a literal sense, a discussion of the effects of technology on urban form and urban history would have no limit, for technology and the civilization in which it exists are inextricably intertwined. As noted in Chapter 1, demographic processes themselves are heavily influenced by technology. The explosive growth of urban populations in third-world countries in this century is, as it was in Europe in the nineteenth century, largely the result of changes in agricultural, medical, and public health technology.

In the United States one of the most powerful forces behind post-World War II urban growth was the mechanization of agriculture. In 1940 the United States had about 11 million farm workers and a rural farm population of 30 million. American farmers fed a population of about 130 million and produced, on a net basis, no surplus for export. At present there are under 4 million farm workers and a rural farm population of about 8 million.[8] American farms feed a population of about 220 million and produce a $25 billion surplus for export. The numbers obviously reflect tremendous increases in agricultural productivity, stemming primarily from technological change.

If U.S. farm output per worker today equaled output in 1940 the United States might require something on the order of 20 million agricultural workers, implying a rural farm population of over 40 million. The rural nonfarm population would also be much larger than it is today for, to a large extent, that population is supported by the earnings from services rendered to the agricultural population. The U.S. rural population, farm and nonfarm, could easily be 50 million larger, metropolitan-area populations correspondingly smaller, and the U.S. urban

---

[8] U.S. Bureau of the Census, *Statistical Abstract of the United States* 1981, Table 1159 p. 657.

situation unimaginably different than it is today. The transformation of American blacks from a predominantly southern and rural population 40 years ago to the most urbanized major ethnic group today is also the result of the mechanization of agriculture. Thus it would not be hard to argue that the single most important event affecting urban areas in recent decades has been the mechanization of agriculture since the end of the Great Depression.

At an equally broad level of discussion per capita income is largely a function of the accumulated effects of many thousands of technological developments. How prosperous people are has major urban consequences. For example, Americans have used their increase in real income to increase their per capita consumption of housing. Average household size fell from 4.2 in 1920 to about 2.7 in 1980. One result has been the rapid growth of the suburbs and, in cases where the urban housing stock could not expand, absolute decline of central-city populations.

The extraordinary mobility of the U.S. population and the ability of people to choose where to live on the basis of taste and amenities, rather than on strictly economic grounds, is due largely to high levels of personal income. For example, one way in which the United States has used rising levels of real income has been to provide generous transfer payments to older citizens, primarily by way of Social Security. Combined with the longevity associated with higher living standards, this has produced millions of individuals and households that are free to live more or less where they want, unconstrained by economic necessity. Transfer payment income from the Social Security has thus been a major force behind the growth of many parts of the sunbelt and has probably been a deurbanizing force in general.

Transportation technologies, which both reduced the cost of transport and made it more flexible, have obviously facilitated movement of population and economic activity away from central places. Improved communications technologies, which reduce both the need for face-to-face communications and the cost of long-distance communications, have powerful decentralizing consequences. The list of these technologies is very long. Since the 1940s we have seen the introduction of long-distance direct dialing, facsimile transmission, closed-circuit television, telex, the long-distance transmission of data between computer systems, and numerous other improvements.

Electronic entertainment media have completed the work begun in earlier decades by the motion pictures in breaking the grip of central places on entertainment. The result has been to increase the relative attractiveness of remote, as compared to centrally located, residential areas.

Technological Effects at the Metropolitan-Area Level Having looked at the matter of technology very generally, let us now consider decentralization and net out-migration at the metropolitan-area level. In many cases both changes have the same or similar causes. Clearly the communications and transportation technology discussed above are *necessary* conditions but not *sufficient* conditions. As the internal-combustion engine, the limited-access highway, and the transistor reduced the cost of travel and communication, more peripheral locations became possible. If we view the matter in terms of agglomeration economies, the advantages of the central city and the metropolitan area weaken. Another way to say it is that the opportunity cost of a noncentral location diminished. Thus, technology is the necessary condition to change, but there may be less consensus about the sufficient conditions.

In part, it seems likely that the technology of earlier periods built up more massive and denser concentrations than the majority of the population wanted. Surveys have consistently shown that much of the U.S. public wanted to live in less dense and less urban situations than it did. For instance, the number of Americans who say they want to live in small towns greatly exceeds the number who actually do.[9] We also know that urban reformers of the late nineteenth and earlier twentieth century viewed deconcentration as a major goal. To some degree the centrifugal forces were always there. Technology simply weakened the centripetal forces and allowed the centrifugal forces to manifest themselves.

The growth of the environmental movement in the late 1960s and 1970s may have had the effect of causing people to want to embrace what was left of the natural world and thus propelled them outward in search for a less synthetic living environment. The growing realization that there is a link between human health and environmental conditions may also have been a factor. Perhaps the perception that one's chances for surviving a nuclear war increase with the distance of one's home from an obvious target was a factor, though the writer is not aware of any research that documents the influence of this consideration.

The very rapid rise in housing prices in the 1970s probably contributed to the growth of nonmetropolitan population. In the 1950s and 1960s personal income grew more rapidly than housing prices, but in the 1970s the situation was reversed. From 1970 to 1979 median family income in the United States rose by 99 percent. But the median selling price of all single-family units rose by 142 percent.[10] The actual monthly carrying cost of a new house rose by even more because of the rise in mortgage rates across the decade. Median home prices in the metropolitan-area rings were approximately 50 percent higher than those in non-metropolitan areas. The price differential would appear to reside, at least in part, in lower construction costs, lower land costs, and weaker land-use controls (see Chapter 8 on the relationship of land-use controls to housing prices). The less expensive and probably more elastic housing stocks of nonmetropolitan areas may have been a major factor in their rapid population growth.

Within metropolitan areas the continuing suburbanization of population seems largely explicable as a continuation of past trends, with technology making dispersion possible and many factors making it attractive to large numbers of people. The list of forces causing those who had the financial ability and the mobility to make the decision to move from central cities is almost endless: the desire for a less-crowded environment, the tax advantages and capital gains possibilities inherent in home ownership (see Chapter 7), the deterioration of many central-city school systems, higher crime rates in central cities, the desire of whites to live apart from large concentrations of blacks, etc. Even the nature

[9] Duane Elgin et al., *City Size and the Quality of Life*, Stanford Research Institute, Menlo Park, California, 1974, p. 29.
[10] U.S. Bureau of the Census, *Statistical Abstract of the United States*, 19, and Table 1360, p. 754.

of modern U.S. highway design may be a factor. In a great many metropolitan areas interstate highways are routed around the central city by means of a loop road, or beltway. The purpose of such a road is to keep through traffic out of the center of the city, but an important side effect is to produce a large increase in suburban accessibility relative to central-city accessibility and thus stimulate the movement of employment and population out of the central city.

Forces behind White Out-Migration from Central Cities

The movement of whites out of central cities during the 1970s occurred on a massive scale. In fact, net white out-migration during the decade was equal to about one-fourth of the total white population in central cities in 1970. One reason for white flight might be the presumed unwillingness of whites to share their living space with blacks. But a much simpler and more universal explanation—and one which does not have pejorative implications—is available. This is simply the income disparity of whites and blacks. Median family income of blacks is about three-fifths that of whites (see Chapter 6). The suburban housing stock, both owner-occupied and rental units, is newer and generally more expensive than central-city housing. Thus in the competition for suburban housing, the income differential alone would give whites a huge advantage. If right-handed people had higher incomes on the average than left-handed people, then one might expect the city-to-suburb migration rates to be higher among right-handed people. It would not be necessary to postulate any antipathy between the groups.

In the case of blacks and whites, antipathy and discrimination do play some part. Undoubtedly some whites do leave the central city because of fear or dislike of blacks. Undoubtedly some blacks who could afford suburban housing remain in the central city for fear of isolating themselves in a sea of whites. Discrimination in the sale or lease of suburban housing may also keep some blacks in the central city. But much of the disparity seems explicable simply on the basis of income differential.

The fact that it is the more affluent race which is leaving the central city at a net rate of roughly 1 million per year strongly suggests that central-city residence is becoming an inferior good. The fact that the central city is now experiencing black out-migration, albeit of a magnitude smaller than for whites, suggests that perhaps blacks' residential preferences are not that different from whites'. They simply have less income with which to express them.

The fact that central-city populations ceased to rise entirely is striking but not out of context with events in previous decades. Part of the reason growth stopped is simply the fall in the birthrate. For several decades central cities have been experiencing net out-migration, but it was more than compensated for by natural increase. When the natural increase slowed, populations began to fall. In Alonso's image the falling birthrate revealed the underlying reality, much as a receding tide reveals the submerged rocks along the shoreline.[11]

---

[11] William Alonso, "The Current Halt in the Metropolitan Phenomenon," in Charles E. Leven, op. cit.

Forces behind the Dispersion of Employment

The dispersion of economic activity has various explanations. Automotive technology and highway construction made possible the suburbanization of manufacturing, just as they facilitated the suburbanization of population. Increased automobile ownership among workers made manufacturers willing to move into areas where public transportation was more limited. Lower land costs in the suburban ring made possible one-story construction, which is cheaper on a square-foot-of-usable-space basis and which facilitates materials handling. The existence of millions of square feet of abandoned multistory manufacturing floor space in urban areas at the same time that one-story facilities are being built in the metropolitan periphery or in nonmetropolitan areas is, in part, testimony to the greater efficiency of the single-story plant.

The suburbanization of retailing was clearly a matter of stores following their customers. As noted, the income gradient in most U.S. metropolitan areas has been growing more pronounced with the passage of time. Thus buying power suburbanized even faster than population. The suburbanization of wholesaling has been a slower process than that of retailing, but here, too, one can clearly see a pull from residential decentralization to the decentralization of retailing to the decentralization of wholesaling.

With services, the story is mixed. For a range of personal services from medical care to dry cleaning the decentralization of population would be expected to produce a corresponding decentralization of employment. For business services decentralization has been much slower. A large range of business services require a high degree of interaction between the personnel of different firms, with the result that—at least until recently—they have tended to resist decentralization. Thus activities like advertising, public relations, investment banking, stock and commodity brokerage, corporate law, etc., have tended to remain in central locations. The transportation revolution of automobile, truck, and limited-access highway was not able to pry them out of their central locations. However, it is possible that the communications revolution based on the transistor will in fact do so, for each improvement in communications probably reduces the need for face-to-face communication.

Forces behind Regional Change

The most striking regional trend has been the growth of the south. The south not only has switched from a net exporter to a net importer of people but exhibited remarkable economic growth as well. As Table 2-10 indicates the south added almost one million manufacturing jobs from 1970 to 1980. The dominance of the northeast and north-central regions in manufacturing has clearly been broken. What accounts for this?

Heavy industry, dependent on rail or water for the bulk shipment of goods with relatively low value per ton, has declined as a percentage of total manufacturing activity. The manufacturing complexes in the major northeastern metropolitan areas were largely built on the strength of water and rail access. Light industry, which can survive on the basis of truck access, has been growing as a share of total manufacturing.

The virtual completion of the interstate highway system in the 1970s has thus made it possible for rural areas in the south to compete with northern industrial centers. Improvements in communications have further weakened the grip of metropolitan areas on manufacturing activity in a variety of ways. They have made it possible for manufacturers in once-remote locations to communicate more readily with customers, vendors, consultants, and colleagues. They have also facilitated the branching of centrally located firms because better communications facilitate the control of distant plants. But if changes in manufacturing itself, in transportation, and in communications have made southern industrial growth possible, this does not explain why it has, in fact, happened.

A close examination of southern manufacturing growth shows that it is not so much a matter of northern firms literally packing up and moving south, though this has happened in some cases. Rather it is a matter of differences in the rates of plant closings, plant openings, and plant growth. The south has been fertile soil for manufacturing. Some of its advantages follow.

1 *Lower wage costs.* Historically, southern wage rates for comparable work have been lower. The increased demand for labor in the south and the decreased demand in the north is closing the gap, but the gap still exists.[12]

2 *Weaker unions.* For reasons of tradition and a more conservative political climate, unions have been weak in the south. Again, the growth of manufacturing and the southward migration of northern workers will probably change this. But until now, it has been an important factor.[13]

3 *Lower construction costs.* Lower wages, milder climates, and generally lower land costs make it cheaper to build facilities in the south.[14]

4 *Lower energy costs.* Southern industry has relied heavily on natural gas (largely as a matter of proximity), while industry in the northeast has relied heavily on imported oil. There has been a price differential for many years. As energy costs rose in the 1970s, the price differential remained roughly the same as a percentage but increased as an absolute amount. The cost advantage of natural gas, combined with the lower space-heating needs in warmer climates, made energy cost differentials significant.[15]

5 *Political climate.* The conservative political temper of the south is undoubtedly attractive to many manufacturers.

6 *Racial matters.* Much southern industrial growth has occurred in predominantly white areas of the south, like the Piedmont area of the Carolinas. Much of the industrial losses in the north have been in areas with substantial black populations, like New York and northeastern New Jersey. Obviously, few

---

[12] Complete wage data by geographic area is not available in any one source for the United States. The best available data is probably found in the *Area Wage Surveys* of the U.S. Bureau of Labor Statistics.

[13] Data on union membership by state can be found in U.S. Bureau of the Census, *Statistical Abstract of the United States,* 1981, Table 690, p. 411. Right-to-work laws—legislation which prohibits contracts requiring a union shop (that is, the worker must join the union as a condition of employment)—are common in the south and absent in the mid-Atlantic and New England region.

[14] A variety of construction cost calculators such as *Means Cost System*, published by R. S. Means in Duxbury, Mass., provide cost indexes by type of structure by city.

[15] For energy costs by energy source see U.S. Department of Energy, *Monthly Energy Review.*

employers are willing to admit to racial motivations for moving, but one is left to wonder. In connection with the movement of manufacturing firms into predominantly white, nonmetropolitan areas of the south Thompson states:

> There are a number of reasons for this new form of racial discrimination, as I gather from conversations with local businessmen. Relocating manufacturers find the hill country white workers are freethinkers who reject unions, while black workers seek the protection of unions. With white labor there is neither a union problem nor a racial problem. This means that we will still have, for some time to come, considerable black migration out of the rural areas and small towns, even in the face of strong growth in the white areas.[16]

7 *Lower taxes*. In general, southern states are low-tax areas. Public services in the south are often not as extensive as in the north, and the wages of public employees tend to be lower. Not only is the tax burden lower, but the structure of taxes is likely to be more regressive, a fact which may be attractive to the executive making the location decision.[17]

8 *Local promotion efforts*. As discussed in Chapter 5, there is a certain amount that a community or state can do to attract industry. Aggressive recruitment of industry is an old southern tradition.

9 *Regional Agglomeration Economies*. The growth of manufacturing in the south may feed on itself to some extent. Given the role of manufacturing as part of the export base of the region (see Chapter 4), its growth stimulates additional population and employment growth. This growth makes the south a larger market, which in turn makes it more attractive as a manufacturing location. Similarly, as manufacturing in the region grows, the availability of suppliers of intermediate products and services grows. The firm that once had to hire consultants from New York or Chicago can now hire the same expertise in Richmond or Atlanta. Just as we argued that agglomeration economies were a force behind urban and metropolitan growth, so too can they be a force behind regional growth.

10 *A Catch-Up in Labor Force Quality*. At one time the quality of public education in the south lagged far behind that of the north. Southern labor was cheaper, but it wasn't as well educated and was likely to be less productive. That differential appears to be largely gone.

When we turn to the growth of employment more generally in the south, many of the same factors noted for manufacturing still apply. In fact, according to the export base model, the growth of manufacturing has in itself been a major stimulus to growth of employment in other sectors. But there are other factors as well. First, warm weather, the increasing number of retirement-age Americans, and a rather generous system of transfer payments to older people have brought large numbers of northerners south to retire. Their transfer incomes bring money into the area just as the sale of manufactured products would outside the region. The expenditure of these transfer incomes in the region builds pools of labor and

---

[16] Wilbur Thompson in Sternlieb & Hughes, eds., *Post-Industrial America: Metropolitan Decline and Inter-Regional Job Shifts*, Center for Urban Policy Research, Rutgers, 1975, p. 190.

[17] See U.S. Bureau of the Census, *State Government Finances in 1980* for comparative data. For comparison of personal income tax rates see *Statistical Abstract of the United States*, 1981, Table 491, p. 294.

capital, which may strengthen the region's competitive position in apparently unrelated ways.

The increasing role that amenities play in influencing the location of employment and residence seems to have favored the south.[18] The improvement in communications has probably favored the south, not by giving it an absolute advantage over other areas but in reducing its relative disadvantage. Whether it is the homeowner's ability to get cable TV and Home Box Office in a small southern town or a consulting firm's ability to communicate with the rest of the business world via telex, some sense of regional remoteness has gone.

Finally, and there seems no good way to quantify this, much of the south's reputation for political backwardness and "redneckism" has vanished. Twenty years ago TV viewers could watch southern sheriffs using dogs and fire hoses to harass civil rights marchers. Today one can argue without seeming absurd that race relations in the south are no worse than they are in the north. The southern universities that only a quarter century ago barred blacks from their campuses now have minority recruitment programs. How much the change in image means is probably beyond quantification. But it seems likely that there are people and companies who will contemplate moving south today who would not have 20 years ago, when Bull Connor and Lester Maddox symbolized the south.

Federal Policy

When regional flows of people and jobs are considered, the role of federal policy and fiscal presence must not be ignored. In several cases policies or actions that appeared to have no geographic intent have actually had far more influence on the location of activity than programs with a specific spatial intent. One might wonder, for example, what the distribution of manufacturing activity would look like if the money that was put into the interstate highway system had been put into the nation's railroads instead. This is not to say it should have been. In fact, it is hard to believe that such an allocation would ever have been politically possible. It is only to say that choices that presumably had no regional intent behind them have had powerful regional consequences.

The pattern of federal taxation and procurement also has important effects. In the mid-1970s the concept of capital export through this route gained prominence.

In this view, the federal government is seen as a huge engine which withdraws taxes from regions and then returns them in the form of expenditures for goods, services, and transfers to individuals. To the extent that some regions pay more than they receive and other regions do the reverse, massive interregional flows of capital are produced, accelerating the growth of some regions and retarding that of others. The size of these flows, if one accepts the concept, dwarfs any federal

---

[18] Numerous writers have commented upon the emergence of amenities as a force in economic location. See Harvey Perloff, "The Central City in the Post industrial Age," in Charles E. Leven, *op. cit.* See also Wilbur Thompson, "Economic Processes and Employment Problems in Declining Metropolitan Areas," in Sternlieb and Hughes, *op. cit.* For a brief summary of this point and a review of the literature on the forces behind industrial relocation, see George A. Reigeluth and Harold Wolman, *The Determinants and Implications of Communities Changing Competitive Advantages: A Review of Literature*, Working paper 1264-03, Urban Institute, Washington, D.C., 1979.

TABLE 2-11
FEDERAL EXPENDITURES AND REVENUES BY REGION, 1979
(In Millions)

Region	Revenue	Expenditure	Deficit or Surplus
Northeast	$107,816	$100,847	−6,969
New England	26,364	28,754	2,390
Mid-Atlantic	81,452	72,093	−9,359
North-Central	$128,584	$101,516	−27,068
East North-Central	93,940	66,457	−27,483
West North-Central	34,644	35,059	415
South	$133,949	$163,548	29,635
South Atlantic*	67,299	90,525	23,225
East South-Central	22,617	29,477	6,860
West South-Central	44,033	43,582	−451
West	$92,183	$96,585	4,402
Mountain	20,583	24,711	4,129
Pacific	71,600	71,874	274

* Includes figures for Washington, D.C.
Source: Government Research Corporation, *National Tax Journal,* Washington, D.C., February 7, 1981. U.S. Bureau of the Census, *Statistical Abstract of the United States,* p. 253.

program that has specific regional or spatial intents. Table 2-11 shows the estimated flows. Developing the data involves many assumptions, such as considering the budget deficit as an added tax so that expenditures and receipts balance and allocating all of an expenditure to the location of the prime contractor. Nonetheless, the numbers are so large that it is hard to believe that the taxing and spending policies of the federal government have not had significant regional consequences.

Taking the figures as a whole, we see a net capital outflow of roughly $34 billion for the north with a corresponding net inflow for the south and west combined. How does one visualize the economic effect of a $34 billion outflow or inflow? One approach is to compare it to an equivalent number of manufacturing jobs. In 1977 total value added by manufacturing in the United States was $585 billion and manufacturing employment was 19.6 million for a value-added-per-worker figure of $30,000 in round numbers.

Thus 1 million workers, if they were employed in manufacturing activity typical of the national mix as a whole and if all of their output were sold outside the region, would bring into a region roughly $30 billion. The computation is very crude and, as noted, the capital export figures themselves involve a number of assumptions and approximations. But as an order-of-magnitude figure, the loss of income to the north via the capital export mechanism might be considered equivalent to the income stemming from 1 million export-sector manufacturing jobs—hardly a trivial loss.

When federal expenditures by region are examined by category, by far the largest variation is in defense. Taken as a whole, about two-thirds of defense expenditures are for procurement and one-third for salaries. The procurement expenditures, like salary expenditures, have the short-term effect of expanding aggregate demand within the region. But, presumably, they also have a long-term effect, which may be more important. A substantial amount of defense procurement monies go for high-technology state-of-the-art equipment and in this process go to build pools of expertise, which then prove to be powerful competitors in nondefense areas. Much of the expertise that now resides in California's Silicon Valley was built on contracts for military electronics. But it can build video games, computer chess players, or minicomputers as well. The writer suspects that in terms of long-run economic impact, a federal dollar spent on high-technology procurement has a much bigger yield than a dollar spent on, say, public-sector employment or income maintenance.

Other federal policies also have powerful regional effects, though they may not always be universally recognized. Cheap water has been an enormous boon to the economy of the southwest. Much agriculture in the region, as well as much of the local activity sustained by agriculture, would be impossible without it. Even some commercial and residential development would be less likely to be attracted to the region without cheap water. Much of the capital that built the delivery systems came from Washington. One suspects the western lawmakers knew what they were getting, but one wonders how many eastern members of Congress saw any link between an irrigation project in the west and an abandoned industrial building in Bridgeport or Newark. In the mid-1970s the northeast and north-central regions became aware of some of these relationships and rather belatedly began to organize. One group set up was the Conference of North East Governors (CONEG). We have also seen the emergence in Congress of a northeast–north-central coalition. But the realization has come rather late in the game.

SOME POLICY ISSUES

To a large extent federal urban policy has been a matter of saving the cities. This has meant helping the cities to retain population and jobs, build new housing and restore old housing, reinvest in urban infrastructure, and remain solvent without drastic cutbacks in services. When federal urban policy has been criticized, it has generally been assailed for not doing enough. The extent of federal urban commitment has varied from one administration to another. If dollars are the true measure, commitment to this goal probably peaked in the Carter administration.

Behind much of our urban policy is the almost automatically assumed position that there is something inherently good about keeping jobs and people in cities. Behind that, though it is not always articulated with crystal clarity, is a view that the city is in some way the best or highest form of human settlement.

The obviously pejorative term "urban sprawl" says a great deal about this viewpoint. We look with envy at the Europeans who have suburbanized far less than we and whose central cities generally appear to be in better shape than ours. We don't expect them to ask themselves why we have been able to provide our working class with free-standing houses on quarter-acre lots while they have not. If we chose to, we could view the massive suburbanization that followed World War II as a major accomplishment of American civilization, in which millions of people got something they obviously wanted. Instead, we often tend to view it as something of a national disgrace. Obviously, there is a very strong feeling that there is something inherently good about the city.

There is little doubt that among those who write about urban questions this sort of view is widespread. A major commitment to preserve central cities in something like their present form may well be justified. But before one accepts that view, there are some serious questions that need to be addressed.

The first is simply this. If the city has the virtues that its defenders and rhetoricians ascribe to it, why are the majority of Americans treating it as an inferior good? If Americans saw the city as its champions do, the middle and upper classes would be using their superior incomes to crowd in and displace the poor into suburbia or exurbia. Instead they are using their superior incomes to flee the city and leave it to the poor.

A second question, discussed in more detail in Chapters 6 and 7, is whether the attempt to strengthen cities and help their populations actually produces a set of incentives for the poor to stay in the cities, both dooming them and the cities in rather different ways.

The third question is whether, in purely economic terms, we need cities in anything like their present form. The physical form of cities changes slowly because the stuff of which they are built—masonry, asphalt, steel—has a very long lifetime. It is thus possible for a city to be drastically out of date in a technological sense. Perhaps another way to put it is to ask, is there some irreducible amount of activity that must, through economic necessity, remain in the city? What is the evidence?

For manufacturing, wholesaling, retailing, and personal services the results seem to be clear, as has been discussed previously. Corporate headquarters still seem, by and large, to need metropolitan areas. But within the metropolitan area there has been a large amount of movement out. In 1968, New York City contained 138 of the Fortune 500 corporate headquarters. By 1980 it contained 73.[19] Most had not left the region. They moved, on the average, 20 to 30 miles to the more affluent New York suburbs. It may be that because it internalizes fewer functions and therefore benefits more from central-city agglomeration economies, the smaller corporate headquarters is more bound to the city than the larger one. But by and large, the direction of corporate-headquarters moves is out, not in.

Possibly there is a core of activity that is still solidly locked to the central city. If so, it has not been identified. In fact, its existence is not certain. It is also not clear, if such a core exists, that it is composed of activities found in all major cities. Some cities may have cores of activity related, say, to foreign trade, finance, advertising, corporate law, and some cultural and artistic activities that are secure for the foreseeable future. This does not necessarily imply that there is an irreducible core in every city—or even in most cities.

Some of the policy issues raised by these speculations are discussed in other chapters, particularly in Chapters 5, 6, and 13.

---

[19] Peter Muller, *Contemporary Suburban America*, Prentice-Hall, Englewood Cliffs, N.J., 1981, p. 149.

CHAPTER 3

THE URBAN LAND-USE PATTERN

James Bohland
College of Architecture and Urban Studies
Virginia Polytechnic Institute and State University

The visitor is often struck with the uniqueness of the city—the distinctiveness of San Francisco, the French imprint on New Orleans, the vastness of Los Angeles, or the old world appearance of Montreal. However, once familiar with a particular city, we find that its overall spatial pattern is very similar to that of other cities. It is these spatial similarities which are the subject of this chapter.

Bourne defines urban form as "the spatial arrangement of individual elements of the built environment as well as social groups, economic activities, and public institutions."[1] His definition includes two seemingly different, yet important, aspects of urban form—that which is visible and has a three-dimensional expression on the landscape and that which is associated with people, institutions, and processes.

It is the built environment that is the focus of this chapter, although we cannot understand its structure without being concerned with social groups, economic activities, and public institutions. We begin with a discussion of general trends in urban form, then turn to a review of different land-use theories, and finally examine different functional components of the city's land uses.

GENERAL TRAITS OF THE URBAN ENVIRONMENT

Before examining the built environment in detail it is useful to identify some general attributes of the form of modern metropolitan America. Such generalizations suggest a common set of processes at work in shaping the structure of the

---

[1] Larry Bourne, "Urban Spatial Structure: An Introductory Essay on Concepts and Criteria," in L. Bourne (ed.), *Internal Structure of the City*, Oxford, New York, 1982, pp. 28–45.

city and serve as a point of departure for comparing those individual cases that do not conform to the general trend.

Horizontal Rather Than Vertical Growth

The modern city is a land-extensive phenomenon compared to earlier settlements; words like "sprawl" or "explosion" are commonly used to describe the growth of the modern city. In this connection see Berry's commuter fields as an illustration of the extensiveness of the modern metropolis (Figure 3-1).

Urban sprawl is associated with urbanization in many parts of the world, but it is particularly acute in the American urban system. Comparisons between countries are difficult because of the lack of any comparable definitions, but what data exist show that American cities have lower population densities than their European counterparts. Hall has found that English cities, which are also in the process of decentralizing, are significantly more dense than comparable American cities (see Table 3-1). Part of the difference may simply be that some key changes have occurred more rapidly in the United States. For example, levels of per capita real income and per capita automobile ownership that were reached in the United States in the 1920s were not reached in England until well after World War II. Of course, there are other differences, including a stronger central planning tradition and much higher population density in England, which may cause the two nations to move along somewhat different paths.

This tendency toward horizontal development and lower population density in the contemporary city contrasts with the morphology of earlier cities in this country. Cities in the eighteenth and nineteenth centuries were compact "walking cities" of high population density. Old Philadelphia and most of the colonial cities on the east coast, with their narrow streets and nucleated commercial district closely surrounded by residential areas, typified the urban structure in America prior to industrialization.

Significance of the Core

With the industrial revolution cities experienced explosive growth of the core, or central business district (CBD). The concentration of economic activity at the core was largely due to the nature of the dominant transportation technologies of the late nineteenth and twentieth centuries. The public transportation lines— trolleys, electric trains, and streetcars—that radiated outward from the center of the city served as conduits to bring the population into the inner city for work and shopping. The growth of CBDs, both vertically and horizontally, led to very high densities and ultimately to congestion and environmental degradation. CBDs became representative of both the best and the worst of the industrial city.

FIGURE 3-1
Commuter fields for major American cities, 1970. The commuter fields in the eastern portion of the country are almost space-filling, indicating that for much of the United States metropolitan dominance is almost complete in terms of area. (*Brian J. L. Berry, "Contemporary Urbanization Processes,"* in Geographical Perspectives on Urban Problems, *National Academy of Sciences, Washington, D. C., 1973, p. 94.*)

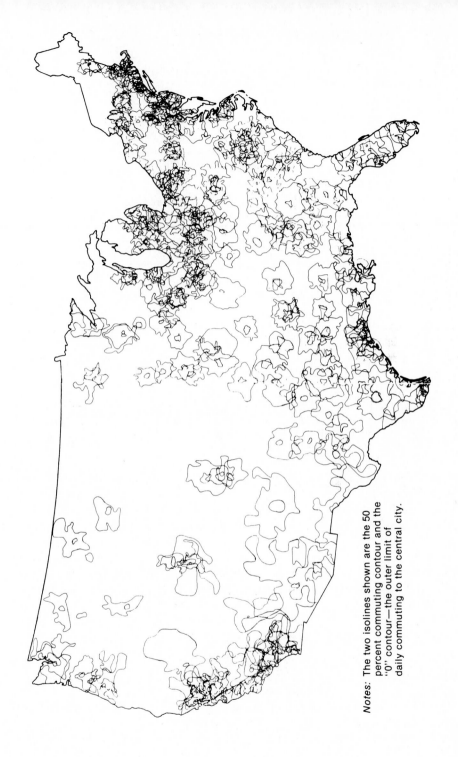

Notes: The two isolines shown are the 50 percent commuting contour and the "0" contour—the outer limit of daily commuting to the central city.

61

TABLE 3-1
COMPARISON OF URBAN DENSITIES IN THE UNITED KINGDOM AND UNITED STATES

	United Kingdom			
	1961		1971	
Area	Population (millions)	Density*	Population (millions)	Density*
Megalopolis in England	32.2	1,651	33.8	1,733
SMLAs within megalopolis England	28.3	2,356	29.2	2,433

	United States			
	1960		1970	
Area	Population (millions)	Density*	Population (millions)	Density*
Northeast U.S. urban complex	34.2	1,084	38.9	1,231
SMSAs within northeast U.S. urban complex	31.7	1,470	35.7	1,653

* Density calculated as number of persons per square mile.
Source: Marion Clawson and Peter Hall, *Planning and Urban Growth an Anglo-American Comparison*, Johns Hopkins, Baltimore, 1973, pp. 63 and 72.

With the emergence of a postindustrial society, the core has lost its relative importance in almost all metropolitan areas and has experienced absolute losses in population and jobs in many. These changes are in large measure due to improvements in transportation and communications technology and to increases in real income, points discussed in the preceding chapters. In most cities, the "urban problem" can be summed up in terms of the decline of the older, more central areas.

But in spite of their losses CBDs are far from insignificant. The urban density gradient, though flattening, still peaks at the core. Nor can historical and political factors be ignored. In most cities the core was the birthplace, the site near the point of original settlement. The symbolism associated with the historic cores of cities like Boston, Philadelphia, or Charleston, to name a few, means that their significance far transcends their economic importance. Thus, the history of the city and the history of the core are intertwined.

Specialization and Segregation of Land Use

Compared to the preindustrial city, the modern city is an elaborate mosaic of highly differentiated land uses and economic activities. Industrialization, particularly as practiced under capitalism, has left in its wake a highly specialized, fragmented society, the spatial manifestations of which are evident in the land-use composition of the modern city.

According to Sjorberg, cities prior to industrialization evidenced little differentiation in land use.[2] Some enclaves of occupational groups may have been evident, but otherwise the compact, crowded preindustrial city was not complex

[2] Gideon Sjorberg, *The Preindustrial City. Past and Present*, Free Press, New York, 1960.

in its land-use arrangement. Radford has argued that the heterogeneity in urban structure accompanying industrialization is a result of three interactive forces:

1 The development of intraurban transportation innovations, which caused the residential options to be opened to residents. Increased options made it possible, operating in the context of the urban property market, for residents to cluster together in neighborhoods that were homogeneous in race, socioeconomic status, and family structure.

2 The factory system in which the separation of home and work eventually led to functional districts, functional hierarchies, and the creation of externalities that further separated the quality of sites within the urban environment (for example, the disamenities to residential uses resulting from the noise, smoke, or traffic of a factory).

3 The rapid expansion of the central business district. The growth of the core imparted to the surrounding areas diversified land uses and created what has been commonly referred to as a zone of transition, a zone which was and is still characterized by marginal economic activities and great land-use variety.[3]

Stability and Change in Land Use

The speed at which land-use patterns can change is often dramatic. The compositions of neighborhoods have been transformed radically within the span of a single year. The spatial structure of retailing within many cities has altered drastically within 2 decades. And industrial decentralization still continues at a rapid pace in many metropolitan areas.

Yet, while change can be dramatic, the basic form of the city has considerable resilience. The large capital investments necessary for the construction of the built environment mean that structures endure long after their original functions have changed. Agglomeration economies, locational interdependencies, and externalities develop through time and act to forestall radical shifts in the character of the land-use mix in an area. Geographic and topographic factors may keep a given part of the city in essentially the same type of land use for very long periods of time.

Even in housing, the land use which we assume is most susceptible to alteration, visible change is slow. Typically, less than 3 percent of the housing stock is less than 1 year old. And, even though some neighborhoods change their social and economic character dramatically and quickly, the social structure and overall residential pattern of the city persists. The core-periphery dichotomies that emerged in the late nineteenth century in the American city have been altered very little up to the present.

The Concept of Relative Location   The concept of relative location is helpful in understanding the dynamics of land-use change. Your home, for example, can be described in relation to your place of work, the school your children attend, the location of the retail center where the family shops. Relative location can be

---

[3] John Radford, "The Social Geography of the Nineteenth Century City," in D. Herbert and R. J. Johnston (eds.), *Geography and the Urban Environment*, vol. 4, Wiley, New York, 1981, pp. 257–294.

modified either by relocation of elements in the network or by changes in travel time brought about by new technological developments.

Changes in the relative location of urban parcels lie at the heart of the dynamics of change in land uses. As the elements in the city's spatial structure undergo reorganization, the value or utility of a particular location also changes.

The spatial mobility of the urban population also fosters change, particularly in residential patterns. Approximately one in five Americans changes address yearly. Yet as high as this rate appears, it is only about one-half the rate for the nineteenth-century city. With the changes in residential structure, the geographic arrangement of market potential and labor supply are constantly being modified. These in turn change the utility of sites with respect to production and distribution activities. Racial or class change in a neighborhood may change the value of nearby commercial land uses.

Decisions that cause land-use change are not without conflict. The growing body of literature on the topic of locational conflict emphasizes concepts such as conflict resolution, power relationship, and multiparticipant decision models as aids in understanding the final resolution of land-use decisions and how land-use change occurs within the political context of the city. And, as we shall see in Chapter 8, many land-use conflicts are ultimately settled in the courts.

Recently an organized movement to slow land-use change has emerged. In the last decade or so there has been increased concern with historic preservation and the restoration of older areas. Preservationists have clashed with those in favor of development over the conversion of land to a new use. The former have argued that we must preserve that which is unique to the character of the American city and American life, while the latter argue that questions of tax base, housing supply, or economic growth should be given precedence.

The preservation movement has not yet gathered the momentum to be a major force in influencing the land-use character of most cities. Yet in isolated cases, for example, Savannah or Charleston, preservationists have had a major role in shaping the present land-use pattern. The willingness of society to fund historic preservation, either with direct grants or special tax treatment like accelerated depreciation, is a tacit acknowledgment that there are positive externalities stemming from historic preservation.

THEORIES OF THE SPATIAL ARRANGEMENT OF URBAN LAND USE

Several general theories of urban land-use patterns have been proposed. While they do not explain or predict the fine detail of land-use patterns, they do provide a general framework for understanding the overall pattern. Three general categories can be identified: (1) urban ecological theory, (2) neoclassical economic theory, and (3) structuralist or Marxist theory.

Urban Ecology

Urban ecology as a theoretical basis for describing land-use patterns originated in the Chicago school of urban sociology of the 1920s. Among the more prominent names associated with the ecological perspective are Burgess, McKenzie, Wirth, and Park.

Urban ecology does not have the mathematical elegance of the neoclassical models, which fuse microeconomic theory and land-use models. However, it offers many useful insights, and the descriptive land-use models associated with the viewpoint have become widely accepted as a reasonably good generalization of the urban land-use pattern in the American industrial city. Moreover, urban ecology has the very important advantage of being dynamic rather than static. Rather than ignoring growth, it focuses on growth.

The human ecologists were concerned with a number of different aspects of the city—social disorder, community organizations, and deviance—as well as land use. In fact, the concern with land use stemmed more from an interest in understanding social aspects of urban neighborhoods than in attempting to build a formal theory of land use.

Urban ecology drew heavily on natural history and social Darwinism. Park defined the ecological perspective in the following way:

> Urban ecology is fundamentally an attempt to investigate the processes by which the botanic balance and social equilibrium are maintained once they are achieved, and the processes by which, when the botanic balance and social equilibrium are disturbed, transition is made from one relatively stable order to another.[4]

Neighborhoods were seen as communities much in the same sense as plant communities. Changes in land use were ascribed to a process of invasion and succession by competing elements of the city. Ecological dominance was achieved when an area had completely transformed itself from one use to another. If the dominance was complete and sufficiently long-lasting, "natural regions" or "natural communities" would come into existence.

The forces responsible for changing urban land uses were immigration, particularly of ethnic or racial groups, and the expansion of the central business district. Both of these activities exerted pressure at the core for space. Thus, the stimulus for land-use change came from the core and precipitated change outward. For example, new immigrants entering the city competed for space with households already established in the core. Over time, the new immigrants would dominate, forcing the previous owners to move to neighborhoods more distant from the core and to compete for residential space with households there.

Descriptive Models of Urban Land Use

The struggle for dominance explicit in the ecological perspective became the important concept underlying early attempts to generalize urban land-use patterns. Burgess's concentric-zone model of land use was the first attempt to generalize the spatial arrangement of land use on the basis of ecological principles. Subsequent descriptions—sector and multiple-nucleus models—while not explicitly linked to ecological theory do nonetheless share some of the basic assumptions and concepts with the concentric-zone model.

As a group they have been criticized for lacking a strong theoretical foundation. Since they were developed 40 or 50 years ago, critics also argue that they do not reflect the current situation. Finally, unsuccessful attempts to apply the three models to cities in different countries has led some to argue that they are not general models of land use but are unique to the U.S. urban experience.

---

[4] Robert Park, "Human Ecology," *American Journal of Sociology*, vol. 42, no. 1, 1936, p. 15.

Some scholars have argued that the ecological perspective and the descriptive land-use models associated with it ignore the economic and political realities of the city. Others, like Firey, have argued that the city cannot be understood in terms of aggregate forces that function according to some type of ecological law.[5] People have symbolic and psychological attachments to place, and to ignore this is to ignore the essence of human behavior.

Despite all the criticisms of the three models, they have endured. Why so? In part, they endure because they provide simple and useful generalizations about land use. They and their descendants do a good job in describing urban land-use patterns in the contemporary American city.

Concentric Rings The concentric-ring or zonal model was first proposed by Ernest Burgess in the 1920s. Burgess makes liberal use of the lexicon of the urban ecologists, using terms like "invasion and succession," "natural areas," and "dominance" to describe the processes and patterns of land use.

Burgess's zonal model was based on observations in Chicago in the beginning 2 decades of the twentieth century. As such, it depicts an American city shortly after its transition to an industrial base. According to Burgess, land use was organized as a series of concentric rings radiating outward from the central business district, as shown in Figure 3-2 (*a*). The zones were originally labeled as follows:

1 *Central business district*. The retail core of the city and a wholesale business district that encircled the retail core.
2 *Zone in transition*. Zone of residential decay occurring in large measure because of the encroachment of industry and business from zone 1.
3 *Zone of independent workingmen's homes*. Working-class neighborhoods occupied by factory workers who needed to be located near their work.
4 *Zone of better residences*. Residential area of the city's middle class.
5 *Zone of commuters*. Smaller towns and communities, occupied by persons who work in the city but can afford to live outside it. In subsequent versions Burgess relabeled this zone the "higher class residential district."[6]

According to Burgess, zonation of land use was the result of pressure for space that originated in zones 1 and 2 because of the growth of the central business district and the influx of large numbers of foreign immigrants into the inner city. The immigrants sought housing in or near the core in order to be near work opportunities. As the central business district grew, its former residents were pushed outward, required to seek space in neighborhoods farther from the central business district. Their moves, of course, precipitated other moves, and a wavelike effect was set into motion by the original pressure from the core. Burgess described the processes as "invasion" and "succession," the latter occurring when the new group eventually obtains dominance in the area.

As noted earlier, Burgess's explanation of land-use zones has been criticized for being cast in a theory that was based on biological analogs rather than human behavior or economic principles. Even if we accept the premises of human

[5] Walter Firey, "Sentiment and Symbolism as Ecological Variables," *American Sociological Review*, vol. 10, no. 2, 1945, pp. 140–148.
[6] E. W. Burgess, "The Growth of the City: An Introduction to a Research Project," *Publications, American Sociological Society*, vol. 18, no. 2, pp. 85–97.

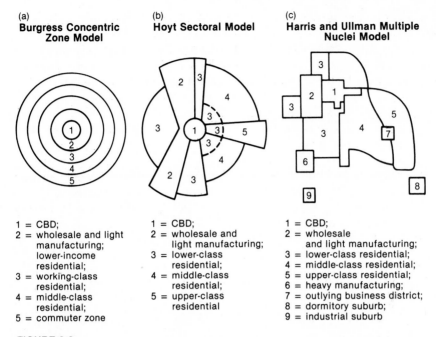

(a)
Burgress Concentric Zone Model

(b)
Hoyt Sectoral Model

(c)
Harris and Ullman Multiple Nuclei Model

1 = CBD;
2 = wholesale and light manufacturing; lower-income residential;
3 = working-class residential;
4 = middle-class residential;
5 = commuter zone

1 = CBD;
2 = wholesale and light manufacturing;
3 = lower-class residential;
4 = middle-class residential;
5 = upper-class residential

1 = CBD;
2 = wholesale and light manufacturing;
3 = lower-class residential;
4 = middle-class residential;
5 = upper-class residential;
6 = heavy manufacturing;
7 = outlying business district;
8 = dormitory suburb;
9 = industrial suburb

FIGURE 3-2
Traditional land-use models. (*Chauncy Harris and Edward L. Ullman, "The Nature of Cities,"* Annals of the American Academy of Political and Social Science, *vol. 242, no. 1, 1945, p. 13.*)

ecology, aspects of land-use conversion remain unexplained. For example, if the city does not grow, or the growth is concentrated in the fringe rather than the core, the process of change implicit in his model is not possible. Moreover, if the focus of the city's economic activity is not the central business district, then the symmetry of the zones would be altered. It is important to recognize that zonal patterns of land use may occur for reasons other than those presented by Burgess and the human ecologists, for example by the workings of the neoclassical model discussed subsequently.

For any limitations it may have the Burgess model does describe much of what one sees on a land-use map of a major metropolitan area. Not only will large elements of a zonal pattern appear at the regional level, but the ring pattern is often recapitulated at a smaller scale within particular urban places in the metropolitan area. For example, one may see elements of a zonal pattern within the cities or older towns in the suburban ring. The concept of succession and the view that land-use change is likely to be particularly rapid in the frontier between zones are useful ideas that describe reality well. For example, the concept of succession seems to describe racial transition very well. For the planner or the community development specialist trying to understand community change the concept of succession may be more useful than more sophisticated models.

Hoyt's Sector Model An alternative to the Burgess model was offered by Hoyt after an analysis of the real estate markets in a number of American cities.

According to Hoyt, urban land use was not arranged in zones around the central business district but in sectors radiating outward from the CBD like wedges, as shown in Figure 3.2(b). The typical city would have a retail core, as proposed by Burgess, but industrial land use would be found in a sector conforming to transportation routes, such as rivers or rail lines. Residential areas would also have wedgelike configurations; for example, working-class neighborhoods would be adjacent to the industrial sector so the workers would be near their work.

Hoyt believed that land-use change was caused both by push factors from the core and pull factors from the periphery. While he recognized the role of the CBD in fostering expansion and change in land use, he believed it less important than did Burgess. Attraction to new housing areas on the fringe was also an important mechanism fostering residential change. Although Hoyt did not coin the term, his discussion of neighborhood change in terms of socioeconomic status is commonly referred to as a "filter-down" process.

In this process, homes eventually filter down the socioeconomic scale, while individuals filter upward. The process eventually leads to a gradient in social status away from the central city if the downward shift in status is radical. However, Hoyt argued that the downward shift in class was slow, and in general the same social-class structure would be maintained over an extensive period of time. The result would be a *gradient in social class* within the general sectors of the model. In effect, the sector model is similar to Burgess's in that zonal gradients are postulated. Thus it has been argued that Hoyt's model is a modification of the original zonal model rather than a repudiation of it.

There are other similarities in the two models. In both, the central business district is the pivotal point. Both are descriptive models whose mechanisms and processes of change are not clearly linked to any formal theory of land-use dynamics. Finally, both models are based on the presumption of urban growth. This presumption raises serious questions about their applicability to declining or stable cities.

Multiple-Nuclei Model   The most recent and yet the least clearly specified of the three models is the multiple-nuclei model offered by Harris and Ullman shown in Figure 3-2 (c). Its major deviation from the previous two is the recognition that the modern city has a number of foci, rather than just the CBD, around which land uses are arranged. The creation of separate nuclei may be the result of planned development that occurs to take advantage of agglomeration economies, the existence of noxious activities, which tend to cluster together to limit externality effects to a few areas, or the site requirements of activities, particularly industrial activities. Because of these and other factors, separate concentrations of specific activities develop that are in turn large enough to influence land-use decisions in the surrounding areas.

Although it lacks well-developed explanatory mechanisms, the multicenter model clearly describes much of what one observes. It is not hard to see commonsense reasons why this is so. The reliance on the automobile tends to prevent monocentric development because the auto works poorly in a congested environment and requires so much space to park. The monocentric development, which is compatible with a rail-based system, is incompatible with an automobile-based system.

In an auto-based transportation system differences in accessibility between parcels are much smaller than in a rail-based system. This reduction allows dispersing forces such as congestion effects and the lower cost of development on previously vacant land to operate more freely. The combination of relative fiscal independence and autonomy in the application of land-use controls among suburban communities tends to scatter development, as discussed in some detail in the section on zoning in Chapter 8. Finally, modern highway design tends to create nodes of high accessibility in numerous locations. The basic strategy in the design of the interstate highway system was to enable through traffic to bypass cities, both to save time and to avoid congesting downtown areas. The result is the now-familiar beltway, such as the one that encircles the District of Columbia. At each point where the beltway intersects a major radial route a point of high accessibility is created and development is likely to follow. Very often a service road will be built parallel to the beltway, creating a band of high accessibility between intersections. Thus the fundamental design of the interstate system is destructive of the monocentric pattern and encourages multinucleated growth.

Neoclassical Land-Use Theory

Neoclassical land-use theory brings the intellectual apparatus of modern micro-economic theory, with its emphasis on adjustment at the margin, to bear upon the distribution of land uses. In this theory urban land uses are primarily a function of urban land values. In turn, land values are largely determined by transportation costs.

The roots of modern urban land-use theory come from the early work of Ricardo and Von Thunen on economic rent as it applied to agricultural land use. In 1903, Hurd began to integrate this earlier work into a theory of urban land use that emphasized the importance of accessibility and location to urban land values.[7] Much of existing theory is based on the work of Muth and Alonso done in the 1960s, including Alonso's seminal book *Location and Land Use*.[8]

Principles of Land Values   Consider a simple model of a single use, for example, residential land use. We make two sets of simplifying assumptions, environmental and behavioral. The environmental assumptions are: (1) the city as a flat plain on which transit costs are solely a function of distance, (2) the concentration of all distribution and production activities at the center of the plain, (3) a uniform distribution of population across the plain, (4) all property in private ownership, and (5) construction and maintenance costs for a building are constant throughout the city. The behavioral assumptions are: (1) uniform tastes by the population in terms of housing size and style and lot size, (2) complete information by the entire population on all locational alternatives, (3) attempted maximization by all residents of the utility they receive from a given combined expenditure on residential space and transportation and (4) no constraints on any segment of the population in purchasing property.

Household costs are defined as housing costs plus transportation costs but

[7] Richard Hurd, *Principles of City Land Values*, The Record and Guide, New York, 1903.
[8] R. Muth, *Cities and Housing*, Chicago University Press, Chicago, 1969; William Alonso, *Location and Land Use: Toward a General Theory of Land Rent*, Harvard University Press, Cambridge, Mass., 1964.

exclude land rents. At the core household costs include only housing costs. However, as we move away from the core a transportation cost element which rises linearly with distance is introduced. A curve precisely like the land-rent curve shown in Figure 3-3 in connection with the Ricardian theory of rent arises. The lower transportation costs associated with more centralized locations are capitalized as higher locational rents. Alonso refers to the plot of all these rents as the bid-rent curve.

While the curve in theory represents the *maximum* rent that householders would *bid* for each location, it in fact becomes the rent gradient because of the competition between households all seeking to maximize utility (behavioral assumption 3). Because there are no nonresidential uses in this simplest of models, the bid-rent curve is determined entirely by households.

A Model for Competing Land Uses   To be more realistic, we need to extend the model to multiple land uses. For purposes of clarity let us consider only three: retail, office, and residential. By inclusion of retail and office we no longer need the assumption that economic activity is at the core, for the model will produce a comparable result without our needing to assume it.

The spatial arrangement of the three uses is determined by the bid-rent curve. In Figure 3-3 the composite curve O'C'B'A' represents the maximum bid-rent

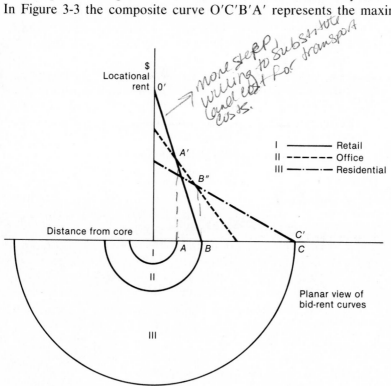

FIGURE 3-3
Bid-rent curves of competitive land uses in the Alonso model. The spatial implications of the bid-rent curves can be seen if we simply transpose the two-dimensional graph to a planar view. Thus, in zone 1 we would expect to find retail activities; in zone 2, offices; and in zone 3, residential units.

curve surface for the three, and thus the land-value distribution for the city. In the model the intercept for each bid-rent curve indicates the relative importance of access to each of the land uses. The slopes of the curves are a measure of the ability of a landowner to substitute land for transport costs. The steeper the slope the more willing the landowner is to substitute land costs for transport costs.

To understand the intercept and slope values for each of the land uses consider the locational factors that are important to each of these three activities. For retail activities, access to consumers is paramount. The more specialized and the higher value of the goods, the more important it is for a store to be located at a point where access to a large market is maximized. Assuming an evenly distributed population, the point of maximum accessibility would be in the center of the city.

Important agglomeration economies also exist for many retail functions because of the need for personal contact between entrepreneurs, comparative shopping behavior of consumers, and the status and prestige associated with being located near certain types of retail establishments. Thus, in addition to a location central to their market, many retail activities favor a location near other retail outlets, even near their competitors.

For office activities a central location is important both for access to labor and to facilitate interaction between the personnel of firms—salespeople and customers, vendors and purchasers, consultants and clients, etc. We assume, perhaps arbitrarily, a bid-rent curve for offices somewhat less steep than for retailing.

We assume the least steep curve for residential uses. The grounds for doing so are that agglomeration economies are absent and that the number of trip ends, trip destination locations, per square foot of household floor space is smaller than for retail or office floor space. Thus, accessibility is relatively less important for the household.

Since retail activities will always outbid the other two in all locations from point O to point A, retail uses occupy this area of the city. Office uses predominate from A' to B', residential uses from B' to C. Beyond C, agricultural land dominates, since it is of no value to the urban user. If we extend the planar view at the bottom of Figure 3-3 to a full 360 degrees we see that the Alonso model generates a pattern of rings similar to that postulated by Burgess.

It is clear that in the model the bid-rent curve determines the configuration of land values and the resultant land-use pattern. While we have described some of the specific location criteria for the three activities used in our example, some general relationships have been proposed which enable us to understand differences in the gradient of the bid-rent curves of various activities. Nourse offers the following generalizations:

1 The gradient is steeper the greater the cost per unit of output for maintaining contact with the center.

2 The gradient is steeper the larger the number of units of output produced per square foot of space.

3 The gradient is steeper the less readily other factors can be substituted for land as its price increases.[9]

[9] Hugh Nourse, *Regional Economics*, McGraw-Hill, New York, 1968, p. 117.

These general relationships are useful in understanding gradient differences between major land-use groups, but what of gradients within a group? For example, we know that household income within metropolitan areas is positively correlated with distance from the center. How does this fit into the theory of urban land values?

According to Alonso the locational choice for residential land represents an attempt by individuals to balance two conflicting preferences: access to the core versus greater living space. The household will maximize its utility subject to the fact that land prices decline with distance from the center and that transportation costs increase with distance from the center. Imagine a household going through a process of evaluating locations successively more distant from the center. As long as the marginal reduction in land costs exceeds the marginal increase in commuting costs the household will consider successively more distant locations. At the point of equality the process will stop and the household will settle.

In principle, the marginal process just described is no different than that which the entrepreneur uses in determining what mix of factors to use in production or the process by which the consumer allocates income among the various competing goods.

Commuting costs are a function only of distance if we ignore the matter of modal choice (see Chapter 9). However, land costs are a function of both distance and the amount of land used. If, as seems entirely reasonable, the amount of land used rises with income the equilibrium distance will rise as income rises. (Note that we have dropped behavioral assumption 1 here.)

This process results in the apparent paradox of lower-income residents living on the highest-valued residential land. But they can do so only by using less space. As a consequence crowding occurs and maintenance costs rise as intensive use accelerates the physical deterioration of the structure.

Of course, commuting has time as well as money costs. Harvey has argued that the bid-rent curve of the wealthy has changed because the relative time and money costs of commuting have changed.[10] If considerations of time were paramount the wealthy would choose access over space and outbid the poor for close-in space. The current income gradient would be reversed (Figure 3-4). In fact, clustering of upper-income households near the core and the concentration of the poor on the periphery is still evident in some cities, particularly in Latin America and Asia. Historically, concentrations of the wealthy were evident near the core in many cities in the United States. When improved transportation lowered the time requirement for commuting, commuting costs rather than time became the decision criterion for the wealthy, and their bid-rent curve changed to that described in the Alonso model.

While Alonso's model emphasizes the income elasticity of demand for space, other interpretations stress the importance of constraints on the supply of housing at the fringe in explaining spatial-income patterns. Both political and legal factors (see Chapter 8) and the costs of new construction hold down the supply of housing for the nonaffluent in outlying areas. The net result is to create what Downs calls

---

[10] David Harvey, *Society, The City and the Space-Economy of Urbanism,* Association of American Geographers, Commission on College Geography, Resource Paper No. 18, Washington, D.C., 1972.

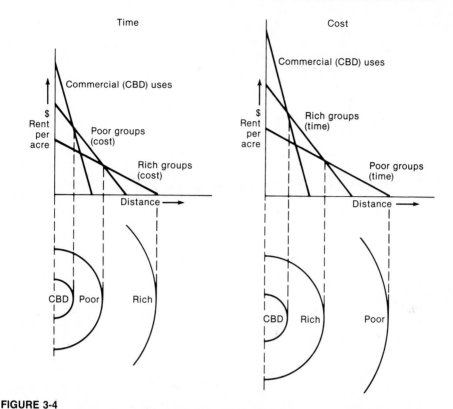

FIGURE 3-4
Bid-rent curves for low- and high-income groups using time versus cost considerations. Harvey's argument is illustrated by the differences in the gradient of the bid-rent curves for the two income classes. If time is important in the locational decision, the wealthy will outbid lower-income residents and be located near the city. If commuting costs are the important element in the decision, the wealthy will select locations on the fringe, leaving inner-city sites to the lower-income residents. (*David Harvey,* Society, the City and the Space-Economy of Urbanism, *Association of American Geographers, Commission on College Geography, Resource Paper No. 19, 1972.*)

the two urban frontiers, the Frontier of Deterioration in the central city and the Frontier of Growth on the periphery.[11]

Locational Interdependencies The Alonso model emphasizes the locational interdependency between the core and other sites in the city but does not deal extensively with the interdependencies between land uses within a local area. What effect, for example, does a block of deteriorating warehouses have on adjacent uses? Though complex, these interdependencies can be modeled by a series of simultaneous equations, which include both the effect of adjacent uses as well as the core effect implicit in Alonso's model. The Alonso model is a static one. It explains how land uses would be distributed if the metropolitan area came

[11] A. Downs, "Alternative Forms of Future Urban Growth in the United States," *Journal of the American Institute of Planners*, vol. 36, no. 1, 1970, pp. 3–11.

into being all at once—that is, if all sites were put up for auction simultaneously and the built environment formed *de novo*. Thus, it can offer no explanation of how growth affects land-use patterns. Finally, we note that the model is patently unrealistic in assuming that all nonresidential trip destinations are located at the core. Yet, for all its limitations the model is useful and worth the time required to comprehend it.

Land Value in the Modern City   How well do the models of land value fit reality? In general the fit is quite good. The major exception is that in reality the land-value curve is much closer to a negative exponential function than a straight line. The model tends to underestimate values in the core and overestimate them in the periphery. Figure 3-5 shows the actual land values for Topeka, Kansas.

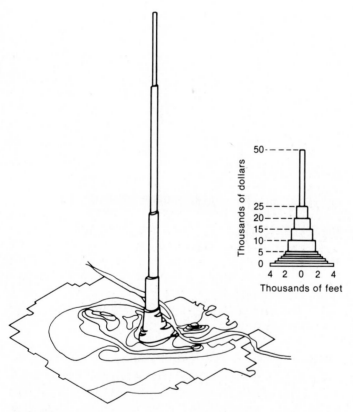

FIGURE 3-5
Land value in Topeka, Kansas. Notice the dominance of the CBD in terms of land values, the steep gradient in values near the core, and the leveling out of the gradient as one moves to the fringe. This distribution of values corresponds more closely with a negative exponential curve than a simple linear curve. Were the study reproduced today, it is highly probable that the price gradient would be somewhat flatter, given the dispersal of population and economic activity in recent years. (*Duane S. Knos, "Isometric Land Value: Topeka, Kansas", University of Kansas, Bureau of Business and Economic Research, 1962.*)

FIGURE 3-6
Land-value cone for metropolitan areas. Land value declines away from the
CBD in the manner described by Alonso. Ridges correspond to major urban
arterial routes, while the secondary peaks occur at the intersection of these
arterial routes and major crosstown streets. (*Brian J. L. Berry,* Commercial
Structure and Commercial Blight, *University of Chicago, Department of
Geography, Research Paper No. 85, Chicago, 1963, p. 35.)*

We have not concerned ourselves in this discussion with the effects of
additional nodes on land values within the city. These can be modeled by
including a local accessibility effect. The influence of secondary nodes is
illustrated in Figure 3-6. The conical-shaped distribution of land value is modified
by higher ridges of values radiating out from the core, representing the greater
access provided by major arterial routes. Secondary land-value peaks exist at the
junction of these arterial routes and circumferential streets, again points of slightly
higher access. Not surprisingly, these secondary nodes were typically the site of
small outlying retail centers, the type of outlying business district existing in the
city prior to the development of the planned shopping malls.

Structuralist or Marxist Perspective

In recent years a growing literature on a Marxist or structuralist interpretation of
urban land use and land values has emerged. Harvey, Scott, and Cassells, among
others, have argued that urban land-use patterns and land values can best be
understood in terms of a Marxist view of society—one that sees society divided
into discrete economic classes, with social change largely the product of class
conflict and government primarily serving the interests of those who possess
capital.[12]

[12] David Harvey, "Class-Monopoly Rent, Finance Capital and the Urban Revolution," *Regional
Studies*, vol. 8, nos. 3–4, pp. 239–255. M. Castells, *City, Class and Power*, Macmillan, London, 1978.
A. Scott, *The Urban Land Nexus and the State*, Pion, London, 1980.

Locational rent as defined in the Alonso model is seen in a different context in the Marxist perspective. In the structuralist or Marxist model rent exists because a class of landowners permits use only in return for a given level of economic benefit. Thus, for example, as Harvey argues, if a surplus of low-rent housing exists, the landlords will create scarcity by disinvestment in areas in order to achieve higher rents as an owner class.[13] When stripped of its ideological content, it could be argued that this is no different from saying that when demand weakens, a freely functioning market is likely to produce a decrease in supply.

Even among non-Marxists, the Marxist critique of neoclassical economic rent theory has provided a basis for new and informative dialogue as to the nature of the urban land market. As an alternative to neoclassical theory it provides the urban scholar with an opportunity to reexamine old concepts and theories.

Public Sector Allocations and Land Use

Increasingly students of urban land uses have come to recognize the importance of public-sector decisions in influencing urban land patterns. As yet no single, integrated theory has been offered to explain public-sector involvement in land-use change. Rather, several different theses or hypotheses have been offered. Pahl, for example, argues in his "managerial thesis" that land-use decisions as well as access to urban resources are controlled by both private- and public-sector managers who seek to maximize some utility function.[14] These managers, or gatekeepers—planners are good examples of such managers in the American context—are able to effect decisions that determine the location of public as well as private investment.

Gale and Moore offer a similar view but place greater emphasis on political power in explaining the decision process. According to their "manipulated-city" hypothesis, the distribution of public resources is controlled by a coalition of private interests, which exerts political influence on public-sector decision makers in order to ensure resource-allocation decisions that are favorable to their interest.[15] This view is consistent with the "elitist" theory of urban politics proposed by Hunter.[16] He argues that the informal power structure of a city, that is, the appointed officials on commissions, boards, and advisory groups, compose a rather small group who make policy decisions that are in their own best interests.

In contrast to this manipulative view of urban politics is the pluralistic view offered by Dahl.[17] Dahl contends that public decisions are influenced by a large number of heterogeneous interest groups, each of which are interested in a rather narrow range of public issues. No single group exerts complete control over decision makers, and, consequently, no group is the sole beneficiary of the allocation decisions.

Regardless of which view one takes, it is clear that these decisions do have a

[13] D. Harvey, op. cit.

[14] R. Pahl, "Urban Social Theory and Research," *Environment and Planning A*, vol. 1. no. 1, 1969, pp. 143–153.

[15] S. Gale and E. Moore, *The Manipulated City*, Maaroufa, Chicago, 1975.

[16] F. Hunter, *Community Power Structure: A Study of Decision Makers*, Anchor, New York, 1963.

[17] R. Dahl, *Who Governs? Democracy and Power in an American City*, Yale University Press, New Haven, 1961.

significant impact on the character and form of the urban environment. While a number of public-sector actions affect urban form, four are particularly important: transportation infrastructure, public utilities, urban services, and direct control over land use. The latter is covered in Chapter 8. The pattern of public investment in the transportation network will be a major shaping force on the city or metropolitan area because it has such powerful effects on the accessibility and value of land. For example, the change from a radial, CBD-oriented infrastructure to one in which circumferential expressways provided quick access between suburbs has contributed to the decline of the central business district. Similarly, the interstate highway system has given urban residents the luxury of "country" living while being able to commute to the city for work. It has thus fostered residential and, at one remove, economic decentralization.

Highway location decisions can also have very direct, often negative, effects on particular areas. In some cases neighborhoods are destroyed or severely fragmented by the construction of urban expressways through them. Even if a neighborhood persists, residents may need to contend with air pollution, highway noise, and congestion. Increases in land values may push out residential uses in favor of commercial ones.

The effect of changes in the transportation infrastructure on neighborhood character is documented by Sennett in his insightful historical analysis of one small area in Chicago.[18] Here the socioeconomic character of the neighborhood undergoes a radical transformation through time because of a change in the orientation of the city's transportation network.

The decision by public officials to extend or withhold public utilities also has a significant influence on the direction of growth and development. For example, sewers are generally necessary for multifamily or even closely spaced single-family development. If households must rely on septic tanks for waste disposal, only relatively low-density single-family development is possible. While most cities do not have an explicit growth policy, city officials use their ability to provide or withhold utilities as a tool to shape and guide growth. In many cases private developers are willing to share in the cost of providing utilities because utility service facilitates development and increases land values. More generally, almost all categories of public investment will shape the city land-use pattern. This is because the location of educational, recreational, social, and other services affects the relative location of every parcel of land within the city.

Not all public-service facilities have a positive influence on adjacent development, however. Noxious facilities, such as sewage treatment plants or sanitation landfills, or stigmatized services, such as prison prerelease centers or community mental health facilities, can have a negative effect on the immediate surroundings, either because of the externalities associated with each or because of people's fear that undesirable residents will congregate around the facilities. Unfortunately, there is a tendency for public officials to concentrate these types of facilities in the same areas within the city, usually in declining or transitional neighborhoods, thus creating a contagious affect that leads to further deterioration.

---

[18] R. Sennett, *Families against the City: Middle Class Homes of Industrial Chicago, 1872–1890.* New York: Vintage Books, 1974.

Because the distribution of public services influences land values, and thus personal wealth, the issue of equity has arisen in connection with the allocation of these services. To what extent do different groups or neighborhoods benefit from the allocation of public services? The "underclass hypothesis," which posits that municipal governments discriminate against poor and minority groups in the provision of public services, has been offered as a point to begin considering the equity question.[19] Empirical evidence for the hypothesis is inconclusive, for some studies indicate that inequities exist,[20] while others have found that many public services are located closer to lower-income areas.[21]

COMPONENTS OF URBAN LAND USE

The factors determining the fine grain of land use are numerous, and no two situations are entirely the same. Though many generalizations are possible, we have not yet been able to formulate a general theory or model of urban land use that has theoretical integrity and is capable of predicting change in a small area.

Because of the difficulties in trying to explain simultaneous changes throughout the entire city, it is more fruitful to consider individual components of urban land use separately and to identify and understand the forces that influence their location. In the following section, two land-use categories, commercial and residential, are discussed in detail.

Commercial Land Use

Commercial land use occupies a relatively small proportion of the area of a city, typically about 7 percent. This compares with 40 percent for residential and 20 percent for transportation (mostly street surface). Yet, as we have seen, the historic commercial center of the city, the central business district, has played a pivotal role in shaping the pattern of other land uses around the city. Thus, its importance exceeds its area.

In an urban economy based on market forces, private ownership, and relatively little central planning, the pattern of commercial land use is the result of numerous individual owners making independent decisions about the location of business activities. Given this rather atomistic decision-making system it is striking that a standard pattern of commercial land-use activities has emerged.

One standard classification of commercial land use has been developed by Berry.[22] He recognized three basic types of commercial activities and several subdivisions within each type, as shown in Figure 3-7.

[19] R. Lineberry, "Equality, Public Policy and Public Services: The Underclass Hypothesis and the Limits to Equality," *Policy and Politics*, vol. 4, no. 2, 1975, pp. 67–84.

[20] K. Cox, *Conflict, Power and Politics in the City: A Geographic View*, McGraw-Hill, New York, 1973. P. Bloch, *Equality of Distribution and Police Services*, Urban Institute, Washington, D.C., 1974.

[21] P. Coulter, "Measuring the Inequality of Urban Public Services: A Methodological Discussion with Applications," *Policy Studies Journal*, vol. 8, no. 5, 1980, pp. 683–697. R. Lineberry, *Equality and Urban Policy*, Sage, Beverly Hills, Calif., 1977.

[22] Brian Berry, *Commercial Structure and Commercial Blight*, University of Chicago, Department of Geography, Research Paper No. 85, Chicago, 1963.

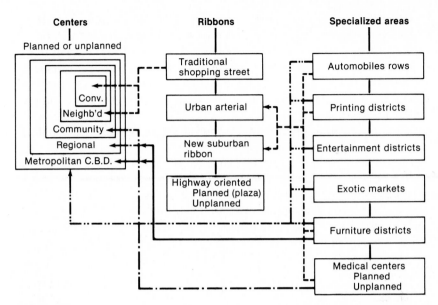

FIGURE 3-7
Berry's classification of intraurban commercial structure. Threefold classification of
commercial activities in urban America. (*Brian J. L. Berry,* Commercial Structure and
Commercial Blight, *University of Chicago, Department of Geography, Research Paper
No. 85, Chicago, 1963, p. 200.*)

Nodes or centers represent those commercial areas in which a number of retailers are congregated in a small area, typically because of agglomeration effects or because they share similar locational requirements. The centers range in size from the very small, one- or two-store convenience nodes to the large central business district.

Ribbons are those commercial activities found strung along streets in any metropolitan area. Retailers gravitate to such locations for a variety of reasons, including to service highway users, to advertise through billboards and storefront signs, to encourage drive-in–drive-out service, or to be more convenient to auto users.

Although nodes have received most attention from geographers and urban economists, it is the ribbon or the ribbon containing a series of nodes that is becoming more prominent. This is simply because of the dominance of the automobile. Reliance on a type of vehicle that can stop anywhere, that does not have a fixed schedule, and that functions poorly in a high-density environment will naturally favor ribbonlike rather than monocentric development.

Specialized areas develop in both centers and ribbons for economic as well as historic reasons. Agglomeration economies are particularly important to the formation of certain types of specialized districts, for example, financial districts, auto sales districts, medical complexes, to name a few. In other cases, as with exotic markets—establishments selling unique or highly specialized goods or services—historic factors may best explain their location within the city.

Central Business District   Of the retail centers, historically the central business district has been the major node. While it is convenient to think of the CBD as a node, in larger cities the CDB consists of several subdivisions or functional districts—financial, entertainment, retail, and publishing, to name but a few. Each contributes to the economic life of the central business district and provides a distinct ambiance to the core. In smaller cities, functional subdistricts are less evident because economies of scale are insufficient for their creation.

Agglomeration economies present in the CBD are important to business activities that require daily personal contact. They are also important in retailing, for individual stores benefit from the presence of shoppers attracted by other stores. Another important factor in the growth of the CBD has been the close proximity of a large labor pool. Finally, the tremendous capital investment in the central business district has caused the local business community to advocate and support local planning and developmental policies that favor the central area. Urban renewal and community development programs have often been designed to favor the growth of survival of the CBD. Zoning regulations and transportation policy are often designed to maintain the dominance of the central business district. However, technological change and some other elements of public policy make some loss of CBD activity inevitable.

The decline in the importance of the central business district as a retailing center is one of the most significant developments in the modern city. It can be traced to a number of interdependent factors. Widespread automobile ownership and the suburbanization of population were preconditions for the decline of the CBD as a retailing center. The expansion of shopping hours into the evenings and to Sunday improved the marketing position of suburban shopping centers with respect to the old retail core. Changes in shopping behavior, brought about in part by changes in the composition of the family, proved to be detrimental to central city retailers. With more and more working wives, convenience and access have become more important in influencing shopping behavior.

The loss of CBD retailing has been accelerated by the advent of the planned shopping center. The central business district and the outlying retail centers that were prevalent in the city prior to the 1950s typically evolved as a consequence of the locational decisions of numerous individual entrepreneurs. In such a decision-making environment, less risk taking was evident, and "satisfactory" rather than optimal locations were the rule. Locational inertia was a major factor keeping retailers in sites that were marginal. The capital required to shift to more profitable sites was beyond the means of many of the smaller owners who comprised the core of the retail trade.

Development firms with professional locational analysts carefully seek out the best locations for shopping centers. The investment required for a large regional shopping center such as Tyson's Corner in Washington or Crossroads Center in Oklahoma City means that the locational decision cannot be left to chance or to trial and error and that a "satisfactory" location may not be sufficient. Maximizing behavior replaces "satisficing" behavior. Because fixed capital needs are met by the developer, downtown retailers can relocate more readily than if they had to have enough capital to own their premises. Developers of centers generally make major marketing efforts prior to opening in order to fill the newly built space. Very often, their prime hunting ground is the nearby downtown.

Outlying Shopping Centers The growth of the outlying shopping center can be attributed to a number of different factors. Certainly, availability of large tracts of cheaper land on the fringe of the city, social problems, and environmental deterioration of the central city area are significant. In some cases tax inducements by suburban communities have been important. However, the two most significant factors have been the decentralization of the urban population and the restructuring of the metropolitan transportation infrastructure.

The modern regional shopping center has been modified and transformed from its earliest stage and is still undergoing change. Initially the regional center tended to be an open space with one or two large department stores serving as the focus of activity, and the remaining stores distributed around a large, central parking area. In the early centers retail establishments and service activities catering to shoppers, for example, restaurants, were usually the only service function present. This early form was soon replaced by the two-level enclosed mall that was anchored by department stores, a design originated by Victor Gruen.

With the advent of a temperature-controlled interior environment, the regional shopping center also became more than a center for retail activities. Art shows, community dances, skating rinks, and other social-cultural activities began to appear with increased frequency. Today's regional centers have become multifunctional, somewhat in the same sense as the old central business district. Entertainment facilities, convention activities, business and office sections, community cultural activities, and other nonretailing functions are now a common part of the shopping center of the 1980s. To stroll along the mall on a Saturday evening and sample the social and cultural life of the community has become a favorite pastime of many suburban families.

Will the growth in the size and diversity of the contemporary shopping mall continue? Surely the supercenters of the 1970s will continue to be an important component of the metropolitan area's retail structure, but a trend toward smaller, more specialized centers has begun to emerge. This trend appears to represent a continuation of the decentralization of retail functions of the central business district. Retail establishments that offer highly specialized, high-valued goods have, so far, been able to maintain a central-city location. However, viewed in the context of continued growth of an affluent suburban population and the emerging development of business and office centers in the suburbs, the new wave of specialty malls threatens a further erosion of the CBD retailing function.

Central Business District Revitalization Faced with competition from suburban shopping centers and the investment losses associated with declining CBD land values, the downtown business community, along with the central city's government, has attempted to revitalize the core. Most commonly, such redevelopment is heavily underwritten by the federal government and, to a lesser degree, by state and local government. For decentralizing forces are so powerful that the process cannot work without considerable alteration of the market. Urban renewal, discussed in some detail in Chapter 8, pumped over $13 billion into urban areas, most of it spent in or near the CBD. Today, community development funds, UDAG grants, and some monies from the Economic Development Administration continue to subsidize CBD development, although these funds are declining in amount.

Revitalization has taken different courses depending upon the particular city and its problems. However, three general redevelopment strategies can be identified: (1) revitalization of the retail structure of the core; (2) expansion of the business and office function; and (3) expansion of the cultural, recreational, and convention activities in the core.

Most attempts to revitalize the retail function have been grand in design and purpose. To attract customers back to the center of the city requires, at least in the minds of planners and architects, the grand architectural statement. Thus, the creation of the downtown shopping mall, similar in design to, but in competition with, its suburban counterpart. The downtown malls range in character and scope. At the one end are the rather simple but effective outdoor malls, such as those in Kalamazoo or Tulsa that utilize existing buildings and simply redesign pedestrian corridors by closing streets, opening areas for walking, and constructing small parks or resting points for shoppers. At the other extreme are the large enclosed centers like Galleria in Philadelphia or Eaton Center in Toronto that are very similar in character to the large enclosed centers in suburbia. In other cases, historic areas have been converted to retail areas, such as the Market Center in Charleston or the Faneuil Hall Marketplace in Boston. Cities with old port facilities have found that restoring these areas into commercial or entertainment districts can provide a stimulus to inner-city economic growth. The Inner Harbor development in Baltimore and Waterside Place in Norfolk are examples of such restoration. The success of the downtown malls has been limited because the underlying forces that have pulled retailing out of the central cities are extremely powerful and, if anything, continue to gain in strength.

Cities have done much better in keeping and adding office spaces. A quick experiment in many cities will verify the character of the new CBD. Visit the CBD on a Saturday midmorning or afternoon and note the level of activity. Do the same on any weekday at noon. In most cities Saturday, the day that was previously the busiest day for shopping, has become a very low-level period of activity. Yet, during the midweek at noon the city bustles with activity as office staffs emerge to engage in social and economic exchange.

The growth of the office function in the CBD is the result of several factors. Agglomeration economies are still very strong for many business functions. Even with modern communications technology, the need for personal contact is still considerable. Because offices are less land-intensive than retailing centers the lure of relatively low-cost suburban land is less important in their siting. Then, too, convenient auto access is less crucial for office than for retail use.

Many cities have attempted to increase the inflow of external money, particularly into the central business district, by attracting tourists or conventioneers to the core. This redevelopment strategy typically involves the construction of convention complexes that include meeting areas, hotels, motels, restaurants, and entertainment centers. The hope is that these facilities will promote the growth of related office and commercial activity. The loss that the municipality takes in building a convention center like Detroit's Cobo Hall or Chicago's McCormick Place will, it is hoped, be made up by increased revenues stemming from the business activity spun off by the facility. Sports and cultural facilities are also often underwritten to enhance the city image, to capture some of the discretionary income of the suburban population, and to attract some of the affluent suburban population back to urban living.

It seems probable that within the next decade the federal government will cut back direct support for redevelopment programs. Without the capital required to meet the costs of grand-scale redevelopment, it appears that the central business districts will have a difficult uphill fight to resist economic decline.

The future of the central business district is even more clouded by the fact that the activities that formed the new economic base of the central business district are beginning to decentralize. The continued rapid advance in electronic communications is profoundly threatening to the integrity of the CBD because it eats away at the CBD's most fundamental reason for being, the need for face-to-face contact. For example, new office construction has begun to increase in the suburbs with the development of the multifunctional shopping area. The continued construction of new office space on beltways around major cities like Washington, D.C., Atlanta, or Boston is a harbinger of a future that will seriously jeopardize the role of the central business district as a business center.

Recently many of the entertainment and cultural complexes located in core areas have been relocated in the suburbs. Increasingly professional sports complexes are being constructed in suburban communities rather than in the old core areas. Large blocks of vacant, easily cleared land, good highway access and the proximity of large numbers of affluent patrons are powerful attractions. Witness, for example, the construction of the Meadowlands sports complex in the New York area, or the new Silverdome outside Detroit or the new sports complex in Kansas City. If the cultural and recreational activities of the core continue to relocate in the suburbs, the growth of the central business district as a convention and recreational center will be seriously jeopardized.

Residential Land Use

When we purchase a house within the city, we buy more than a structure. We also purchase a location and membership in a neighborhood. The relative location of the home activities and the composition of the neighborhood all have a significant effect on our well-being. Expenditures on travel to work, the quality of our children's education, personal safety, the quality of our social interaction, and our prestige and status, to mention a few, are all influenced in some manner by our neighborhood and its location within the city. It is a cliché among real estate brokers that the three most important factors in determining the value of a house are location, location, and location. Like most clichés it has a basis in experience.

Neighborhood Composition   In this section we will focus on two aspects of the urban neighborhood: the composition and spatial arrangement of neighborhoods and the process of neighborhood change.

Several neighborhood typologies have been proposed, including those based on stages in neighborhood decline, the perception of neighbors about their area, and the functions a neighborhood performs. They have all been used at one time or another to classify neighborhoods. Warren, for example, recognized six functions of neighborhoods—sociability, organizational base, status, social contact, mutual aid, and interpersonal-influence center—that could be used to develop a typology of urban neighborhoods.[23] In general, though, the principal basis for organizing and classifying residential areas within the city has been the socioeconomic attributes of residents. A number of descriptive typologies of the social and economic structure of residential areas have been devised to analyze the structure of urban residential space. Most of these are based on the early work in social-area analysis by Shevky and Bell.[24] According to social-area theory, neighborhoods can be differentiated on the basis of three residential attributes: social status, urbanization (family status), and race or ethnicity.

Of the three dimensions, social status—or, as it is sometimes termed, social rank—has received the most attention. Typically income, occupation, and educational variables are combined in an index to measure class or social status. In studies of urban residential space, census tract data for these variables are collected, mapped, and analyzed in order to ascertain whether any general spatial patterns are evident (Figure 3-8). The existence of social class as a major attribute in neighborhood classification stems from the fragmentation and specialization of society resulting from industrialization and urbanization. As noted earlier, preindustrial cities evidenced less specialization and class structure, and consequently more homogeneity, in the class structure of their neighborhoods. While we can assign to industrialization responsibility for greater class differentiation in society, the question still arises why persons from similar classes tend to cluster together.

One explanation is economic, based principally on the manner in which the housing market functions. If most individuals who purchase a house view it as an investment as well as shelter, then the decision can be seen as one of maximizing rate of return or minimizing risk. Given the fact that the market value of a house is a function of its neighborhood as well as its physical characteristics, it is in the best interests of an individual investor (homeowner) to select a home in a neighborhood of comparable or higher-valued housing. By doing so, the possibility of appreciation is maximized.

Because of the investment motivation, developers tend to construct tracts in which all the houses are of roughly comparable value. If the values in a tract varied widely, the builders would experience great difficulty in selling the top-of-the-line units. In a large city, the demand for housing within a particular income range is sufficiently high to permit the construction of homogeneous neighborhoods. In a small community, the market is not large enough to permit this behavior. Thus, in smaller communities there is typically greater diversity in the class structure of neighborhoods. In many suburban communities the structure of the zoning ordinance is such as to suggest that the community is behaving like a

[23] Donald Warren, "The Functional Diversity of Urban Neighborhoods," *Urban Affairs Quarterly*, vol. 13, no. 2, 1977, pp. 151–179.
[24] E. Shevky and W. Bell, *Social Area Analysis*, Stanford University Press, Palo Alto, Calif., 1955.

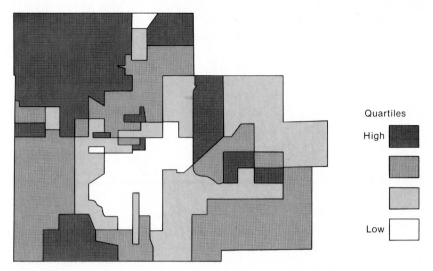

FIGURE 3-8
Socioeconomic status in Oklahoma City, 1980. Status is plotted by census tract. Note the cluster of low-status tracts in central areas and the more peripheral location of higher-status tracts.

club whose policy is to admit no new member whose status or income is not equal to or higher than that of the average member.

Class segregation may also stem from status considerations. One's neighborhood can say much about one's position in the social hierarchy. To the person concerned with status, it may be important to live in a neighborhood that has the desired reputation.

The desire to interact socially with persons of similar values, attitudes, and preferences is important to many people. Living in neighborhoods composed of persons from the same class can increase the level of "neighboring" and of informal support among neighbors.

Family Status Life Cycle   Differences in life cycle also produce residential differentiation. Family status life cycle is usually measured by a combination of age, housing composition, and family structure variables such as absence or presence of children.

Differences in family status lead to homogeneous neighborhoods because various life cycles are associated with particular housing needs. Households with children, particularly children of school age, generally require larger homes than childless households. The location of schools and other activities for children will be important to some households but not to others. Persons whose lifestyle is oriented more to work than to family are likely to have a different set of preferences regarding location, neighborhood type, and recreational and cultural amenities.

Typically, family or life-cycle homogeneity is not as great as for either socioeconomic status or race and ethnicity. This is because life-cycle changes occur rather rapidly and typically may not require an adjustment in housing. For example, as a middle-aged family's children leave, a new life cycle begins, but the older residents are still able to meet their needs within the existing house. Many families remain over an extended period of time and "age in place," while others in the neighborhood may have moved and been replaced by younger families with children. Thus, some diversity in family status persists.

Race or Ethnic Status   U.S. urban history is closely linked to immigration. At the beginning of the twentieth century large numbers of foreign immigrants from eastern and southern Europe took up residence in cities, particularly those in the northeast and midwest. In excess of 1 million a year entered the country for several years during the first 2 decades of the 1900s. Restrictions on immigration enacted during the 1920s sharply curtailed this flow, and the cities experienced much less immigration during the 1930s. However, the rapid mechanization of agriculture following the end of World War II promoted massive black migration to the cities in the 1950s and 1960s. Today the influx of blacks has been replaced by Latin-American and Asian immigration. Because of the changing mix of minorities and the fact that assimilation and acculturation of each has not been completed, the social geography of the city is a cultural and ethnic mosaic. This diversity and persistence of minority culture within the city has led many to use the metaphor a "cultural stew pot" rather than "melting pot" to describe the cultural pluralism of the American city.

Living in a racially or ethnically homogeneous neighborhood has been the common experience of numerous newcomers to the city. The existence of segregated black or Hispanic neighborhoods is a trait that has come to character-ize most, if not all, American cities. Yet, the segregated neighborhoods represent only the contemporary version of a pattern of residential space that has been prevalent throughout much of the history of this country.

Although residential segregation is common to most minorities, variations in the degree of segregation are evident. A commonly used segregation index ranges in value from 0, for total integration, to 100, for total segregation. Using this index with data from census tracts or blocks, the segregation index of blacks in American cities typically ranges between 70 and 90, for Hispanics between 40 and 60, and for European minorities between 30 and 60.

A number of factors are responsible for racial and ethnic enclaves. Some segregation is voluntary in that many people find it more comfortable to live in neighborhoods with those of a similar culture. When urban immigrants speak a different language, are unfamiliar with the culture of the city, or have moved to avoid persecution in their home area, the ethnic enclave can be a haven, a starting point for becoming familiar with and adjusted to the life and rhythm of the city. "Understanding a city" or "reading a city" is a process that all residents must undertake. For many minorities this can be done less stressfully in the context of an enclave composed of persons of a similar kind.

The enclave as a haven can, however, eventually become confining for the person who wishes to become part of the mainstream culture. Old customs, traditions, and family responsibilities protect, yet they also bind one to a way of life that is not always commensurate with upward mobility. In many cases, the strong ethnic enclaves that prevailed in the early decades of this century have been weakened by the migration of younger residents to the suburban communities of the 1950s and 1960s.

While some racial or ethnically homogeneous neighborhoods have come into existence as havens, in other instances segregation exists because of constraints imposed on the housing alternatives available to minorities. Certainly, the segregation of blacks in the city has been largely a function of discrimination in the housing market. While the term *ghetto*, meaning forced restriction of living space, was initially applied to the Jewish population in Europe, many consider its use appropriate to the black experience in American cities. Discriminatory practices have in fact traditionally limited the black population to a restricted area of the city.

Discriminatory practices in the housing market have taken many forms and have been used against different minorities, but the efforts directed against blacks have been most severe and visible. Neighborhood covenants and point systems were used extensively against blacks throughout the 1940s and into the 1950s. Covenants generally involved a binding commitment by a white owner not to sell property to a member of a particular race. Point systems were special forms of covenants wherein a prospective buyer was evaluated on a variety of attributes— race, religion, occupation, etc.—and accumulated points for or against their purchase of a home on the basis of the "correct" answers to these items.

Discriminatory practices in the sale and rental of housing and in the granting of credit are illegal under the Fair Housing Act of 1968. Congress has since strengthened the provisions of the 1968 act with regard to discriminatory lending practices. This legislation includes the Equal Credit Opportunity Act of 1974, the Home Mortgage Disclosure Act of 1975, and the Community Reinvestment Act of 1977. In addition to federal legislation most states have enacted similar and, in at least some instances, even stronger legislation. Thus, while some discriminatory practices persist, their incidence has been greatly reduced.

The "Tipping Point" Phenomenon   Although the incidence of explicitly discriminatory practices has been sharply cut back, integrated neighborhoods are still often difficult to maintain. Some urban scholars have argued that a "tipping point" exists at perhaps 30 percent, and if the black percentage reaches this threshold, white flight and complete transition occur.

Maintaining stability in the racial composition of a neighborhood is made more difficult by the blockbusting tactics of some realtors and neighborhood groups. In blockbusting, after a black family has purchased a home in a neighborhood, panic selling is encouraged by realtors who threaten a lowering of property values in the future. As panic selling occurs, a self-fulfilling prophecy of lower market values for homes takes place, adding to further panic selling. The homes that are sold at below market value are quickly resold to new families at inflated prices; thus after the initial drop in property values occurs because of panic selling, values typically rise above the original price. The consequences of blockbusting are that neighborhoods undergo complete racial transition rather quickly, sizable profits occur for a few unscrupulous realtors, and animosity between racial groups is heightened. The practice is illegal, but the quick profits it offers make it hard to stamp out entirely.

Given the civil rights revolution of the last 2 decades and the general increase in affluence, many blacks have been able to secure housing in the suburbs. However, even though suburbanization of blacks increased in the last 2 decades, the American city continues to be two societies—a suburban white one and a minority inner-city one. Since residential patterns often display considerable stability, the patterns spawned by past discrimination may be with us for many years to come.

Neighborhood Change Neighborhood change typically is discussed in the context of an increase or decrease in the social status of residents or in the physical quality of the housing stock. One such model, developed by Downs, has been used extensively by HUD.[25] The model classifies neighborhoods into five periods, progressing from health to abandonment.

> **Stage 1:** *Healthy neighborhood.* Minimal physical decay, good property maintenance, replacement of older residents by persons of similar economic status.
> **Stage 2:** *Incipient decline.* Reduction in the economic status of residents, poor maintenance practices, beginning of conversion of owner-occupied units to rental ones.
> **Stage 3:** *Decline.* Major repairs needed in housing, definite reduction in economic status of residents, financing for home purchases and renovation becomes difficult, neighborhood gains external reputation as one in decline.
> **Stage 4:** *Accelerated decline.* High rate of vacancy and absentee ownership, extremely low level of economic standing of residents, high turnover rates.
> **Stage 5:** *Abandonment.* Large portion of structures abandoned and condemned, "home of the homeless."

The five-stage model has been criticized because it explains neighborhood change as resulting primarily from the decisions of individual households and ignores the role of other urban institutions. Naparstek and Cincotta have, for example, proposed a different model of neighborhood change that is based on stages in the investment policies of a city's financial institutions.[26] The model begins with a healthy neighborhood, progresses through a beginning stage of disinvestment, and then to a stage of redlining. This is a situation in which banks refuse to lend within the redlined area regardless of the condition of individual properties or the financial situation of the applicant. In time, no private capital is forthcoming without public guarantees. The process terminates when complete abandonment has occurred; the area is razed and reinvestment occurs. Redlining is illegal under the Fair Housing Act of 1964 and succeeding legislation mentioned earlier. Whether or not it still persists on a significant scale has been the subject of some debate among scholars. The Naparstek and Cincotta model raises the more general questions of what causes neighborhood change or decline, but it is still

[25] Anthony Downs, *Urban Problems and Prospects*, Markham, Chicago, 1970.
[26] A. Naparstek and G. Cincotta, *Urban Disinvestment: New Implications for Community Organization, Research and Public Policy*, National Center for Urban Ethnic Affairs, Washington, D.C., 1976.

incomplete in that it only focuses on one causal agent in this process, the withdrawal of investment capital.

The two views appear quite different at first glance because one focuses on individual behavior and the other on institutional behavior. However, the differences may be smaller than first appears. The homeowner or landlord may fail to invest in his or her property because it appears that the neighborhood is deteriorating and therefore the investment will be lost. If the banks redline they do so for analogous reasons. They fear that with neighborhood decline the value of the mortgaged property will sink far enough to wipe out the owner's equity. Then if the bank must repossess because the owner fails to make payments (a likely event once the owners' equity is gone), the bank will not be able to recover the full amount of the debt when it resells the property. Both the owner's and the bank's behavior thus stem from the same perception of the area's future.

Neighborhood decline is an inevitable outcome of the filtering-down process. If we define decline in socioeconomic terms, then this is true by definition. If the filtering-down process is slowed, for example, when new housing construction slows, neighborhood transition is also slowed. While decline through filtering is common, it is not inevitable. If the neighborhood has particular advantages of location or amenity housing, it may not filter down at all. In fact under conditions of inelastic supply and rising demand it may filter upward as discussed below. In recent years increases in new-house prices have exceeded the average rate of increase in personal income. As the effects of increased new-house prices are reflected in the prices of used housing considerable reverse filtering may occur.

Upgrading and Gentrification   The physical condition of a neighborhood can improve for a variety of reasons. One may be a rise in the incomes of the residents. Then as long as the income elasticity of their expenditures on housing exceeds zero some upgrading will occur. Another factor may be that conditions in real estate markets are making the area itself more valuable—for example, the growth of federal employment in the 1960s and 1970s made housing in the Georgetown area of Washington D.C. more valuable. This makes owners more willing to invest in their properties. It is just the converse of the proposition that falling demand encourages disinvestment. If the housing supply becomes inelastic, investment in existing properties is likely to increase. Thus one effect of excessively restrictive zoning or of growth management policies may be the diversion of capital from new construction to renovation and rehabilitation.

Reinvestment in existing properties has often been fostered by local governments, which provide low-interest credit for this purpose. One common strategy is to use Community Development Block Grant (CDBG) monies to bring down the interest rates that banks charge for home improvement loans and to guarantee such loans. Where such loans are made to homeowners there is often a means test to direct the limited-subsidy funds to owners who would be less likely to make the improvements unaided. Often such loans are directed into fringe or transition areas to slow the invasion and succession phenomena noted previously.

The upgrading of neighborhoods has caught the attention of the popular press and is often termed *gentrification*. The word is derived from the English term *gentry* and refers to the migration of higher-income individuals into a neighborhood of lower economic status. Housing in the neighborhood is restored and renovated, and the neighborhood rather quickly changes from what had been a lower-income into a higher-income neighborhood.

The gentrifiers, for the most part, have consisted of young, single, or childless couples, middle-class professionals who have moved from other areas in the city. A prevailing misconception of gentrification is that it represents a return back from the suburbs to the central city. The data on movers indicate, however, that the prior residence of most gentrifiers is the central city, not the suburbs. It does appear, however, that many of the younger participants were originally from suburban families.

Most city officials view the gentrification process with considerable enthusiasm and anticipation because it represents a reversal of a long trend of downward change in urban residential environments. The increase in tax base, owing to the appreciation of residential property, is obviously desirable. The enthusiasm for gentrification should be tempered by two realizations. First, what little data exist suggest that gentrification does not involve large numbers. A survey by the Urban Land Institute in 1975 indicated that approximately 48 percent of all cities over 50,000 were experiencing renovation, either incumbent or gentrification. On a percentage basis, gentrification was more common in larger cities (over 500,000). Furthermore, the institute estimated that for the 7-year period between 1968 and 1975 approximately 55,000 units were renovated either through gentrification or incumbent upgrading.[27] This total represents a rather small number in comparison to the over 2 million new units that were constructed in the cities studied during the same time period. It seems clear that, even when taking into account a recent increase in the process, gentrification involves a small percentage of the persons establishing new residential quarters in the metropolitan area.

The second point is the human cost of gentrification: the displacement of the prior residents of the neighborhood. In many cases the displaced population consists of a disproportionate share of the elderly, many of whom were persons who have aged in place in their old neighborhood. The disruption in lives and the economic and social costs resulting from displacement are problems that concern many planners and city officials. Proponents of gentrification argue that the number of persons displaced is small, particularly in comparison to the relocations caused by the normal operation of the housing market. Programs have been suggested to pay for the moving costs of persons displaced in the gentrification process, but in most cases cities have not instituted a formal procedure for assisting in this manner. In some ways gentrification involves not so much a solving of problems but a relocation of problems.

Two explanations for gentrification are commonly proposed. A demographic-ecological theory of gentrification emphasizes changes in the demographic character of the urban population, in the economic structure of the central business district, and in the operation of the urban housing market. The coming of age of the baby boom has placed a stress on the urban housing market, causing

[27] J. Thomas Black, "Private-Market Housing Renovation in Central Cities: An Urban Land Institute Survey," in S. Laska and D. Spain (eds.), *Back to the City. Issues in Neighborhood Renovation*, Pergamon, New York, 1980, pp. 3–13.

shortages and rising costs. In such an atmosphere there are cost advantages to purchasing an older, cheaper home and renovating it. More couples choosing to remain childless and more women participating in the labor force further encourage gentrification. In general, there has been a reduction in the "familialism" that was so important to the growth of the suburbs. In many cities, growth of corporate activity has increased the number of professional workers and thus added to pressures for gentrification. Older inner-city neighborhoods, many of them of historic value or with distinctive architectural styles, become attractive residential alternatives because of their low cost and accessibility to work.

A second explanation stresses the economics of gentrification. Here both traditional and Marxist interpretations have been offered. The traditional view stresses the importance of rising transportation costs, inflation in the suburban housing market, and the relative low costs of purchasing old homes in the inner city. The Marxist interpretation stresses the argument that the housing market is manipulated by politically powerful individuals to enhance their investment. They point to the practice of landlords who squeeze out renters by various practices in order to convert rental structures to owner-occupied units in the gentrified areas. They also argue that financial institutions have encouraged the disinvestment in certain neighborhoods. This has led to neighborhood decline, which enables investors eventually to purchase the land very cheaply. At this point gentrification is fostered by favorable loan practices. One who is skeptical of Marxist interpretations might ask how this view of the property owners acting as a class squares with the highly fragmented and poorly capitalized structure of property ownership in poorer neighborhoods as revealed by such students of urban housing markets as Sternlieb.[28]

It is clear that gentrification offers, to the risk taker, the opportunity for sizable investment profits. Homes have been known to increase in value by 300 percent within a year at certain stages in the process. This investment potential, however, occurs for only a brief period of time. In the later stages of gentrification more attention is directed toward protection of property value rather than speculation.

Can we expect gentrification to continue and perhaps accelerate? Because of its positive effect on a city's tax base, one can be certain that local governments will continue to encourage gentrification. The key to future development will not be the actions of local government officials, however, but rather the condition of the urban housing market. Increases in the real costs of new housing and transportation should favor gentrification. On the other hand, loss of central-city office employment and increasing familialism as the baby-boom generation enters the foothills of middle age will have the opposite effect. The rapid construction of new housing on the urban fringe, a condition which typified much of the 1970s, would dry up the demand for old inner-city housing by the middle class and the gentrification will have been only a slight aberration in the dynamics of the urban residential market.

---

[28] George Sternlieb and Robert W. Burchell, *Residential Abandonment: The Tenement Landlord Revisited*, Center for Urban Policy Research, Rutgers, N.J., 1973.

CHAPTER 4

MODELS OF THE URBAN
ECONOMY

In this chapter three models of the urban economy are presented: export base, input-output, and econometric. The explanations offered in the text of the chapter are verbal and intuitive. Some mathematical detail is presented in the appendix. None of the models are entirely satisfactory in the sense that all involve considerable simplifications of reality and none are guaranteed to predict employment and other economic trends with great accuracy, particularly over long time periods. Nevertheless, all of them can be useful in a variety of ways.

For many purposes of public administration and planning a concept of how the local or regional economy works is essential. There is almost no end to the sorts of policy and planning questions that can be illuminated by such an understanding. For example, in the making of a master plan, population projections are essential. There is a rough relationship between population and employment. Therefore, if we can accurately project employment we may be able to make acceptable projections of total population. If we are grossly wrong about employment trends, then population projections are likely to err significantly.

In transportation planning, estimating future employment is a key item because peak-hour travel volume is largely determined by the size of the workforce. And it is the peak-hour requirements that determine the necessary capacity of the transportation system.

Insight into how the local economy works is useful in economic development planning (see Chapter 5). Suppose a city has limited funds to spend on economic development and can finance site improvements to facilitate one of two projects. The first is a factory that will employ 50 people and sell its products outside the metropolitan area. The second is a shopping center that will employ 100 people and sell primarily to city residents. The question arises as to which project will promote a greater increase in total employment within the city. Without some model (sophisticated or otherwise) of how the local economy works the question cannot even be addressed.

A municipality may confront a major economic event such as the loss of a large employer, the opening of a new industry, or a shift in the demand for the products of local industry. A model of the area's economy will help to explore the probable effects as a guide to policy planning. European demand for U.S. coal increased drastically when the price of oil almost doubled in 1979. The limiting factor in U.S coal exports is port capacity, not production capacity. Thus it seems inevitable that east coast coal-loading capacity will be substantially increased in the near future. One place under consideration is the port of Hampton Roads, Virginia, where it has been proposed that some tens of millions of tons of coal-loading capacity be added. What will be the effect on the economy of the Hampton Roads area in terms of employment, population, the fiscal status of local governments, additional land needed for residential and commercial use, vehicular traffic, etc? Use of one or more economic models to estimate employment and income change can provide some numbers and some insights into the probable course of events. If the defense build-up proposed by the Reagan administration involves major new aircraft procurement, what will be the effect on the economy of Seattle, the home of a major US aircraft manufacturer? How will the effects of increased employment in the aircraft industry reverberate through the metropolitan economy? These and many other questions can be addressed through an economic model.

THE EXPORT-BASE MODEL

The oldest, most commonly used, and in many ways the easiest to use of the three models mentioned earlier is the export-base model. The most central concept in the export-base model is the division of the economy of a city or region into an export and a local sector. Often, the term *basic* is applied to the export sector and *nonbasic* to the local sector. In brief, the export sector is the sector that produces goods or services for sale outside the area and thus brings income into the area. Local-sector activity is essentially production for local consumption.

Export-base theory, in its pure form, gives unquestioned and total primacy to the export, or basic, sector, though the sophisticated modern user of the technique may be more flexible. The logic of assigning primacy to the export sector is the simple fact that any city or metropolitan area must export or die. No small area can be self-sufficient, and thus it must export to pay for its imports. If the community does not produce its own food and raw materials, it can only grow to the extent that it can import these necessities. And it can only import these necessities to the extent that it can pay for them. Since the imports are paid for by exports, the size of the export sector determines the size of the local economy. If exports were equal to zero, then total economic activity would be zero. According to this logic, if the community loses a factory that produces for export, the local economy will contract. But if a store that sells only to the local populace closes, this does not portend shrinkage. Either a new one will open in its place or other stores will expand their sales to pick up the slack. The volume of transactions in the local sector will not be affected, since it is the income earned from exports that determines local-sector activity. In the language of statistics, the export sector is the independent variable and the local sector as the dependent variable.

The Multiplier

The other central concept in the export-base model is that of the multiplier. The *multiplier* is the ratio between total activity and export-sector activity. If for every $1 of export-sector activity there were $2 of local-sector activity the multiplier would be 3, since total activity would be 3 times export-sector activity. In practice, it is very difficult to determine money flows in the two sectors of the economy but relatively easy to approximate employment. Therefore, employment is generally used as a proxy for the value of economic activity. Assume that total employment = 30,000 and export sector employment = 10,000. Then we have:

$$\text{Multiplier} = \frac{\text{total employment}}{\text{export sector employment}} = \frac{30,000}{10,000} = 3$$

For any given city or metropolitan area, the multiplier can be determined empirically. Several techniques for this will be shown shortly. But one can ask, in principle, what causes the multiplier to be a particular size. Consider a highly simplified situation. Assume that the local economy is composed entirely of firms and households. Firms obtain all the factors of production (labor, capital, etc.) from households. Conversely, households obtain all their income in the form of wages, interest, rent, etc., from firms. So far, there is no government sector, no exporting or importing, and no saving. This rather unrealistic system is shown in Figure 4-1(*a*). Income is precisely equal to the value of the output of local firms because each dollar received by the firm is entirely exhausted in wages, interest, rent, profit, etc., all of which constitute the income of local households. The flow of payments from firms to households is the same as the flow of payments from households to firms. This equality must necessarily prevail at any level of economic activity, for there is no way money can leak from the system and no way that money can be injected into the system. In principle, the model is in equilibrium at *any* level of activity.

Let us now take one step in the direction of reality and complicate the model slightly. Assume that for every $1 of income received the consumer spends 33.33 cents on imported goods and services. To pay for imports we must assume some export activity. This new condition is depicted in Figure 4-1(*b*).

There is now a leakage from the system in the form of expenditures on imports and an injection into the system in the form of earnings on exports. For the system to be in equilibrium imports (leakages) must equal export earnings (injections). If leakages exceed injections then the system will shrink to a smaller size. If injections exceed leakages the system will expand until the two are equal.

Intuitively, we can see that the system has a multiplier of 3, in that $1 of additional export activity will be exactly sufficient to balance $1 of additional imports generated by $3 of additional income. If exports are equal to $100 then total activity will be equal to $300. If exports rise to $101 then total activity will be equal to $303, and so on. For each level of export-sector activity there will be a uniquely determined level of total activity.

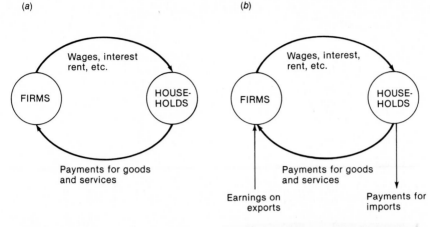

(a)

Because the system is closed, the flow of money from firms to households is necessarily the same as that from households to firms. Therefore, the system is in equilibrium at any level of activity.

(b)

At equilibrium, the "leakage" in the form of payments for imports must equal the "injection" in the form of earnings on exports. Exports are determined by an exogenous factor (external demand). This fixes the level of imports. Since imports are assumed to be a constant percentage of income this, in turn, fixes income. Total income can change only if exports change or if the percentage of income spent on imports changes.

FIGURE 4-1
Two highly simplified models of the local economy.

The above can be expressed in very simple algebra. Let us use Y for total income, IM for imports and X for exports. Recall that at equilibrium imports must equal exports. Then:

→ 33% of income spent on imports

$$.33Y = IM = X$$

and, therefore:

$$Y = 3X$$

Thus if export activity = $100, total activity must equal $300. If export activity = $150, total activity must equal $450. And so on.

To make a simple physical analogy, one might imagine a sink in which water enters at a constant rate but drains out at a rate that varies with the height of the standing water in the sink. Equilibrium would be the height at which the rate of outflow exactly equals the rate of inflow. If the height of the standing water is above that level, then outflow will exceed inflow and the water level will fall. Conversely, if the height is below the equilibrium height, inflow will exceed outflow and the water level will rise.

The model can be made more complicated by introducing savings and taxes as additional "leakages" and government expenditures and investment as additional "injections." An algebraic model incorporating these elements is shown in the appendix to this chapter.

Taking the above model at face value, we see that there are two paths to growth for the local economy. The first, expansion of exports, has been discussed. In the above example, imports were 33.33 cents of every $1 of income and the multiplier was 3. To increase total income from $300 to $400 export activity would have to be increased from $100 to $133.33. The second path is import substitution, the replacement of imported goods and services by locally produced ones. Assume that some formerly imported goods were produced locally so that imports shrank from one-third to one-quarter of total activity. Then $X = IM = .25Y$ and $Y = 4X$. Thus the multiplier has been increased from 3 to 4. Therefore, $100 worth of export activity will now sustain $400 in total activity. The same increase in total activity that was obtained through an increase in exports has now been achieved by substituting locally produced goods and services for imported goods and services.

The export-base model is a demand-driven model. Demand for the export products of the community is assumed to determine the size of the export sector, and this determines the total amount of economic activity for a given multiplier. Much criticism of the model, to be discussed shortly, focuses upon this emphasis on demand. The fact that import substitution, as implied above, is another path to growth is one of the weaknesses in using export-base theory, particularly over a long time period.

Place Size and Multiplier Size   The concept of import substitution suggests that there is a relationship between the size of the local economy and the size of the multiplier. As the local economy grows, the size of local markets grows and more and more goods and services that were formerly imported can be produced locally. This should be true both for consumer goods and services and for producer goods. Thus, one would expect larger places to have larger multipliers. Studies of U.S. metropolitan areas that use employment data have indicated that this is the case.[1] The same principle can be seen on the national level. In fact, it may be somewhat more convincing at the national level, since exports and imports are much more clearly documented there than at the subnational level. Thus it is not necessary to use employment as a proxy for the value of goods and services. For the United States, exports of goods and services are about one-eighth of GNP. For France, they are about one-quarter of GNP. For Luxembourg, they are over one-third of GNP.[2] Thus, if one were to compute multipliers by dividing total activity (GNP) by exports one would get figures of 8, 4 and somewhat less than 3 respectively.

Estimating the Size of the Multiplier   As noted, obtaining dollar figures for export and local-sector activity is exceedingly difficult, due primarily to the

---

[1] Britton Harris, "Comment on Pfouts Test of the Base Theory," *Journal of the American Institute of Planners,* November 1958.

[2] For the reader interested in examining briefly the relationship between size of the national economy and exports or imports as a percentage of GNP the International Statistics section of the 1981 *Statistical Abstract of the United States* should provide adequate data.

openness of the local economy to the national economy. However, employment figures are readily obtained from standard statistical sources. Thus, employment is used as a proxy for economic activity and sector size.

The simplest technique for splitting employment into export and local shares is to categorize each sector of the economy as either one or the other. For example, one might categorize manufacturing as export and retailing and wholesaling as local. In fact, this was the technique used in the first applications of the model. But such a crude approach has obvious disadvantages. Some manufacturing may be for local consumption. Some wholesaling may be to retailers located outside the area. Even some retail sales may be to customers outside the area. Similar problems might arise with business services. For example, one attorney might specialize in wills or divorces, which are essentially services delivered to local residents. His or her work would properly be classed as local-sector activity. But another might furnish legal services to firms engaged in export-sector activity and therefore properly be placed in the export sector. Comparable comments might also be made about construction. The building of a house is clearly local-sector activity but the building of a factory is not.

The Location Quotient A second and much superior technique is the use of location quotients. The philosophy here is to look at each sector and determine whether it appears to be larger than needed for local consumption. If so, the excess is regarded as export activity. For any given industry employment is calculated in that industry as a percent of total employment in the study area. This

---

BOX 4-1

ESTIMATING EXPORT SECTOR EMPLOYMENT

The following table shows employment in finance, insurance and real estate (FIRE) for New York City and for the United States. In addition, the table shows the location quotient for FIRE in New York City and the percentage of New York City FIRE employees estimated to be employed in the city's export sector.

	Total employment (in thousands)	Employment in FIRE (in thousands)	FIRE as % of total employment	Location quotient	% of FIRE workers assigned to export sector
Nation	97,270	5,860	6.02	—	—
New York City*	2,918	349	11.96	1.98	49.7

*The New York City data is for place of residence rather than place of work and is illustrative only. If place of work data were used the LQ would be higher.

Source: Statistical Abstract of the U.S. and General Characteristics of the Population, Bureau of the Census, Department of Commerce, Washington, D.C.

The LQ is 11.96/6.02 = 1.99. This means that 99 out of every 199 or, roughly, 49.7 percent of all workers in FIRE in New York City are considered to be export sector workers. Applying that percentage to a total FIRE employment of 349,000 yields an estimate of approximately 173,000 FIRE workers in the export sector.

number is then divided by the industry's percent of total employment nationally. Specifically, the LQ for industry X equals:

$$LQ = \frac{\text{Percentage of local employment in industry X}}{\text{Percentage of national employment in industry X}} \quad \begin{array}{l} =1 \ local \\ >1 \ export \end{array}$$

The technique is based on the assumption that those employees up to the point of percentage equivalence with the national labor force are producing for local consumption. Those workers past that point are producing for export. Buried in this are three corollary assumptions.

> **1** Consumption of all goods and services in any particular area is proportional to employment. That is, if area X has twice as many workers as area Y, then it consumes twice as much of good 1, twice as much of good 2, and so on.
> **2** Output per worker in any given industry is the same from one area to another. That is, there are no differences in productivity.
> **3** Production for export does not begin until local demand has been satisfied. Given assumptions 1 and 2, this is equivalent to saying that no industry with a location quotient of less than 1 exports goods.

All of the above are questionable to some degree, assumption 3 particularly so. An industry may have a location quotient of more than 1 and yet supply only a part of local demand, with the remainder of local demand supplied by imports. In the Detroit SMSA the location quotient for passenger cars is far greater than 1. But many automobiles purchased in Detroit are made overseas or in other parts of the United States. Similarly, the fact that an LQ is less than 1 does not mean there is no export activity. It may well be that local demand is filled by imports and that most or all of local production is exported.

In an effort to improve on the LQ technique, some urban economists have resorted to the minimum-requirements approach. Here the analyst looks at a number of comparably sized places and for a given industry finds the smallest LQ in the set. This LQ is then assumed to be what is required for local consumption, while higher LQs indicate export activity. A variant on this technique is to use the LQ of some place slightly above the lowest figure rather than the absolutely lowest figure. For example, one might arrange the LQs for a particular industry in size order and then take the LQ of the fifth percentile. But whatever the precise mechanics employed, there is an element of arbitrariness about the technique.

Several points about the LQ technique or the minimum-requirements approach should be noted. First, as industry data is disaggregated, the apparent amount of export activity increases. As an example, in 1978 about 21.5 percent of U.S. employment was in manufacturing, about 12.9 percent in durable goods and 8.6 percent in nondurable goods. Assume that in city X 21.5 percent of all workers are in manufacturing. If one does not disaggregate manufacturing at all there appears to be no export activity. However, assume that in this city 19.0 percent of all workers are in durable-goods manufacturing and only 2.5 in nondurable-goods manufacturing. Using the location quotient technique

$$LQ = 19.0/12.9$$
$$= 1.47$$

in durable-goods manufacturing. Roughly one-third of all durable goods manufacturing workers are now assignable to the export sector. One might disaggregate durable-goods manufacturing still further and find that the LQ for primary-metals manufacturing is below 1 but that the LQ for electrical machinery is above average. Some additional export activity is revealed. When industries are aggregated, those with LQs of less than 1 mask those with LQs of more than 1. As disaggregation proceeds, this masking effect is diminished. But however far the disaggregation procedure is carried, there is presumably some masking effect left undiscovered.

In principle, the most effective way to accurately measure the size of the export sector would be by asking firms to identify their customers so that the actual destination of their output could be tracked. But the problems here are formidable. The first, obviously, is cost. Beyond that, many firms may not know where their customers are located. Manufacturers of nuts and bolts who sell to wholesalers may not have the slightest idea where their products ultimately go— nor may they care. The survey approach is thus likely to end with a great deal of "guesstimating" in spite of its apparently empirical nature.

Projecting Export-Sector Employment   Projecting export-sector employment is crucial given its centrality in the export-base model. Unfortunately, it is not easy. In general, projecting the activity in a given sector of a local economy will involve all of the uncertainty that attaches to projecting that sector's activity at the national level and changes in the locality's competitive position vis-à-vis other areas. Attempts to ascertain what other categories of activity the area may subsequently attract or lose add still another dimension of uncertainty.

Clearly, there is no standard technique to be recommended across the board.

BOX 4–2

USING THE EXPORT-BASE MODEL

The use of export-base studies to provide the baseline numbers for large-scale planning is extremely common. Consider a given SMSA in which total employment is 325,000 and export-sector employment is 90,000. The multiplier is thus 3.6. Assume we project export-sector employment to grow to 130,000 in 5 years and that the multiplier will remain unchanged. Total employment is now projected at 468,000 (3.6 × 130,000). If demographic studies predict total population to equal 2.2 times the workforce then we have a projected total population of 1,030,000. If projections based on future household size yield a figure of 2.8 in 5 years, this suggests a total of about 368,000 households. With a reasonable assumption about vacancy rates, this in turn suggests a total housing stock of perhaps 380,000 units. If current experience places automobile ownership at 1.2 per household, then total automobile ownership should be in the 440,000 range in 5 years. If the average automobile in a comparable SMSA is driven an average of 11,000 miles per year, this suggests an annual total of 4.8 billion vehicle miles. If traffic studies show peak hour-trips average .6 per household then peak hour-trips should be in the 220,000 range in 5 years. If demographic studies project an average of one person age 5 to 17 for every two households in 5 years, then the school system will probably have to accommodate in the range of 231,000 students. If per capita water consumption is 150 gallons per day, residential water demand should be in the 150-million gallon range. And so on.

The economist or planner must examine the particular situation and try to select a method appropriate to it. If the study is being done in-house or if funding is relatively limited, the estimation of changes in final demand and export-sector activity will necessarily be done in a fairly informal manner. If an econometric model or an input-output framework with some econometric features is used, a more formal and mathematical approach to estimating changes in final demand may be taken. The input-output model is discussed on page 109, the econometric model on page 118, and a hybrid model on page 121. In general, most agencies find that an input-output or econometric model require the services of an outside consultant with special expertise. Some informal approaches follow.

One approach might be to list the major export activities and obtain national projections for future activity in these sectors. Econometric models of the national economy are a useful source for such projections. (National models have been developed at various universities such as the Wharton School of Business at the University of Pennsylvania. They have also been developed by consulting organizations such as Chase Econometrics or Data Resources Incorporated.) One might then examine the recent past to determine how the area has done in competing for these activities, that is, whether the area's share of these activities has fallen or risen.

But the continuance of past trends is never guaranteed. Some effort should be made to identify probable future events or situations that will effect local export industries. The strength of potential competitors might be considered. Home computers, for example, are an obvious growth industry, and the metropolitan area with industries well situated in that field might consider itself fortunate. But before extending rising trends too far into the future one might wish to do some research on the prospects for foreign competition. It would be foolhardy to ignore the inroads that overseas producers have made in other areas of consumer electronics. Supply-side limitations, if any, can be identified. Obviously, this will vary tremendously from place to place. For example, in many parts of the southwest availability of groundwater might cast a shadow over some types of industrial and commercial development, as well as agricultural activity. In the suburbs of a major metropolitan area the price of housing might suggest that some industries will have difficulty in recruiting an adequate labor supply. The ability of a producer to use the environment to dispose of waste products can be regarded as a supply factor. Thus the potential costs of meeting environmental standards may be a factor. Likely changes in the cost of energy relative to other areas are another factor. And so on.

Interindustry linkages should be considered. If industry A requires inputs from industry B, then the growth prospects of the former are likely to influence the growth prospects of the latter. A great deal of the above will require insights into particular industries that are not readily obtained from the outside. Thus the economist or planner would do well to obtain as much advice from those inside key industries as possible.

When all is said and done, a great deal of uncertainty will attach to any projections of export-sector growth. The national and regional demand for the product, the strength of competing areas, the cost of productions factors, the cost of capital, changes in the cost of labor, changes in production technology, etc., all introduce uncertainty. Nevertheless, an informed guess is likely to be better than an uninformed guess.

Shift-Share Analysis

Beyond the question of trying to assess the area's prospects on a sector-by-sector basis it may also be worthwhile to try to assess the general competitive strength or weakness of the area. A commonly used technique is shift-share analysis.[3] The technique is mathematically quite simple and can be done from standard sources. In this technique the analyst compares the actual performance of the area's economy with what would have happened had the area simply gotten its proportional share of national growth. The term *shift* refers to the difference between the actual employment change and the change that would have been expected on a *share* basis.

When the figure for shift has been obtained it is broken into two components: that which is attributable to the area's competitive strength and that which is attributable to its industry mix. As an example, assume that in a certain time period industrial employment has grown by 8 percent nationally, but by 12 percent in a particular city. Has the city's growth been more rapid because it has an industry mix that is more heavily weighted with rapidly growing industries than is the national mix? Or is it because the area is competitively successful in that its particular industries are growing at an above-average rate? If the area has lagged behind the national growth rate or even shown absolute employment decline, is this because it has specialized in slow-growing industries (unfavorable industry mix) or because its industries are not holding their own in competition with the same industries in other parts of the nation (competitive weakness)? Or is it some combination of the two? A shift-share analysis will provide a numerical answer to the question.

The findings of such an analysis may have some policy uses. For example, if the area shows competitive strength but has experienced slower than desired growth because of an unfavorable industry mix, an active program of industry recruitment might be indicated. If the main problem has been competitive weakness, a strategy designed to attack the sources of this weakness makes most sense. A demonstrated finding of competitive weakness might provide the motivation for searching out details of this weakness—tax structure, energy costs, land and development costs, wage rates, labor force quality, inadequate infrastructure, etc.—with a view to remedying those that are within the province of government to change.

The Limits of Shift-Share Analysis It must be remembered that the technique is only a simple arithmetical procedure using local and national employment in a base year and an end year. It will yield insight into what has happened. But whether or not past performance will be a useful guide to the future is a matter for informed judgment. For example, a shift-share analysis of a coal-producing area in Appalachia done in the mid-1970s might have shown a very gloomy picture, with

---

[3] A discussion of shift-share analysis and a numerical illustration of the process can be found in Edgar M. Hoover, *An Introduction to Regional Economics*, Knopf, New York, 1971, pp. 292–295.

the area exhibiting competitive weakness in a declining industry. But the perceptive analyst, observing the increase in world oil prices, might well have decided that world coal demand was going to increase sharply and that past events would prove to be a very poor guide to the future. The analyst might have gone one step further and speculated that much of the increase in demand would come from western Europe. This should favor eastern coalfields because of their relative proximity to eastern ports such as Hampton Roads.

Shipbuilding has been a declining industry for a number of years, as foreign shipyards have underbid American yards on contracts for freighters and tankers. A shift-share analysis of a U.S. city heavily specialized in shipbuilding would show rather discouraging prospects, at least on an industry-mix basis. But, again, a perceptive analyst aware of recent changes in the nation's defense posture and

---

BOX 4-3

THE TECHNIQUE OF SHIFT-SHARE ANALYSIS

Shift-share analysis is generally carried out over a wide range of industries, for example, all of manufacturing. But for simplicity let us assume that the entire manufacturing sector of a given SMSA is composed of only three 2-digit SICs, as shown in the table below. (SIC is an abbreviation for Standard Industrial Classification.)

	Employment (in thousands)		National % change	Expected employment, based on national % change
	1972	1978		
Nation				
Primary Metals	1,260	1,206	−4.3	
Fabricated Metals	1,560	1,653	6.0	
Transportation equipment	1,853	1,956	5.6	
Total	4,673	4,815	3.0	
SMSA				
Primary metals	26	28		25
Fabricated metals	140	160		148
Transportation equipment	150	175		158
Total	316	363		331

Source: National figures from the U.S. Bureau of the Census, *Statistical Abstract of the United States,* 1979.

Let us first find the shift component. Nationally, employment grew 3 percent. If employment in the SMSA had grown at this rate, it would have been 325,000 in 1978. In actuality it was 363,000. Subtracting 325,000 from 363,000 yields 38,000 for the shift.

The question is how to apportion the 38,000 between a mix and a competitive component. We note from the lower right column of the above table that if each industry in the SMSA had grown at the national rate for that industry, total employment in the SMSA would have been 331,000. Because of its relative specialization in faster growing industries the SMSA, without any competitive advantage, will show more rapid employment growth than the nation as a whole. Specifically, the difference between 331,000 and 325,000 is attributable to its more advantageous industry mix. Thus of the 38,000 shift noted before, 6,000 is attributable to a favorable industry mix. That leaves 32,000 attributable to competitive advantage.

the requirement that all military vessels be built domestically would at least be wary of relying too heavily on the results of shift-share analysis.

Shift-share analysis is a useful technique as long as its limitations are understood. But to assume uncritically that the past relationships it reveals will necessarily continue is to misuse the technique.[4]

An Evaluation of the Export-Base Model

The export-base model has been in existence, in one form or another, since the 1920s. It has undoubtedly been used more often than any other model of the local economy and has exercised considerable influence upon economic development policy. As might be expected it has been subject to a great deal of criticism, much of it quite well founded. Criticisms and limitations of the model are presented here, not to demolish or debunk it but simply to make the reader more sophisticated about it.

The most fundamental criticism of the model is that it ignores supply-side considerations entirely. In a powerful and influential criticism of the model Blumenfeld wrote:

> A large metropolitan area exists, survives, and grows because its business and consumer services enable it to substitute new "export" industries for any that decline as a result of the incessant vicissitudes of economic life.
>
> These services are the constant and permanent, hence the truly "basic" and "primary" elements of the metropolitan economy; while the ever-changing export industries are the "ancillary" and "secondary" elements. The relation assumed by the method is, in fact, reversed.[5]

In a biological analogy one might compare the local sector to the root system of a plant and the export sector to the stems and leaves. It is true that the leaves and stems provide the nutrients on which the root system grows. But it is also true that the root system is capable of generating a new above-ground system if the old one is lost. It is this capacity for regeneration and sustenance that is ignored by the export-base model.

The history of many urban areas is a history of losses and regenerations. In assessing the long-term future of a metropolitan or urban economy, the capacity of that economy to generate new activity may be more important than the future of demand for its current export products. ⟶ local economy

An export-base analysis of the Boston area done in the mid-1940s would have presented a rather grim picture. The area was heavily dependent on shoe and textile manufacturing. Neither was rapidly growing at the national level, and Boston did not show competitive strength vis-à-vis other areas. But the area was able to generate a thriving electronics industry largely located on Route 128, a circumferential road around the city. A major factor in its success in doing this was the presence of the right infrastructure for attracting high-technology industry—namely, the presence of MIT and Harvard and a large skilled labor

---

[4] A highly critical view of the shift-share technique can be found in Harry Richardson, *Regional Economics,* University of Illinois Press, Urbana, Ill., 1978, pp. 202–206.

[5] Hans Blumenthal, "The Economic Base of the Metropolis," *Journal of the American Institute of Planners,* vol. 2, Fall 1955, pp. 114–132.

force and a quality of life that facilitated personnel recruitment. No export-base analysis could have predicted such a development.

Writing in the mid-1960s about the importance of supply factors, Wilbur Thompson noted:

> While a demand orientation has been the more fashionable for the past decade, the existence of a supply side to urban-regional economic development has long been recognized, even antedating the demand (export-base) model. A supply orientation is implicit in the typical "inventory" of local resources with which many area development studies begin—and too often end. A supply approach need not be naive, for it holds considerably greater potential for unraveling the pattern and determinants of urban growth than does the relatively static export-base logic.
>
> We might generalize to the effect that the longer the time period under consideration, the greater the relative importance of supply—local resource endowment and industrial culture. The recent New York study, for example, highlighted the fact that the New York metropolitan area grew by incubating new functions, nurturing them and finally spinning them off to other sections of the country, all the while regenerating this cycle. The flour mills, foundries, meat packing plants, textile mills and tanneries of the post-Civil War period drifted away from New York, their place taken by less transport-sensitive products, such as garments, cigars, and office work. Currently, New York is losing the manufacturing end of many of its most traditional specialties, as garment sewing slips away to low-wage Eastern Pennsylvania leaving only the selling function behind, and as printing splits away from immobile publishing. But New York's growth never seems to falter, as the new growth industries are much more than proportionately regenerated in its rich industrial culture.[6]

As it happened, employment growth in New York City continued until about 1969 and then headed downward. In the 1970s the city was unable to generate new activity as fast as old activity was lost, and there was a net job loss of about half a million. Some reasons are discussed in Chapter 5. But the fact is that for well over a century employment in New York City climbed steadily while one industry after another was lost.

The supply-side analysis, as Thompson notes, is the first step in designing a municipal or a regional economic development program. The operative questions are, "What are our strengths and what can we attract?" and "What are our weaknesses and what are we likely to lose?" This is not to say that an export base and shift-share analysis cannot be valuable by illuminating the past and indicating where present trends will take the area. It is just to say that by itself the demand-side analysis is only one blade of the scissors.

Another criticism of the export-base model is that it is most applicable to the single-industry small area and that it loses applicability as place size increases. Blumenthal in his critique of the economic-base method cites the example of a copper mining town as being appropriate for economic-base studies. It is a single export industry that exports all of its product. If that industry is lost it cannot be replaced with another industry. There are no external sources of income other than copper exports. Here the economic-base model should work well.

But in a complex and larger economy the predictive power of the model weakens. If demand for a primary export product shrinks, labor and capital

---

[6] Wilbur R. Thompson, *A Preface to Urban Economics,* Johns Hopkins, Baltimore, 1965, pp. 37.

devoted to its production may well flow into other area, with the result that total export activity does not decline. The falling wages resulting from job losses in one export sector may lead to expanded employment in other export sectors as lower wage rates improve the position of other export firms relative to their competitors in other localities. The diversion of capital from a lost export activity may stimulate investment in the production of products that were formerly imported. Investment in the area may rise or fall for reasons unrelated to the demand for export products. And so on.

The Limits of the Multiplier Concept   For any economy one can calculate an export multiplier. For example, U.S. exports of goods and services are equal to about 12 percent of GNP. Therefore the calculated multiplier would be about 8. But to attempt to estimate next year's, or even next decade's GNP on the basis of projected U.S. export activity would be absurd. If U.S. exports fall by 20 percent next year, this hardly implies that GNP will fall by 20 percent next year. If U.S. exports double in the next few years, this does not imply doubling of GNP. In predicting GNP supply factors, including labor force, capital, past rates of productivity change, etc., would be far superior to any trade-based measure. All other things being equal, the larger the place the more important internal transactions and relations become relative to external ones. At one extreme, consider the household. There are no internal monetary transactions the multiplier is 1. The household exports labor; hence, export earnings constitute 100 percent of income. At the other extreme, consider the planet. There are no exports, so one can think of the multiplier as being infinite, clearly not a useful idea. Past some not precisely defined scale the concept of the export multiplier loses meaning.

The Importance of Nonexport Earnings   One other limitation of the model is that it presumes that all money that flows into the area come from export earnings. Not only is this not so, but it is becoming less so with the passage of time. Consider personal income. About $1 in every $8 of personal income comes from government transfer payments of one kind or another. These are, in general, payments that attach to the individual wherever he or she resides. Social security, veterans benefits, pensions, annuities, etc. all move with the individual. Another roughly equal share of personal income comes from dividends and interest. Thus, altogether about one-quarter of personal income is essentially portable.[7] To the extent that this is so it reverses the logic of the export-base model. In the model, employment growth stemming ultimately from increased demand for export goods stimulates population growth. Individuals who live on transfer payments can move into an area without regard for employment opportunities. Their expenditures then stimulate local-sector employment. Sunbelt growth has been powerfully stimulated by exactly this process. One can go further and suggest that stimulation of the local economy by expenditures from transfer payments builds

---

[7] Data is from the *Statistical Abstract of the United States.* In 1979 transfers amounted to $252 billion out of a personal income of $1,924 billion, or 13.1 percent. Interest and dividend payments amounted to another $245 billion, or 12.7 percent. Thus, very roughly, one-quarter of personal income was relatively portable.

capital, labor force, and infrastructure, which then facilitates the development of export activity. The entire sequence is reversed.

Cautions for the User   The above are major criticisms or fundamental limitations of the model. There are also a number of minor points which, in the writer's view, do not invalidate the model but which the user of the model should be aware of.

As noted before employment is generally used as a proxy for economic activity. In fact, not all export workers are equal in terms of effect on the local sector. Workers who are more highly paid will, all other things being equal, have a larger effect on the local sector, for they will make more purchases. In New York City both stock brokerage and garment manufacturing are export industries. There is little doubt that one stockbroker sustains considerably more of the local sector than one garment worker. All other things being equal the industry that has more links to local suppliers will have a larger multiplier effect attached to it than one that imports most of its inputs. In short, the use of employment in calculating the multiplier obliterates real distinctions between types of export-sector activity.

The multiplier is generally taken as fixed but, as noted, may change as the area begins to produce goods that were formerly imported or, conversely, begins to import goods that were formerly produced locally. For an economic development agency seeking to stimulate total employment, steps that promote import substitution or resist the loss of industry producing for domestic consumption may be just as effective in maintaining or elevating total employment as steps that bring in new export activity. Finally, but as a caution for the user, definition of the area is critical for correct use of the model. The theory is based on the idea of interarea trade and should be used with this thought firmly in mind. For example, the Indianapolis SMSA is a relatively distinct entity, which trades with its largely agricultural hinterland and with the rest of the world beyond. It is not possible to say precisely where the area ends in an economic sense, but the census definition is not far wrong. On the other hand the Gary-Hammond-East Chicago SMSA shares a border with Chicago and is thus powerfully affected by changes in the Chicago economy. Analyzing the Gary SMSA as if it existed in isolation would obviously be a major departure from reality.

Similarly, if only a piece of the SMSA is subjected to conventional economic-base analysis, the technique is being misused. Consider, for example, a suburban county. What sustains the local economy? First, there will be some export activity exactly as discussed earlier. But a great deal of the local economy is likely to be sustained by the expenditures of local residents who work elsewhere. Calculating the multiplier in the traditional way produces a misleadingly high figure because a great deal of local activity is incorrectly attributed to traditional export-sector activity. Consider the following example from Westchester County in the New York metropolitan area. In the early 1970s its population was about 900,000, but this constituted only about 5 percent of the regional population. Total employment in the county was about 350,000, and export-sector employment about 50,000.[8] A naive use of the export-base technique would thus indicate a multiplier of about 7,

---

[8] Estimates by author.

a very high figure. The reality was that each day about 120,000 residents commuted out of the county to work while about 70,000 out-of-county residents commuted in. The county was thus a net exporter of labor to the extent of 50,000 workers. Thus, much of the local sector is sustained by the income earned by commuters rather than by traditional export-sector activity. In fact, as is often the case in suburban counties, those who commuted out had higher average earnings than those who worked locally or commuted in. Thus the economic stimulus of money earned outside the county was even larger than simply the net labor export figure suggested.

But let us go further. Assume that an agency seeking to promote economic development in a suburban county wishes to estimate the multiplier effect of new export activity. The agency is mindful of the fact that labor export figures heavily in the maintenance of the local sector and therefore decides not to try to compute a multiplier. Instead, it reviews the literature and observes that SMSAs with populations comparable in size to the county typically have multipliers in the 3 to 4 range. It then decides to use a multiplier of 3.5. Are events likely to show this to have been a wise choice? The answer is no. The figure will prove far too high because much of the multiplier effect will be captured by the rest of the region and not by the county itself. In-commuters will carry some of the multiplier effect out of the county in their pay packets. Service businesses located outside the county will capture part of the effect. At the regional level, the 3.5 figure may prove relatively accurate. At the county level, leakages into the rest of the region will make it much too large.

The moral of this illustration is that the export-base technique cannot be used off-the-shelf in part of a region. If it is to be used at all at the subregional level, careful modification must be made. For example, one might estimate regional multiplier effects and then try to estimate how much of that effect will be captured by the subregional area in question. To the writer's knowledge, such a procedure is a trip through relatively uncharted territory.

Pros and Cons Summarized   From a practitioner's viewpoint what can be said about the model? On the positive side the model is inexpensive to use. The theory behind it is easily mastered and easily explained to the noneconomist. For specialists who wish to see their work used rather than shelved, general comprehensibility is an important consideration. The data used by the model is obtainable from standard sources and is generally fairly accurate. The model can be current. In many states employment data is available on a quarterly or even monthly basis, with a lag of perhaps a few months. Annual county data is also available from the federal government, though with somewhat more time lag. The very exercise of building the model will reveal the main outlines of the area's economy. If one couples this with insight into the local economy derived from other sources one can often get some idea of potential growth and problem areas. Shift-share analysis is easily done and can be combined with the export-base analysis to evaluate changes in the export base *if recent trends continue.*

The model is weak in that it ignores supply factors. If export demand rises but supply proves inelastic, the local export activity may not expand much. There is nothing in the model that addresses the question of the area's ability to generate new export activity. Blumenthal made these points a quarter century ago, but in no way has the passage of time invalidated them.

There is also nothing in the model that addresses the strength of competing areas. Area X may have a substantial widget manufacturing establishment, and

---

BOX 4–4

EXPORT-BASE THEORY AND KEYNESIAN ECONOMICS

Export-base theory fits very comfortably with Keynesian economics. As it happens, export-base theory was developed first and Keynesian theory appeared about a decade later. Though their development was largely independent, the fact that export-base theory is intellectually consis-tent with Keynesian theory has presumably given it a certain amount of support. The economist or student or planner who understands basic principles of Keynesian economics is likely to grasp the export-base concept with ease and to feel comfortable with it. The intellectual ground has already been prepared. If one believes in "the unity of ideas," then export-base theory draws strength (albeit not necessarily validity) from Keynesianism.[9]

In the appendix to this chapter it is shown that the export multiplier can be demonstrated with the same algebraic formulations as can the Keynesian investment multiplier. All that is needed for the transformation is a change in symbols. The Keynesian marginal propensity to save simply becomes the marginal propensity to import. But beyond the mechanical similarity there is also a philosophical similarity. Both are demand-driven. In the export-base model the demand for export products determines export-sector activity, which in turn determines total economic activity. In Keynesian economics aggregate demand plays a central role in that changes in aggregate demand are a major factor in determining the level of output. In practice, Keynesian economic policy is to a large degree a matter of demand management. In both models the supply curve or supply function is taken for granted. The source of change in the system is on the demand side.

There is a certain parallelism between the criticism of export-base theory typified by the Blumenthal article two and a half decades ago and the recent attack on Keynesian economics by the supply-siders. Blumenthal criticized the export-base theory for ignoring the capacity of the local economy to generate new activities—for seeing the local economy only as a passive responder to externally determined changes in demand for its products. The supply-siders have attacked Keynesianism for viewing all changes in supply merely as responses to new demand conditions. They have argued that supply can evoke demand and that the decisions on production are based as much on supply conditions as on demand conditions. They have thus emphasized entrepreneurship, incentives, work effort, and other supply-side factors that are largely neglected in conventional formulations of Keynesian theory. For example, where the Keynesian might argue that the path to increased output is increasing aggregate demand by more expansionary fiscal policy, the supply-sider would argue in favor of measures that facilitate investment, free entrepreneurs from regulation, increase incentive, stimulate higher rates of labor force participation, etc.[10]

Perhaps the symmetry of the Keynesian model and the export-base model accounts for the fact that the criticisms directed against them have much in common.

---

[9] For a general statement of the Keynesian model of the reader is referred to any modern introductory text. *Economics* by Paul Samuelson and a book of the same title by Campbell McConnell, both of which have appeared in numerous editions, contain excellent presentations.

[10] Probably the most widely read presentation of the supply-side position is to be found in George Gilder, *Wealth and Poverty*, Basic Books, New York, 1981. The supply-side criticism of Keynesian-ism was noted here because of its resemblance to criticisms made of the export-base theory. An entirely different but long-standing and powerful source of criticism of Keynesianism has been that directed at it by the monetarists, the most prominent of whom is Milton Friedman.

the demand for widgets may be rising. But if area Y has a different constellation of widget supply factors and is just reaching the point at which it can undersell area X in national markets, the outlook for area X may be quite pessimistic. However, here it must be admitted that the same comment can be made regarding any other subnational area model.

In general, export-base models have more predictive power in the short run that over the long run, in large measure because they ignore the supply side. They look at the leaves and stems and ignore other potential stems the same system of roots may be capable of sending out. Although the model ignores the supply side, this does not mean that the model user must also ignore it. The model, for all its limitations, is still a highly useful tool for the eclectic.

INPUT-OUTPUT MODELS

The input-output (I/O) model differs from the export-base model in several important practical regards, but it also has some underlying similarities. I/O models provide a vastly more detailed vision of the workings of the local economy than do export-base models. Thus, at least in principle, the I/O model can yield a much more powerful insight into the effects of change in a particular sector. On the other hand the model has been much more expensive and time-consuming to use. It requires much more data and a higher level of mathematical skill. Though the concept of the input-output model predates the computer and simple models can be done by hand, any model large enough to be useful requires a computer.[11] Because of the data requirements of the input-output model, most models have come out with a time lag of several years. A base year must be selected, data gathered as of that base year, and then calculations done as of that base year.

The underlying similarity between the I/O model and the export-base model is that both are driven by the demand for the export products of the area. Hence, the projection of export demand and thus export employment are as critical to the input/output model as to the export basic model. Therefore, in spite of the very sizable mechanical differences between the models, it would not be stretching the truth much to regard the input-output model as a highly disaggregated export-base model. We shall return to this point subsequently. In the meantime, let us turn to the mechanics of the I/O model.

The Transactions Matrix

The central element in the input-output model is the transactions matrix. This matrix shows relationships among all the sectors of the economy that are included in the model. If the output of any one industry changes, the amount of change required of every other industry in the model is revealed. This capacity to demonstrate the detailed ramifications of change in any one sector is the special strength of the model.

Table 4–1 shows a hypothetical two-sector model to illustrate some of the

[11] The concept of the input-output table was developed in the 1920s by Wassily Leontieff, but widespread use did not begin until the advent of the digital computer several decades later. Extended discussions of input-output techniques are available from a number of authors. In particular see the works of William Miernyck.

transactions matrix .

TABLE 4-1
A TWO-SECTOR INPUT-OUTPUT MODEL

Producing sectors	Consuming sectors		Final demand	Total demand
	Industry	Agriculture		
Industry	20 +	5	40 =	65
Agriculture	10	10	80	100

outside demand (export)

principles involved. Assume the economy is divided into two sectors, industry and agriculture.

To the left of the vertical line is the transactions matrix. It specifies the interindustry relations. The model in Table 4–1 is quite simple, but a larger model contains a massive number of relationships. For example, in a 500-sector table there are 250,000 cells (500 × 500) in the transaction matrix.

Consider just the industry row of Table 4–1. We observe that industry consumes 20 units of industrial products and 5 units of agricultural products. In other words, to produce 65 units of industrial goods requires the use of 20 units of industrial goods and 10 units of agricultural products. The agriculture row shows that to produce 100 units of agricultural products the agricultural sector requires the consumption of 5 units of industrial products and 10 units of agricultural products. These relationships simply indicate the interdependency of production processes. Agriculture requires the use of machinery. Industrial production makes use of raw materials. Machinery is used in the production of machinery, and agricultural products—for instance, seed—are used in the production of more agricultural products.

To the right of the transactions matrix is the final-demand column. In this illustration it can be considered to be export activity, that which is produced for sale outside the area. The total demand column is simply the horizontal addition of all the preceding columns.

The Effects of Changes in Final Demand   So far the model is simply a picture of the local economy at one time, presumably constructed empirically. Suppose we now raise the question of what the local economy will look like if the final demand for industrial products rises from 40 to 60 units.

Total industrial production will have to rise by more than 20 units because some industrial products will be needed in the manufacture of the additional industrial goods to be exported. We also know that since agricultural products are used in the production of industrial goods, an expansion of agricultural production will be needed. That expansion will also require more industrial output, since industrial products are required in the agricultural sector. Table 4–2 shows the effect of readjustment to the new level of final demand. Note that every cell in the table has changed. The mathematics for producing Table 4–2 are shown in the appendix.

Table 4–2 shows that exporting 20 units more of industrial products has required the production of 34.25 more units of industrial products and 5 more units

TABLE 4-2
REVISED TWO-SECTOR INPUT-OUTPUT MODEL

Producing sectors	Consuming sectors		Final demand	Total demand
	Industry	Agriculture		
Industry	29	5.25	60	94.25
Agriculture	14.5	10.5	80	105

of agricultural products. In addition to determining the increase in total output we also observe the changes in interindustry relationships: how much more agricultural output is needed by the industrial sector, how much more industrial output is needed by the agricultural sector, and how much more production is required in each sector for use by that sector itself.

To examine a few uses of the table let us arbitrarily assume that each unit of output has a market value of $1 million. Let us also assume that it takes one industrial worker for every $50,000 of industrial products and one agricultural worker for every $100,000 of agricultural products.

We can thus compute the increase in employment resulting from the increase in final demand. Comparing Tables 4–1 and 4–2 we see that in order to export $20 million more of industrial products total industrial production had to rise by $29.25 million. This will require an additional 585 workers ($29,250,000/50,000 = 585). The increase in agricultural production will require an additional 50 workers ($5,000,000/100,000 = 50). Thus total employment will rise by 635. In this instance a $20 million increase in industrial final demand has resulted in the creation of 635 new jobs, or 31.75 jobs per $1 million of final demand.

Had we hypothesized, instead, an increase in agricultural demand rather than industrial demand or an increase (or decrease) in both demands, the jobs-per-dollar figure and the interindustry relationships would be different, but the principles would be the same. Simple as the above model is, it does indicate the far greater specificity provided by I/O analysis than by export-base analysis. However, the reader should note one common element. In both the export-base model and the illustration above, changes in the demand for exports are the factor that cause change. Both the economic-base model and the input-output illustration provided here are demand driven.

The Technical Coefficient The term *technical coefficient* refers to a technical relationship, for example, the amount of agricultural machinery required to produce $1 of agricultural products. As used here the term refers to national models which are relatively closed systems. At the subnational level the term *regional purchase coefficient (RPC)* is more appropriate. It can be considered to be the technical coefficient adjusted for the percentage of the factor that is produced locally.

One very useful product that emerges from the construction of an I/O model is a table of technical coefficients. These figures show how much of the output of one industry is needed by another industry to produce 1 unit of output. For

TABLE 4-3
TECHNICAL COEFFICIENTS FROM TABLE 4-1

	Consuming Sectors	
Producing sectors	**Industry**	**Agriculture**
Industry	.307	.05
Agriculture	.154	.10

example, if 100 units of agricultural output require 5 units of industrial products (machinery, fertilizer, etc.), the technical coefficient is .05 (5/100 = .05). Table 4–3 shows the technical coefficients based on figures in Table 4–1. The figures in the table are computed as follows:

$$20/65 = .31$$
$$5/100 = .05$$
$$10/65 = .154$$
$$10/100 = .10$$

The table of technical coefficients is useful in that it indicates the strength of interindustry relationships. The size of the coefficients provides a gauge of how much expansion in one industry will require in the way of inputs from another industry. For example, in Table 4–3 we see that increasing industrial output by a given amount makes about three times as much demand upon the agricultural sector as increasing agricultural output by the same amount makes upon the industrial sector.

BOX 4–5

THE VANCOUVER MODEL

Table 4–4 shows an 18-sector table constructed for the economy of metropolitan Vancouver in British Columbia. In basic form the table resembles the 2-sector model, but some differences should be noted. First, we observe that the single final-demand column of the 2-sector model has been replaced by a group of columns extending from household consumption to exports, rest of world. But the basic principle of adding horizontally to arrive at total output remains the same.

Below the transactions matrix, which is indicated by the horizontal double line, are a group of inputs. To see how much labor, imported factors of production, etc. each producing sector used, simply read down the column for that sector. In other words, read the table vertically to examine that sector in its consuming role. Read the table horizontally to see how the output of any industry is consumed. For each industry the column total is the same as the row total. That is, for each industry the total output is the sum of all the inputs used. Another way to state this is that the value of the output is the sum of all the value added. The total value added by, say, the chemical industry is the sum of all the factors of production it purchased from the other sectors plus the labor it employed plus the factors of production it imported plus miscellaneous items covered under the entry "other value added." The reader may wonder how, if the value of the industry output is precisely equal to the sum of value added, the industry can make a profit. The answer is that profit is included in the "other value added" row and is a balancing item.

The Uses of Input-Output Models

The use of the model in estimating total employment change and employment change by sector was described briefly in connection with the two-sector model. Once the model has been constructed employment multipliers for each sector can be constructed. Multipliers from the Vancouver model are shown in Table 4–5. Note the rather substantial range within the table. Using these multipliers the employment implications of any hypothesized pattern of final demand may be explored.

The model lends itself to exploratory uses and to tracing the ramifications of major events through the local economy. For example, a 500-sector model of the Philadelphia area was used to trace the effects of the cessation of Vietnamese war expenditures on the local economy.[12] The model was run both with actual wartime and assumed peacetime patterns of federal expenditure. The outputs of the runs were then compared. A model of the south Florida area is being used to estimate the impact of a pipeline that will divert traffic from, and thus reduce economic activity in and around, Port Everglades.[13] Another study is being used to estimate the effect of shale oil development on a group of counties in Colorado. Still another is being used to estimate economic losses in the Harrisburg area resulting from the Three Mile Island accident. If economic activity can be projected, then light can be shed upon population change, revenue change, and change in the demand for public services. Input-output techniques are thus of considerable use to local government.

The model can be used to identify new problems and pitfalls in advance. For example, it seems very likely that the demand for oil-drilling equipment will rise sharply. A metropolitan area in which the manufacture of this equipment is a significant part of the local economy wishes to forecast the effects. New final-demand figures are substituted for the old ones and the model is run. By observing the changing levels of activity in each sector it may be possible to identify any supply-side constraints before the market makes them visible in the form of rising prices and lengthening delivery times. Because of the sector-by-sector detail the I/O model produces it is far superior to the export-base model for this particular purpose.

Similarly, if loss of some export market seems inevitable, the effects on the local economy can be simulated. If forewarned, there may be ways in which the community can soften the blow.

Assume an area is designing an economic development program. The input-output model might be used to estimate employment multipliers for various industries. If development funds are limited (as they inevitably are), then informed decisions can be made about where to spend scarce capital funds or subsidy monies.

A land-use planner might use an input-output model to gain information on the

---

[12] This and other matters pertaining to the Philadelphia model are discussed in considerable detail in Walter Isaard and Thomas W. Langford, *Regional Input-Output Study: Recollections, Reflections and Diverse Notes on the Philadelphia Experience,* MIT Press, Cambridge, Mass., 1971.

[13] Benjamin H. Stevens, David J. Ehrlich, and James R. Bower, ''Draft Report to South Florida Regional Planning Council,'' Regional Science Research Institute, Amherst, Mass., 1980.

TABLE 4-4
THE VANCOUVER MODEL

Table of interindustry transactions, metropolitan Vancouver, 1971 ($1000—producers' prices)	1. Agriculture, forestry, fishing and mining	2. Construction	3. Food and beverages	4. Wood industries	5. Paper and allied products	6. Chemicals and petroleum
1. Agriculture, forestry, fishing and mining	795	304	12,923	0	0	0
2. Construction	1,920	592	258	205	243	718
3. Food and beverages	824	0	20,935	1	2	0
4. Wood industries	230	17,408	0	21,909	505	0
5. Paper and allied products	29	2	19,523	223	19,497	1,067
6. Chemicals and petroleum	1,013	329	1,085	2,364	2,689	7,367
7. Nonmetallic products	71	20,070	11,705	112	0	173
8. Metal fabricating	116	12,558	19,824	2,132	451	909
9. Printing and publishing	369	347	712	76	231	518
10. Manufacturing, nec	1,585	5,022	468	103	639	2,073
11. Trade and transport	1,389	10,647	10,385	4,173	3,716	1,614
12. Communications	451	2,339	932	1,562	558	450
13. Utilities	1,221	1,642	5,886	3,229	2,730	17,134
14. Finance, insurance, and real estate	755	11,255	2,710	2,788	3,311	1,512
15. Health and welfare	19	0	9	0	0	43
16. Education	129	250	693	42	327	767
17. Business services	421	7,590	1,400	3,372	2,291	3,149
18. Other services	31	484	232	1,838	1,675	19
Total intermediate purchases	11,368	90,839	109,680	44,129	38,865	37,513
Imports	18,744	93,680	172,598	140,771	54,484	406,040
Wages and salaries	8,651	300,257	89,712	123,453	41,403	25,516
Other value added	26,939	87,942	76,596	54,961	37,167	26,098
Total value added	35,590	388,199	166,308	178,414	78,570	51,614
Total input	65,702	572,718	448,586	363,314	171,919	495,167

TABLE 4-4 *(Continued)*

Table of interindustry transactions, metropolitan Vancouver, 1971 ($1000—producers' prices)	16. Education	17. Business services	18. Other services	Total intermediate demand	Household consumption	Gross private capital formation
1. Agriculture, forestry, fishing and mining	0	0	281	15,174	10,819	0
2. Construction	520	45	1,212	27,666	9,188	314,495
3. Food and beverages	837	0	1,602	25,082	217,381	0
4. Wood industries	0	0	992	47,180	2,633	8,364
5. Paper and allied products	1,017	298	786	69,210	10,533	0
6. Chemicals and petroleum	343	116	208	45,831	52,790	0
7. Nonmetallic products	738	0	140	41,520	1,021	0
8. Metal fabricating	0	73	132	84,063	7,879	2,328
9. Printing and publishing	5,122	7,613	398	59,314	18,766	0
10. Manufacturing, nec	2,208	82	1,029	49,664	12,560	3,197
11. Trade and transport	1,856	614	789	114,379	531,187	27,381
12. Communications	2,482	3,718	5,817	59,126	65,834	0
13. Utilities	4,577	1,630	3,791	80,679	92,168	0
14. Finance, insurance, and real estate	1,251	5,393	4,825	116,045	394,432	6,574
15. Health and welfare	0	0	0	107	82,902	0
16. Education	1,689	33	0	4,609	27,495	0
17. Business services	7,308	10,997	2,239	96,032	31,212	0
18. Other services	0	572	6,667	16,657	293,049	0
Total intermediate purchases	29,948	31,184	30,908	952,338	1,861,849	362,339
Imports	18,635	22,079	52,620	1,567,976	995,811	394,611
Wages and salaries	153,437	150,827	193,655	2,683,052	46,710	—
Other value added	78,691	142,712	147,526	2,079,902	338,258	—
Total value added	232,128	293,539	341,181	4,762,954	384,968	—
Total input	280,711	346,802	424,709	7,283,268	3,242,628	756,950

Source: Reprinted by permission from H. Craig Davis, *An Interindustry Study of the Metropolitan Vancouver Economy,* University of British Columbia, Vancouver, 1975.

TABLE 4-4 *(Continued)*

7. Nonmetallic products	8. Metal fabricating	9. Printing and publishing	10. Manufacturing, nec	11. Trade and transport	12. Communications	13. Utilities	14. Finance, insurance, and real estate	15. Health and welfare
494	11	0	0	366	0	0	0	0
682	300	580	314	14,206	1,739	1,212	1,413	1,507
30	0	0	0	645	0	0	49	157
162	2,139	0	3,012	600	46	0	0	177
888	1,082	17,488	1,222	5,820	251	0	16	1
2,893	1,332	2,148	1,488	14,653	1,960	3,462	229	2,152
7,441	0	0	370	159	196	345	0	0
2,295	18,613	614	17,852	2,056	4,069	1,730	0	639
97	137	7,364	1,045	23,307	1,832	33	8,696	1,417
3,825	16,953	245	7,285	4,440	530	1,385	379	1,413
4,397	3,079	2,608	10,410	40,189	1,344	1,646	9,203	6,320
301	1,164	1,841	2,112	24,176	742	1,663	7,925	893
2,028	7,022	817	1,992	15,837	643	6,445	1,581	2,474
2,438	1,880	2,018	2,993	33,091	4,335	2,079	32,646	765
0	6	0	0	0	0	0	30	0
0	0	0	0	0	20	0	14	645
1,155	1,318	3,835	7,043	27,631	5,129	4,158	5,441	1,555
0	183	1,227	138	1,952	276	0	468	895
29,126	55,219	40,785	57,276	209,128	23,112	24,158	68,090	21,010
5,379	77,863	52,301	182,722	122,124	29,541	64,245	31,790	22,360
22,001	69,865	50,720	173,115	800,608	89,373	39,142	182,132	169,185
20,470	39,879	12,217	89,674	586,462	76,727	113,700	375,374	86,767
42,471	109,744	62,937	262,789	1,387,070	166,100	152,842	557,506	255,952
76,967	242,826	156,023	502,781	1,718,322	218,753	241,245	657,386	299,322

TABLE 4-4 *(Continued)*

Federal, provincial, and local government purchases	Exports, rest of BC	Exports, rest of Canada	Exports, US	Exports, rest of world	Exports, total	Total final demand	Total output
3	11,197	7,465	21,043	0	39,706	50,528	65,702
208,087	10,847	2,418	17	0	13,282	545,052	572,718
7,662	39,574	70,735	49,531	38,621	198,461	423,504	448,586
1,532	21,990	43,663	123,593	114,359	303,605	316,134	363,314
3,448	27,068	61,252	229	179	88,728	102,709	171,919
11,493	366,927	15,248	2,320	558	385,053	449,336	495,167
192	30,021	0	4,222	0	34,243	35,456	76,976
8,896	82,426	42,142	9,294	5,798	139,660	158,763	242,826
1,724	54,664	15,883	0	5,672	76,219	96,709	156,023
18,772	170,792	234,438	9,348	4,016	418,594	453,123	502,787
14,901	357,535	309,647	209,811	153,481	1,030,474	1,603,943	1,718,322
1,864	64,347	27,582	0	0	91,929	159,627	218,753
9,335	59,063	0	0	0	59,063	160,566	241,245
9,203	94,960	17,272	13,032	5,868	131,132	541,341	657,386
201,707	14,395	211	0	0	14,606	299,215	299,322
213,123	11,075	22,635	847	927	35,484	276,102	280,711
27,744	153,208	24,971	5,284	8,351	191,814	250,770	346,802
2,298	39,729	54,290	16,714	1,972	112,705	408,052	424,709
741,984	1,609,818	949,852	465,285	339,802	3,364,758	6,330,930	7,283,268
47,873							
148,936							
—							
—							
938,793							

TABLE 4-5
METROPOLITAN VANCOUVER EMPLOYMENT MULTIPLIERS, 1971

Sector	Employment Multiplier*
1. Agriculture, forestry, fishing, and mining	155.21
2. Construction	90.05
3. Food and beverages	61.80
4. Wood industries	70.70
5. Paper and allied products	60.69
6. Chemicals and petroleum	15.03
7. Nonmetallic products	91.12
8. Metal fabricating	69.39
9. Printing and publishing	76.81
10. Manufacturing, nec	74.32
11. Trade and transport	160.70
12. Communications	89.19
13. Utilities	53.30
14. Finance, insurance, and real estate	85.99
15. Health and welfare	138.38
16. Education	136.25
17. Business services	93.39
18. Other services	145.04

* Figures refer to jobs per $1 million of sales.

types of industrial growth to expect. Different industries have different land-use demands in terms of location, site requirements, number of workers per acre, utility services needed, etc.[14] Again, a pattern of final demand would be assumed and the model run to see how the local economy might change sector by sector.

Input-output models lend themselves to "sensitivity analysis" because of the capacity of the computer to run the model repetitively to explore the effects of changes in one or more variables. If the state of Kentucky expected major increases in coal demand and had a functioning model of the state economy, it could run a series of trials at different production levels to see how sensitive the economy of the state was to changes in the activity of this industry.

Limitations and Problems

Having described some uses of the model, we should say a few words about its limitations and problems. The first input-output models were developed to study the national economy. While the national economy is not sealed off from the rest of the world, it is far more closed than a local economy. Herein lies a major

[14] For some space requirements of various types of industrial development see F. Stuart Chapin and Edward J. Kaiser, *Urban Land Use Planning*, 3d ed., University of Illinois Press, Champaign, Ill., 1979. For additional information on space requirements, traffic generation, and the like as related to employment see John M. Levy, *Economic Development Programs for Cities, Counties and Towns*, Praeger, New York, 1981, chap. 7; Joseph D. Chiara and Lee Koppleman, *Planning Design Criteria*, Van Nostrand Reinhold, New York, 1969; Donald C. Lochmoeller et al., *Industrial Development Handbook*, Urban Land Institute, 1975; and Arizona Department of Transportation in cooperation with U.S. Dept. of Transportation, *Trip Generation Intensity Factors*, Federal Highway Administration, Washington, D.C., 1976.

problem. At the national level we can learn the appropriate interindustry relations or technical coefficients by looking at production processes. For example, it is not difficult to learn how many tons of coke are used to produce 1 ton of pig iron. But to analyze the economy of, say, Pennsylvania we need to know how much of the coke used in Pennsylvania steel mills comes from Pennsylvania coal mines. The size of the increase in total employment will depend on the source of inputs to the steel industry. If Pittsburgh steel mills run on coal from eastern Pennsylvania, the multiplier effect will be larger than if they run on coal from Kentucky or from the mountain states.

Thus national technical coefficients cannot be applied to the local economy. Instead, the source of the inputs to local industry must be determined with some degree of accuracy. In general, until the last few years the construction of input-output models has involved heavy use of surveys to develop this information. This made input-output studies quite expensive and caused them to come out with a substantial time lag. But even when substantial interviewing and surveying is done, there is still a considerable amount of uncertainty left. In many cases firms do not know where their factors of production originate.

Fairly recently mathematical techniques have been developed that may reduce or obviate the need for survey data.[15] These permit the construction of input-out models at a fraction of their former cost. Essentially, these techniques involve mathematical estimates of regional purchase coefficients (RPCs) for local industry without the need for surveying local firms. The RPC indicates what percentage of one sector's inputs from another sector come from local sources. One approach has been to combine Bureau of the Census Survey of Transportation data on interregional freight shipments, using variables like population density and weight-to-value ratios to develop regression equations that predict RPCs. According of one of the developers of the technique, when an I/O model of the State of Washington based upon indirectly developed RPCs was compared with one using coefficients developed by extensive surveying, the differences were trivial.[16]

Another approach to estimating multiplier effects without the use of survey data is the regional industrial multiplier system (RIMS) developed in the mid-1970s by the Bureau of Economic Analysis (BEA), a branch of the Department of Commerce. Essentially, the RIMS system uses existing BEA personal income data and earnings data to construct location quotients, which are used to estimate the percentage of the inputs to each sector that are supplied locally. The RIMS system is in wide use and is well regarded. When an updated version of the system, RIMS II, was tested against survey-based estimates it was found that most of the industry-specific multipliers from RIMS were within 10 percent of the survey-derived values.[17]

If I/O models based upon indirectly developed RPCs become generally

[15] Benjamin H. Stevens, George I. Treyz, and David J. Ehrlich, "On the Estimation of Regional Purchase Coefficients, Export Employment, and Elasticities of Response for Regional Economic Models," Regional Science Research Institute Discussion Paper Series, no. 114, December 1979.
[16] Communication with Benjamin Stevens.
[17] Joseph V. Cartwright and Richard M. Beemiller, "RIMS II Regional Input Output Modelling System: A Brief Description," Bureau of Economic Analysis, Department of Commerce, Washington, D.C.

accepted the major barriers to the use of these models—cost and time—will be eliminated and the I/O model may become very commonplace, perhaps replacing the traditionally simpler export-base model for many planning and projecting purposes.

Like the export-base model, the I/O model is demand-based. One can postulate new final-demand figures and then use the model to explore their consequences. The degree of insight and detail obtained will far surpass that available from the export-base model. But whether or not projections made in this manner will be accurate will depend upon the quality of the assumptions about final demand. If the assumptions are bad, then the model may produce a finely detailed exploration of a set of imaginary conditions. As noted before, forecasting export demand for subnational areas is difficult indeed.

Earlier the technical coefficient as the specifier of interindustry relations was described. When the two-sector model was readjusted for new final demand for industrial products, the technical coefficients were implicitly assumed to remain constant. This point is not apparent from the text but is apparent in the mathematical appendix.

In fact, of course, technical coefficients may change. If the price of coal changes relative to the price of oil, then the technical coefficient specifying the use of coal in the generation of electric power will change. Beyond price changes for existing products of commodities, technological changes will alter technical coefficients. In some cases simple change in industry size may change the technical coefficients, for example, if higher levels of output permit shifting to more capital-intensive techniques. Some I/O models have the capacity to accept changes over time in technical coefficients. This flexibility is useful. However, the accuracy of the results will be determined by the accuracy of estimates of future changes in technical coefficients. The model itself cannot offer assistance on that key element.

ECONOMETRIC MODELS

Econometric models constitute a diverse class and the discussion of them here will be rather general. In an econometric model a system of equations is constructed in order to model the performance of the economy. The equations may be constructed from time series data, cross-sectional data, or both. Time series data is data about the same area collected over a number of time periods. For example, in the construction of national econometric models, extensive use is made of quarterly data going back over a period of many years. Cross-sectional data is data gathered from a number of places in the same time period.

In virtually all econometric models of subnational areas there are some exogenous factors, that is, factors whose value is determined outside the model. For example, a model might require figures for rate of growth of real GNP, rate of inflation, interest rate, national production of durable goods, etc. A number of regional econometric models are designed to work in conjunction with national

THE INGREDIENTS OF A LARGE-SCALE ECONOMETRIC MODEL

Presentation of an econometric model in detail is beyond the scope of this chapter. For example, a large econometric model of the Philadelphia regional developed by Glickman is composed of 228 equations.[18] It uses 30 exogenous variables related to the U.S. economy, many of them supplied by the Wharton Annual and Industry Forecasting Model, and another 17 exogenous regional variables. The model contains numerous simultaneous relationships, both within and between major blocks of the model, and a number of lagged relationships in which events in one time period are partially determined by events in a preceding time period. To illustrate the building blocks that the model is constructed of, we have shown a few equations. Output of apparel and related products in the Philadelphia SMSA is shown by

$$QAPP = -134.4014 + .0391 \text{ POP} - 2.5085 \text{ TIME} + 6.1551 \text{ QAPP*}$$

where QAPP = output
POP = population
QAPP* = national output of apparel, an exogenous variable derived
from a model of the national economy

The equation indicates that the output of textiles is positively related to population (local market) and national textile production (an indicator of export demand) and negatively related to the passage of time (i.e., if all other factors were held constant the industry would be in decline in that SMSA). Population is predicted by

$$POP = 1494.0555X + 5.2379 \text{ NATG} + 0.3861 \text{ AVERN} + .0433 \text{ GRO}$$

where POP = population
NATG = natural growth (births − deaths
AVERN = average earnings
GRO = gross regional product

Glickman notes the hypothesis here is that increased earnings and output will increase in-migration. NATG is exogenous while the other two independent variables are developed within the model.

The equation which predicts unemployment is an example of a relationship in which lagged data are used.

$$UNR = 3.307 + .6361 \text{ UNR*} + .3004 \text{ UNR} (-1) - .0164 [ET - ET(-1)] - .0002 \text{ GRO} (-1)$$

where UNR = unemployment rate for the region
UNR* = unemployment rate nationally
ET = total employment within the region in thouands
GRO = gross regional output in millions

The symbol (-1) following the acronym for a variable indicates use of that variable from the preceding time period.

To illustrate how the equation would work assume the national unemployment rate is 6 percent, last year's regional rate was 7.5 percent, this year's employment within the region is 1.9 million, last year's was 1.85 million; gross regional output is $20,000 million. The equation becomes:

$$UNR = 3.307 + 6.0 + .3004 (7.5) - .0164 (1,900-1,850) - .0002 (20,000) = 6.74$$

If GRO were to change to $21 billion, then the last term in the equation would become $-.0002$ (21,000) and the predicted unemployment rate would be 6.54.

[18] Norman Glickman, *Econometric Analysis of Regional Systems*, Academic, New York, 1977, p. 38.

econometric models. That is, the national model generates some or all of the exogenous factors required for the subnational model.

Econometricians can be somewhat more eclectic in their choice and use of economic theory than, say, those who are constructing an export-base model. For econometricians the main question is whether or not the relationship proves out empirically. For example, if analysis of time series data shows that adding the percent population growth in time period t-1 to one-half the percent population growth in time period t-2 yields a good predictor of housing starts in time period t, the econometrician can use that relationship whether or not a clear theoretical explanation for it can be formulated. Obviously, one does not wish to carry this emphasis on predictability rather than theory too far. If a relationship clearly violates established theory, a great deal of skepticism and caution are called for. In Glickman's words:

In contrast to economic base and input-output models, econometric models are not necessarily based on a specific theory of urban structure. . . . This is especially true in the case of economic base models, where a constraint is placed on the analyst by a theory of urban structure. With input-output, too, inflexible assumptions concerning production techniques restrict the range of investigation. In both instances, the analyst only searches for the parameters of a model dictated by the particular theory. Econometricians, however, are free to work with the relationships between variables that are shown to hold for a given region. They are constrained only by the broad bounds of economic theory itself.[19]

Like the input-output model, the econometric model lends itself to detailed exploration of the effect upon the economy of various hypothesized events. The exogenous variables can be changed singly or in groups to see the effect upon the entire model. For example, in the Philadelphia model the output of the textile industry is predicted partly by national textile output. Assume that city officials are concerned that increasing overseas competition will sharply diminish U.S. textile production. A new value for national textile demand can be introduced and the model run again. As in the case of the input-output model the effects will ramify through the entire model. For instance, the effect upon textile output will affect earnings. This in turn will affect population growth, which will affect all those variables for which population is a part of the predictive equation, etc.

To a degree, the econometric model might be viewed as something of a competitor to the input-output model, in that both offer a degree of detail and insight beyond that which an export-base model can offer, but both are also more expensive to construct. In the past the econometric model had a substantial cost advantage, in that most of its data come from standard sources rather than field research. However, if the practice of developing regional purchase coefficients indirectly, as discussed previously, comes to be generally accepted the cost advantage of the econometric model vis-à-vis the input-output model is likely to vanish.

---

[19] Ibid.

BOX 4–7

A HYBRID MODEL

Although input-output and econometric models have been presented as entirely separate types, they can be combined. A hybrid, developed at the Regional Science Research Institute, Amherst, Massachusetts, by George I. Treyz, Benjamin A. Stevens, and David J. Ehlich is pictured in Figure 4–2.

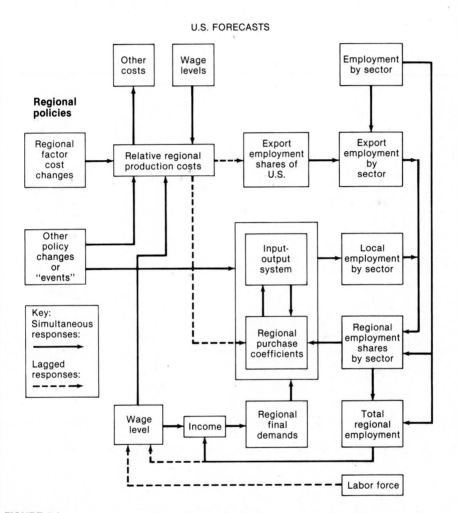

FIGURE 4-2
The regional forecasting and policy simulation model. Simultaneous responses are indicated by solid lines, and lagged responses are indicated by broken lines. (*B. A. Stevens, "A Brief Description of the Core Forecasting and Policy Simulation Model,"* Regional Science Research Institute, *Amherst, Mass., 1981. Reprinted by permission.*)

At the center of the model is an input-output table using the indirectly developed RPCs discussed earlier. The model is structured so that both national and regional events can provide information that influences the results generated by the I/O model. Consider, for example, the block labeled Export Employment by Sector. If we trace back the inputs to this block we see that it is fed both by national employment forecasts (derived from a national econometric model) and cost factors. Some of the cost factors are also generated by the national model but others are specific to the region. Thus a very wide variety of variables ranging from national employment trends to, let us say, local tax policy, can be factored into the calculation of export-sector employment.

We also note that the RPCs are not fixed but rather are affected by changes in relative regional production costs. Thus, if the costs of production in the region rise relative to other areas, local firms will increase their purchases from suppliers outside the region and the RPCs will fall. Conversely, if regional costs fall relative to other areas, the RPCs will rise.

Labor demand is generated inside the input-output block, but that in turn affects wage levels, which affect relative production costs, which in turn affect the RPCs and thus ultimately the employment level. The upward pressure that growth may put on labor costs (or the downward pressure of shrinkage) is fed back into the input-output block of the model, producing a more realistic estimation of multiplier effects than would be obtained without such a loop.

The model contains both simultaneous relationships, shown by solid lines, and lagged relationships, shown by broken lines. For example, wage costs immediately affect production costs. But there is a time lag between changes in relative costs and RPCs, since it presumably takes producers time to adjust to changes in relative costs.

Because the model is structured so that both national and regional events and trends are taken into account, it appears well suited to sensitivity analyses and the exploration of different scenarios.

MATHEMATICAL APPENDIX: The Multiplier

One way to view the multiplier is as the sum of an infinite series. Let us assume that the only external source of income for an area is earnings from exports. Further assume that the only way in which money leaks from the economy is through expenditures on imports (no taxes, savings, etc.). Finally, we assume that expenditures on imports are 20 percent of income. Thus for every $1 brought in by the export industry 80 cents are spent on locally produced goods and services, and 20 cents on imported goods. The 80 cents spent locally ends as income to local residents, who spend 64 cents on locally produced goods and services and 16 cents on imports. Of that 64 cents, 51.2 cents is spent on local goods and services and 12.8 cents on imports. And so on.

We can view this process as continuing until the sums involved become infinitesimal. It is not necessary to accumulate these sums to see where the process ends because there is a standard formula for computing them out to infinity. The sum of an infinite series is

$$A(1/1 - r)$$

where A is the first term and r is the ratio between terms. Thus for $1 of export earnings in the above example, the sum would be

$$1/(1 - .8) = 1/.2$$
$$= 5$$

The multiplier is thus 5.

This explanation is consistent with the more intuitive explanation given in the text, where $5 in income would be required to generate $1 in imports, which would balance $1 of export earnings. The export multiplier can also be arrived at algebraically by a logic identical to that shown for macroeconomic multipliers in textbook presentations of Keynesian economics.

In the standard Keynesian presentation for an economy in which the only leakage is through savings and the only injection is through investments we have the following:

where Y = income
     C = consumption
     b = the propensity to consume
  $1 - b$ = the propensity to save
     I = investment

$$\text{Then, } Y = C + I$$

But we know that $C = bY$, so we can rewrite the first equation as

$$Y = bY + I \qquad \rightarrow mps$$
$$\text{Then } (1 - b)Y = I$$
$$\text{and } Y = I/(1 - b)$$

To convert the above macroeconomic formulation into the export multiplier formulation for a subnational area it is necessary only to change the symbols. Replace I (investment) with EX (export earnings) and consider that $1 - b$ instead of representing the propensity to save, now represents the propensity to import. Identical algebraic manipulations are followed resulting in

$$Y = EX/(1 - b)$$

If the latter is written as

$$Y = EX1/(1 - b)$$

it is obviously identical to the formula given earlier for the sum of an infinite series.

A slightly more complicated model can be constructed. Let us say that income is equal to export earnings plus consumption minus imports. In other words, income is the sum of exports plus production for local consumption.

$$Y = EX + C - IM$$

where EX = export earnings
     C = consumption
   IM = imports

If b = propensity to consume and d = propensity to import where both are functions of income, then we can write

$$Y = EX + bY - dY$$

This can be rearranged to

$$(1 - b + d)Y = EX$$

and then further rearranged to

$$Y = EX\ 1/(1 - b + d).$$

Note that as b, the propensity to consume, rises the multiplier increases, while as d, the propensity to import, rises the multiplier falls. This is in keeping with the intuitive arguments made in the chapter. Looking at the formula in toto, we see that and increase in EX or a decrease in d will both increase Y. This is an algebraic expression of the point made in the text that expansion of export-sector activity and import substitution are both paths to economic growth.

A Simple I/O Model

There are a variety of ways to produce a new input-output table after a postulated change in one or more of the final demand values. One way is to think of the table as constituting a set of simultaneous equations, one for each sector. The solution of these equations after new final-demand values are entered yields the new total-demand values. For convenience Table 4–1 and Table 4–3 are reproduced below. Table 4–1 shows a two sector table with the actual values for intermediate and final quantities. Table 4–3 shows the technical coefficients derived from the data present in Table 4–1.[20]

TABLE 4-1
A TWO-SECTOR INPUT-OUTPUT MODEL

Producing sectors	Consuming sectors		Final demand	Total demand
	Industry	Agriculture		
Industry	20	5	40	65
Agriculture	10	10	80	100

TABLE 4-3
TECHNICAL COEFFICIENTS FROM TABLE 4-1

Producing sectors	Consuming Sectors	
	Industry	Agriculture
Industry	.307	.05
Agriculture	.154	.10

To represent the industrial sector let *Ind* equal total industrial output. Then

$$Ind = .307\ Ind + .05\ Ag + 40$$

From left to right these figures are the technical coefficient for the use of industrial products in the production of industrial products, the technical coefficient for the amount of industrial output necessary for 1 unit of agricultural output, and the final demand for industrial products. The equation can now be rearranged to form equation (4–1).

$$.693\ Ind - .05\ Ag = 40 \tag{4–1}$$

[20] A good numerical illustration of this process can be found in Norbert Oppenheim, *Applied Models in Urban and Regional Analysis,* Prentice-Hall, Englewood Cliffs, N.J., 1980, chap. 3.

Similarly, using *Ag* to represent total agricultural output we can write

$$Ag = .154 \, Ind + .1 \, Ag + 80$$

This can be rearranged to form equation (4–2).

$$-.154 \, Ind + .9 \, Ag = 80 \tag{4–2}$$

We now multiply equation (4–2) by 4.5, which yields equation (4–3).

$$-.693 \, Ind + 4.05 \, Ag = 360 \tag{4–3}$$

[handwritten: $Ag = \dfrac{360}{4} = 90$]

Adding equation (4–1) to equation (4–3) drops out the term for industry and leaves 4.00 *Ag* = 400, or *Ag* = 100. We can now insert the value for *Ag* in equation (4–1) and solve for *Ind*, obtaining a value of 65. The two values obtained and those given for total demand in Table 4–1 indicate that the equations are correct.

To obtain the new table one simply replaces the old value of final demand for *Ind* with the new value in equation (4–1) and solves again in exactly the same manner. Specifically, if we assume final industrial demand will rise to 60, we get

$$.693 \, Ind - .05 \, Ag = 60$$
$$-.693 \, Ind + 4.05 \, Ag = 360$$

Then 4.00 *Ag* = 420 and *Ag* = 105. We now substitute the value for *Ag* in either equation and obtain a value of 94.5 for *Ind*.

To construct a new I/O table we immediately write in the newly calculated total-demand figures and the assumed final-demand figures. The figures for the transactions matrix are readily developed by applying the technical coefficients to the final-demand figures. For example, we know that 10 units of industrial output were necessary to produce 100 units of agricultural output. Therefore, if the technical coefficient remains constant we know that 10.5 units of industrial output are necessary to produce 105 units of agricultural output. This figure thus fills the lower right cell of the transaction matrix. The other cells are filled in a similar manner. The results are the same as shown in Table 4–2 on page 111.

Another method for obtaining the total-demand figures is matrix multiplication. Below is shown the problem expressed in matrix form with the symbols to be used subsequently written above the matrices. For simplicity, all coefficients are rounded to two digits.

$$\begin{matrix} Y & X & A & Y \end{matrix}$$

[handwritten: new demand]

$$\begin{bmatrix} Ind \\ Ag \end{bmatrix} = \begin{bmatrix} 60 \\ 80 \end{bmatrix} + \begin{bmatrix} .31 & .05 \\ .15 & .1 \end{bmatrix} \cdot \begin{bmatrix} Ind \\ Ag \end{bmatrix}$$

The above expresses the idea that the total demand is the sum of the final demand plus total demand multiplied by the technical coefficients. Using the symbols written above the matrices, we have

$$Y = X + AY$$
$$Y - AY = X$$
$$(I - A) \, Y = X$$
$$Y = X/(I - A)$$
$$Y = X(I - A)^{-1}$$

The matrix of technical coefficients A is

$$\begin{bmatrix} .31 & .05 \\ .15 & .1 \end{bmatrix}$$

This is subtracted from the identity matrix I

$$\begin{bmatrix} 1 & 0 \\ 0 & 1 \end{bmatrix} - \begin{bmatrix} .31 & .05 \\ .15 & .1 \end{bmatrix} = \begin{bmatrix} .69 & -.05 \\ -.15 & .9 \end{bmatrix}$$

The matrix is inverted to obtain

$$\begin{bmatrix} 1.462 & .081 \\ .250 & 1.125 \end{bmatrix}$$

Then, total demand is obtained from the relationship $X(I - A)^{-1} = Y$, as follows:

$$\begin{array}{ccc} (I - A)^{-1} & X & Y \end{array}$$

$$\begin{bmatrix} 1.462 & .081 \\ .250 & 1.125 \end{bmatrix} \cdot \begin{bmatrix} 60 \\ 80 \end{bmatrix} = \begin{bmatrix} 94.2 \\ 105.0 \end{bmatrix}$$

The values of Y are, with rounding error, the same as those obtained by the simultaneous-equation method shown previously. In fact, the matrix algebra shown is simply another method for solving simultaneous equations. For a very small number of sectors, as shown here, the first method is probably simpler. As the number of sectors or equations grows, the matrix method is easier. Another advantage of the matrix method is that once $(I - A)^{-1}$ is obtained, new values for total demand may be obtained simply by substituting new values in X and multiplying.

For example, suppose we assume that new final demand for industry will be 70 and new final demand for agriculture will be 110. Then to obtain the new total demand we simply multiply as follows:

$$\begin{bmatrix} 1.462 & .081 \\ .250 & 1.125 \end{bmatrix} \cdot \begin{bmatrix} 70 \\ 110 \end{bmatrix} = \begin{bmatrix} 111.25 \\ 141.25 \end{bmatrix}$$

Thus we see that meeting final demands of 70 for industrial products and 110 for agricultural products will require total outputs of 111.25 for industry and 141.25 for agriculture.

Still another method of obtaining total demand is an iterative one in which successive increments of production are computed and added. When the increments become sufficiently small the process is stopped. The iterative method lacks the elegance of the matrix multiplication approach but for reasons of cost is commonly used in practice.

PROBLEMS, POLICIES, AND PROSPECTS

CHAPTER 5

LOCAL ECONOMIC DEVELOPMENT PROGRAMS

In Chapter 4 several models of the local economy were described. Though they differ considerably in detail and technique, these models are all demand-driven and thus can present a somewhat misleading picture in which events in the local economy are determined entirely by events beyond local control.

The export-base model, for example, takes changes in the demand for a locality's exports as an independent variable. Its movement determines the size of the export sector, which, through the multiplier mechanism, determines local-sector employment. Thus both components of employment are determined by the exogenous variable of demand for the city's exports. The input-output model can be viewed in a similar light. The user of the model postulates a change in final demand for one more export product and then observes the output of each sector. Thus an external event, change in export demand, has resulted in changes in the local economy.

Econometric models are not as easily summarized because of their great variety. The majority of them, however, are essentially Keynesian, and they too are likely to convey a sense that events in the local economy are determined by factors beyond local control. The econometric model typically presents a picture of fixed endogenous (internal) relationships and exogenous variables like interest rates, inflation, growth of GNP, etc., the latter all apparently beyond local control.

However, none of the models presented in the preceding chapter should give the reader the impression that the fate of the local economy is entirely determined by exogenous factors or fixed internal relationships. Though they do not appear as variables in any model of which the author is aware, factors such as municipal entrepreneurship, civic effort, and the joint efforts of the local business communi-

129

ty can greatly influence the fate of the local economy. Though we speak of demand for the export products of municipality X, the demand is actually for the products made by firms that happen to be *located* in municipality X. The municipality can do little to affect the national demand for, let us say, office furniture. But it may be able to do a great deal to encourage manufacturers of office furniture to locate there instead of somewhere else. There is little that the state of Maryland can do to affect the national or worldwide demand for semiconductors. Nevertheless, Maryland did engage in a massive campaign to attract California-based semiconductor manufacturers, apparently with some success.[1] There is little an American city can do to affect the European demand for U.S. coal. But it is clear that any east-coast city that can capture a major share of the coal trade will receive an enormous stimulus to the local economy. In fact, at the end of the 1970s and beginning of the 1980s, before energy prices softened and world demand for U.S. coal sagged, it appeared that considerable intermunicipal competition over coal trade was shaping up.

At the city, town, county, metropolitan area, and state level there is intense interest in fostering economic development, and the attitude toward economic growth is anything but passive. The local effort to promote local economic growth is an old American tradition, probably as old as the republic itself.

THE IMPACT OF LOCAL ECONOMIC DEVELOPMENT EFFORTS

The extent of the efforts to attract economic activity is striking. There are an estimated 15,000 organizations in the United States devoted to the promotion of local economic growth. They range from small-town chambers of commerce to state agencies with large staffs and multimillion-dollar budgets. And they occur in bewildering variety—governmental, quasi-governmental, nonprofit corporations, local development corporations, community development corporations, etc.

The activities of such organizations and the political jurisdictions they represent include advertising and promotion, subsidization, tax abatement, issuance of tax-exempt financing, acquisition of federal funding, land acquisition, construction of facilities, personnel training, development planning and development promoting capital expenditures, among others.

In general, the competition among municipalities and states for economic activity is intense—just as intense as the competition between the firms who are the economic developers' quarry.

It is not possible to say precisely how much is spent annually on the promotion of local economic development, in part because of the many jurisdictions involved and in part because much of the spending takes the form of tax abatements or tax expenditures, which do not show up as line items in budgets. Then, too, the problem is further complicated by the problem in defining precisely an economic development expenditure. Assume a city spends money on road improvements, which it believes will provide access to potential industrial sites and thus attract

---

[1] The campaign included much recruitment activity and a well-published visit by the state's governor to California's silicon valley. It has been covered periodically in the business section of *The Washington Post.*

new industry. Is that an economic development expenditure? Or should that simply be considered another highway and traffic expenditure, like widening the street in a residential subdivision?

Recently, New York State advanced by some years the completion of a 3-mile stretch of the Sprain Brook Parkway, partly because it feared that the Union Carbide Corporation, which has a major office facility near that stretch of parkway, might leave the state if access to the site was not improved. Does one classify this as a form of subsidization? The question is not easily resolved.

Conservatively, local economic development expenditures run into many billions of dollars. There is the cost of operating the 15,000 or so agencies mentioned before. Federal grants to local economic development total several billion dollars a year.[2] Federal revenue forgone (tax expenditures) on tax-exempt industrial revenue bonds (IRBs) or industrial development bonds (IDBs) amount to well over $1 billion a year and the figure is growing very rapidly.[3] Local property tax abatements and state investment tax credits are another massive but not precisely known sum. A significant amount of development occurs on land that has been acquired and improved with public monies and is then made available to firms at below cost. The municipal industrial park is a very widespread institution. In many cases there has been substantial absorption of front-end cost by the municipalities. Among southern states, publicly funded workforce training programs designed specifically to meet the labor needs of incoming firms are common. And this list is far from complete.

The Why of Local Development Programs

The motivations behind local economic development programs are not hard to discern. Softness of the local labor market is probably the most common.

Labor Market Considerations   If jobs are too few, if wages are too low, if labor force participation rates are depressed because workers have dropped out of the labor force in discouragement, if people are working part-time because full-time jobs are not available—an economic development program that brings in jobs seems like an obvious answer. If net loss of jobs appears inevitable, then an economic development program, which may at least slow the loss of jobs, seems like an obviously good idea.

The need to improve the local labor market is probably also the most respectable reason for mounting a local economic development program. Labor market effects are the item most commonly discussed in scholarly literature that has attempted to evaluate the aggregate effects of local economic development efforts. Those federal programs that furnish direct financial assistance to local

---

[2] This total includes funding for EDA and UDAG—each of which was generally funded in the $.5 billion range at the end of the 1970s—as well as some portion of CD funding, since these funds may be and frequently are used for economic development purposes, and funding for regional commissions and miscellaneous smaller programs.

[3] Office of Management and the Budget, *Special Analyses, Budget of the United States*, annual. For data on the face value of IRBs issued (over $8 billion in 1980), as well as a detailed discussion of the process generally, see Congressional Budget Office, *Small Issue Industrial Revenue Bonds*, Washington, D.C., 1980.

economic development efforts contain eligibility requirements based directly upon labor market conditions or upon poverty, a factor obviously connected with labor market conditions.[4]

Tax Relief A second major reason for the local economic development program is property tax relief. To one municipal government the interest in economic development may come from rising citizen resistance to increases in property taxes. That such resistance is increasing nationally is hardly arguable given the Proposition 13 phenomenon of the late 1970s. For another municipality the interest may stem from having reached its constitutional taxing or debt limitation. As noted in Chapter 10, government is a highly labor-intensive activity and few of its functions appear to have significant economies of scale attached to them. A variety of forces, including inflation, rising interest rates, the loss of industry and more affluent citizens to other jurisdictions, and the increasing unionization of municipal labor forces, have placed many municipalities in increasingly difficult financial straits. Thus, economic growth to expand the tax base—to yield a fiscal surplus in which the revenues gained from new economic activity exceed the costs imposed—becomes attractive.

In suburban areas that share a common labor market but have independent fiscal structures, tax-motivated development programs are very common. Most of the community's employed residents do not work in town and most of those employed in town live in other jurisdictions. Thus there is little the community can do about its own labor market but much it can do about its own fiscal condition. For such a community a facility that carried a high assessment but had few workers, generated little traffic, and required few services would be preferred. An expensive mausoleum would be almost ideal.

Other Motivations To a smaller degree, other and generally less praiseworthy motivations for development programs may be found. Local property owners may favor such a program because it will bid up rents and land prices. The development process may come to be dominated by those who have a financial stake in accelerating local economic growth. The local political structure may favor an economic development program because it generates favorable publicity and enables government to borrow a certain prestige from the private sector. In some instances local development programs are mounted because growth "seems like a good idea" without any particular goals being clearly defined.

THE HISTORY OF LOCAL DEVELOPMENT EFFORTS

In the pre-Civil War period most efforts took the form of providing transportation infrastructure. Overland transportation was far more expensive relative to the

---

[4] Most EDA-eligible areas became so on the basis of either poverty or unemployment. Details on the basis of eligibility can be found in the annual reports of the agency. The basic eligibility criteria are specified in the Public Works and Economic Development Act of 1965, as amended. Two of the six UDAG eligibility criteria are poverty and unemployment. The others essentially refer to growth lag. UDAG criteria are spelled out in the *Federal Register,* vol. 43, no. 56, Wednesday, March 29, 1978.

cost of production than it is at present (see Chapters 1 and 2). Thus states and cities correctly perceived that the key to economic growth was obtaining low-cost access to their agricultural hinterlands. The spate of canal building in the early nineteenth century was largely financed with monies raised by cities and states seeking to steal a march on their competitors in what one writer describes as an age of "urban mercantilism."[5]

There is little question that many of these efforts paid off very well. New York City leaped ahead of its two major rivals, Philadelphia and Boston, largely on the strength of the superior access the Erie Canal (completed in 1825) gave it to the midwest. The canal-building era ended about 1840 with the emergence of a superior technology, the railroads. Again, the enormous commercial advantage of superior access was quickly perceived, and much railroad building was capitalized by municipalities seeking competitive advantages. In some cases, cities and towns bought railroad bonds. In other cases, they guaranteed them, thus making them marketable. In still other instances they actually took equity positions (purchased stock) in railroads. Municipal competition to attract railroads was intense. The New York and Oswego Midland Railroad, built shortly after the Civil War, as described by one writer

> zigzagged across the state in search of municipal bonds which were its principal source of capital. . . . Syracuse, which refused to subscribe, was left on one side and the Midland managed to cross the state for nearly 250 miles from Cornwall on the Hudson to Oswego on Lake Ontario without ever passing through a single major city.[6]

This particular railroad's bankruptcy, as might be expected, was not long in coming. But the intermunicipal competitiveness and the heavy reliance on municipally raised funds it illustrates is typical.

In an age when the transportation network of the country was far from complete and a railroad or canal could offer ton-mile costs equal to only a few percent of those offered by horse and wagon, the concentration on transportation was entirely rational.[7] A single project could cut the Gordian knot that held back municipal growth and give the municipality an overwhelming advantage over its competitors.

In the later part of the nineteenth century, with the nation's railroad network well developed, the focus of municipal competitiveness shifted. Subsidization of industry became common in less heavily industrialized parts of the country. For example, textile plants were brought south from New England in part with capital raised by municipalities and groups of residents who saw the economic advantages of industrialization and diversification.

During the Great Depression the state of Mississippi initiated a Balance Agriculture with Industry (BAWI) program under which localities, with the consent of the state, could issue bonds whose proceeds could be used to acquire sites and build plants to be leased to firms at below cost.[8] To complement the local

---

[5] Alfred Eichner, *State Development Agencies and Employment Expansion,* University of Michigan Press, Ann Arbor, Mich., 1970.

[6] Ibid., p. 15.

[7] See Chap 1, p. 21.

[8] Eichner, op. cit., p. 20.

effort, the state mounted a promotional campaign designed to interest industry in the state. In its emphasis on subsidization, promotion, and state and local cooperation, the BAWI program might well be regarded as the progenitor of much modern local development activity.

The Federal Presence in Local Economic Development

In the last two decades another feature has been added to the local economic development effort. This is the substantial participation of the federal government, a relationship that requires a few words of explanation.

During the Great Depression the nation's primary economic problem was massive cyclical unemployment. The emphasis in federal policy was, simply, job creation.[9] With the coming of World War II the unemployment problem disappeared. Labor force participation rates rose dramatically and measured unemployment fell to as low as 2 percent. After the war, rather than lapsing backing into 1930s-like stagnation, as some feared might happen, the nation entered into a period of sustained prosperity. Per capita income grew rapidly, inflation rates were modest by recent standards, and unemployment rates were relatively low. The proper economic role of government, it appeared, was to manage aggregate demand in such a manner that national prosperity continued.

It took a while for it to become apparent that some areas of the nation seemed unable to participate in the general prosperity. In Appalachia, for instance, it almost appeared that the Great Depression had never ended. It also became apparent that although the population as a whole was becoming more affluent, there were subgroups of the population that were not.[10]

The term *structural unemployment* began to be heard. It applies to a relatively permanent (not cyclical) mismatch betweeen the demand for labor and the supply of labor. This mismatch has two main dimensions. One is geographical. Populations tend to be less mobile than capital, so some unemployment may result simply from the fact that workers do not immediately migrate in the face of changing labor market demand. In fact, if labor were perfectly mobile the natural workings of the market would eliminate interarea wage and unemployment rate differentials. Little, if any, case could then be made for local economic development on the basis of labor market considerations.

The second dimension of structural unemployment is the matter of skills. If the demand for coal miners has fallen while the demand for systems analysts has risen, then coal miners may be chronically unemployed while systems analyst jobs go unfilled.

The perception of structural unemployment as a national problem is at the root of the federal presence in local economic development efforts. At present federal programs provide funding for various types of local economic development efforts, labor training, and job creation activities. In almost all of these programs

[9] William E. Leuchtenburg, *Franklin Delano Roosevelt and the New Deal, 1932–1940*, Harper & Row, New York, 1963.

[10] A book that greatly increased the nation's sensitivity to the question of poverty was Michael Harrington's *The Other America*, Penguin, Baltimore, 1969.

eligibility and the extent of funding are conditioned by unemployment or poverty statistics.

At first structural unemployment was seen as being largely a problem of bypassed nonmetropolitan areas—for example, coal-mining areas that had been hard-hit by the nation's switch from coal to oil after World War II or agricultural areas losing jobs because of mechanization. However, the loss of jobs from central cities and the arrival in those cities of a large displaced agricultural labor force began to change that perception. Today, structural unemployment is seen largely, though certainly not entirely, as an urban problem.

THE STRUCTURE OF FEDERAL AID TO LOCAL ECONOMIC DEVELOPMENT

Because structural unemployment has two dimensions—place-related and skills-related—the federal effort to combat it is likewise bifurcated. There have been a series of programs designed to promote place prosperity and another series designed to narrow the gap between the skills of the labor force and the demands of the job market. However, even the so-called people-related programs generally have an element of place relatedness about them in that the amount of funding may be conditioned by the characteristics of the place and the program is generally run by or through local government.

Place-Related Programs

With the growing realization in the late 1950s of the persistence of unemployment in particular areas, the so-called pockets of poverty, pressure mounted for federal action to deal with the problem. The first result was the creation of the Area Redevelopment Administration in 1961. The role of the agency was to stimulate lagging areas by using federal funds to provide development infrastructure and subsidize industry. The ARA lasted for 4 years and was then superseded by the Economic Development Administration (EDA), created as a branch of the Department of Commerce.[11]

The Economic Development Administration   Essentially, EDA served to deliver federal subsidies to eligible areas. There were a number of criteria for eligibility, of which unemployment and poverty were the primary ones. The agency provided grants for development infrastructure, loans for firms in eligible areas, technical assistance for economic development planning, and a variety of specialized assistance.

A prototypical EDA-assisted project might have been the following. A community wished to see an industrial park developed on property it owned. However it realized that the cost of providing the necessary site improvements was such as to make that site uncompetitive with sites in other communities if the entire cost had to be borne by the entrepreneur. The community determined that if an initial investment of $2 million could be made in site improvements, such as access,

---

[11] Public Works and Economic Development Act of 1965.

drainage, sewering, grading, etc., the site would then be competitive with other sites. The municipality applied to EDA for a grant for this purpose. If EDA approved the project as planned, it funded a share of total cost, generally 50 percent. EDA put up $1 million, and the city the remaining $1 million, some of which may have been services in kind rather than cash. The site was improved and then leased for long terms to firms that built and operated facilities on the site. The city justified its expenditures on the grounds of increased property and sales tax revenues and the private gains to city residents who were employed on the site or who otherwise benefited from increased local economic activity.

EDA originally had a rural and small-town orientation owing, perhaps, to the original perceptions of structural unemployment as being largely a phenomenon of bypassed nonmetropolitan areas. As urban structural unemployment became more evident the agency has become more active in urban areas as well.

EDA has operated largely at the county level. However, for the last several years it has encouraged the formation of economic development districts (EDDs), composed generally of five to ten counties, with a view toward encouraging a more comprehensive approach to economic development planning.

Regional Commissions   The federal government has also attempted to deal with the structural unemployment question (and associated problems of poverty, poor housing, healthy, and education) through the creation of regional commissions. The first such commission was created for Appalachia. In 1964 the President's Appalachian Regional Commission termed the region ''an island of poverty in a sea of affluence,'' referring to the contrast between the endemic poverty of Appalachia and the wealth of the eastern seaboard on one hand and the industrialized midwest on the other. (Given the economic difficulties of the northeast and north-central regions noted in Chapter 2, the phrasing might be somewhat different were the report written today.) The Appalachian Regional Commission (ARC) was subsequently authorized under the Appalachian Regional Development Act of March 1965. The commission covers a 13-state area extending from the southern-tier counties of New York to eastern Mississippi. The commission has taken a broad-based approach to the problems of the area, including funding highway development, vocational training, housing, and health services.

It was believed that a major impediment to development in the region was the relative isolation of Appalachian communities owing to the often steep topography of the region and its limited road network. Thus highway construction has accounted for the major share of expenditures. Given that the ARC and subsequent commissions have been largely oriented toward nonmetropolitan areas, an extended discussion would be out of place here.

In the years after the founding of ARC nine other regional commissions were set up. The regional-commission approach did not find favor with the Reagan administration, and the nine no longer exist. The ARC, perhaps in part because it includes parts of 13 states, had enough political support to survive.

Department of Housing and Urban Development Programs   The Department of Housing and Urban Development (HUD) has been involved in urban economic development for many years, first through urban renewal and then through community development (CD) programs (see Chapter 8 for a discussion of both). Though neither program was or is intended purely for economic purposes, substantial monies from both have been used for economic development. In 1977 the urban development action grant (UDAG) program to be administered by HUD was created by congressional action.

UDAG funding requires that area eligibility be established by criteria relating to poverty, unemployment, and some variables that are proxies for what loosely might be termed urban stagnation. UDAG funds can then be used for a wide variety of purposes, which have the effect of lowering private costs enough to "make the numbers come out right" and thus cause private investment to occur. UDAG funds can be used to acquire property, to clear land and make site improvements, to pay the relocation expenses of firms and individuals moved from the site, to provide a variety of public services, and to pay the nonfederal share of other federal programs.

A typical use of UDAG monies might be the following. A city determines that development of a downtown hotel would be a major stimulus to local business activity but that the economics of the project are such that no entrepreneur will undertake it if he or she has to absorb all the costs. The city obtains a UDAG grant, which it uses to acquire the site, clear it of existing structures, and compensate the site's present business or residential occupants for their relocation expenses. At this point the city leases or sells the cleared site to a hotel developer at a fraction of cost. As a matter of fact, a large number of UDAG grants have been used for hotels and convention centers, with the idea that these tend to act as magnets bringing other types of activity into downtown areas.

Changes under the Reagan Administration   Most of the programs described above have not been viewed favorably by the Reagan administration as a matter of political and social philosophy. The administration has proposed a "zero budget" for the EDA in fiscal 1985. This means that after the beginning of the fiscal year the agency could complete projects already "in the pipeline" but could not begin any new projects. Whether the administration will get its way remains to be seen since the agency has substantial congressional support. As noted, regional commissions have, with the exception of ARC, been disbanded and no proposal has yet been made to replace them. UDAG has not been viewed favorably either, but it has received strong support from city officials and it appears that it will continue for the foreseeable future.

The Reagan administration is more inclined to the enterprise zone (EZ) concept. This concept, which would apply to the poorest areas of a limited number of cities, is discussed in Chapter 6.

People-Development Programs

At the same time that structural unemployment has been attacked by funneling federal money into places, it has also been attacked through direct expenditures on people. The programs are designed to alleviate the poverty of individuals directly rather than to help individuals by the indirect mechanism of helping places. They are discussed in Chapter 6.

THE LOCAL ECONOMIC DEVELOPMENT PROGRAM

Before describing local economic development efforts let us consider what localities can and cannot reasonably be expected to do. Very obviously, they cannot change many important locational considerations like climate or location with regard to market areas. However they can do a considerable amount in regard to marketing the area, to changing its "business climate," and to subsidizing and otherwise facilitating local economic development.

In most areas the major share of economic growth is internally generated. A figure of 80 percent is commonly quoted, though its origin is uncertain. Bringing a new industry into the area may be the most visible and most "glamorous" thing that the local economic developer can do. Yet in looking back over several years of work many economic developers find that the most useful thing they have done for the community is to retain and nurture the industrial and commercial base that was there to begin with.

"Selling" the Locality in an Imperfect Market

For the firm choosing a location, whether it entails a 1000-mile move or finding a new site in the same community, developing enough information to make a rational choice is often very difficult. The amount of data on sites, construction costs, labor costs, tax rates, utility costs, land-use controls, environmental controls, etc. necessary to choose among possible locations can be very large and quite expensive to gather.

The fact that the information costs time and money creates room for advertising, public relations, and sales efforts. In the economist's perfect market, one characteristic of which is that buyers and sellers all have complete information, the salesperson has no role because there is nothing he or she can say that is not already known. But the markets for land, buildings, labor, etc. are far from perfect in this regard. Thus all serious local economic development efforts include a public relations and marketing effort. In effect, the community is a product that the economic development agency "sells."

The Ombudsman Function Government has considerable power to obstruct development, and this power is often exercised unintentionally. The delay that appears trivial from the bureaucracy's viewpoint may be crushing to an entrepreneur. For example, at 20 percent, one day's interest on a $10 million loan is just short of $5,500. Many agencies thus perform an ombudsman function, seeking to smooth relations between government and industry and to minimize delay and conflict. Political climate is a major consideration in the minds of many businesspeople and the development agency will seek to produce as cooperative and nonthreatening a climate as possible.

The Provision of Infrastructure The provision of infrastructure is a major shaper and cause of land use and development. The use of the capital budget to make development possible is a basic economic development fuction even though it is not always referred to as such. In suburban areas, for example, highway access is often the number one determinant of economic location. Public investment in roads and interchanges thus shapes and facilitates economic development. In central cities land clearance and assembly is often a way in which government can combine its capacity to make capital expenditures and its legal powers (for example, right of eminent domain) to set the stage for subsequent private development. Land assemblage, clearance, and subsequent sale or lease at below cost was the central mechanism in urban renewal (see Chapter 8).

In many municipalities, both urban and nonmetropolitan, public funds and legal powers may be used to acquire land for industrial parks. The community uses its funds to purchase land (or to pay the condemnation awards) and then makes necessary infrastructure improvements such as roads, grading, provision of water and sewerage, storm water drainage, etc. After this, land is made available through long-term leases, generally below cost, to industrial users. On a larger scale, municipalities or groups of municipalities may invest in major facilities, which will serve to attract economic activity. The Dallas-Fort Worth Airport, for example, was developed as a major stimulus to the development of the two-city area. The Houston Ship Canal, which made Houston a port city, represents a massive capital investment to facilitate economic development.

The Subsidization of Industry

Subsidization will rarely be decisive in the choice between two radically different locations; however, where differences between places are relatively small, it may well be the deciding factor. Thus subsidization to affect the location of industry is extremely widespread in the United States.

In some instances the locality itself provides the subsidy. In other cases the subsidy, though routed through the development agency, comes from higher levels of government. The pursuit of federal grant monies is a major function of many economic development agencies. In some instances the subsidy may take the form of a direct expenditure by the locality or higher level of government. In other instances, the subsidy takes the form of a tax expenditure. This term, which appears frequently in discussions of taxation and public finance, merits definition. A *tax expenditure* occurs when, through special provisions of the tax law, income or property that would normally be subject to taxation is exempted. Thus the subsidy takes the form of a failure to collect revenue from the beneficiary rather than a payment from government to the beneficiary. Because of the implicit nature of the tax expenditure as opposed to the explicit nature of a direct subsidy tax expenditures are less visible and estimating the precise value of the subsidy can be difficult.

Some of the major types of subsidy are listed below. This list is far from exhaustive.[12]

1 *Tax abatement.* Many localities offer property tax abatements for new industrial and commercial structure. In most cases the abatement is time-limited. In some localities abatement is offered on all new development, whereas in others it may be offered selectively. State laws regarding the financial relations between

---

[12] For more detailed discussion of these techniques see John M. Levy, *Economic Development Programs for Cities, Counties and Towns,* New York, Praeger, 1981, chaps. 9 and 10.

government and business vary greatly; there is no uniform pattern. Offering the subsidy only to selected firms for whom it is believed it will be a decisive factor will reduce the number of windfalls and is obviously a more efficient use of public funds. But it also opens up possibilities of corruption and favoritism. The advantages and disadvantages of offering the same subsidy to all are essentially the opposite of the selective subsidy.

Investment tax credits are also common. These are comparable in principle to federal investment tax credits. The firm is allowed to deduct some percentage of eligible investment from its corporate income tax payment. Because relatively few substate units of government levy corporate income taxes this form of abatement for purposes of affecting the location of economic activity is usually a state-level activity. Essentially the same comments as above can be made regarding the selectivity issue.

2 *Tax-exempt financing.* In this process the locality issues bonds whose interest is tax-exempt.[13] The revenues from the bonds are then used to finance the construction, acquisition, or equipping of commercial and industrial properties. A common arrangement is for the issuing agency to become the "owner of record" of an industrial property, which it then leases to the firm. The lease payments from the firm retire the bonds. When the bonds have been paid off, the property is transferred to the firm for a nominal sum, often $1. In effect, the development agency serves as a legal shell that makes the low-cost financing possible.

The subsidy comes about because the buyer of the bonds is willing to accept a lower interest rate because of the tax exemption feature. Tax-exempt bonds typically carry interest rates of about three-fourths that carried by taxable securities of comparable term and quality.[14] The cost of the subsidy is borne by the federal government, since it is the Internal Revenue Service that forgoes the collection of tax on interest that would otherwise be subject to tax.

An interesting feature of the bond-issuing process is that although the subsidy (in the form of a tax expenditure) comes from the federal government, the issuing agency commits the federal government to such subsidy without prior consultation. It issues the bonds and subsequently notifies IRS of its actions. Like all tax expenditures, the cost does not appear as a budget item because there is no flow of funds from any unit of government, only a diminished collection of revenues.

At the end of the 1970s interest rates rose sharply and hence the absolute magnitude of the spread between taxable and tax-exempt interest rates increased substantially. Tax-exempt financing became much more attractive to firms, and the amount of tax-exempt financing increased greatly. By 1981 the estimated annual revenue loss from these tax expenditures was over $1 billion. Tax expenditures for industrial revenue bonds, sometimes referred to under the more generic term *exempt small issues*, became the subject of congressional hearings.

---

[13] For description of state-enabling legislation see Mark Rollinson, *Small Issue Industrial Revenue Bonds,* Capitol, Chicago, 1976. All state legislation is necessarily keyed to the provisions of the IRS code, which permits tax exemption for such issues. See section 103(b) (6) (D).

[14] Estimates by author. Made by comparing interest rates on all IRBs issued in New York State during 1979 and 1980 with yields on taxable corporate bonds of comparable quality issued during the same period. The figure cited also corresponds with the impressions of bankers familiar with tax-exempt issues.

With the the passage of the Tax Equity and Fiscal Responsibility Act of 1982, the industrial revenue bond provisions of the Internal Revenue Service code were changed so as to bring the process to an end as of December 31, 1986.[15] TEFRA was passed during a period of extremely high federal deficit when there was heavy pressure to find and close "loopholes." Whether this particular loophole, if that is what it is, will stay closed remains to be seen. Industrial revenue bonds have been widely used, and they have a very large constituency both in industry and on the public side of the fence within the economic development community. Thus there is already substantial pressure to permit continuation of industrial revenue bond issues beyond the current 1986 "sunset" date.[16] In fact, the Senate version of the 1984 tax bill, the Deficit Reduction Act of 1984, contained provisions which would have extended the sunset date to 1990.

3 *Loans and loan guarantees.* Loans and loan guarantees for firms that cannot obtain credit through conventional sources are quite common. To the extent that government absorbs the losses on defaults or lends at rates lower than its own borrowing costs, there is an element of subsidy in the direct loans. It can also be argued that if government borrows its loan funds through the issuance of tax-exempt securities, there is an element of subsidization as in the case of tax-exempt financing discussed previously.

Loan guarantees in general have two effects. First, they make it possible for firms that could otherwise not obtain credit to do so. Second, they reduce the cost of credit. Part of the cost of credit is a risk premium. The more risky the loan, the higher the interest rate the lender is likely to demand. When the public guarantees repayment, risk is essentially eliminated.

The ultimate source of guarantee may be the municipality, the state, or the federal government. In some cases a revolving loan fund may be self-financing. Here the lending agency sets its interest rate sufficiently above its own borrowing costs so that it can cover an occasional default. Of course, the agency following the self-financing course will have to be more selective in its choice of borrowers than an agency with an outside source of funding. In short, the self-financing operation will have to behave far more like a conventional lender.

The amount of subsidy in public loan and loan-guarantee programs varies considerably. In some cases it may be quite large. For example, the Small Business Administration (SBA) finances local development corporations (LDCs). Loans made by LDCs include both SBA and conventional funds. In mid-1980 the SBA portion of such loans was at 8.25 percent. The prime rate was closer to twice this figure. Since these funds could not be used for firms that were able to obtain credit elsewhere, SBA funds were being lent to firms with marginal credit ratings for not much more than half the rate that blue-chip corporations were paying for conventional financing.

4 *Second-mortgage financing.* In this process the state or locality provides

---

[15] For arguments pro and con and an insight into congressional thinking on this subject see the *Congressional Record,* Hearings before the Senate Budget Committee, March 17, 1982. For the TEFRA provisions pertaining to IRBs see *U.S. Code and Administrative News,* West, Mineola, N.Y., no. 7, September 1982, p. 152.

[16] Communication with staff of House Ways and Means Committee. New York Senator Alphonse D'Amato has been a particularly strong supporter of IRB financing.

money for the second mortgage, while money for the first mortgage comes from conventional lenders. The process reduces the risk to the prime lender because less of its money is at risk and because, should the firm fail and foreclosure become necessary, it will be paid before the state. Second-mortgage programs may also have the effect of lowering the total interest rate on the project somewhat, since the state can use its tax-exempt borrowing privileges to finance its own lending. Very often, such programs include a front-end charge, which includes administrative costs and a risk premium, so the cost to the state for the program can be very low. To the extent that it uses its tax-exempt borrowing powers to finance the second-mortgage issuing agency, an element of cost is being shifted back to the federal government and then, at one remove, to the nation in general.[17]

5 *Direct grants and write-downs.* This category includes a very large variety. In many cases local development is stimulated by public acceptance of part of the cost of developemnt. As noted, much downtown development occurs on cleared land whose cost has been written down. A local government or a development agency will obtain land through purchase or condemnation, clear the land, perhaps make certain basic infrastructure investments such as roads or sewers, and then sell or lease the land to a private developer at some fraction of its cost. In many instances, monies will also be used for the building of structures to render the remainder of the site more desirable—a municipal parking structure or convention facility, for example. Funds may come from local sources or the federal government. At present, HUD funds may be used for these purposes. In the past, urban renewal and model cities funds have been so used.

Many industrial parks have been developed with the use of public funds for a variety of front-end expenses including land acquisition, site preparation, and provision of access and utilities. In some cases funds have been raised locally. In other cases funding has come from federal agencies. The Economic Development Administration, the Department of Housing and Urban Development, and various regional commissions such as the Appalachian Regional Commission made grants for this type of investment.

Although far from complete, the above listing should give some notion of the extent and variety of subsidization. Though the programs have been discussed separately, many projects involve more than one type of subsidy. Part of the skill of the economic developer may lie in his or her ability to use several programs to put together a total package that is sufficiently attractive to induce development. For example, EDA matching funds might have been used to subsidize site preparation for an industrial park. For some firms the cost of construction and equipment might be subsidized with tax-exempt bonds. Firms whose credit was not strong enough for tax-exempt financing might be helped to purchase buildings with state-provided second-mortgage financing. Investment tax credits might be offered by the state for the firm's expenditures on both structures and capital equipment. Some firms might make use of SBA financing for working capital or

---

[17] In the author's opinion New York State's Job Development Authority has been a particularly effective user of second-mortgage financing as described here.

equipment. Additional inducement may be provided by local property tax abatement. Workforce training funds might be used to reduce labor costs. And so on.

BOX 5-1

WHO REALLY GETS THE SUBSIDY

So far, we discussed the effect of subsidies on the national economy. Another dimension of subsidization is the amount of the subsidy that reaches the intended recipient. The late Arthur Okun likened the giving of subsidies to carrying water in a leaky bucket. In general, it is not possible to subsidize any group of individuals or activities without some leakage along the way. Consider the following example.

A firm wishes to build an $8 million facility. Rather than finance the facility with conventional loans at 20 percent, it locates a city that is eager to have the plant and that agrees to finance the plant with tax-exempt industrial revenue bonds issued by that city's economic development agency. A consortium of buyers for the bonds is found, and an interest rate of 14 percent is agreed upon. Assume that the average buyer in the group is in the 50 percent marginal tax bracket. Let us consider the size of the subsidy (tax expenditure) and how it is divided.

If the financing had been a conventional one with taxable bonds at 20 percent, interest payments would have been $1,600,000 annually. But the investors, paying a marginal tax rate of 50 percent, would have received an after-tax annual yield of only $800,000. The other $800,000 would have been paid by them in taxes. Since the bonds are not taxable, one can consider the $800,000 that the federal government does not collect as the tax expenditure.

How is the tax expenditure divided? The firm gets its financing at 14 percent rather than 20 percent. This reduces its annual interest costs from $1,600,000 to $1,120,000. It thus captures $480,000 of the subsidy. The bond buyers would have retained only $800,000 after payment of federal income tax. With the tax-exempt bonds they receive $1,120,000. If we add the $480,000 captured by the firm and the $320,000 thus captured by the bond buyers we arrive at the total subsidy of $800,000. The subsidy continues until the bonds are paid off.

Of course, this is not the end of the matter. One can trace almost endlessly the ripple effects of the subsidy. Some unemployed members of the local labor force benefit by gaining jobs at the new plant. Other members of the local labor force may give up lower-paying or otherwise less attractive jobs to take the newly offered jobs. This in turn leaves job openings that are filled by other workers, who are thus presumably indirect beneficiaries of the subsidy. The general tightening of the labor market, which begins when the new plant begins to hire may exert upward pressure on wages, thus benefiting workers in many other enterprises. The increase in economic activity will affect rents, land values, the profitability of retail and service businesses, etc. An almost endless chain of events can be shown.

If one could line up all of the beneficiaries of the subsidy they would include the bond buyers, the corporation's stockholders, merchants, property owners, some workers who had previously been employed, some previously unemployed workers, some workers from prosperous households, some workers from households formerly below the poverty line, etc. What percentage of the subsidy was delivered to its intended recipients is not easy to say.

To this confusion about the distribution of the benefits is added some confusion about the "disbenefits." If community A gains a plant that would otherwise have gone to community B, then a complementary set of losses may be shown. If one postulates that subsidies will be used only by those communities most in need of additional employment, perhaps the benefits to the winning community may exceed the disbenefits to the losing community. But suppose that in the competition for this particular plant an impoverished community with a serious unemployment problem was beaten by a relatively prosperous community whose interest in economic development stemmed from the desire of its generally prosperous population to hold down property tax rates. In this case, the losses may exceed the benefits.

It should be evident that Arthur Okun's "leaky bucket" is readily demonstrated.

The Realities of Intermunicipal Competition

Perhaps the most salient point in the matter of intermunicipal competition is simply the strength of that competition. Literally thousands of political jurisdictions have economic development programs. There are far more municipalities seeking to bring in firms than there are firms looking for locations. If one regards the municipality as a seller, then, by and large, it is a buyer's market, a fact that is not lost upon the business people who are experienced in dealing with local development agencies.

Second, most of the subsidizing tools that are available from the federal government are available very widely. For example, industrial revenue bond financing is made possible by provisions of the IRS code, which necessarily apply nationally. State-enabling legislation is also necessary, and it exists in 47 of the 50 states. Community development funds from the Department of Housing and Urban Development can be used for economic development among other purposes. CD funding is based on formulas designed to favor poorer areas, but some CD funding is available in virtually all communities. Eligibility for UDAG grants is determined by several statistics, some of which are related to labor market conditions. But the number of communities that are able to meet these requirements is very large. Thus there is some degree of targeting in the program, but not very much. A number of Small Business Administration programs can also be used for economic development purposes. In general, they do not have geographic restrictions. EDA grants are conditional upon the locality meeting eligibility requirements, but when national unemployment rates went up in the late 1970s areas containing about 85 percent of the US population became eligible.[18]

At the state level, there is an enormous range of programs available for economic development. These include investment tax credits, loan guarantees, interest rate write-downs, and second-mortgage financing, as noted earlier. In general, the degree of targeting within the state is small. This is hardly surprising, for if the goal is to stimulate the economy of the state, a finely targeted program that made assistance available only in the most distressed areas would be counterproductive.

At the local level there is a great deal of subsidizing of economic development, both by direct expenditures and by tax abatement. Whether, in general, there is more of this activity in distressed than in relatively prosperous areas is not known. Distressed areas are likely to be more motivated but prosperous areas are likely to be more capable.

The situation is complicated by the fact that a great many communities mount economic development programs for tax-base rather than labor market reasons. One can find many prosperous municipalities that do not have a serious structural unemployment problem engaged in the promotion of their own economic development. Quite often, the more prosperous community can outcompete a less prosperous one. The more prosperous community may be in better condition financially and can, therefore, expend more on economic development. Often,

---

[18] For a map showing eligible areas of the United States by county see the annual reports of the EDA.

though not inevitably, it may have a lower tax rate. If the municipal fiscal structure is sounder, municipal bond ratings will be higher and borrowing costs will be lower. Thus a given amount of debt service will finance a greater amount of investment in development infrastructure (roads, water and sewer facilities, land acquisition and clearance, etc.).

The very fact of municipal prosperity may be attractive to firms because it promises a certain stability, whereas a poor and overburdened community involves more risk. If the community is financially strained and losing economic activity, firms may fear that major increases in taxes will be forthcoming as social service and poverty-related expenditures rise and the tax base shrinks. If it appears that bankruptcy is possible, firms may fear that the municipality will be unable to raise capital to make necessary infrastructure investments and provide adequate basic services like fire and police protection. New York City's brush with bankruptcy in the mid- and late 1970s is believed to have had an adverse effect in just this way. In fact, for a brief time there were fears that a New York City bankruptcy might drag New York State under and this made the task of attracting activity to any part of the state more difficult.[19]

LARGER CONSIDERATIONS

For the city or town engaging in the subsidization of economic development, the question is whether the process is worth the cost at the municipal level. If the primary motivation is softness in the labor market, then the question is whether the public expenditures are adequately counterbalanced by the additional income that will accrue to its own residents. If the primary goal is tax relief, the question is whether the anticipated new revenue from development will exceed the anticipated increase in public expenditures needed to attract and service the new industry.

A slightly more sophisticated view would include some side effects such as environmental quality and housing-market consequences. Formal cost-benefit studies are rare. But cost-revenue studies, often referred to as fiscal-impact studies, are quite common.[20] In many instances no study is done, but it is simply presumed that the benefits of economic development will exceed its costs. In any case, evaluating the desirability of subsidizing development is essentially a matter that ends at the municipal line. Externalities are simply not considered. In fact, if economic developers took to wondering out loud about the effects of their town's development program on adjacent and perhaps competing towns, they would soon be likely to find themselves seeking other employment.

However, if we transcend the question of local interest and look at the effect of subsidizing local economic development upon the national economy, some theoretical questions soon arise.

---

[19] Observation by author, who was active in local economic development in New York State during the mid-to-late 1970s.

[20] For an example of a simple fiscal-impact study see Chapter 12 in Levy, op. cit.

The Efficiency Question

Among economists it is widely assumed that the subsidization of local economic development is economically inefficient—that we pay a price in total output for the privilege of achieving a pattern of location that is different from the pattern the market would achieve.

> Persons and firms consume and produce in patterns and by methods they would prefer not to adopt, but do adopt, just to minimize their tax bills. The losses in consumer satisfaction and in productive efficiency that result from being thus induced to act in non-preferred ways are, in the economist's term, an "excess burden." Such a burden is an efficiency loss and represents an unproductive use of the real national income of the economy.[21]

Though the above was written in regard to the distorting effects of unequal taxation it applies as well to the effects of subsidizing some activities or places but not others. Consider the case of a firm making a fixed amount of a product for sale to a national market. Presumably, if there is no public interference with market forces, the firm will choose the least-cost location. From the firm's point of view this is a profit-maximizing decision, but from a national point of view it also maximizes GNP by producing a given output with minimum resource costs.

Now assume that a municipality that is not a least-cost location offers the firm a subsidy that is at least as large as the cost differential between itself and the least-cost location. The subsidizing jurisdiction now becomes the profit-maximizing location and the firm locates its operation there. But in terms of the national economy there has been a loss because more than the minimum amount of resources are now being used to produce a given output. The difference in production cost between the subsidized location and the least-cost location is the measure of this waste. In fact, one can argue that the difference understates the waste because delivering the subsidy necessarily involves some transactions costs. One can argue a priori that if a subsidy is necessary to attract or retain a firm, the subsidizing jurisdiction is not the least-cost location. The extension of this is that the more we subsidize economic location, the further we move away from an efficient pattern of economic location.

The above argument is really a particular case of the general proposition that subsidizing the production of some goods but not others moves us away from an efficient pattern of resource allocation by producing too much of the former and too little of the latter. In this case we are saying that if community A offers subsidies and community B does not, then too much activity will be located in community A and too little in community B.

It could be argued that since many communities offer economic development subsidies, the overall pattern of activity is not greatly altered by subsidization. Rather, the net effect of local subsidization efforts is simply a subsidy to capital investment, which, viewed nationally, increases investment and hence increases total output. For example, industrial revenue bond financing is available in

---

[21] Jerry J. Jasinowski, "The Economics of Federal Subsidy Programs," in Lowell C. Harriss (ed.), *Government Spending and Land Values,* University of Wisconsin Press, Madison, Wisc., 1973, p. 13.

thousands of communities in all but a very few states. It lowers interest rates by perhaps one-quarter on the average. Why not simply regard it as a subsidy to investment generally. Investments that would not have been profitable with conventional financing become profitable with tax-exempt financing. Hence more investment occurs.

However, as convincing as the above may be, it is easily countered. One could achieve the same effect by reductions in corporate income tax rates or expanded investment tax credits. It can be further argued that as funds available for loan flow into the tax-exempt market, the supply of such funds elsewhere must necessarily shrink, thus exerting upward pressure on other interest rates. Thus investment in other activities is discouraged. With local subsidization a large subsidy is delivered to a limited number of firms, not because they are necessarily particularly deserving but for reasons generally unrelated to the efficiency with which the firm utilizes resources.

What has been said in regard to tax-exempt financing can also be said with only minor modifications for grants, loan guarantees, and other forms of assistance.

Efficiency and Market Imperfections Though the majority of economists would probably agree to the efficiency arguments stated above, there is an efficiency argument that can be made in favor of subsidization of local economic development. It turns on the imperfection of labor markets. Two necessary characteristics of the perfect market are: (1) full and immediate mobility of all the factors of production, and (2) no impediments to the immediate adjustment of prices. If these conditions were met, structural unemployment as a function of geographic distribution would not exist. When an area lost jobs, wage rates would fall as the demand for labor weakened. As a result there would be an out-migration of workers to other areas. This would reduce the supply of labor until the original level of wages had been restored. However, as noted before, labor is not instantly mobile. Thus as jobs are lost, workers will become either unemployed or employed in activities in which their earnings are lower because their marginal productivities are lower.

About 20 years ago, using the above line of reasoning, Moes constructed an argument to the effect that local subsidies to economic development actually increase GNP.[22] He gave the following example. Assume that in a given area the wage for industrial labor is $1 per hour but that a new firm will not come into the area if it has to pay more than 90 cents an hour. In other words, he is assuming that wages are not flexible downward. Assume further that the marginal product of labor in agriculture is 15 cents per hour, a figure he claims was accurate for a part of the southeast at that time. If the community furnishes a subsidy that effectively reduces wage costs by 10 cents per hour, manufacturing will move in and labor will be shifted from an activity in which its marginal product is worth 15 cents per hour to one worth 90 cents per hour. This accounts for a net productivity gain of 75 cents at the margin. Thus Moes argues that allowing communities to

[22] John Moes, "The Subsidization of Local Industry in the South," *Southern Economic Journal*, vol. 28, pp. 187–193. See also comments on Moes's article by Goffman and Thompson, vol. 29, pp. 111–126.

subsidize industry actually contributes to the performance of the national economy.

His critics argued that he neglected to consider the jobs that would be lost elsewhere when the firm moved to the jurisdiction offering the subsidy. His rejoinder was that employment is not a fixed total nationally and that job loss elsewhere cannot be assumed. At this point the argument turns upon how the national economy works. If one takes a strict Keynesian view that total activity, and hence total employment, is a function of aggregate demand, then the local subsidization of economic activity must be a zero sum game. One community's gain is another community's loss. In this case Moes's critics have the better side of the argument. If one takes, as Moes did, a neoclassical view that unemployment results from the lack of downward flexibility of wages and that local subsidization can constitute a substitute for this downward flexibility, as in the above example, then the zero sum game argument falls.[23]

A long digression on the merits of Keynesian economics would not be appropriate here. To summarize, we might say the following. Most economists regard the subsidization of local economic development as inefficient because of the cost-of-production arguments made earlier. Some case for possible efficiency gains can be made along the lines of the Moes argument. The key point here is whether or not one should consider total employment nationally as being fixed by outside factors, that is, aggregate demand. On this point, opinions among economists differ. Thus, this is as far as the theoretical road will take us at present.

Changing the Rules of the Game

Even if we accept the idea that the subsidization of local economic development might be very useful at the national scale because of its capacity to reduce structural unemployment, we must note that it is far from certain that the net result of subsidization is to strengthen the weakest areas. For the economic development game is played by both strong and weak areas and it is not clear who the winners are on balance.

The reader may respond by saying that a logical course of action would be highly targeted programs and rules that limited the use of subsidies to obviously needy areas. For example, tax-exempt financing is probably the single most powerful subsidizing device available to the economic developer.[24] Why not simply amend the provisions of the IRS code, which make this device possible, to

---

[23] The neoclassical view that employment can be expanded by downward movement of wages was dominant until the Keynesians argued that if workers accepted lower wages the expected increase in output and employment resulting from lower production costs would be at least partly negated by decreased aggregate demand. For a discussion of pre-Keynesian theories of employment and the Keynesian attack upon it see Campbell McConnell, *Economics,* 9th ed., McGraw-Hill, New York, 1984.

[24] The technique delivers a fairly large subsidy. The process is noncompetitive in that there is no fixed pot from which monies come and therefore no ranking, or "prioritizing," of projects. If the project meets the requirements of the law and buyers for the bonds can be found, then the subsidy can be had. Finally, the process is quick because there is no grant application process and therefore no waiting for a response from a governmental agency. In fact, there is no direct participation by the federal government in the process at all.

limit it to designated areas rather than allowing it to be used ubiquitously? In a similar vein, why not have tightened EDA requirements for eligibility so that instead of being available to areas with 85 percent of the population EDA funding was available only to the most distressed 10 or 20 percent?

To a large extent, the answer is to be found in the realities of politics. The more ubiquitous a program is, the more political support it is likely to have. For example, late in his first term President Nixon sought to abolish EDA. But he was unable to do so because its congressional support was too strong. Too many congressional districts had either gotten EDA grants or had prospects for getting them. The fact that the agency's funding efforts were not narrowly targeted gave it more political strength. The survival of UDAG under the Reagan administration appears based upon its widespread support among mayors, a breadth of support it would not have were it targeted to, let us say, only the most impoverished 10 percent of U.S. cities.

The People versus Places Question

Because promoting the welfare of places as a means of promotion the welfare of individuals involves such a long path and one so fraught with leakages and uncertainties, it has been argued that perhaps we ought not to worry so much above places and instead concern ourselves directly with people. The people versus places controversy has been with us for almost as long as have been place-oriented programs. Table 5–1 summarizes some of the major points in the people versus places argument. Let us consider the various points in order.

Do Places Matter?   We might take a strongly individualistic view and assert that there is no public interest apart from private interests, that is, what we call the public interest is no more and no less than the sum of private interests. Without arguing the rightness or wrongness of this view we simply note that it is a position held by a number of economists, political theorists, and other scholars.[25] We might go further and add that as long as the individual has adequate skills and mobility he or she can deal with problems in the social or economic environment by adapting or moving. If we assert the above, we have accepted much of the case for a "people" rather than a "place" strategy.

On the other hand we might assert that there are indeed elements of the public interest that are not simply the sum of individual interests. We might also assert that places matter as places and not just for the effects they may have on their present inhabitants. Then we might argue that individuals are powerfully influenced by their social and economic environments. If we accept these latter statements we have accepted much of the case for place-oriented programs.

How Important Is Efficiency?   The conventional view that place-related programs are inefficient raises the question, "How important is efficiency?" How much productivity and output are we willing to give up in order to achieve equity gains?

---

[25] For example, the "public choice" school, of whom James Buchanan and Gordon Tullock are probably the best-known members, takes precisely this view.

TABLE 5-1
THE PEOPLE VERSUS PLACES CONTROVERSY

Issue	People prosperity	Place prosperity
Rationale	Only individuals matter. Individual welfare is relatively independent of place condition	Places also matter. The welfare of individuals is relatively dependent upon place condition
Presumed efficiency effects	Not certain. Might increase GNP by improving labor force quality nationally	Inefficient. Lowers GNP if orthodox view is correct
Effects on interarea migration	Probably accelerates it	Retards it
Strategy	Bottom up. May take a "worst-case-first" approach	Top down. May focus on places with most development potential (within eligible area)
Benefits to the nonpoor	Undoubtedly some. Probably not as many as in other case	Clear and substantial benefits to the nonpoor (see Box 5-1)
Most obvious drawback	Does little to mitigate the social and psychological costs of economically forced migration. May do little to aid the survival of dying places	As a strategy to aid the long-term poor it is at least partly defeated by labor force mobility and elasticity
Political support	Relatively weak, particularly if programs bypass local political structure	Very strong support from the political establishment of eligible areas
Relation to recent locational trends	No necessary conflict	Definitely swimming against the tide

In the 1960s and early 1970s there seemed to be something of an unspoken consensus that a considerable sacrifice in efficiency might be acceptable. Perhaps that consensus came in part from the post-World War II economic history of the United States, which, by and large, was one of continued growth in productivity and affluence. If we could take productivity growth for granted then we could relegate efficiency questions to the back seat and concentrate on equity.

However, during the 1970s several complacency-shattering events occurred. Productivity growth began to stagnate. Total U.S. real GNP still rose but that was primarily due to increases in the size of the labor force rather than increasing output per worker. In the mid-1970s a number of nations passed the United States in per capita GNP—a startling event for most Americans.[26] The view that there is a nexus between inflation and stagnating productivity became widespread, and many came to believe that inflation could better be dealt with when productivity was growing. At the end of the decade there appeared to be a weakening of

[26] In 1970 the United States had the highest per capita GNP in the world. By 1978 the United States had been passed by Switzerland and Sweden and the German Federal Republic had caught up with it. The reader should be aware, however, that international comparisons of GNP are not entirely definitive. GNP is first computed in terms of the nation's own currency. Prevailing exchange rates are then used to put all figures in terms of a common denominator. To the extent that a nation's currency is over- or undervalued on world markets the data is distorted. For comparative data on GNPs see the International Statistics section of the *Statistical Abstract of the United States.*

détente and a forming consensus in favor of substantially increased U.S. defense expenditures. Very obviously, such an effort will cause less pain and require less sacrifice in a growth environment than in a nongrowth environment.

The penetration of U.S. consumer goods markets, perhaps most notably in automobiles and consumer electronics, by foreign producers also heightened concern with efficiency. Low productivity implied not only lower living standards for all but unemployment for those in industries that were not competitive internationally. Thus the growth of world trade creates efficiency demands that would not exist in a more insular economy. The vision of the "age of limits," which the environmental movement has made widespread, may also have increased the emphasis on efficiency by suggesting that we cannot have both more equity and more output.

Urban America in the Eighties, a report published by the President's Commission in the last days of the Carter administration, noted:

> National economic policies that seek to increase productivity, to expand markets, to create jobs, and to nurture new industries also have the potential for conflict with urban revitalization efforts. Policies aimed at increasing the productivity and competitive position of industry (such as business tax cuts and accelerated depreciation allowances) may well lead to the outmigration of firms or to their secondary expansion away from distressed locations, where the costs of doing business are prohibitively high. Conversely, vigorous pursuit of a national urban policy—with its current emphasis on restoring economic vitality to distressed localities and regions—may undermine a more general effort to revitalize the national economy—with its relative deemphasis on what happens in specific places.[27]

Often taken by the press as a recommendation to abandon America's older cities, the report was the subject of widespread and sometimes scathing criticism. An editorial on it in *The Washington Post* headlined Offing the Frostbelt: A Stupid Idea Whose Time Has Come typifies press reaction. Yet, the report raises some questions that are not easily dismissed. The report's authors in effect accepted the argument that there is an aggregate loss when activity is directed into non-least-cost locations. They then make it clear that they give preference to efficiency over the matter of geographic distribution.

The Question of Migration   The two approaches clearly differ in their effects on migration. A people-oriented policy may well encourage migration by helping employable individuals to relocate in areas where jobs are more plentiful. In fact, assisted migration is often proposed by those who favor people-oriented strategies. For example, the President's Commission cited earlier stated:

> The United States is virtually the only developed capitalist nation without policies or programs that assist the migration of people who are willing to follow employment opportunities. In Europe, mobility assistance programs are relatively well developed and enjoy considerable legitimacy. Presumably some portions of such people-to-jobs policy strategies could be imported.[28]

---

[27] President's Commission for a National Agenda for the Eighties, *Urban America in the Eighties,* U.S. Government Printing Office, Washington, D.C., 1980, p. 3.

[28] President's Commission, op. cit., p. 59.

The report then went on to suggest a number of strategies that we might consider. These included a national jobs clearinghouse and a variety of housing and financial assistance devices to ease the strain of migration on individuals and families.

Place-oriented strategies are clearly designed to reduce out-migration from declining areas and thus reduce interarea migration. The proponent of place-oriented programs might argue that migration forced, or at least strongly encouraged, by economic forces has large personal costs: shattering the web of personal relationships within the community, the fragmenting of families, cultural shock for the migrant and sometimes for the receiving community as well. The black experience in American cities following the post-World War II mechanization of agriculture offers powerful evidence that migration forced by economic necessity can subject individuals and families to tremendous stresses, and the damage done may last for quite long periods of time. In addition, it might be argued that when economically bypassed places die we lose some element of cultural diversity and are poorer for it as a society.

The advocate of people-oriented policies might say that the growth and death of places has being going on for as long as we have records and is a natural process from which we need no protection. It might also be argued that for a nation of immigrants with a long tradition of high geographic mobility there should be nothing frightening about interarea migration in pursuit of economic opportunity. It is, after all, an old and honorable national tradition.

Worst Case or Best Prospect?   People-oriented policies are likely to take a worst-case first approach, as did the new CETA discussed in Chapter 6. A place-oriented program presumably will seek to target aid to those areas needing it most, though, as noted, there are political reasons why the targeting may not be extremely precise. But within those areas it is likely not to funnel aid into the most distressed places. Rather, it is quite sensibly likely to focus on those places that show most promise for growth. For example, in the last several years of its existence the EDA encouraged the formation of multicounty economic development districts (EDDs), which were to have designated "growth centers" within them. The "growth-pole" concept is central to the work of many regional development theorists, such as Hansen and Perroux.[29]

Windfalls and Accidental Enrichments   As Okun emphasized with his leaky-bucket metaphor, the giving of subsidies inevitably involves some leakage along the way. Place-related programs seen almost inevitably to involve large leakages to the nonpoor simply because the nature of the subsidy is to offer inducements to those who have the capital to make the necessary investments (see Box 5-1 on page 143). We also note that if one gives a subsidy to induce action it is always possible that the action would have been taken anyway. In that case, the subsidy is pure windfall. It is in the interest of the firm seeking a subsidy to convince the subsidizer that it will not act without the subsidy. In the writer's experience it is often very difficult to tell, even after the transaction is completed, whether or not the subsidy was or was not decisive in motivating the firm.

[29] Niles Hansen, *Intermediate-Size Cities as Growth Centers*, Praeger, New York, 1971.

Given their bottom-up orientation it seems likely that people-oriented programs will provide somewhat fewer enrichments for the already prosperous. The author must admit, however, that he is not aware of any work that proves this supposition.

Inherent Drawbacks   The most obvious drawback of the people-oriented approach is the matter of migration and place stagnation, noted earlier. The most obvious drawback of the place-related strategy is that labor force mobility and the elasticity of the local labor supply may prevent it from helping those most in need. Assume subsidies succeed in the bringing a new branch plant of the XYZ Manufacturing Corporation into an area of high unemployment. The plant opens and proceeds to hire 100 workers. Who will they be? Some will be workers who migrate into the area because of the new jobs. Some will be local people who were not previously in the labor force but who are drawn into it because of the increased probability of finding a job now that the new plant has begun to hire. Finally, some of the newly hired workers may be formerly unemployed local workers. The salient point is that the in-migration of new workers plus the expansion of the local labor force will probably cause the reduction in unemployment to be much smaller than one might at first suspect. In summarizing the experience of small towns that attracted new industry Summers found that the percentage of newly hired workers who had been formerly unemployed in that area ranged from close to zero up to about 25 percent.[30] In no cases were the majority of new jobs taken by formerly unemployed local workers.

Writing about the opening of industrial jobs in the rural south, Wilbur Thompson noted:

> Relocating manufacturers contend that they do not have to depend on workers already in town. . . . In almost any Southern town from which blue collar workers have migrated . . . some would like to return, but they need a good job. When a new plant comes in, they come back. In fact, the hard corollary of this easy mobility is that local growth does not really lick the unemployment problem—all it does, in the long run, is enlarge the local labor force. Since it is the returning skilled workers who win away most of the new jobs, the town just gets bigger, still struggling with its chronic unemployment problem—its "unemployables."[31]

The growing southern towns of which Thompson writes are not perfect analogies for stable or shrinking central cities. But the quote does emphasize the point that labor force mobility will, to some degree, defeat the labor market goals of place-related programs.

Political Support   Place-related economic development programs tend to get strong support from local governments that have some probability of receiving funding, as noted earlier. A purely people-oriented program is not likely to have such wide support. This is particularly true if the program appears to encourage

---

[30] Gene Summers, *The Invasion of Non-Metropolitan America by Industry: A Quarter Century of Experience*, Praeger, New York, 1976.

[31] Wilbur Thompson, "Economic Processes and Employment Problems in Declining Metropolitan Areas," in George Sternlieb and James W. Hughes (eds.), *Post-Industrial America: Metropolitan Decline and Job Shifts*, Center for Urban Policy Research, Rutgers, 1975, p 190.

migration, for example, if the program trains workers in lagging areas and then helps them move to other areas. Few politicians would care to lose constituents, and it is dubious that politicians in potential receiving areas would be anxious to see outsiders come in to compete with residents for limited job openings.

Relationship to Present Realities of Economic Location   The last point in the table is the question, "Which approach fits in with present realities in the location of employment?" There is no conflict so far as people-related programs are concerned. The person who is trained or otherwise helped to be more competitive in the labor market is made more mobile and is more likely to have the confidence and skills necessary to move out of a lagging area and into an area where the labor market is tighter. The place-related strategy is, by definition, an attempt to swim against the tide. Apart from the issues noted above, there remains the matter of whether the swim will be successful.

Obviously there are arguments on both sides of the issue. The Reagan administration has clearly been unfavorably disposed to place-related programs. Its ideological commitment to a smaller role for government in the making of economic decisions necessarily predisposes it against programs that seek to alter the pattern of capital allocation. Its concern with cyclical unemployment and international competition also predisposes it against programs whose rationale is equity rather than efficiency. But which way the pendulum will move in the next few years is far from certain.

CHAPTER 6

POVERTY AND THE CITY

THE CONCENTRATION OF POVERTY IN URBAN AREAS

Poverty is central to any discussion of urban problems for many reasons. Perhaps most important is that there has been a marked urbanization of poverty in the last 2 decades or so. In 1959 central cities had only 83 percent as many poor people as they would had if the poverty population of the nation had been homogeneously distributed. By 1978 central cities had 135 percent of their proportionate share of the nation's poor. In 1959 central cities had 1.5 times as many people per thousand in poverty as did the communities making up the suburban ring. By 1978 that ratio had risen to 2.4. In 1959 the incidence of poverty in central cities was 54 percent of what it was in nonmetropolitan areas. By 1978 that figure had changed to 114 percent.

For the city, the concentration of the poor in or near its center is a serious economic handicap. The provision of services for the poor places a financial burden on the city that must necessarily show up in higher tax rates or reduced expenditures for other activities. Either alternative makes the city less attractive as an economic or residential location for those who have other options.

Beyond that, many of the nonpoor seem to have a strong aversion to living close to the poor. One may decry this but that does not alter the fact. One reason for this is that the poor and what has been called the "underclass" tend to live in the same areas. According to Auletta, the underclass is an ill-defined and ill-counted group which is made of four subgroups.[1]

1 The passive poor, primarily long-term welfare recipients
2 Street criminals

[1] Ken Auletta, *The Underclass*, Random House, New York, 1982, p. 43.

3 Hustlers; people who are generally not violent but who earn their livings in the illegal side of the "hidden economy," which is discussed later

4 The traumatized; alcoholics, deinstitutionalized mental patients, drifters, shopping-bag ladies, etc.

The poor are a much larger group than the underclass and are by no means synonymous with it. For example, a substantial percentage of the poor who are eligible for public assistance never avail themselves of it, whether as a matter of pride or for other reasons.[2] Among those who do, the majority are pushed into it by a specific event such as a divorce or separation, loss of employment, or an uninsured medical emergency and get off as soon as they can. If we track a cohort of welfare recipients, we observe a great deal of mobility, with an average stay on the rolls in the range of 2 to 3 years. The permanent welfare recipient is a distinct minority of all recipients. Similarly, not all of the underclass is poor. But there is considerable overlap and in urban areas they tend to occupy the same physical space. Poor neighborhoods tend to be high-street-crime areas, even though most of the poor aren't criminals and not all criminals are poor. When nonpoor citizens move out of the city, they take their buying power with them, thus enriching the suburban or exurban service economy and weakening that of the central city. When they arrive at their new destination their presence strengthens the suburban and exurban labor force and weakens the city's labor force. In time this begins to influence the locational decisions of firms that constitute the export base of the central city. Every survey of the causes of industrial and commercial relocation places labor availability fairly close to the top of the list.[3] The feedback effects are not difficult to see. The out-migration of working-class and middle-class residents softens the economy of the central city, thus promoting poverty, pushing some members of the larger class of poor toward an underclass existence, and encouraging still more out-migration.

There are a number of reasons why poverty is increasingly an urban phenomenon.

1 The U.S. internal migration mentioned before in connection with the mechanization of agriculture. Agricultural employment dropped by about two-thirds between the late 1940s and the early 1970s. A rural population, often ill-prepared for urban life, poured into the cities. A large percentage of the migrants were southern blacks, the poorest segment of the population in what was then the poorest region of the country.

2 The loss of employment, particularly manufacturing and other blue-collar jobs, to suburban and nonmetropolitan areas.

3 The presence of large amounts of relatively low-cost rental housing in central cities. Since metropolitan areas tend to grow from the center, the housing stock

---

[2] David W. Lyon, *The Dynamics of Welfare Dependency: A Survey*, Institute of Policy Sciences and Public Affairs, Duke University, 1977. See also various reports of the Panel Study of Income Dynamics, Survey Research Center, Institute for Social Research, University of Michigan, Ann Arbor, for detailed analyses of the amount of mobility in the poverty and welfare populations.

[3] See, for example, Reigeluth and Welman, *The Determinants and Implications of Communities Changing Competitive Advantages: A Review of Literature*, Working Paper 1264–03, Urban Institute, Washington, D.C., 1979.

near the center is often the oldest and least expensive in the region. The supply of centrally located low-cost housing is often increased by public housing policy and sometimes by rent controls as well (see Chapter 8).

4 The provision of more adequate public services in urban areas. Cities may provide services like public hospitals and public transportation that are not available in rural or suburban areas. But providing services to aid the poor may have the effect of increasing number of poor within the city.

5 Tax and other public policies that increase the opportunity cost of renting for middle-income and upper-income persons (see Chapter 7). The net effect is to encourage the selective suburbanization of the prosperous and thus increase the urban poor as a percentage of the total urban population.

6 Suburban land-use controls. For reasons explored in Chapter 8, a large number of suburban communities have used their land-use controls—sometimes intentionally and sometimes unintentionally—to prevent the construction of low-cost housing. This amplifies the effect discussed in item 3.

THE FACTS OF POVERTY

Before turning to the question of urban poverty per se, we should discuss poverty in general. We begin with a few definitions and some comments on what the statistics mean.

Counting the Poor

When statistics on poverty are quoted, they generally refer to the federal poverty line. In the 1960s it was estimated that a family with a moderate income spent about one-third of its income on food. Using data furnished by the Department of Agriculture, the cost of a minimum but nutritionally adequate diet was determined. This figure was then multiplied by 3 to establish the so-called poverty line.[4] That figure is adjusted annually for changes in the consumer price index (CPI). When the decennial census is taken, each household's income as indicated on its questionnaire is compared with the poverty line for a household of that size and age composition. Thus figures on the number of households, the number of families, and the number of individuals below the poverty line are generated. For other years estimates are made by survey techniques.[5]

Limitations of the Federal Poverty Level   Although it is the most widely used and probably the most useful measure of poverty available to us, the federal poverty line has some distinct limitations.

First, it is an absolute measure. The cost-of-living adjustment essentially keeps

---

[4] For a discussion of the process of determining the poverty line see Mollie Orshansky, "Counting the Poor: Another Look at the Poverty Profile," Social Security Bulletin, U.S. Social Security Administration, January 1965. This article and a number of others on related subjects are reprinted in *The Measure of Poverty*, Technical Paper 1, Department of Health, Education, and Welfare, Washington, D.C., 1977. For a discussion of the correction of poverty figures for in-kind payments see Background-paper 17, "Poverty Status of Families under Alternative Definitions of Income," CBO, January 1977, as well as the work by Timothy Smeeding footnoted under Table 6-2.

[5] See Series U.S. Bureau of the Census, *Current Population Reports*, various years.

the purchasing power of a poverty-line income constant over time, regardless of how average incomes are changing. Thus, if the shape of the income distribution curve were to remain constant but real incomes were to rise, the percent of the population below the poverty line would fall. In fact, this is exactly what happened in the 1960s and early 1970s.

Whether an absolute or a relative poverty measure is best is arguable. If one is concerned about whether people can meet minimum needs for food, shelter, medical care, etc., then clearly an absolute measure is appropriate. On the other hand, if one is concerned about people's images of themselves, their feeling of self-worth and accomplishment, the extent to which they feel that society and life itself have treated them well, a relative measure may be best.

The preference for one type of standard rather than another may be partly an ideological choice. The conservative who seeks to defend the existing system is likely to prefer an absolute standard because it demonstrates a long-term reduction in poverty. The radical, whose ultimate agenda is a massive redistribution of wealth and power, may prefer a relative standard, which emphasizes inequality regardless of the absolute level of income.

The federal statistics are statistics of "income poverty" and take no account of other factors that contribute to living standards. If family A and family B have the same age and sex structure and the same cash income, their poverty status will be evaluated in the same manner. The fact that family A lives in rented housing while family B lives in a paid-off home will not make a difference. The value of housing services delivered to family B by the asset it owns are ignored. Similarly, the value of services in kind like free medical care, reduced-rate school lunches, or the difference between rent paid and true costs in subsidized housing is not counted. The value of food stamps, which as will be shown subsequently come very close to being a cash transfer, is also not counted.

How Accurate Is Poverty Data?   According to the Bureau of the Census itself, data on wage and salary income is more accurate than data on business income or transfer payment income. Thus income data for the middle-class, middle-income household is likely to be more accurate than for those at either end of the income distribution curve.

Income that is not reported to the Internal Revenue Service is not likely to be reported to the Bureau of the Census in spite of the Bureau's long history of protecting confidentiality. Estimates of the so-called hidden economy of the United States place the income it generates at over $300 billion, well over $1,000 per capita.[6] A sizable part of this figure comes from activities that are in themselves illegal, but the majority comes from legal activities that are concealed for tax purposes. The physician taking a fee in cash and failing to report it and the welfare mother who works 2 days a week "off the books" as a domestic are both

---

[6] The first widely cited estimate appeared in an article by Peter M. Gutmann, "The Subterranean Economy," *Financial Analysts Journal*, Nov.-Dec. 1977, pp. 26–34. Gutmann placed such transactions at about 10 percent of GNP. Subsequently, a number of articles on the subject have appeared in a variety of scholarly and business periodicals, generally indexed under the term "underground economy." Other estimates of the size of the underground economy range from somewhat smaller to substantially larger than Gutmann's.

TABLE 6-1
U.S. POVERTY POPULATION, 1959–1982
(Figures in Millions)

	1959	1969	1979	1981	1982
U.S. population	177.9	202.7	225.1	229.8	
Population below the federal poverty line	39.5	24.1	24.5	31.8	34.4
Poverty population as a percent of total population	22.2	11.9	11.0	13.8	14.8

Source: U.S. Bureau of the Census, *Current Population Reports*, ser. P 60, no. 124 and *The New York Times*, August 3, 1983, p. 1.

participants in the hidden economy. The existence of the hidden economy is deduced largely from indirect evidence. For example, the public's demand for cash has gone up considerably in recent years, whereas the development of new types of checking accounts and the widespread use of credit cards would cause one to expect it to have gone down. Because it is something that cannot be easily surveyed and measured directly, it is not possible to say how the earnings of the hidden economy are distributed or how the census income figures would be changed if earnings from the hidden economy could be factored in.

Trends in Poverty

In the 1960s U.S. per capita GNP rose rapidly, and the shape of the income distribution curve remained relatively constant. This situation, combined with an absolute poverty standard, produced the substantial decrease in poverty shown in Table 6-1. In the 1970s real per capita GNP increased much more slowly, so the incidence of poverty measured by the Bureau of the Census declined more slowly. With the coming of the recession in 1981, the poverty figure turned upward.

However, it can be argued that a better measure for poverty—namely income statistics that are adjusted for income in kind—would have reflected substantial improvement over the decade. Annual in kind payments increased from a few billion in the late 1950s to about $60 billion by the end of the 1970s. The effect of income transfers and services in kind on poverty is shown in Table 6-2.

Column 1 shows the effect of counting the market value of in kind payments upon the number of people who would be counted as poor. Note that by this measure the number of people under the poverty line is cut almost in half. Column 2 shows the reduction in poverty if instead of counting the cash value of payments in kind we calculate the estimated cash value to the recipient. As is discussed in the appendix on welfare economics, the value of a payment in kind to the recipient may be less than its cash value.[7] Thus the reduction in poverty is smaller but still far from trivial.

[7] See Lester Thurow, "Cash Versus In-Kind Transfers," *American Economic Review*, May 1974, pp. 190–195.

TABLE 6-2
1979 POVERTY POPULATION AND POVERTY RATE USING
VARIOUS MEASURES
(Figures in Millions)

	Valuation techniques		
	Market value (1)	**Value to recipient** (2)	**Poverty budget** (3)
Money income only (census income definition)	23.6 (11.1)	23.6 (11.1)	23.6 (11.1)
Money income plus food and housing in kind	19.9 (9.4)	20.2 (9.5)	20.7 (9.8)
Money income plus food, housing, and medical care (excluding institutional) in kind	14.0 (6.6)	18.4 (8.7)	18.9 (8.9)
Money income plus food, housing, and medical care (including institutional) in kind	13.6 (6.4)	17.3 (8.2)	18.9 (8.9)

Note: Figures in parentheses are percentages of the total U.S. population.
Source: Timothy M. Smeeding, *Alternative Methods for Valuing Selected In-kind Transfer Benefits and Measuring Their Effect on Poverty,* Technical Paper 50, U.S. Department of Commerce, U.S. Bureau of the Census, March 1982, p. 00.

The approach in column 3 is more restrictive. It only counts the value of in kind payments up to the level at which these goods and services are normally consumed by those at or near the poverty level. Timothy Smeeding, the researcher who developed the estimates, explains this approach. "It assumes that in-kind transfers in excess of these amounts are not relevant for determining poverty status because an excess of one type of good (e.g., housing) does not compensate for a deficiency in another good (e.g., medical care)."[8]

Assume we adopt the middle position shown in column 2, value to the recipient. In that case we observe that from 1959 to 1979 the poverty rate has been reduced from 22 percent (shown in Table 6-1) to 8 percent. (Because of the small size of in kind assistance at the beginning of the time period the adjustment for them in 1959 would be quite small.) Thus in 20 years poverty, measured by an absolute standard, has been reduced by two-thirds. In the period up to 1970, the reduction was accomplished primarily by income transfers and real income growth. Since 1970 the reduction has been accomplished primarily by income transfers and a marked rise in transfers in kind.

The Feminization of Poverty

The poverty population of the United States has also undergone a major change in composition. These changes have been referred to as the *feminization of poverty,* a term that simplifies the situation but still captures a great deal of truth.

---

[8] Timothy M. Smeeding, *Alternative Methods for Valuing Selected In-Kind Transfer Benefits and Measuring Their Effect on Poverty,* Technical Paper 50, U.S. Department of Commerce, U.S. Bureau of the Census, March 1982.

Of all children in families below the poverty line, about three-fifths are in female-headed households, a remarkable change from the situation at the end of the 1950s, when the comparable figure was about one in four. The age group that in percentage terms, is most overrepresented in the poverty population is young children. Until recent years the other overrepresented age group was people over 65. That is no longer the case, thanks largely to transfer payments from the Social Security system.

As Table 6-3 indicates, an enormous amount of change occurred in the space of a generation, and all indications are that the trend is continuing. Several factors combined to produce this result. First, the incidence of poverty has traditionally been higher among female-headed than male-headed families. For one thing, males in general earn more per hour than females. Then, too, the male head of household is more likely to be employed full-time than the female head because of differences in child-care responsibilities. Finally, a male-headed household is much more likely to be a multiple-earner household than a female-headed household.

A second point is that the incidence of female-headed households has gone up over the last 2 decades. There has been a modest increase among whites and a very large increase among blacks. Finally, the increase in real incomes, combined with the use of an absolute poverty standard, has meant that the probability of any household with a full-time wage earner falling under the poverty level has decreased. By the late 1970s the Bureau of the Census estimated that only 2 percent of all households with a full-time wage earner fell under the poverty line. Thus a type of household that made up a substantial portion of the poverty population 20 years ago—a household headed by a male employed full-time—has diminished greatly as a proportion of all households in poverty. Putting all of the above together, the increasing concentration of poverty in female-headed households is not hard to understand.

Where the Poor Live

The place of residence of the poor has changed drastically over the last 2 decades. Table 6-4 shows the urbanization of poverty from 1959 to 1978.

Note the large decline in poverty in nonmetropolitan areas and in the suburban ring versus the relatively small decline in central cities. Another way to look at the same data is shown in Table 6-5.

TABLE 6-3
FAMILY COMPOSITION BELOW THE POVERTY
LINE, 1959 AND 1976
(Percent)

	1959	1976
Male head, wife absent	4	3
Female head, husband absent	20	50
Husband-and-wife family	76	47

Source: U.S. Bureau of the Census, *Current Population Reports,* ser. P 60, nos. 115, 1959, and 124, 1978.

TABLE 6-4
THE CHANGING GEOGRAPHIC DISTRIBUTION OF POVERTY, 1959–1978
(In Millions)

	1959			1978		
	Total population	Poverty population	Poverty rate (%)	Total population	Poverty population	Poverty rate (%)
Total U.S.	176.5	38.8	22.0	215.7	24.5	11.4
Metropolitan	111.0	17.0	15.3	145.7	15.1	10.4
Central city	57.2	10.4	18.2	60.5	9.3	15.4
Suburban ring	53.9	6.6	12.2	85.3	5.8	6.8
Nonmetropolitan	65.4	21.7	33.1	69.9	9.4	13.4

Sources: U.S. Bureau of the Census, *Current Population Reports,* ser. P 60, nos. 115, 1959, and 124, 1978.

Poverty and Race

One might ask, "Why discuss the racial aspects of poverty at all?" If it is a misfortune to be poor, then presumably it is equally a misfortune whether one is black or white. Why not be color-blind? Perhaps one day we will be. But at present American society seems to have collectively decided to regard the disparities between the races as a very serious matter and to regard the reduction or elimination of such disparities as a major social goal. Whether one looks at federal funding requirements for social programs, equal opportunity regulations for government contractors, or requirements for the receipt of federal funds by school districts or universities, questions of race are omnipresent. From *Brown v. Board of Education* to *Bakke v. University of Southern California,* much of the most important litigation in the last several decades has been concerned with issues of race.

At present, as has historically been the case, blacks are disproportionately represented among the poor. In 1959, 22 percent of the white population and 55 percent of the black population was below the poverty line. In 1978 the comparable figures were 9 percent and 31 percent. With the urbanizing of the black population, the percentage of all black poor located in central cities has risen sharply, from under 40 percent at the end of the 1950s to about 60 percent at present. There has been some increase in the percentage of the white poor living

TABLE 6-5
GEOGRAPHIC SHARES OF THE POVERTY
POPULATION, 1959–1978, IN PERCENTAGES

	1959	1978
Metropolitan areas	43.9	61.5
Central cities	26.9	37.9
Suburban rings	17.0	23.7
Nonmetropolitan areas	56.1	38.5

Sources: U.S. Bureau of the Census, *Current Population Reports,* ser. P 60, nos. 115, 1959, and 124, 1978.

in central cities during the same period, but at present about two-thirds of all white poor live outside central cities.

In the last 2 decades urban poverty has increasingly become a matter of black poverty. In 1978, 49 percent of all poor families in central cities were black. Whites made up 48 percent and other races the remainder. The black urban poor population is a younger population than the white urban poor, both because the black population of the United States is somewhat younger than the white population and because heavy white out-migration from urban areas selectively drains off children and younger adults. A substantial percentage of the white urban poor are over 65, a situation not the case with the black population. Studies of the concentration of population in poverty areas within central cities (census tracts in which 20 percent or more of the population is under the poverty line) indicate that the black poverty population is substantially more concentrated than the white poverty population. The migration trends discussed in Chapter 2 and the differences in age structure suggest that the black share of urban poverty will continue to grow for a considerable time to come.

The income of blacks has lagged behind that of whites for as long as statistics are available and reasons are not hard to find. The majority of American blacks are descended from slaves freed at the end of the Civil War.[9] A population that in many ways was ill-prepared to make its way economically soon had to contend with the additional burden of restrictive legislation and custom generally referred to as Jim Crow—a structure which probably reached its most complete and repressive form at about the end of the nineteenth century.[10]

Until the end of World War II most U.S. blacks were southern and rural or small-town. They lived in the least prosperous part of the country under conditions that guaranteed that they would be less prosperous than the surrounding white population. The massive black migration to the cities began in the 1940s and persisted through the 1960s. Thus the majority of urban blacks are perhaps no more than 3 decades from their rural or small-town roots. The dismantling of the legal apparatus of segregation in the south is not too far behind us. By and large, the south made the transition from the age of Jim Crow to the age of affirmative action no more than 2 decades ago. In the north the formal structure of Jim Crow never existed, but discrimination in hiring, college admissions, etc. was prevalent. And while discrimination today is much reduced, it is far from eliminated in many areas of life.

Why Hasn't the Income Gap Closed? The income gap is thus not hard to understand. However, one aspect of the gap has caused puzzlement and distress. In spite of the enormous progress made in civil rights, equal opportunity, and affirmative action in the last 2 decades, the median family income of blacks bears about the same relationship to that of whites that it did 20 years ago. In 1959 black median family income was 53 percent that of whites. By 1969 it was 61 percent,

---

[9] Among American blacks not descended from slaves freed at the end of the Civil War—primarily blacks descended from slaves freed in the decades before the Civil War and immigrants from the Caribbean—the incidence of poverty is much lower. For a discussion of this point see Thomas Sowell, *Ethnic America*, Basic Books, New York, 1981.

[10] Sowell, Ibid.

TABLE 6-6

MEDIAN FAMILY INCOME BY RACE AND FAMILY STRUCTURE, 1979

	All families	Married couples	Male with female absent	Female with male absent
White	$20,618	$21,858	$18,608	$11,847
Black	$11,853	$16,939	$13,850	$ 7,100
Black income as a percent of white income	57	77	74	60

Source: U.S. Bureau of the Census, Current Population Reports, ser. P 60, no. 126, 1979.

and by 1979 had dropped back to 57 percent. Given that the ratio is subject to the workings of the business cycle—generally rising in good times and falling in bad times—there is little evidence of closure.

The explanation that seems to be gaining acceptance at present is that many of the potential gains stemming from the civil rights revolution have been negated by a massive increase in female-headed families among the black population.[11] Table 6-6 shows median income by type of family for whites and blacks in 1979.

Table 6-7 shows family composition for whites and blacks in 1979. Note the much larger proportion of female-headed families among blacks. If the income figures from Table 6-6 are combined with the family composition figures of Table 6-7, it is apparent that almost half of the black-white income gap would disappear if the family compositions were similar. Among those younger blacks with intact family structures, most of the income gap has vanished. For example, among husband-and-wife families in which both work and in which the husband is between 25 and 34, median income for whites in 1979 was $21,445 and for blacks $19,166, a gap of 11 percent. For blacks who were in a position to take advantage of the gains of the last 20 years much of the gap has been closed. But partly

TABLE 6-7

FAMILY STRUCTURE AND RACE, IN PERCENTAGES, 1979

	All families	Married couples	Male with female absent	Female with male absent
White	100	82	3	15
Black	100	56	4	40

Source: U.S. Bureau of the Census, Current Population Reports, ser. P 60, no. 126. 1979.

[11] The relationship between black poverty and family structure first received public notice with the publication of Daniel Patrick Moynihan's The Negro Family: The Case for National Action, U.S. Government Printing Office, 1965, more commonly referred to as "The Moynihan Report," in 1965. Some critics of the report argued that extended families were more common among blacks than whites and that, therefore, by focusing on census-defined family data Moynihan understated the strength of the black family. Others reacted quite negatively to the report in part because they believed that by laying much of the blame for the situation at the door of the black family Moynihan furnished arguments for those who would deny the need for national action. For a discussion of the reaction to the report and the changing reaction to it over time see Ken Auletta, op. cit.

because of a weakening in family structure much of the black population is not able to take advantage of newly achieved economic opportunities.

The causes of the rapid increase in female-headed households among blacks are not fully understood. Perhaps some are related to the rapid urbanization of the black population in the 1950s to 1970s and the stresses to which it subjected individuals and families. The experience of the nineteenth-century white immigrant groups strongly suggests this is as at least part of the explanation.[12]

Whether the income gap will close in decades to come remains to be seen. Sowell notes that white ethnic groups that immigrated to the United States in the nineteenth century typically took several generations to catch up to the native population in terms of income. On the more pessimistic side we note that in the period when the Irish, Italians, Poles, Jews, and other white ethnics arrived in greatest numbers cities were growing and the demand for labor, particularly work that did not require a great deal of specialized education or prior experience, was greater. There were fewer protections against individual misfortune (unemployment insurance, public assistance, antidiscrimination legislation, medicare, food stamps, etc.), but there was also more opportunity.

WHAT HAS BEEN DONE

The United States has a long history of attempts to eradicate or reduce poverty. At least five major strands can be identified.

1 Direct transfers of income.
2 The provision of goods and services either at no cost or at reduced cost. This category is generally referred to as "services-in-kind."
3 Job creation.
4 Measures to improve the labor market performance of the poor.
5 The expenditure of public funds in economically lagging areas.

Most Americans would probably prefer an approach to poverty that achieved its goals through the last three items. One has only to listen to an election-year debate to realize how uncomfortable many politicians and citizens feel with direct transfers. But the fact of the matter is, a substantial part of the population cannot be helped by the last three items and can be helped only by transfers or in kind assistance. This group clearly includes those who are incapable of functioning in the labor market because of age or psychological or physical disability.

Beyond that, poverty among the population of those who can function in the labor market can only be eliminated if enough jobs are available. Quite evidently, this is not the case. In fact, very large increases in employment may still leave substantial pools of unemployment. From 1970 to 1980 the nation created almost 19 million jobs. Employment rose by 23.8 percent, while the U.S. population increased by only 11.4 percent. Paradoxically, the unemployment rate rose from 4.9 in 1970 to 7.1 in 1980.[13] What happened? First, as a result of the baby boom of the 1950s the working-age population increased faster than the total population.

[12] Sowell, op cit.
[13] See U.S. Bureau of Labor Statistics, *Employment and Earnings*, various years.

Second, female labor force participation rates increased enormously. If 1970 female participation rates had prevailed in 1980 the US labor force would have been 6 million smaller than it actually was.[14] The biggest increase in labor force participation was among white women from middle- and upper-income households. The number of two-income households went up sharply, but there was no decrease in the number of no-income households.

The 1970s were atypical in the number of baby-boom children reaching working age and, perhaps, also in the very large increases in female labor force participation rates. Yet they do indicate that labor force elasticity may at least partly defeat the unemployment-reducing effects of increases in total employment.

Direct Income Transfers and In-Kind Payments

"Transfer" refers simply to a payment made as a matter of entitlement rather than in return for a service performed. Social Security or public assistance falls in this category. If the transfer is given only when need can be demonstrated, then the transfer is said to be "means-tested." Social Security retirement payments are not means-tested, but public assistance is. "Payments in-kind" refers to payments that take the form of goods or services, like subsidized housing or free medical care. Payments in-kind may or may not be means-tested. For example, Medicare, which provides free or reduced-cost medical care to all persons over 65, is not means-tested. Medicaid, which provides free or reduced-cost medical care to those under 65 if they fall below certain income levels, is means-tested.

Direct income transfers go back many years. Even before the Great Depression a number of states had programs for assisting the blind, needy mothers and children, and the aged. By 1920 the great majority of states had enacted some form of worker's compensation. In 1935 the Social Security Act established the groundwork for most of the main elements in the present income maintenance structure of the United States. These included unemployment insurance, old age insurance, and matching programs to aid the states in providing assistance to mothers with dependent children and to the blind and disabled. Unemployment insurance (UI), Aid for Families with Dependent Children (AFDC), Supplemental Security Income (SSI), and Old Age Survivors, Disability, and Health Insurance (OASDHI) all had their origins in this act. In 1980 federal government expenditures on income transfers in kind amounted to 10.3 percent of the GNP and 46.8 percent of federal expenditures. If we include comparable expenditures by state and local governments, the share of GNP would increase to about 13 percent.

In 1970 comparable direct transfers and in-kind payments were approximately 6.1 percent of GNP and 30.6 percent of federal outlays. Inclusion of state and local expenditures would raise the total share of GNP for 1970 to about 8 percent. Table 6-8 shows selected federal programs. Note the very large percentage increases in in-kind assistance, specifically Medicaid, food stamps, and subsidized housing.

Although the making of transfers and the provisions of services in-kind (medical care, food stamps, below-cost housing, etc.) are clearly separate in the accounts of the federal government, the line between them is much more blurred

---

[14] Calculation by author made by applying 1970 and 1980 labor force participation rates to 1980 population statistics.

TABLE 6-8
FEDERAL EXPENDITURES FOR INCOME SECURITY, 1970–1980
(In Billions)

	1970	1980
Total cash	$48.6	$200.3
Social Security	29.0	118.6
Federal employee retirement	5.8	27.8
Public assistance	3.9	13.7
Veterans' benefits	5.3	11.8
Unemployment insurance	2.9	17.9
Other*	1.7	10.5
Total in-kind	$11.6	$70.9
Food and nutrition	1.6	14.0
Food stamps	0.6	9.1
Health care	9.6	50.0
Medicaid	2.6	14.0
Other†		
Housing‡	0.5	5.4
Total	$60.2	$271.2
Total federal outlays	$196.6	$579.6
GNP	$992.7	$2,626.1
Total income security as % of:		
Federal outlays	30.6	46.8
GNP	6.1	10.3

*Railroad retirement and miscellaneous programs.
†Primarily expenditures for Medicare, a non–means-tested program largely for persons 65 and over.
‡Includes both public housing and rent and mortgage income supplements.

Sources: Compiled from Tables 416, 522, 699, *Statistical Abstract of the United States,* 1981.

in reality. For example, if you use food stamps to obtain food you would otherwise have bought with cash and then use the cash to make other purchases, how much difference is there between receiving cash and receiving food stamps? The relative merits of direct transfers versus payments in-kind, is discussed at some length in the appendix of this chapter.

Job Creation and Labor Force Development

We discuss both job creation and labor force development together because even though they are conceptually separate they are very commonly combined in practice. Job creation has been with us, with interruptions, for almost 6 decades. Serious attention to training is of somewhat more recent origin.

Job creation programs date from the early years of the Great Depression. By the end of 1933 over 4 million Americans were employed in federally funded jobs, a huge figure for a population about half its present size.[15]

[15] William E. Leuchtenburg, *Franklin Delano Roosevelt and the New Deal,* Harper & Row, New York, 1963.

The problem to be dealt with was clearly that of cyclical unemployment and the person to be helped was, by and large, the male head of household with some prior work experience. The present concept of targeting assistance at particular segments of the population was absent. Terms like *Structural unemployment, pockets of poverty,* the *economically disadvantaged,* and *underemployment* did not exist. Job creation as a major role of the federal government lasted through the 1930s and then became superfluous with the coming World War II.

After World War II the country entered into a prosperous period characterized by low unemployment and rapid growth in GNP. The general feeling was that the main economic task of government was to maintain aggregate demand at a level sufficiently high to guarantee full employment. The labor force was visualized as being like a queue arranged from the most to the least productive.[16] The greater the demand for labor, the further down the queue hiring would go. The way to help those at the end of the queue was to stimulate aggregate demand and hence the derived demand for labor. This view was expressed in President Kennedy's inaugural address in 1961 by the phrase "A rising tide lifts all the boats."

The Recognition of Structural Unemployment   But in spite of the general postwar prosperity, it gradually became apparent that the entire society did not seem to partake of the general prosperity.[17] Structural unemployment, or "pockets of poverty," could exist in the face of sustained high employment and general prosperity. In the late 1950s, pressures for programs targeted both at individuals and at places mounted. Place-oriented programs were discussed in Chapter 5. On the labor side, the pressure culminated in the passage of the Manpower Development and Training Act (MDTA) in 1962. Underlying the act was the premise that there existed a mismatch between the needs of employers and the skills of workers. The original thrust of the act was to provide living expenses for heads of households while they went through job-training programs to acquire new skills. The program appealed both to liberals, who had been pushing for training programs, and to conservatives, who saw the bill as a way to reduce relief and unemployment rolls, increase productivity, and perhaps even shift the Phillips curve in a favorable direction.[18] Subsequently the MDTA was gradually restructured into a broad-based labor bill with youth programs, residential-training programs, on-the-job training, and vocational education.

The MDTA, as amended, remained the mainstay of federal labor policy until the passage of the Comprehensive Employment and Training Act (CETA) at the end of 1973. CETA lasted until 1983. Very briefly, it provided federal money to be

---

[16] See Garth L. Mangum, *Employability, Employment and Income,* Olympus, Salt Lake City, Utah, 1976.

[17] Michael Harrington, *The Other America: Poverty in the United States,* Macmillan, New York, 1962.

[18] The curve represents a postulated inverse relationship between the unemployment rate and the inflation rate. Thus macroeconomic stimulus designed to reduce the former will increase the latter. If the curve were shifted by attacking structural unemployment, a given unemployment figure would be obtainable at a lower inflation rate. Belief in the existence of the curve has been somewhat weakened in the last few years by the simultaneous existence of high unemployment figures and high inflation rates. For a discussion of the curve see a standard introductory economics text such as those by Samuelson or McConnell.

spent by locally designated agencies on job training (both classroom and on-the-job) and job creation within the local public sector. The various CETA programs were means-tested, but it was widely believed that wholesale evasions of the intent of the means testing occurred within the public sector.

> *CETA funds have not been clearly aimed at those who need help the most.* The previous Administrations used CETA as a form of backdoor revenue sharing. In some cases, CETA funds were used to shift city workers from local to federal payrolls. Architects and city planners were kept on the payroll through CETA funds ostensibly designed to help the disadvantaged. Local governments could supplement CETA dollars without any limit, and, as a result, some CETA workers were middle-class professionals.[19]

In 1978 the act was substantially revised and the resulting "new" CETA contained much stronger provisions for targeting jobs to the most needy. How well the new CETA succeeded in this regard now seems a moot point.

The "War on Poverty"   Though MDTA and its successor, CETA, were both designed to improve the labor market performance of the poor through training, the most comprehensive attempt made to improve the competitive ability of the poor was the "war on poverty," as initiated by the Economic Opportunity Act (EOA) of 1964.[20] The philosophical underpinning of the effort was the view that simply transferring income did nothing to end the fact of dependency—and, in fact, might exacerbate it. What was needed, then, were programs designed to free the poor from dependency.

It was thought that the poor lacked vocational skills, so vocational training programs were started. For young men and women from poor households, the Job Corps was begun. In the words of the Office of Economic Opportunity, "No miracles are worked for these young people, rather, they are given the raw materials to make their own miracles: education, good work habits and a well ordered life." It was noted that the children of the poor generally did less well in school, an obvious handicap in a society in which there were shortages of systems analysts and surpluses of people with strong backs. So the Head Start program for preschool children was begun to give the children of the poor the mental stimulation they supposedly weren't getting at home. It was thought that often the poor do not get their fair share in American society because they cannot afford good legal representation. So programs providing free and low-cost legal services to the poor were begun. It was thought that mothers in fatherless homes couldn't participate in the labor market because good child-care facilities were beyond their financial reach. So day-care programs were begun. It was thought that children from poor homes sometimes did poorly in school because of poor nutrition. So school nutrition programs were begun. It was believed that poor neighborhoods often lacked the political and social cohesion that more prosperous neighborhoods possessed. So the federal government funded thousands of community action programs (CAPs) to bring this cohesion into being.

---

[19] Former Secretary of Labor Ray Marshall, U.S. Department of Labor press release, Feb. 1, 1979.
[20] A description of the "war on poverty" and evaluation of a number of programs can be found in Robert H. Haveman, *A Decade of Federal Anti-Poverty Programs: Achievements, Failures and Lessons*, Academic, New York, 1977.

The war on poverty, initiated by the EOA of 1964 and run by the Office of Economic Opportunity (OEO), lasted until 1974 with expenditures for it peaking during the early years of the Nixon presidency. In 1974 the OEO was disbanded, and remaining programs transferred to the Community Services Administration (CSA).

In general, those who have done retrospective studies on the "war on poverty" do not judge it to have been particularly successful.[21] Its defenders assert that it was never adequately funded, and its critics often assert that the problems it attacked were simply far more complex and less amenable to direct action than its creators envisioned. Like all major social programs, it appears to have produced some paradoxical results. For example, the number of families receiving AFDC roughly doubled from 1964 to 1970 in spite of the fact that national economy grew at a rapid rate during the period. Part of the explanation that has been offered is that the legal services and community organization had the effect of mobilizing the poor to claim what was legally theirs, and thus the rate of welfare participation among the eligible poor climbed sharply. It is dubious that securing such an increase was the intent of the legislators who voted for the EOA of 1964.

Current Labor Force Development Initiatives Disappointed with CETA, particularly its weak performance in placing program participants in private, unsubsidized employment, the Reagan administration ended the program. It has been replaced by the Jobs Training Partnership Act (JTPA). JTPA, which began in fiscal 1984, lacks CETA's public-sector employment aspect entirely and will emphasize training rather than job creation. A very major participation by industry in the program is envisioned. At this writing JTPA is just beginning and thus its superiority or inferiority to CETA cannot be judged.

Some Miscellaneous Programs

There have been a number of experimental programs targeted to small parts of a municipality or to subgroups of the population. In general, the amount of money devoted to such programs has been small compared with the sums devoted to the programs mentioned above and miniscule compared to the sums devoted to income transfer programs. However, a few such programs merit brief attention here.

The "black capitalism" movement was an attempt to encourage black entrepreneurship, since entrepreneurial activity is relatively less common among blacks than whites. The Small Business Administration has directed capital to black-owned firms through the Office of Minority Business Enterprise, with a view to alleviating the situation. There has also been limited philanthropic activity along these lines. To date, neither the sums of money involved nor the results have been massive. We might also note that just as place-related programs involve a very conspicuous demonstration of Okun's leaky bucket, so too may black capitalism programs. The immediate beneficiary of the program is the black entrepreneur who is far enough up the economic ladder to make use of the

[21] Haveman, Ibid.

program. Benefits to the poorest strata of black society will be trickle-down effects.

Community development corporations (CDCs), the best-known of which is Bedford-Stuyvesant Restoration in Brooklyn, New York, have been set up in a number of cities. Funding has come from the federal Community Services Administration, from philanthropic organizations such as the Ford Foundation, and from local sources within the area to be served. Such organizations encourage job development by advancing capital, often provide a variety of services such as job training and day care, and often engage in housing rehabilitation. In the case of Bedford-Stuyvesant Restoration, a good deal has been accomplished, particularly in housing. But such organizations are not often very effective in preventing job losses because their resources are small compared to the forces behind the decentralization of employment. As a former official of the agency said to the writer, "Why do you think we should be able to do what no one else can do?" The point is unarguable.

A proposal that has received some support from the Reagan administration is the enterprise zone.[22] These would be areas within a limited number of cities. The zone might be made up of one or more census tracts with particularly high poverty statistics. Within the zone there would be federal tax abatements for firms that located there. There would also be local tax abatements, presumably sales and property, and there might be other financial inducements as well. In addition there might be relaxation of some local land-use controls to permit densities, degrees of site coverage, or mixes of uses not normally allowed. The scheme would be different from most place-related programs discussed in the preceding chapter in that reliance would be placed solely on tax expenditures rather than grants. Thus the supervisory role of government would be far smaller. Then, too, the program would be very tightly targeted. However, in that it involves expenditure of federal and other governmental funds in order to convert non–least-cost locations into least-cost locations, it is perhaps not as different from other approaches as might at first appear to be the case.

Whether it will prove more effective than other place-oriented techniques remains to be seen. In the writer's view its effects are just as likely to be diluted by labor force mobility as are the effects of any other place-related program. In fact, given the small size of the zones it would be very surprising if this did not happen. The plan, presumably, will also be subject to doubts regarding displacement effects. If an enterprise zone in the South Bronx attracts a business that would otherwise have located three subway stops away in the North Bronx, exactly what useful purpose has been accomplished?

POLICY ISSUES AND DIRECTIONS

Clearly the question of urban poverty, like poverty itself, has not been solved. Our inability to solve the problem does not stem from lack of trying. Rather, it stems from the fact that the problem is an immensely difficult one. For example,

---

[22] The legislative proposal for enterprise zones that has probably received most notice is the Kemp-Garcia bill.

we observe that increases in available jobs may be absorbed primarily by increased labor force participation rates among the nonpoor rather than by the hiring of the least-employable members of the labor force. We also note that one good may be the enemy of another good. We may take satisfaction in the opening up of many parts of the labor market to women during the 1970s while simultaneously admitting that the entrance into the labor market of millions of white women has probably pushed up unemployment rates for black males and widened the white-black income gap.

As noted, income transfers form the lion's share of the total antipoverty effort in the United States. For this reason we turn first to the income transfer system.

Dissatisfaction with the Transfer System

One could argue that the country can be proud of the effort made against poverty. Altogether, in 1980 the federal government spent about twice as much on income support and services in kind than it did on national defense. Though much income support was not means-tested, federal and state contributions to means-tested programs were well over $60 billion, or roughly half the defense budget. So we can hardly be accused of stinginess as a society. Yet there is and apparently always has been dissatisfaction with our efforts to combat poverty. The phrase "welfare mess" is heard often enough in public discourse that one almost begins to think of it as a single word. Neither CETA nor the food stamp program has met with widespread public approval. In fact, the only major income transfer program that seems to enjoy widespread approval is Social Security, which is not means-tested and which has many of the aspects of a compulsory insurance system.

To generalize, it seems that we are upset by three fundamental aspects of our attempts to deal with poverty.

1 *Equitableness.* It seems only fair that people in similar circumstances be treated similarly. This is clearly not now the case. At present, there is approximately a 4 to 1 ratio in the levels of public assistance benefits from the least to most generous states.[23] Some types of payments in kind, for example, housing assistance, are available only for a fraction of those who are potentially eligible. Thus one family might receive substantial assistance, while another family with the same income receives none.

2 *The side-effects of income redistribution.* It is widely believed that giving aid reduces work effort and induces dependency. We are concerned that we are creating a "culture of poverty," in which people settle for a life of low income and less effort—a life which is ultimately unsatisfying to them and a weight upon society as a whole.

Many conservatives have little doubt that this is precisely what has happened. For example, George Gilder, probably the most prominent exponent of supply-side economics, takes exactly this position.[24] He argues that by offering the

[23] In 1980 average monthly AFDC payments in the United States were $280, with a high of $399 in California and a low of $88 in Mississippi. See Social Security Administration, *Annual Statistical Supplement to the Social Security Bulletin,* 1981.
[24] George Gilder, *Poverty and Wealth,* Basic Books, New York, 1981. The same point is one of the main themes in a less well known book of Gilder's, *Visible Man,* Basic Books, New York, 1978.

mothers of young children an income that is comparable to what a relatively unskilled male can earn from full-time labor, one has rendered the male economically superfluous. The result is a shattering of family structure and a dimunition of male work effort. The empirical evidence on the relationship of transfer payments, work effort, and family structure is not yet conclusive, and Gilder's views are hardly universal.

3 *Efficiency.* If for every $1 appropriated to fight poverty, 5 cents went into administrative costs and the remainder all went to deserving individuals without in any way diminishing their efforts to fend for themselves, most of us would concede the system to be efficient. But such is not the case.

For two reasons it is not possible to target aid purely to the poor. As a practical matter, the poor don't constitute a powerful political constituency. Therefore, any program will have a better chance of passage if it scatters its largesse a bit more widely. On a theoretical level, targeting money purely to the poor and cutting off all aid as soon as the target population hits the poverty line produces major disincentives among the near-poor, as will be discussed subsequently. But this means that precise targeting of aid to the poor is not practical. There have been attempts made to condition aid upon effort to find work, but in general the results have not been good. One may compel someone to go to a job interview, but one cannot compel him or her to look eager. Then, too, we face the fact of less than full employment. Worker willingness does not automatically bring jobs into being.

"Reforming" the Transfer Payment System

"Reform" of the present system would mean achieving greater horizontal equity, providing less disincentive for work effort, increasing family stability, delivering assistance with minimum administrative costs, and targeting aid only to the needy. We might add to this list the avoidance of efficiency losses. This means avoiding the inducement to migration simply to obtain higher benefits and avoiding expenditures on goods and services that society would not purchase if it were not for particular characteristics or requirements of the income redistribution system.

The above is a tall order and there is no consensus as to how it might be achieved. The proposal that attracted most discussion among economists was the guaranteed annual income, or negative income tax (NIT). The terms are used interchangeably, since the key element in a negative income tax is a guarantee of the minimum annual income. Proposed in the early 1960s by Milton Friedman, a conservative Nobel Prize-winning economist, the idea rapidly gained currency, culminating in the Nixon administration's Family Assistance Plan (FAP). This passed the House of Representatives twice but was unable to clear the Senate. The idea of guaranteed annual income, or NIT, has also been the subject of a series of social experiments spanning the years 1968 to 1976 and costing about $70 million. These make it probably the second most costly social experiment ever performed in the United States. The move to a negative income tax, or guaranteed annual income, would have made a major change in the fundamental philosophy of income distribution in the United States as well as the institutions involved in achieving redistribution.

Under a negative income tax scheme each household would file a tax return even if it had no income. Below a crossover point the household receives a payment (negative tax) from the IRS. Above the crossover point the household pays tax. The structure of the system is such that the marginal disincentive to work is not overwhelming, and thus, in theory, the reduction in work effort is small. (Again, we note the extreme difficulty or perhaps the impossibility of designing a transfer system with no disincentive at all.)

Friedman characterized the advantages of the plan as follows:

> The advantages of this arrangement are clear. It is directed specifically at the problem of poverty. It gives help in the form most useful to the individual, namely, cash. It is general and could be substituted for the host of special measures now in effect. It makes explicit the cost borne by society. It operates outside the market. Like any other measures to alleviate poverty, it reduces the incentives of those helped to help themselves, but it does not eliminate that incentive entirely, as a system of supplementing incomes up to some fixed minimum would. An extra dollar earned always means more money available for expenditure.
>
> No doubt there would be problems of administration, but these seem to me a minor disadvantage, if they be a disadvantage at all. The system would fit directly into our current income tax system and could be administered along with it. The present tax system covers the bulk of income recipients and the necessity of covering all would have the by-product of improving the operation of the present income tax. More important, if enacted as a substitute for the present rag bag of measures directed at the same end, the *total administrative* burden would surely be reduced.[25]

When he uses the phrase "outside the market" Friedman means that the scheme does not distort patterns of production, consumption, or location. Thus, we do not add the cost of efficiency losses to the cost of the NIT itself. (The concept of efficiency losses associated with in-kind aid is discussed in some detail in the appendix to this chapter.)

Figure 6-1 shows a hypothetical negative income tax system. As is the case with means-tested programs, the benefits are adjusted for household size. In this hypothetical system the guaranteed income for a family of four is set at roughly half the 1981 poverty line ($9287), or $4500. The reason it is not set at the poverty line itself will become apparent shortly.

Line OC in Figure 6-1 represents the relationship of income and earnings in the absence of the NIT. The 45-degree slope of the line indicates that income received equals income earned. Line MB represents a system with 50 percent work incentive and a guarantee of $4500 in the absence of any remunerative work. For each $1 the family earns, payments under the NIT are reduced by 50 cents. Thus payments do not disappear until earned income equals $9000. The loss of 50 cents in NIT on each dollar of income earned is far from a trivial disincentive. Suppose we wished to keep the same minimum guarantee of $4500 but advance the work incentive from 50 percent to 66.7 percent. This structure would be represented by line MC. Note that in this case transfers under NIT continue out to an earned income of $13,500. Suppose we want a system with a 100 percent work incentive. That is represented by line MD. It runs parallel to line OC and means that all

---

[25] Milton Friedman, *Capitalism and Freedom*, University of Chicago Press, Chicago 1962. p. 192.

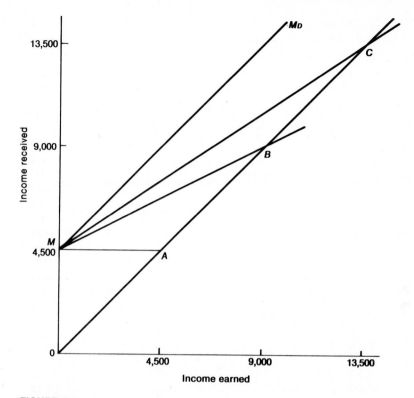

FIGURE 6-1
The negative income tax. The income guarantee, set at $4500—or roughly
half of the 1981 poverty level for a family of four—is shown by point *M.* The 50
percent tax rate is shown by line *MB.* The size of the payment to the family
varies with income and is represented by the vertical distance between lines
OB and *MB.* Note that payments cease at an earned income of $9000. A 33
percent tax system (67 percent work incentive) is shown by line *MC.* Payments are represented by the vertical distance between *OC* and *MC* and continue out to an earned income of $13,500. Line *MD* represents a flat "demo-
grant" comparable to the McGovern proposal in 1972. These payments
continue regardless of the amount of earned income but are recovered from
families above some income level by the higher tax rates necessary to finance
the demogrants.

families, no matter how wealthy, receive the $4500. Finally, let us consider the
other extreme, a system that provides the $4500 minimum but no other work
incentive. That is represented by line MA. Under that system each $1 earned
results in the loss of $1 of NIT.

Consider some of the alternatives. The 100 percent work-incentive scheme is
incredibly expensive. There are now about 80 million households in the United
States, so the scheme would cost well over $300 billion, a sum greater than the
IRS now collects in personal income taxes. For families at a crossover point the
system would break even, in that their gains from the NIT, or "demogrant,"
would be cancelled by the higher taxes necessary to finance the system. Beyond

that point, the additional tax burden would outweigh the demogrant, producing net loss. Thus even though the system in the first instance aids all individuals without regard to income, it is, in totality, progressive.

The system with the 66.7 percent work incentive would not be quite as expensive, but it would still mean distributing at least some income to perhaps 35 or 40 percent of all families, hardly a politically or fiscally feasible solution. At the 50 percent work incentive we are now confining transfers to those at or below the poverty line, and the drain on the public purse is not as enormous. However, the work disincentive is now substantial. For the worker at the minimum wage of $3.35 per hour the marginal return on labor is $1.68 before any subtractions for the expense of working or payment of other deductions such as FICA. The most narrowly targeted and presumably least-expensive program, represented by line MA, provides overwhelming disincentives to work for low-income workers. For a worker who might be able to work full-time 50 weeks a year at the minimum wage, the marginal return on work is less than $1 per hour (50 × 40 × $3.35 − $4500)/ 2000. For the worker who puts in, say, 20 hours a week at the minimum wage there is a 100 percent disincentive to work. This is so because as long as his or her annual earnings are under $4500, every $1 earned would cause a loss of $1 of NIT. If working entailed some costs, as it usually does, the disincentive would exceed 100 percent.

The example above should indicate how difficult it is, even in principle, to design an acceptable program, that is, one that is not ruinously expensive and does not destroy work incentive.

The model in the figure is actually not very different from the Nixon Family Assistance Plan (FAP), which passed the House of Representatives in 1969 but died in the Senate. That plan called for a guarantee of $1600 for a family of four, a 50 percent work incentive (corresponding to line MC) and a statutory provision that defined $720 of income per year ($60 per month) as working expenses not to be counted as income. In addition, families eligible for aid under FAP would also be eligible for food stamps, medical treatment, and public housing. In that sense, the program was not as thoroughgoing a change as suggested by Friedman when he introduced the concept in the early 1960s.

With the failure of the FAP to pass Congress, the effort to pass a major "reform" of the public assistance–income transfer system of the United States weakened. In the 1972 presidential campaign George McGovern broached the idea of a demogrant of $1000 per person, a variant of the NIT that corresponds in principle to line MD on Figure 6-1. McGovern was unable to explain his plan convincingly or demonstrate where the revenues to pay for it were to be found. McGovern's overwhelming defeat—possibly one made a bit more overwhelming by the above proposal—further reduced the chances of moving to a guaranteed annual income.

What has happened since then? The most important changes in the system have been quantitative rather than qualitative. As shown in Table 6-8 the in-kind components of the system have grown enormously, making the system far more generous than it was a decade ago. Medicare (for all Social Security recipients over 65) and Medicaid (a means-tested program for those under 65) totaled close to $60 billion by the end of the decade. The food stamp program grew from about $.5 billion in 1970 to about $9 billion in 1980. Though classified as an in-kind

BOX 6-1

A NEGATIVE INCOME TAX EXPERIMENT

The concept of a guaranteed annual income or negative income tax has been the subject of a number of experiments funded by the Department of Health, Education, and Welfare (HEW). The largest experiments in the series were the Seattle Income Maintenance Experiment (SIME) and the Denver Income Maintenance Experiment (DIME), which ran from 1970 to 1976, cost about $70 million, and involved 4800 families.

On a panel of recipient families and controls the study tested basic combinations of guarantee and tax rate.[26] Highlights of the findings, some expected and some not, are noted below.

First, it was found that income supplementation did reduce work effort. The reduction was greater for both high levels of guarantee than for low levels of guarantee and for the 70 percent tax rate than the 50 percent tax rate. Thus for families with a guarantee equal to 50 percent of the poverty level and a 50 percent tax rate, the reduction in work effort was 196 hours per year. For families with a 100 percent guarantee and a 70 percent tax rate, the reduction in work effort was 308 hours per year.

The provision of guaranteed income increased the rate of interarea migration and caused those families migrating to give more weight to climate and less weight to income than the control families. In general, those aided also made longer moves and spent more on moving than did the controls.

These results are not surprising. They show low-income families behaving toward increases in income in a rational manner. They used their income to "purchase" more leisure and more desirable living environments.

The surprising—and distressing—finding was that for most experimental groups the provision of guaranteed income increased the rate of separation and divorce. It had long been believed that the AFDC program, by largely restricting benefits to female-headed households (the so-called man-in-the-house rule), provided a strong incentive for family breakup. By eliminating this incentive, NIT was expected to strengthen family structure. The project staff explains the result in the following way. They postulate on the one hand that there is an income effect that enhances family stability. This is based upon the observation that cross-sectional data of the population as a whole shows a positive relationship between income and family stability. On the other hand, they postulate a destabilizing "independence" effect. When income is available from a source other than the husband, it is easier for the wife to separate. The actual result is the sum of these two opposing forces.

Altogether, the results of the experiment have produced some disillusion with the guaranteed annual income–NIT concept. If the guaranteed annual income increases dependency and breaks up families, why is it better than the system we have now? Daniel Patrick Moynihan, Democratic senator from New York, who was one of the driving forces behind the FAP when he was an advisor to President Nixon in the late 1960s, appears to have acquired many doubts.

Even Moynihan has subsequently backed off his proposal. "Our proposition was that a condition that was normal and universal would not have the effect of creating dependency," he said in an interview. "Experiments have cast doubt on this." . . . "Current research, as I understand it, says it creates more problems than it solves."[27]

program and not included in census estimates of income poverty, food stamps approach a pure cash transfer for the reasons discussed in the appendix.

The present system is thus a mixed one with several major elements. Social Security provides massive transfers, most of which are not means-tested but

---

[26] For a detailed account of the experiment and its findings see Philip K. Robbins, et al. (eds.), *A Guaranteed Annual Income: Evidence from a Social Experiment*, Academic Press, New York, 1980.
[27] Moynihan quoted in Auletta, op. cit.

which still produce a major reduction in income poverty. The food stamp program constitutes the closest thing we have to a national NIT. Public assistance, primarily AFDC, is a means-tested program with both federal and state contribution. Its generosity varies widely from state to state, making it hard to deny the charge of horizontal inequity. Various means-tested programs, including Medicaid, public housing, and rental allowances, make substantial transfers to the poor and the near-poor. But, as noted, for the last two the degree of horizontal inequity is very high.

How much of a work disincentive the entire system contains is not known with certainty. It has been pointed out that in principle marginal disincentives to work of over 100 percent can be shown for the family that benefits from several programs. Yet empirical studies show that administrative discretion and recipient ingenuity reduce the actual disincentive to perhaps 50 or 60 percent, a range not far different from the work incentive rate in the FAP.

Present Income Transfer Proposals   At this writing the NIT is very much on the political back burner. Current proposals by the Reagan administration would, in fact, move us in somewhat the other direction. The Reagan agenda appears to be the following. The federal government will pick up the full cost of Medicaid and food stamps. AFDC—what most people mean when they say "welfare"—would become a state function. The latter proposal represents a long-term Reagan view that the power and presence of the federal government is excessive and that many powers and responsibilities should be turned back to the states and localities. Perhaps it also represents a conservative view that the amount of income transfer is excessive and that turning the program back to the states will, over time, reduce benefit levels.

Employment Training and Job Creation Programs

There is no question that employment training programs have helped many thousands of individuals and families and have pulled many people out of poverty by making them competitive in the urban labor market. A number of studies of employment training programs have been done to assess the effect of the training program on trainee incomes and then compare that figure to program costs. Often these studies show quite favorable cost-benefit ratios. There are serious methodological problems in estimating what trainee incomes would have been in the absence of the programs, and there are also problems in separating job placement and "credentialing" effects from actual training effects. Nonetheless, if one just looks at trainees many programs appear successful.

Whether employment training programs have much effect in reducing poverty in toto is not so clear. For one thing most such programs do little to retain jobs. The writer is not aware of any study that shows that the presence or absence of federal employment training programs is a significant determinant of industrial location decisions.[28] Beyond that, there is the question of how much of a zero sum

---

[28] See, for example, Reigeluth and Wolman, op. cit. See also John M. Levy, *Economics Development Programs for Cities, Counties and Towns*, Praeger, New York, 1981, for a discussion of factors affecting the choice of commercial location.

game is played with job training. If job training helps a member of the city's poverty population get a job, who didn't get the job because he or she did? In general those who have evaluated the effectiveness of training programs have admitted that they cannot deal with these displacement effects.

> Manpower policies are disaggregative, "particularistic," and selective; they operate primarily on the supply side of the market and function in the local labor market context. In contrast, fiscal and monetary policies operate on aggregate demand, are broad-gauge and diffused in their impact, and operate in the context of the national economy. While manpower, fiscal, and monetary policies are all directed at full employment, economic growth, and price stability goals, the impacts of local manpower policies cannot be measured by the direct indicators of these goals. This is due in part to the relatively small size of manpower programs. More important is the fact that adequate labor market theory for accounting for displacement effects on non-participants is not yet available.[29]

Job creation programs are also subject to a variant of the efficiency argument used against place-related programs. It is easily argued that job creation programs frequently cause the production of goods or services that society would not ordinarily consume or would consume in smaller quantities. There may thus be an efficiency loss comparable to that of locating firms in non–least-cost locations as discussed in the previous chapter. The charge that job creation programs lead to wasteful activities goes back to the Great Depression and the invention of that colorful term of uncertain origin, "boondoggle."

Place-Related Programs   We have also tried pumping public money into poor areas in order to create jobs. For example, HUD's urban development action grant program has been spending money in urban areas at very roughly $.5 billion annually for several years to do exactly this. Undoubtedly it has done some good. But in an economy with a GNP of close to $3 trillion, the amount of funding is small. And, as with most forms of subsidy, one should admit that some of the activity might have happened in any case, even though administrators do their best to avoid windfalls. One must also note that there may be displacement effects here. The downtown hotel built on a site acquired and cleared with UDAG monies may take some customers away from hotels elsewhere in the same city. If they then lay off workers, the employment gains from the new facility are partially canceled. Finally, we must note that the labor market effect of all place-related development strategies are partly undone by the mobility of labor, a point discussed in Chapter 5.

The Enrichment-versus-Dispersal Debate

The problem of attacking central-city poverty has led to a long running argument sometimes referred to as the "enrichment-vs-dispersal debate." The debate is enlightening in that it indicates the difficulty of the urban poverty problem. Its frustrating quality is reminiscent of a line the writer heard when he was a small boy: FIRST HUNTER: "Don't shoot, the gun ain't loaded." SECOND HUNTER: "I gotta shoot, the bear won't wait."

---

[29] Garth Mangum and David Snedeker, *Manpower Planning for Local Labor Markets*, Olympus, Salt Lake City, Utah, 1974. p. 185.

Those on both sides of the issue point to the same set of facts but interpret them in opposite ways. The facts themselves are clear. There has been an erosion of the central-city job base and an accumulation of the poor within the central cities. There is also a jobs-skills mismatch, in that central-city job losses have been most severe in manufacturing and other blue-collar employment. In a number of cities white-collar jobs have increased, but a very large percentage of these jobs have been taken by better-educated and more-experienced suburbanites rather than by the central-city poor. Discrimination by employers against blacks, Hispanics, and other minority group members may further tilt the hiring process against central-city residents. We also know that metropolitan-area transportation systems, particularly the public components, are designed to bring workers from the periphery into the center, not to distribute workers from the center to scattered peripheral locations. Thus these systems give suburbanites reasonably good access to central-city jobs but give central-city residents much poorer access to suburban jobs. Finally, we note that land-use controls in suburban communities are often used to block the development of low-cost housing and thus reduce the opportunity of the central-city poor to move closer to suburban job markets.

There is some empirical support for the view that residential segregation does impose job losses on poor inner-city populations. In the 1960s Kain tested this hypothesis vis-à-vis urban blacks.[30] He assumed a statistical relationship between location of work and location of residence. He then compared the actual number of black workers at various work sites with the number that would be expected if blacks were distributed in a random rather than a segregated pattern. According to his estimates residential segregation imposed over 20,000 job losses on blacks in the Chicago metropolitan area and about one-third that many in the Cleveland area. Kain's data are now quite old, and it is not known what the results of a comparable study would be today. However, we do know that black residence is still concentrated in the central cities and the dispersion of economic activity has continued and possibly accelerated. Thus the dynamic that produced Kain's findings is still in force.

Those who take the enrichment side of the debate conclude that the only way to aid the poor is with a variety of job creation, training, and other programs that will "enrich" the areas in which the poor now live. They argue that this is necessary because it is unrealistic to believe that the requisite amount of dispersal will occur.

Those who favor a dispersal strategy argue that if the jobs and the best school systems are outside of the central cities, the way to aid the poor is to help them get out of the central cities. They assert that it is unrealistic to believe that the necessary amount of enrichment will occur.[31]

With enrichment the question is simply, "Where would the funds come from?" Central cities now contain about 30 percent of the U.S. population. Is it likely that

[30] John F. Kain, "Housing Segregation, Negro Employment and Metropolitan Decentralization," *Quarterly Journal of Economics*, May 1968, p. 176.

[31] For a presentation of the dispersing argument see Anthony Downs, *Urban Problems and Prospects*, Markham, Chicago, 1970, chap. 2. For an argument for enrichment written from a radical perspective see Thomas Vietorisz and Bennett Harrison, *The Economic Development of Harlem*, Praeger, New York, 1970. See also Bennett Harrison, *Urban Economic Development*.

the other 70 percent will consent to being heavily taxed in order to pour funds into central places?

With dispersal the first question is, "How would we induce suburban communities to accept the inner-city population?" Zoning and land-use controls are, by and large, firmly under local control. Thus the receiving communities have enormous capacity to block the construction of housing that the inner-city poor could afford. Beyond that, even if there were no suburban resistance to dispersal, substantial housing subsidies would be needed to render suburban housing affordable to the city poor. Where would they come from? Looking further at the matter we wonder what position most big-city mayors would take on this issue. If housing subsidies are in limited supply, as is inevitably the case, how many big-city mayors will favor seeing them diverted to the suburbs. Furthermore, astute mayors may wonder whether the dispersion program will really rid them of their poor and most economically helpless residents or merely strip the ghetto of its most talented, energetic, active members, thereby simply compounding the city's problems. Thus while there is a logical case for dispersion, it is hard to show the political constituency to make it happen.

Is the above a counsel of utter hopelessness? Not necessarily. The strategies are not mutually exclusive, and one might argue that however much of either can be done should be done. The reader should not be left with the impression that nothing is being or has been done. Many of the programs discussed, such as UDAG and CD, are, in effect, enrichment programs. On the dispersal side, both the federal government and the courts have moved on a number of fronts to reduce residential segregation. A number of these efforts are discussed in the chapter on housing.

APPENDIX: A Digression on Welfare Economics

To understand some of the discussion of public policy related to poverty, and particularly the academic literature thereon, it is necessary to understand the rudiments of welfare economics.* The same principles developed here in connection with individuals will also be useful in understanding some of the theoretical points made in connection with grants and local governments in Chapter 11. We are about to submerge in what appears to be an abstract and unrealistic discussion, but have faith. We will surface in the real world quite shortly.

Imagine the following dialogue between the manager of a public housing complex and an applicant for an apartment.

Applicant: I understand that you have a vacancy. I am a member of the deserving poor, the very sort of individual you seek to help, and am here to apply for an apartment.

Manager: (After perusing application form) You are, indeed, a member of the deserving poor, and we will be happy to rent you an apartment. However, since we would

---

* Numerous books contain more detailed presentations on welfare economics. See, for example, D.M. Winch, *Analytical Welfare Economics*, Penguin, New York, 1971; Stanley Kaish, *Microeconomics*, Harper & Row, New York, 1976; Jack Hirschleifer, *Prince Theory and Applications*, Prentice-Hall, Englewood-Cliffs, N.J., 1976; Walter Nicholson, *Microeconomic Theory*, Dryden, New York, 1972.

like you to be grateful as well as deserving, we want you to know that the apartment we are prepared to rent to you for $2000 per annum actually costs us $5000 per year to provide.

Applicant: I am grateful—to the extent of $3000 per annum as a matter of fact—but it occurs to me that I would derive as much satisfaction from $2000 a year spent in a manner of my own choosing. Why don't I tear up the lease, you give me $2500, and we'll both be $500 ahead. I'll come back again this time next year and we'll repeat the transaction.

Manager: An obviously rational course of action but . . .

The dialogue may sound foolish, but the question it poses is a serious one. Why, in fact, do we give payments-in-kind rather than just giving cash. In principle it can be shown without too much difficulty that from the viewpoint of the recipient, a payment in cash is always as good as the equivalent in-kind payment and usually superior.

The analytical device with which much of welfare economics begins is the indifference curve shown in Figure 6-2. The curved lines convex to the origin are referred to as indifference curves. Each line represents a combination of quantities of A and B that are all equally satisfying to the consumer. The curvature of the line occurs because of the law of diminishing marginal utility. At some point in the consumption of anything, additional increments of that good or service begin to produce smaller and smaller marginal amounts of satisfaction. This statement is offered without proof, but the reader might test its plausibility by trying to think of an exception. Returning to the diagram, we might imagine that the horizontal axis represents food and the vertical axis shelter. Point X represents consumption of a very large amount of food and very little shelter—say eating each meal in a fine French restaurant and then returning home each night to sleep in a pup tent. Point Y might represent consuming a very large amount of housing but very little food—say, living in a splendid mansion but dining each night on fried dog food. Clearly the consumer at point X might be willing to give up quite a bit in the way of food to obtain modest but decent housing. Similarly, the consumer at point Y might be willing to give up quite a bit of

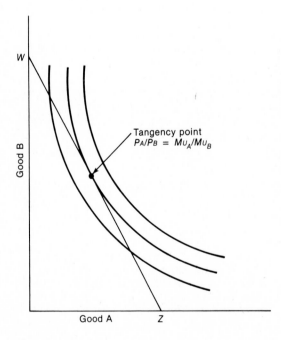

W

Good B

Tangency point
$P_A/P_B = MU_A/MU_B$

Good A   Z

FIGURE 6-2
The indifference curve. Each curve represents combinations of goods that the consumer finds equally satisfying (hence, the term "indifference"). They owe their convexity to the law of diminishing marginal utility. Higher curves farther from the origin represent higher levels of satisfaction because they represent higher levels of consumption. The budget line represents the consumer's ability to purchase. The distance of point W from the origin (measured in units of good B) is the budget divided by the price of B. A comparable statement can be made for the distance of point Z from the origin. The tangency point is an optimal allocation of the budget because it places the consumer on the highest possible indifference curve for a given budget.

housing to obtain modest but decent food. Thus the slopes of the line are different at the two points.

The family of indifference curves shown simply represent different levels of satisfaction. As long as we posit some positive marginal value to additional consumption, a curve further from the origin will represent an increase in satisfaction, and the rational, self-interested consumer will want to be, viewing things from the origin, on as distant an indifference curve as is possible.

Which indifference curve consumers can reach is a function of two things: Their budget and the prices of A and B. In Figure 6-2 point Z represents the amount of good A that could be purchased if consumers spent their entire income on A. Similarly point W represents the amount of good B that consumers would purchase if they spent all their income on good B. The line connecting the two points represents all possible combinations of expenditures on A and B.

If the two axes representing the two goods are scaled equally—the same space for a unit of A as for a unit of B—then we can determine the relative prices of the two goods from the slope of the line. In Figure 6-2 we see that the slope of the line is such that the intersection with the horizontal axis is only half as far from the origin as the intersection with the vertical axis. Thus, the unit price of A is twice the unit price of B.

The point of tangency between the budget line and the indifference curve represents an optimal pattern of expenditures, given a set of prices, a budget, and a particular set of preferences, as expressed by the indifference curves. It is optimal because it represents the highest curve that particular consumer can reach.

This optimum, the tangency point, has a particular characteristic. At that point, and only that point, the indifference curve and the budget line are parallel. That is, they have the same slope. This means that at this point only the consumers' preferences and the market prices have been brought into a certain alignment. Specifically, the ratio at which consumers would substitute one good for another is the same as the ratio of their prices. For example, we noted that the slope of the budget line indicated that the price of A was twice the price of B. Because the slope of the indifference curve at the point of tangency is the same as that of the budget line, we can say that at that point consumers are willing to exchange two units of B for one unit of A.

Therefore, we can write $PA/PB = MUA/MUB$, where PA and PB are the per unit prices of A and B and MUA and MUB are the marginal utilities of A and B at the tangency point. Again, because the tangency point is the only point where the slopes are the same it is the only point where this equality holds.

Allowing consumers to equalize the ratio of prices and marginal utilities thus permits them to maximize the satisfaction they get from a given amount of income. To emphasize this point, suppose we compel consumers to consume a combination of goods at which this equality does not exist. In Figure 6-3(a) that might be points A or B. These points will give consumers the same satisfaction they get at the tangency point, but we note that they cannot reach these points unless we increase the budget. The larger budgets required to keep the consumer on the same indifference curve if we move them off the tangency point are shown by the dashed lines. The amount of waste involved is the amount by which we must increase the budget to obtain the same satisfaction.

Conversely, assume we insist upon a ratio of MUA to MUB different from the ratios of prices but do nothing to alter the consumer's budget. This is shown in Figure 6-3(b) by moving consumers along the budget line to points C and D. Thus consumers are forced down to lower indifference curves. In this case, the measure of waste is the difference in satisfaction offered by the two curves.

The point of the above argument is that there is a strong prima facie case for allowing consumers the freedom to allocate their income in such a way as to be able to make the

(a)   (b)

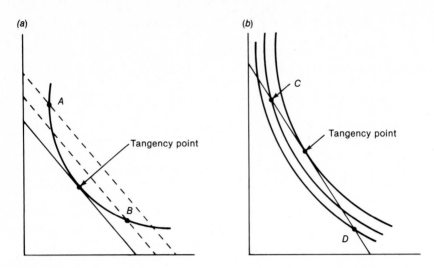

FIGURE 6-3
The efficiency effects of distorting consumer choice. (*a*) Points *A* and *B* represent ratios
of consumption of A and B other than that which the consumer would choose freely. If
these different ratios were forced upon the consumer, he or she would be able to remain on the same indifference curve only at a higher level of expenditure, as shown by
the dashed lines indicating higher budget lines. (*b*) The consumer is held to the same
expenditure total but forced into a different expenditure pattern as indicated by movement away from the tangency point to position *C* or *D*. Note that displacement from the
tangency point necessarily imposes a welfare loss by moving the consumer to a lower
indifference curve.

equilibration between the ratio of prices and the marginal rates of substitution, as discussed
previously. That, in turn, makes a prima facia case for aiding the poor through transfer
payments rather than services in kind or subsidized goods and services. We shall return to
that point shortly.

The reader may wonder how much use the above line of argument is, given that the
illustration only discusses two types of goods and that few people carry indifference curves
as part of their normal psychic apparatus. The answer to the first point is that the thinking
behind the indifference curve is easily extended to more complex cases. Rather than good
A and good B, we can just as well think of good A on one axis and all other goods as being
on the second axis. We also note that three good cases can be drawn though the picture is a
good deal more complex. A third axis is necessary for the third good. The budget line
becomes a flat plane intersecting all three axes, and the indifference curve becomes a
curved plane still convex to the origin. The tangency point between planes will still
represent an optimum. If one goes beyond three goods, pictorial representation is no longer
possible, but there is no reason that we cannot think about a case with *n* goods and *n* prices
in which *n* is very large.

While it is true that the indifference curve is an abstraction not to be found in many
heads outside of the economics profession, we can say that all of us necessarily behave in
ways that are consistent with the indifference curve concept. We all necessarily make
decisions at the margin about our expenditures on various types of goods, regardless of
whether the term *marginal* is part of our vocabularies. Many of us have some control over
how much work effort we make. In that case we are making a choice, at the margin,
between income and leisure.

If we say that the indifference curve comes from consumers' psyches and the budget line from the realities of their income and the prices of goods and services, then it is clear that society can operate with relative certitude upon the budget line but not upon the indifference curve. Let us consider how public intervention may change the former portion of the diagram.

In Figure 6-4(*a*) we see the effect of a direct cash transfer with no restrictions on how the increment is to be spent. The budget line shifts to the right parallel to its original position.

Figure 6-4(*b*) shows the effect of reducing the price of good A. In this case the amount of B that could be purchased (if all income were spent on B) is unchanged, so the intersection of the budget line and the vertical axis is unchanged. The intersection on the horizontal axis moves to the right, since a given budget can now buy a larger quantity of A. Figure 6-4(*c*) shows the situation in which consumers are authorized to receive at no cost a quantity of A. They may or may not choose to purchase additional amounts of A at the market price. Here, the effect is similar to the cash transfer in that the budget line is shifted to the right. The only difference is the flat section at the top. That section can be considered to represent the situation in which consumers spend all their income on B but still receive a certain quantity of A free. One way to interpret the last figure would be to say that if one provides a good free in lesser quantity than the consumer would have purchased in any case, the effect of providing the good is identical with that of providing an equivalent cash transfer. Food stamps would be a good example of this in that in many cases the amount of food they supply free is less than the household would purchase in the absence of stamps. In this case, the stamps are conceptually indistinguishable from a cash transfer. They are, of course, different from a cash transfer in the accounting of the federal government and in the computation of income poverty. In the psychology of the recipient they may also be different.

With no more change than a relabeling of lines, the indifference curve apparatus described in connection with the consumer can be transformed into a statement about production. Assume that there are two factors of production, labor and capital. One axis is

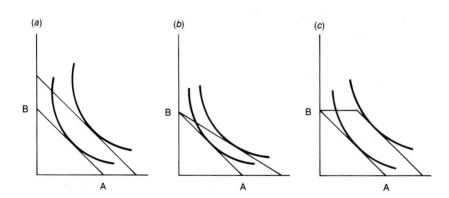

FIGURE 6-4
Public policy and the indifference curve apparatus. (*a*) The effect of an unrestricted transfer, which increases the recipient's disposable income by 50 percent. Note that the budget line simply moves parallel to its former position. (*b*) The effect of subsidizing good A. In this case, the subsidy reduces the price of A by 33.3 percent, permitting the recipient to purchase 50 percent more A for a given sum. As drawn, the subsidization has the effect of sharply increasing the purchase of A, while leaving the amount of B purchased relatively unchanged. Contrast this with the effect of the unrestricted transfer shown in (*a*). (*c*) The effect on the budget line of providing an amount of one good free. The effect is similar to that of the unrestricted transfer (*a*) except for the flat section at the top. This occurs because the maximum amount of B that could be consumed is unchanged by the free provision of good A.

labeled for each factor. The budget line represents the combinations of amounts of the factors which can be had for the producers budget. Each curve, now referred to as an isoquant, represents different combinations of the two factors that will produce a given amount of product. The curve is convex to the origin because of the law of diminishing returns, which, in terms of the geometry of the diagram, plays the same role as that played previously by the law of diminishing marginal utility. If producers purchase the factors of production free of subsidies, differential taxes, legal or administrative constraints etc. they will purchase at the tangency point, thus achieving maximum output for given cost, analogous to the consumer achieving maximum satisfaction for a given budget. If they are forced away from the tangency point—perhaps by subsidization of one factor or an excise tax on another factor—then either less output will be achieved at a given cost or the same output will be achieved at a higher cost.

The principles illustrated for the case of a single consumer or single producer can easily be extended to the case of two consumers diagrammatically and then, conceptually, to a situation of n consumers and m goods when n and m have no upper limit. A simple graphical device for a two-consumer two-good situation is the Edgeworth Box devised by the English economist of that name.

In Figure 6-5 we see consumer X and Y positioned at diagonally opposed corners of the box, and we note that the total quantities of good A and good B available in this economic system are represented by the sides of the box. Thus any point in the box divides up all the goods in the system. The indifference curves of consumers X and Y radiate out of their respective corners. The question now is to consider whether there is some logic by which we can look at a given point and decide whether it is possible that the point may be an optimal division of goods. What is meant by "optimal" will become apparent.

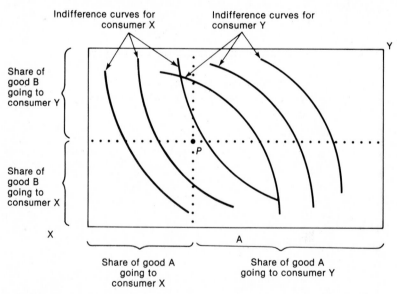

FIGURE 6-5
The Edgeworth box. The borders of the box represent the amount of good A and good B available in this two-good, two-person economy. The two individuals are located at opposite corners of the box. Note that any point within the box divides up all the goods in the system. If point P represents the allocation of goods, then the shares of A and B going to consumers X and Y are as shown on the edges of the box.

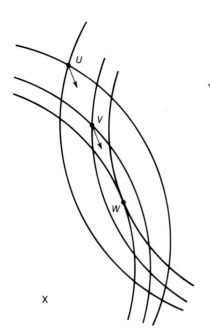

Y

FIGURE 6-6
Optimal and suboptimal positions on an indifference
map. This figure shows an enlarged portion of Figure
6-5. Consider an initial distribution of goods at point
U. It is not an optimal position because it is possible
to locate another point that places both consumers
on higher curves. If the two consumers in the system
were free to trade, they would do so. The move to V
shows both consumers on higher indifference curves
than was the case initially. Position V, though an improvement, is still not optimal, in that movement to W
places both consumers on still higher indifference
curves. At position W, however, an optimum has
been reached, for the only way that one consumer
can rise to a higher indifference curve is if the other
moves to a lower curve.

Consider point U in Figure 6-6. Is it possible that it may represent an optimal distribution of goods? The answer is no, for a very simple reason. If the point is moved in the direction of the arrow, both X and Y are moved to higher indifference curves (the height of the curve being measured from their respective corners). If movement of the point is able to improve the lot of both parties, clearly it is not an optimal distribution. Consider next point V. Again the same argument can be made. The point can be moved again in such a manner that both X and Y are placed on higher indifference curves. When we reach point W, however, we observe that it is no longer possible to relocate the point in such a manner that both parties are placed on higher indifference curves. If we are to place one party on a higher curve, it can be done only by placing the other party on a lower curve. If we said that our criteria for suboptimality was that a movement that which improved the condition of both parties was possible, then we cannot demonstrate that point W is suboptimal, and we must admit the possibility that it is optimal.

The geometrical characteristic which defines point W is the back-to-back tangency of the indifference curves of X and Y.

Figure 6-7 shows a series of these points forming a line referred to as the contract curve. The curve represents a series of optima like point W above. What is the meaning of the contract curve? For any distribution of goods off the curve, it is possible for both parties to improve their positions through trade, analogous to the movement from U to V or V to W, discussed above. For any point on the curve there are no mutual gains to be realized from trade. Thus all points in the curve represent optimum distributions. In Figure 6-7 point C represents an optimum distribution, given that the two parties have roughly comparable incomes. Point D represents an optimum given that X is rich and Y is poor.

The situation in which no party's welfare can be improved without reducing the welfare of some other party is referred to as Pareto optimal, after the economist Vilfredo Pareto. The Edgeworth box-indifference curve-contract curve apparatus presented above is simply a graphical illustration of the concept of Pareto optimality.

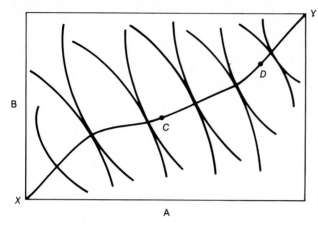

FIGURE 6-7
Optimal allocations of goods. The contract curve, which represents optimal distributions of goods for all possible income distributions between X and Y, is formed by the back-to-back tangency points. Point *C* is an optimal distribution given that *X* and *Y* have similar incomes. *D* is optimal given that *X*'s income is larger than *Y*'s.

If any point on the contract curve is an optimum, then which point is best? For us to be able to answer that we would need to be able to say what the optimum distribution of income is, and that judgment takes us beyond the realm of marginal economics and into questions of social justice, the relationship of one human being to another, etc. Presumably the economist is neither more nor less qualified than the noneconomist in these realms.

But even though we beg the ultimate question here, the foregoing analysis still has some philosophical implications. When Friedman, quoted earlier, argues that one advantage of the NIT is that it works "outside the market" he is saying, in effect, "let us redistribute income in a single stroke and then let the market operate with complete freedom." What is being advocated is a system in which the gains of trade can be realized so that we settle at some point on the contract curve. The evenness of the distribution of wealth will be determined in part by how much income we chose to redistribute before the trading begins. But we will not try to bias the terms of trading in order to achieve distribution gains.

The poor but worthy applicant in the beginning of this appendix was, in effect, proposing the sort of process suggested above, namely, that we make a single effort at income distribution outside the market and then let the process of trade allow for a final distribution of goods that fall on the contract curve. In the discussion on the indifference curve, we noted that by relabeling, it could be transformed into a statement about production called an isoquant. That discussion suggests an efficiency loss when we cause producers to alter their factor proportions for reasons unrelated to the true cost of these factors. This suggests that subsidizing or differentially taxing particular factors or particular production processes because of the presumed equity effects entails an efficiency loss. That is, it is more efficient to help poor people by giving them money that they then take into an undistorted market place than by distorting the market place in order to lower the prices of the goods that the poor are prone to buy.

Yet in spite of these arguments, which are widely accepted within the economics profession, society does provide many goods at below cost, does provide services in-kind rather than cash, and does distort the market place for distributional or equity reasons. Why do we do this? The answer has two parts. First, there are some valid economic reasons for intervening, and, second, there are some serious noneconomic reasons for intervention rather than just simply redistribution. Let us consider the former class of reasons first. Three cases where direct intervention may be justified follow.

1 The rationality of the recipient is in doubt. Here it is possible that society, by gross measures such as provision of free goods or alteration of market prices through subsidies and taxes, can do a better job of maximizing the utility from a given total expenditure than the consumer (recipient) working alone.

2 Significant externalities exist. Thus the pattern of consumption that maximizes individual utility will not maximize total utility, and it is desirable to alter the consumer's (recipient's) behavior accordingly. We thus subsidize, in one sense or another, the consumption of goods with positive externalities and tax the consumption of goods with negative externalities. This is illustrated in Figure 6-8.

3 If the consumption of a particular good or service appears in the utility function of the donor as well as the recipient. If society as a whole derives some satisfaction from observing a given recipient of assistance consume good A, let us say, but not good B then perhaps distorting the recipient's behavior by providing assistance in some form other than an unrestricted transfer makes sense.

Beyond the "economically respectable" reasons offered above, there are a number of practical reasons why aid to individuals often comes in other than cash terms. One reason is political acceptability. Even if the disguise is fairly thin, casting what is essentially income redistribution in other terms may make it more acceptable politically. For example, food stamps are the closest thing we have to a national guaranteed income system. But the name disguises it just a bit and makes it a little more palatable politically. The name also suggests that the program is benefiting farmers by increasing the demand for food. Thus it enlists some legislative support from farm state representatives even though the truth may

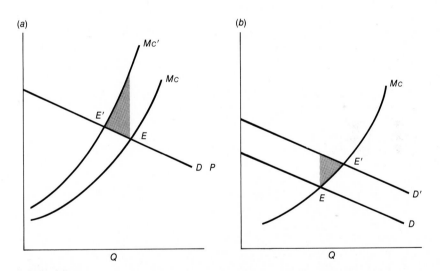

FIGURE 6-8
Externalities and market intervention. (a) MC represents the marginal costs as seen by the producer, while MC' represents those costs adjusted for the negative externalities the production or use of the product imposes upon third parties. If said externalities are not incorporated into the cost of the product the market will be in equilibrium at E. The shaded area represents the loss to society (true marginal cost exceeding marginal utility). If the negative externalities are incorporated into the cost of the product, the market will come to equilibrium at E' and the waste represented by the shaded area will be eliminated. (b) D represents demand and D' is demand adjusted for the positive externalities that the production or use of the product produces. If the market comes to equilibrium at E, the shaded area represents a loss stemming from the failure to continue producing while the true benefits exceed the cost of production. Such a situation may justify subsidization in order to move the equilibrium to E'.

be that they increase the demand for food about as much as unrestricted transfers of the same amount. The rental-assistance payments discussed in the housing chapter have a large element of income transfer in them. In fact, if the recipient continues to occupy the same housing as previously, it is hard to see them as anything other than a direct cash transfer. But the way they are named and the way they are delivered blurs the issue a bit and may bring in some political support from housing and construction interests. In many cases an in-kind program has about it an aura of worthiness. After all, food and housing are more "worthy" goods than, say, beer. The fact that having part of your housing or food budget picked up by a third party may then liberate some funds for your beer budget may not be readily apparent to the casual observer.

Finally, providing aid through a variety of programs tends to obscure the total amount of aid given and deprives the opponents of aid of a single target. If the entire combination of means-tested direct transfers and in-kind payments were replaced by a single transfer scheme of, say, $75 billion, it would give the opponents of redistribution a single, clear target to shoot at. The fact that the program is scattered and partly disguised gives it some protection against a single, devasting legislative blow.

CHAPTER 7

URBAN HOUSING

HOUSING CHARACTERISTICS

Housing is a peculiar good in many ways with characteristics that are almost unique among all the manufactured objects in common use. Though these characteristics are generally apparent on some reflection, it is well to make them explicit.

1 *Fixity.* In most cases it remains on its original site for its entire life and in most cases it was produced on that site.

2 *Durability.* It is in general more durable than any other important, widely used class of manufactured objects. Not only is it durable, but with sufficient investment it can be given an almost indefinite life.

3 *Slow rate of technological change.* Thus housing tends to become obsolete more slowly than most other manufactured objects.

4 *Proneness to neighborhood effects.* Unlike movable objects, the value of housing is greatly affected by the place at which it is constructed or installed. Thus its value as an asset over time is only partially within the control of its owner.

5 *Sensitivity to credit.* Because housing is a large expenditure it is generally financed with long-term credit instruments, and thus the availability and cost of credit weigh very heavily in its construction and purchase—far more so than with any other item commonly purchased by households.

6 *Speculative motive in ownership.* Most goods that are purchased by households are purchased solely for use. A house, whether it is free-standing or a unit in a larger structure, has a dual function. It provides housing services, but it also holds out the possibility of speculative gain in the same sense as a stock or a bond.

7 *Merit good.* To some degree we have viewed housing as a merit good, as something whose consumption has beneficial effects beyond the satisfaction it brings to the user.

8 *Small scale of producing units.* Although many components in most houses are factory-produced and although some housing itself is factory-produced (mobile homes), most producers of housing are small relative to the national market and generally also relative to the local market. The average construction firm in the United States in 1977 had slightly fewer than ten employees, and there were over half a million self-employed construction workers.

9 *Fragmented ownership.* Not only are there about 52 million owner-occupied units; there are literally millions of owners of rental units. And the largest owners of rental units control only fractions of a percent of the total rental stock.

10 *Visibility.* The condition of people's housing is continuously visible to a degree that is not true of any other good, a fact that seems to have something to do with the matter of public concern.

The durability and fixity of housing almost guarantee that some of it will be in the "wrong" place and of the "wrong" type. Given rapid population growth and technological change, any large manufactured object that can't be moved and that may last for a century has some potential for being the wrong object in the wrong place. The durability of housing also guarantees that there will be some dissatisfaction with at least part of the housing stock, for as real incomes have risen over time, our standards of what constitutes acceptable housing have risen.

Neighborhood effects sharply limit the ability of owners to affect the value of their property. Forces beyond the owners' control may present them with windfalls or impose substantial losses on them. In the windfall case some may be outraged by the earning of an "unearned increment," but in general no damage to the quality of the housing stock is likely to result. In the case of the loss, the decrease in property value or income potential may be such as to make further investment or adequate maintenance unprofitable, and this can have major quality effects extending to, in the ultimate case, arson or abandonment.

The credit sensitivity of housing makes construction rates highly responsive to changes in money markets, as shown in Figure 7-1. Note the powerful inverse relationship between construction rates and interest rates. Thus macroeconomic policy decisions such as those made by the Federal Reserve Board often affect housing markets more than legislation or administrative action directed specifically at housing. Because interest rates generally peak at or near the top of the business cycle construction usually has a somewhat countercyclical pattern. This may be desirable in terms of reducing the amplitude of the business cycle. However, it seems likely that large swings in construction activity reduce the efficiency of the housing industry and elevate costs.

The fragmentation of ownership and of supply tends to make housing markets relatively competitive in the economist's meaning of the term.[1] Since housing

---

[1] See U.S. Bureau of the Census, *Statistical Abstract of the United States, Table 1363*, 1981, for data on construction firm size.

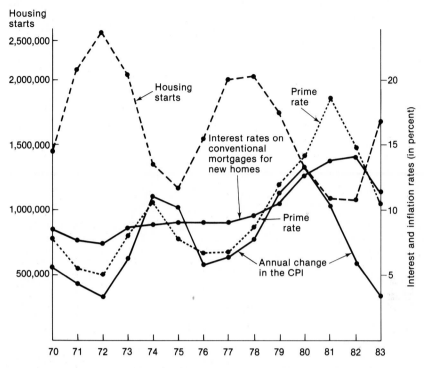

FIGURE 7-1
Inflation, interest rates, and housing starts. Note the generally opposite movement of housing starts and the prime rate throughout the 1970s and into the early 1980s. Mortgage rates generally moved with the prime but, as is typical of rates in long-term instruments, were somewhat less volatile. Underlying the movement of the prime was the change in the inflation rate. In the very early 1980s tight money policy maintained after the rate of inflation declined caused the inflation rate and interest rates to move oppositely but for most of the time period their movements coincided reasonably closely. (Survey of Current Business and Federal Reserve Bulletin, *various issues.*)

units cannot be identical, if only because they are located on different sites, the monopolistic competition model (many buyers and sellers with a mild degree of product differentiation) describes the market well. Monopolistic competition as a market model was first described by Chamberlin in the 1920s but is covered in most standard introductory texts.[2] The fragmentation of ownership also means that each owner cannot capture the positive externalities resulting from improvement of his or her own property and, therefore, in declining areas owners as a class may underinvest. This situation, in which a group of individuals are blocked from acting in their own best interest either because they cannot communicate with each other or because they cannot trust each other to act in accordance with agreements, is sometimes referred to in discussions of game theory as "the prisoner's dilemma."

[2] Edward Chamberlin, *The Theory of Monopolistic Competition*, 8th ed., Harvard University Press, Cambridge, Mass., 1965.

If an entire area were in single ownership the owner-monopolist might reason that money spent on property A increases the value of property B, C, and D. Thus the owner-monopolist will be more likely to invest than will the owner who holds only property A. (The student of microeconomics might note that this is one instance in which a monopolist or oligopolist might allocate resources more efficiently than would a large number of pure competitors.)

The possibility of speculative gain makes the purchase of housing subject to a different set of motivations than any other good commonly purchased by households. In the 1960s and 1970s the possibility of speculative gain presumably elevated the price of owner-occupied units and may have accelerated the process of suburbanization somewhat. It also appears to have reduced demand for rental housing significantly. But where the possibilities of speculative gain exist, so too do the possibility of speculative losses. In the 1980s falling real prices of houses and high carrying costs owing to high interest rates appear to have imposed losses on many purchasers of housing.

Viewing housing as a "merit" good (one whose consumption yields benefits beyond the immediate satisfaction delivered to the consumer) has numerous implications for public policy. If we did not so regard housing, it would be hard to explain why we subsidize it in a variety of ways, both direct and indirect, and why we have created such a variety of institutions to facilitate its financing.

Housing's visibility tends to focus public concern upon it and, perhaps, causes us to give more attention to housing problems than we would if they intruded less continuously upon our collective consciousness.

The Mechanics of Housing Stock Change

The driving force behind the growth of the housing stock, both in number and quality of units, is the long-term increase in demand. Estimates of the income elasticity of housing demand generally place it between .7 and 1 percent, though figures may vary from one time period to another, from one class of household to another, and from one housing type to another.[3] This means that, typically, for each 1 percent that personal income rises national expenditures on housing rise by between .7 percent and 1 percent. (See the section on housing finance at the end of this chapter for more details on elasticity.) Thus housing expenditures rise almost as rapidly in percentage terms as do real incomes. This, combined with population growth itself, continually shifts the demand curve for housing to the right. Changes in the structure of the population may also affect the demand for housing. The maturing during the 1970s of children born during the baby boom of the 1950s increased housing demand by accelerating the rate of household formation.

The Effects of New Construction New construction adds units, generally toward the upper end of the price and quality scale, while abandonment and demolition remove units, generally further down on the price and quality scale. The process of construction accelerates the loss of older units for two reasons. First, particularly in higher-density areas, a certain amount of demolition occurs

---

[3] For a discussion and review of recent findings see J. M. Quigely, "What Have We learned about Housing Markets?" in Peter Mieskowski and Mahlon Straszheim (eds.), *Current Issues in Urban Economics*, Johns Hopkins University Press, Baltimore, 1979.

to make room for new construction. Second, new construction shifts the supply curve of housing to the right, exerting downward pressures on prices and rents. This lessens the market value of the existing stock, pushing marginal units in the direction of abandonment or demolition. This is no more profound than saying that the building of new cars puts downward pressure on used-car prices and hastens the junking of the least valuable members of the used-car fleet.

Conversion and Renovation   The inventory is also changed by conversion and renovation. A certain number of residential structures are converted to nonresidential uses, and, similarly, there are conversions in the other direction. The number of housing units in a given structure can also be changed through renovation. A large apartment might be made from two or more small ones. More commonly, large units may be converted into smaller units. Single-family units once occupied by upper-middle-class households may be converted into multifamily units occupied by poorer families, a phenomenon often seen in transitional neighborhoods.

In recent years the number of two-family units in the nation has increased more rapidly than can be accounted for by construction of new units alone. The difference is made up by conversions, some of them illegal, of single-family units. Where demand is increasing, construction costs are high, or the housing stock is relatively inelastic, the motivation to increase the number of units by conversion may be great.

Investment and Disinvestment   At the same time that the above processes are adding and subtracting units the entire housing stock is subject to qualitative change through the process of investment and disinvestment. A variety of factors including tax treatment, owners' expectations of future change in the market conditions for that area, the cost of capital, and, in the case of rental properties, present cash flow all affect owners' willingness to maintain or improve their properties. Where expectations of future demand are pessimistic or where cash flow is weak, disinvestment is likely and quality will decline. "Disinvestment" means that the owner puts less into maintenance than is necessary to sustain the quality of the structure. Cash flow is improved at the cost of the future quality of the property. Where expectations of future demand are good and cash flow is adequate, net investment may occur and the quality of existing units may improve.

The Filtering Process   The so-called filtering process is one of the most basic and widespread mechanisms at work in housing markets. The force behind the filtering process is the generally greater attractiveness of new housing relative to old housing. Why should this be?

Because there is a long-term rise in real incomes and because the income elasticity of demand for housing exceeds zero with the passage of time the real amount the average family spends on housing will increase. Thus it is likely that units built to meet recent demand will be of higher quality than units built some years back. For this reason alone recently built units are likely to be more attractive than older units. This tendency will be augmented by periodic technological improvement, for example, central air-conditioning or the so-called superinsulation developed in response to energy price increases. It will also be augmented by the physical deterioration of housing over the years.

The tendency of new housing to be of higher quality than older housing is also reinforced by public policy. This control takes various forms. Building codes specify structural and mechanical standards such as room size, window size, insulation, fire resistance, plumbing systems, and the like. Zoning laws and subdivision requirements specify lot size, street geometry, provision of open space, setbacks, height of structure, etc. Thus the law reinforces those market forces that make new housing more valuable than existing housing and new neighborhoods more attractive in design than older neighborhoods. In fact, if there were a significant demand for new low-quality, low-cost housing, building codes and zoning laws would act to prevent that demand from being met.

Most municipalities do attempt to maintain the quality of older housing through housing codes and other devices. However, the enforcement of standards is much more effective for new than for existing units.

It is easy and costless for the permit-issuing jurisdiction to deny a building permit for a plan that does not meet the ordinance requirements. Similarly, it is easy to deny a certificate of occupancy for a new structure that has been put up in a manner that violates the law.

For old housing enforcement of standards is much more difficult. Although local government can, and often does, put pressure on property owners (generally owners of rental property) to meet standards, it is hard to compel compliance. This is particularly so of dwellings in which the income potential is low. (Where the income potential is high little or no compulsion may be necessary.)

For all of the above reasons with the passage of time the occupants of a given housing stock generally are less wealthy, at least in relative terms, than earlier occupants. At some point in the filtering process the rent-paying capacity of the occupants may fall so low that either the structure has no economic value at all or its economic value falls below the value of its underlying debt. As an example of the latter situation, assume an investor buys an old apartment house for $100,000, putting up $30,000 of his own capital and taking out a mortgage for $70,000. With the passage of time the neighborhood becomes poorer. As a result, the rent that can be obtained from apartments in the building falls, and this reduces the market value of the building. When the value of the building drops to $70,000, or whatever the remaining balance of the mortgage is at that time, the owner's equity has been entirely lost. If the value of the building falls still further, he has not only lost all equity but is also in the position of owing more on the building than it is worth. It will thus be in his financial interest to free himself from his mortgage debt one way or another. If he can, he may file bankruptcy and transfer his losses to the bank that holds the mortgage. Or he might simply abandon the building and disappear. If the building is insured for more than its actual market value, an unscrupulous owner might resort to arson. It is not surprising that arson is a common crime in many slum areas, where the filtering process is at its end.

A Housing-Based Explanation of the Urban Income Gradient   In Chapter 3 a simple mathematical model based on the work of Alonso was presented to explain why, in general, there is a positive relationship between personal income and distance of residence from the central place. The model is a static one in that it has no time dimension. It explains why, in equilibrium, the result should be found but not the sequence of events leading to that result. The economist and urbanist Anthony Downs offers a simpler explanation.[4] In general, new housing is built toward the periphery of the region, since it is cheaper to build on vacant land, to avoid both clearance costs and the cost of absorbing the remaining economic value in existing real property. Since new housing is generally more desirable than old housing and since it can be afforded only by those on the upper portion of the income distribution curve, the well-known gradient is produced.

Downs notes that in societies where there are no quality controls on new housing the gradient may be reversed, with the poor living on the periphery in low-cost, low-quality housing, often of their own construction. This pattern is seen in a number of South American cities. He also notes that the prohibition against the construction of low-quality new housing tends to bring about greater segregation among income classes because the threshold effect of new-house prices effectively excludes lower-income people from newly developed areas.

Housing Markets and the Neighborhood Life Cycle   The fact that we build for the more prosperous also tends to produce a typical neighborhood life cycle. When the filtering process has gone on long enough the incomes of the new occupants (whether of rental or owner-occupied properties) may be insufficient to generate the cash flow necessary for adequate maintenance. At this point the area begins to deteriorate physically. Ultimately the remaining economic value in the area's housing stock may sink low enough to permit clearance and redevelopment. Downs suggests a typical life cycle of 40 to 60 years for the process.[5] But, as noted in Chapter 3 if the area has particular characteristics that make it specially desirable, demand for location there may remain high enough to prevent the process. Thus areas with particular amenities or locational advantages may resist this cycle for an indefinite period of time.

HOUSING TRENDS

Table 7-1 shows changes in the number of housing units by region from 1960 to 1980. Note the much more rapid growth in the south and west than in the east and north-central regions. In both the 1960s and 1970s we also observe much slower housing growth in central cities than in the suburbs and in nonmetropolitan areas. In fact, in the east and north-central regions the growth of the central-city housing stock almost ceased. In the 1970s another trend became evident, the rapid growth of the nonmetropolitan housing stock. All of the above housing stock changes are consistent with the migration patterns discussed in Chapter 2.

Table 7-2 reveals a number of national housing trends. One striking point is that during the decade the nation's housing stock increased much more rapidly in percentage terms than did its population. In fact, for every 100 additional residents the United States added 86 new housing units. Concurrent with the rapid

---

[4] Anthony Downs, *Urban Problems and Prospects*, Markham, Chicago, 1970.
[5] Anthony Downs, *Urban Problems and Prospects*, 2d ed., Rand McNally, Chicago, 1976, p. 90.

TABLE 7-1
GROWTH OF HOUSING STOCK BY REGION, 1960–1980
(In Thousands)

	1960	1970	1980	% change 1970 to 1980
Total United States	58,326	68,672	88,207	28.4
Northeast	14,798	16,642	19,272	15.8
Central city	6,005	6,212	6,293	1.3
Suburban	5,829	6,824	8,231	20.6
Nonmetropolitan	2,964	3,606	4,748	31.6
North-Central	16,798	18,971	22,800	20.2
Central city	5,695	5,978	6,244	4.1
Suburban	4,818	6,228	8,271	32.8
Nonmetropolitan	6,284	6,765	8,305	22.8
South	17,173	21,000	29,057	38.4
Central city	5,208	6,166	7,519	21.9
Suburban	3,844	5,486	8,637	57.4
Nonmetropolitan	8,121	9,379	12,901	37.6
West	9,558	12,029	17,078	42.0
Central city	3,531	4,252	5,475	28.8
Suburban	3,701	5,143	7,827	52.2
Nonmetropolitan	2,325	2,634	3,778	43.3

Source: U.S. Bureau of the Census, Annual Housing Survey, pt. A, 1980 and earlier years. Survey data above may not agree in detail with results of the 1980 Census of Housing.

increase in housing stock was a decline in average household size of almost .4 persons, the largest ever recorded in a single decade.

The decrease in household size has an important implication for urban population because it means that increases in housing stock are necessary simply

TABLE 7-2
SUMMARY OF HOUSING STATISTICS
(Figures in Thousands Where Appropriate)

	1970	1980	% change
U.S. population	205,100	227,700	11
All housing units	68,672	88,207	28
Vacant, seasonal, and migratory	973	2,183	124
Occupied units			
Owner	39,886	52,516	31
Renter	23,560	27,556	17
Vacancy rates[a]			
Owner	1.2	1.4	
Renter	6.6	5.1	
Average household size	3.14	2.75	
Median household size[b]			
Owner	3.0	2.6	
Renter	2.6	2.0	

TABLE 7-2 *(Cont'd.)*

	1970	1980	% change
Percent "overcrowded"[c]			
Owner	6.4	3.1	
Renter	10.6	6.2	
Percent of units without complete plumbing			
Owner	4.2	1.4	
Renter	7.8	3.5	
Consumer price index	100	212	112
Construction costs index			
Union labor	100	201	101
Materials	100	236	136
Prepared single family building lots	100	304	204
Median single family house prices[d]			
New	$23,400	$64,500	175
Resale	$23,000	$62,200	170
Median contract rent[e]			
Annual Housing Survey	90	203	126
Bureau of Labor Statistics			70
Median household income			
Owner	$9,700	$19,800	104
Renter	$6,300	$10,500	67
Median value/income ratio	1.7	2.5	
Median rent/income ratio	.20	.27	
Percent of new single family houses with			
Less than 1200 sq ft floor area	36	21	
More than 1600 sq ft floor area	37	50	
Sources of housing stock change, 1970–1980			
Net growth	19,535		
Units begun 1970 through 1979[f]	17,858		
Losses through demolition and disaster	2,461		
Unspecified sources of increase[g]	3,995		

[a] Units vacant and available for sale or rent as a percent of the total housing stock.

[b] Medians are computed as if the number of persons per household were a continuous variable. For example, two-person households are rated as if they were homogeneously distributed from 1.5 to 2.5. Because numbers far above the center of the distribution have no more effect than numbers just slightly above the median, the figures for median numbers of persons per household are lower than the figures for the average number of persons. Thus the median figures cannot be reconciled with the average figures immediately above them.

[c] "Overcrowded" is defined as 1.01 or more persons per room.

[d] Because the new and resale prices come from different sources, they may not be directly comparable.

[e] There is a large discrepancy between the results of the Annual Housing Survey and the results of Bureau of Labor Statistics compiled in connection with the development of the consumer price index. For this reason both sets of values are cited. When the housing questions from the 1980 census are tabulated the discrepancy should be resolved.

[f] This represents 10 years of starts. The assumption is that units started in 1970 would not have been completed and counted in that year but that units started in 1979 would have been completed and counted in the 1980 survey.

[g] This is a balancing item. It includes conversions from residential to nonresidential uses (and vice versa), losses through condemnation, gains from bringing condemned units back into the housing stock, and conversions that change the number of units in a structure. It is such a large positive number partly because of the conversion of single-family units into multifamily units. It may also cover a variety of sources of statistical error, such as building permits missed in the tabulating of national data and units constructed without the filing of building permits. See front matter in Annual Housing Survey, Part A, for further details.

Sources: U.S. Bureau of the Census, *Annual Housing Survey,* various years through 1980; Bureau of Labor Statistics, *Monthly Labor Review;* U.S. Bureau of the Census Construction Report ser. C-20; unpublished data from the Division of Construction Statistics, U.S. Bureau of the Census; National Association of Realtors, "Existing Home Sales"; and E. H. Boeckh, building cost index.

to maintain population stability and that stability in the housing stock implies population decline. For example, if average household size in a given city declines from 3.0 to 2.6 (a typical change for the 1970–1980 decade) and the number of occupied units remains constant, the household population shrinks by slightly over 13 percent. Thus the approximate stability in the size of the housing stock in northern cities was consistent with their often substantial population declines.

A number of factors contributed to the rapid expansion of the housing stock in the 1970s. First, there was substantial increase in real income. From 1970 to 1980 the nation added almost 20 million jobs. Thus, even though productivity per worker did not rise much, total personal income increased substantially. Second, the maturing of the baby boom children noted earlier greatly increased the rate of new household formation. Third, as we shall see subsequently, a constellation of economic of forces made home ownership extremely attractive as a financial proposition. Note that despite the increase in housing stock, vacancy rates actually declined slightly across the decade.

Another change to note is the increase in owner-occupied units as a percentage of all units. This phenomenon results from the mix of units built, the demolition of multifamily units in urban areas, and, to a lesser degree, the conversion of rental units to condominiums and cooperatives.

How well people are housed is always a somewhat subjective matter, but the mass of available evidence suggests that there was substantial improvement during the decade. In fact, given the amount of new construction and the relationship between the building of new units and the retirement of old units, it would be surprising if this were not the case. Let us look at the matter in a little detail. Through 1960 the Bureau of the Census asked its enumerators to classify housing as sound, deteriorating, or dilapidated. Tests run after the 1960 census indicated that different interviewers evaluated the same properties differently and this type of evaluation was dropped. At present, estimates of housing quality rely upon more objective but perhaps more limited measures. One item, which in years past correlated with a high incidence of deteriorating or dilapidated units, was the absence of complete plumbing. As Table 7-2 indicates, the number of units with incomplete plumbing facilities declined by about half during the decade. The number of overcrowded units, admittedly not a structural characteristic but still an important aspect of people's housing situation, also declined to about half of its 1970 level. The size of new single-family units increased substantially from 1970 to 1980. Note the decrease in the percentage of new units with under 1200 square feet of floor space and the increase in the number of new units with more than 1600 square feet of floor space.

Construction costs increased somewhat more rapidly than the consumer price index. The most rapid increase among the major factors was land costs. The relationship between land costs, land-use controls, and public capital investment is discussed in the next chapter.

Interesting and major financial changes occurred over the decade. The price of new and used owner-occupied units increased much more rapidly than CPI. They also increased more rapidly than household incomes, with the result that value/income ratios rose.

For rental units the situation was different. Depending upon which data one uses (two sources are shown in the table) rents either rose by slightly more or considerably less than the CPI. In any case, the rise in rents was far smaller than the rise in the values of owner-occupied units. Yet in spite of the relatively moderate rise in rents, rent/income ratios rose. The only way this can be explained is if renters, as a class, became poorer. This is precisely what happened. Note that the family incomes of owners increased by 104 percent from 1970 to 1980, while those of renters grew by only 67 percent. Given the increase in the CPI during the period, the real incomes of renters declined significantly. It appears that the more affluent renters were selectively drawn into home ownership for reasons discussed later in this chapter.

The Housing Problem

Do we have a housing problem and, if so, what is it? While a diverse collection of people will tell us that we do have a problem, we are far from a consensus on what that problem is.

Someone concerned largely with the physical cities might argue that of course there is a problem. If we have any doubts we might simply drive through any one of a number of urban areas and observe the substantial number of deteriorated and substandard units.

The advocate of the urban poor would point to the fact that in spite of the general improvement in housing quality in recent decades a significant number of poor families still live in substandard housing. This might lead to a discussion of the "housing poor." As a rule of thumb housing economists have considered households to be spending too much of their income on housing if housing costs exceed 25 percent of income. The rule has been around since the 1930s, but its origin and precise rationale are unclear.

Recent statistics suggest that the housing poor are quite numerous in the lower-income brackets. In 1980, for example, 57 percent of central-city renter households with incomes under $3000 spent more than 25 percent of their income on housing and 38 percent of these households spent more than 35 percent on housing. For households in the $10,000 to $15,000 range the comparable percentages are 51 and 17. By the time we reach the $25,000 to $35,000 bracket the comparable figures drop to 6 percent and less than 1 percent.[6]

Clearly, many poorer households spend what are widely considered to be inordinate percentages of their incomes on rent. The only question is whether we regard this as a housing problem or an income problem. That takes us back to the issue of payments-in-kind versus straight transfers discussed in Chapter 6.

Middle-income people may complain that the price of what they consider acceptable housing either is beyond reach or can be purchased only with an inordinately large share of total personal income. But the skeptic might ask what is sacrosanct about these wants or where the term "inordinately" comes from. Our skeptic might also ask what goods or services the complainant cares to give up in return for cheaper housing.

The planner may believe that the basic problem is that we have built too much suburban housing, thus siphoning off the middle class from the cities, eating up

---

[6] U.S. Department of Commerce, *Annual Housing Survey*, pt. C, Table A1, 1980.

hundreds of thousands of acres of precious farmland, and creating an energy-intensive lifestyle, which will ultimately be a geopolitical disaster. But the planner's critic might argue that our massive suburbanization gave millions of households what they seemed to want, that the loss of farmland is not a cause for concern because our agricultural problem is one of overproduction, not underproduction, and that expert opinion on future energy supplies and costs is far from unanimous.

Do We Have Too Much Housing? Of late some have been wondering whether part of the American housing problem is that we have too much housing. Consider Mr. X, who used to make a good income working on an assembly line at General Motors. Right now he is driving downtown in his Toyota to pick up his unemployment insurance check and wondering how he will keep up the payments on his new house in an attractive suburban subdivision. Being a philosophical fellow, he wonders if the American housing problem isn't that we invested too much capital in housing, leaving too little for machine tools and industrial robots. Perhaps if only we got rid of those tax expenditures for housing and provided more generous tax treatment for capital investment and corporate profits he'd still be working. His house might be smaller, but he wouldn't be wondering how to meet next month's payment.

An Inconclusive Conclusion Do we have a housing shortage? If we accept the economist's definition of a shortage—quantity supplied less than quantity demanded at the prevailing price—the answer is no (perhaps with the exception of places with rent controls, but more on this point later). If we accept a more commonplace though less precise meaning—not enough of the product available at what we somehow consider to be an acceptable price—then the answer is maybe. If we ask whether most of us are well housed by world standards or by past U.S. standards, most writers on the subject of housing would say yes. It we ask whether too many of us, particularly poor urban renters, are spending too large a percentage of our incomes on housing, many housing economists would answer yes, but whether we should regard that as a housing or an income problem is arguable. If we ask whether we have met the goal expressed in the 1949 Housing Act, however vague it may be, of a "suitable home and a decent living environment" for every family, the answer is obviously no. Since there is no consensus among the experts, the reader should not be overly troubled by the inconclusiveness of the above discussion.

PUBLIC POLICY

Housing markets, the housing industry, and the housing customer function in an environment of almost omnipresent public intervention. Building codes, zoning laws, and environmental regulations decree what may be built and where it may be built. The value of land on which housing is built is heavily influenced by public capital expenditures for roads, sewer lines, water mains, etc. Much construction for rental purposes is subsidized in one way or another. There are few direct subsidies behind home ownership, but the homeowner enjoys massive tax expenditures. Housing finance is accomplished through a complex set of institutions and regulations, which have been evolving since the Great Depression. No builder or investor makes a significant commitment without paying serious attention to the relevant portions of the IRS code. The very fact of inflation, both our willingness to tolerate it and our periodic attempts to control it, has been a major element in the financial backdrop of housing markets and the housing industry.

At the federal level the most important actions affecting housing have been decisions regarding the tax treatment of housing, the creation of institutions to facilitate the financing of housing, and direct expenditures for housing. Let us begin by making a fundamental distinction: direct expenditures versus tax expenditures.

The Distinction between Grants and Tax Expenditures

A grant is generally unambiguous. Money is spent on or given for some clearly identified good or service. There is little doubt about the amount of the grant or the ostensible purpose for which it is made. (If a grant commits government to future expenditures whose cost cannot be accurately estimated there may, however, be considerable doubt about the long-term costs of the program.)

A *tax expenditure* is not quite so simple or clear. Just as government may foster an activity by direct grants, it may also foster the same activity by taxing it more lightly than it would normally have done. In some cases the tax forgiveness may go directly to the party performing the desired act. For example, investment tax credits (a subtraction from the firm's corporate income tax liability) go directly to firms making certain types of capital investment. In other cases, the tax expenditure may indirectly benefit the party performing the desired act. For example, provisions in the IRS code permit school districts to issue tax-exempt bonds, the proceeds of which are used to construct new facilities. In this case, the immediate beneficiary of the tax code provisions is the individual or organization which buys the bonds because they receive tax-exempt interest income. The school district benefits secondarily, since it can market its bonds at a lower interest rate because the interest on the bonds is exempt from federal taxation.

A grant either exists or does not exist and there is no doubt as to the situation. With tax expenditures, the case is not always quite so clear. This is because of the potential ambiguity embedded in the phrase "would normally have done" in the paragraph immediately above. With tax expenditures there is also some ambiguity about size. For example, if a school district issues $1 million in tax-exempt bonds we cannot specify the immediate revenue loss to the federal government unless we can specify, among other things, the marginal tax bracket of each of the buyers.[7]

Tax expenditures occur because of provisions—sometimes quite obscure ones—in the IRS code. As a result they have received less public and legislative attention than direct grants of comparable magnitude. However, this situation has

[7] Estimating revenue losses from tax expenditures is complicated. See, for example, Harvey Galper and Eric Toder, *Modelling Allocation Effects of the Use of Tax Exempt Bonds for Private Purposes*, Office of Tax Analysis, U.S. Department of the Treasury, OTA Paper 44, December 1980.

begun to change. For the last several years the Office of Management and the Budget (OMB) has made estimates of federal revenue loss from tax expenditures. For 1981 the figure was slightly over $231 billion, or about 38 percent of federal recipts from all sources in that year.[8] The power of the tax code structure (quite apart from the amount of money collected) to shape the nation's allocation of resources should thus not be taken lightly.

Tax Expenditures and Housing

As it happens tax expenditures in support of housing are a much larger sum than direct grants, so let us begin with them. Most writers on the subject of housing have pointed out that the tax treatment of homeownership is a major force in increasing owner-occupied housing as a percent of all housing, and, since the 1940s, a powerful force in the suburbanization of America. It has also been suggested that this tax treatment has increased the total amount of housing in the United States and that it partially accounts for the strong positive relationship between family income and the prevalence of owner-occupied housing. It is also a powerful force in promoting the conversion of existing housing units from rental to condominium and cooperative status.

The tax expenditures for owner-occupied housing arise from provisions of the IRS code, which permit homeowners to deduct mortgage interest and real property taxes from their taxable income. These features of the tax code are not unique to owner-occupied housing in that, in general, interest payments and taxes paid to subnational units of government are deductible from one's federal taxable income.

How does this work? Assume a particular household is in the 30 percent marginal tax bracket and lives in a house for which property taxes are $1000 annually and mortgage interest is $4000. When the household itemizes its federal income tax returns, these two deductions lower its taxable income by $5000 and the amount of the tax it owes to the federal government by $1500 ($5000 × .30). The matter is slightly more complicated in that in order to make use of its housing deductions the household must itemize its deductions rather than use the standard deduction. If it happens that in the absence of the housing deductions the household's itemized deductions would have not have added up to as much as the standard deduction, that difference would have to be subtracted from the $5000 to get the actual reduction in taxable income. For example, the standard deduction for a family is $3200. Assume that its itemizable deductions other than for housing would have been $2800. Then the reduction in taxable income because of the deductibility of the housing expenses is $5000 − (3200 − 2800), which equals $4600. Therefore, the reduction in tax liability is $1380 ($4600 × .30).

In any case, the tax treatment of mortgage interest and real property taxes is a large savings for many households. Estimates by the Office of Management and Budget for 1981 place revenue losses for the federal government from the above deductibility at $28.7 billion—about twice the total of all the expenditures of the Department of Housing and Urban Development (HUD) in that same year.

---

[8] U.S. Office of Management and the Budget, *Special Analysis, Budget of the United States, 1981.* Summary data is reprinted in the *Statistical Abstract of the United States*, Table 433, 1981.

TABLE 7-3
HOUSEHOLD INCOME AND TENURE STATUS, 1980
(Percent)

Tenure status*	Under $10,000	$10,000–24,999	$25,000 and over	Median
Own	23	40	37	$19,800
Rent	48	42	11	$10,600
Condominium	19	35	46	$23,600
Cooperative	35	36	30	$15,400

*Own category excludes condominium and cooperative owners. Figures may not add to 100 percent due to rounding.
Source: U.S. Bureau of the Census, *Annual Housing Survey*, pt. C, 1980.

In connection with deductibility note that the reduction in federal tax liability is a function of two main items: (1) the amount spent on mortgage interest and property taxes, and (2) the marginal tax bracket of the taxpayer. Because of the latter item the incentive to own rises with personal income. This relationship is believed to be a major factor in the strong relationship between home ownership and personal income noted earlier and summarized in Table 7-3. In Canada, where personal income is comparable to that of the United States but where such items are not deductible, the relationship is much weaker.

The Concept of Imputed Rent Some students of housing markets have suggested that there is another tax expenditure in favor of homeowners, possibly on a scale comparable to those just discussed. This is the failure to tax imputed rents. Homeowners can be considered to play two roles: one as investors who have some equity in an asset that yields a stream of salable services (that is, housing services from the house); and another role as renters. Homeowners, in effect, rent the house from themselves. The value of the services they rent to themselves could be imputed from the rental they would collect if they were to rent the house to someone else. We note, parenthetically, that those who have developed the national income accounts take the concept of imputed rent seriously enough to include it in the gross national product.[9]

If we were to treat homeowners as we treat other investors we would count as part of their gross income the value of the housing services their house yields. Thus, if a house could rent on the market for $500 per month we would then consider that the homeowner's gross income was raised by $6000 a year. Then, we would count as expenses property taxes, mortgage interest, maintenance, and depreciation. These would be subtracted from the homeowner's gross income to obtain net income. (Note that we would not count amortization or expenses for capital improvements because these, in effect, represent income that the owner will collect at the time of sale.) If, for example, these expenses came to $300 a month, then we would make a $3600 subtraction from the owner's gross income to arrive at net income. In this illustration the difference of $2400 escapes taxation

[9] Richard Ruggles and Nancy D. Ruggles, "Integrated Economic Accounts for the US, 1947–80," *Survey of Current Business*, Bureau of Economic Analysis, U.S. Department of Commerce, May 1982.

and the tax expenditure would be the product of $2400 multiplied by the owner's marginal tax bracket. For example, at a 30 percent marginal tax bracket the tax expenditure would be $720 ($2,400 × .30).

Some years ago Aaron, using 1966 tax return data, estimated the tax expenditure stemming from the failure to tax imputed rent at about $4 billion.[10] Given that prices have roughly tripled from 1966 to this writing and that the number of owner-occupied units has increased by roughly 40 percent from then to the present, a current estimate in the $15 to $20 billion range might be reasonable.

Again, we note that the value of this tax expenditure goes up very rapidly with income. Not only does the amount of housing consumed rise with income, but the marginal tax bracket rises.

The Effect of Tax Expenditures on Housing Markets

Figure 7-2 shows the effect of tax expenditures on housing markets. The effects can be viewed from either the supply side or the demand side. The supply-side approach is shown in Figure 7-2(*a*). If we view the long-term supply of housing as completely elastic, then there is only a quantity effect. The price remains the same and all of the tax expenditure is captured by the buyer. If we view the supply curve as being of less than infinite elasticity, then the tax expenditure is divided between the buyers of housing and the sellers of housing. In both cases there is an expansion of quantity and a decrease in price. If we view the supply curve as less than infinitely elastic then the tax expenditure is divided between buyer and seller as shown in Figure 7-2(*b*). As the elasticity of supply decreases, the share captured by the seller increases.

Alternatively, we can view the effect of the subsidy as increasing the demand for housing, that is, shifting the demand curve to the right as shown in Figures 7-2(*c*) and (*d*). Again, if we view the long-term supply curve of housing as being infinitely elastic, all of the tax expenditure is captured by the buyers.

In much literature supply is shown as infinitely elastic.[11] The argument is that since housing is built of ubiquitously available materials and with labor that is not in short supply, there is little reason to believe that constraining factors will cause the supply curve to have an upward slope. In the writer's view these observations may be true so far as construction costs are concerned. However, land availability is subject to considerable constraint (see subsequent materials on zoning), and therefore the supply of housing is far from infinitely elastic. In support of this view it should be pointed out that land costs increased more rapidly in the 1970s than any other major housing supply factor.

The increase in the nation's housing inventory promoted by tax expenditures is presumably one factor behind the rapid suburbanization of the nation. That makes it, at one remove, a factor behind the plight of many central cities.

As is suggested at a number of points in this book, the unintended effects of federal policy often have more powerful effects on cities than do specifically urban policies. The magnitude of the tax expenditures just discussed suggests that this is

---

[10] Henry Aaron, *Shelter and Subsidies*, Brookings Institution, Washington, D.C., 1972.
[11] Aaron, Ibid.

(a)

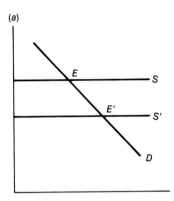

(c)

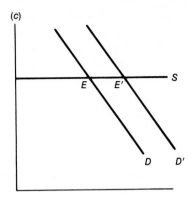

(b)

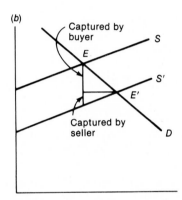

(d)

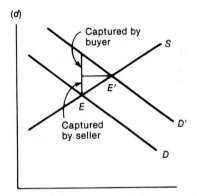

FIGURE 7-2
Tax expenditures and housing demand. (*a*) The tax expenditure is represented by
a decrease in the supply price. Supply is assumed to be infinitely elastic, and
therefore the supply curves are horizontal. The equilibrium moves from *E* to *E'*,
and the buyer captures all the tax expenditure. (*b*) The supply curve is shown
having less than infinite-elasticity. The equilibrium moves from *E* to *E'*. The decrease in price is less than the size of the tax expenditure (represented by the
vertical line from *E* to *S'*). In this case the tax expenditure is divided between buyer and seller. (*c*) The effect of the tax expenditure is represented as a rightward
shift of the demand curve and the supply is assumed to be infinitely elastic. The
equilibrium shifts from *E* to *E'*. Since price is unaffected, the entire tax expenditure is captured by the buyer. (*d*) Supply is represented as less than elastic. In
this case price rises as equilibrium moves from *E* to *E'*, and the tax expenditure is
divided between buyer and seller, as shown.

true. Again, we note that the tax code provisions pertaining to homeowners are
not specifically designed to have spatial consequences. In fact, it is questionable
whether there has ever been any clearly articulated purpose behind them. In
general, interest payments (whether on a house, a car, a boat, a vacation loan,
etc.) are deductible. Similarly, most taxes (sales taxes, personal property taxes,
etc.) paid to subnational units of government are deductible from federal taxable
income. The tax treatment of owner-occupied housing is thus not unique. It was of

little importance until the 1940s when federal tax rates rose sharply to finance World War II and then remained high after the war to finance a variety of military, social, and other federal programs. There is thus a somewhat accidental quality to the situation. There is also, quite obviously, a very large political constituency behind the present tax treatment of owner-occupied housing, which would make it difficult to change regardless of the merits of the case.

Financing Institutions

Whether the tax expenditures described above are the most powerful federal policies favoring the building of owner-occupied housing is arguable, for there are also another set of federal actions that work in the same direction. Unlike the tax expenditures, these have come into being in quite an intentional way. Before the Great Depression there was little federal involvement in housing finance.

> Lenders considered a ten-year home mortgage to be long-term. Many mortgages ran only one, two, or three years, with most of the loan amount due in one large payment at the end of the short term. At the end of this short period, the home purchaser faced great uncertainties. Could he persuade the lender to renew his mortgage? At what interest rate? If he failed to get a renewal, he often lost his home. The standard plots in the melodramas of the time were not entirely fiction: this type of financing greatly contributed to the record level of home mortgages foreclosed during the Great Depression.[12]

Beginning during the early years of the Roosevelt administration and continuing into the 1970s the federal government has created a series of institutions that have changed the face of real estate finance and made home ownership possible for millions of households. To a much lesser degree, it has also facilitated the financing of renter-occupied housing.

Essentially the federal government has intervened in two major ways. First, it has insured mortgages so that lenders are willing to extend financing for much longer terms and with much less owner's equity. Second, it has created secondary markets for mortgages. This means that a bank can sell a mortgage to a federally created agency. The bank continues to "service" the mortgage and collects a small fee for doing so. However, the bank's own funds are not tied up permanently. This tends to make the bank more willing to lend long-term because it reduces the possibility of opportunity cost losses. If a bank lends long-term and interest rates subsequently rise, but its capital is tied up, it can't take advantage of the higher rates. The difference between the actual and the potential interest payments constitutes the opportunity cost. This is simply one instance of the general idea that the true cost of doing anything is the value of that which had to be forgone in order to do it. As we shall see, to a very large degree federal actions brought into being the financial instrument that built much of America's suburbs—the long-term, *low*-fixed-interest-rate, constant-payment, fully amortizing mortgage.

[12] Carter M. McFarland, *Federal Government and Urban Problems*, Westview, Boulder, Colo., 1978, p. 117.

A Brief History of the Federal Presence in Housing Finance A quick history of the federal presence in housing finance follows. It is far from complete but will indicate the main thrust of federal policy. In 1934 the Federal Housing Administration (FHA) came into being, and the following year it began to insure home mortgages against default by the borrower. The importance of FHA insurance stemmed from the fact that where there is no insurance lenders are likely to be more selective in whom they lend to and are not likely to lend for as long a term. They are also likely to demand a large down payment. The latter point motivates the borrower to make every effort not to default and lose his or her equity in the property. It also reduces the lender's "exposure," meaning that if there is foreclosure and subsequent sale of the property at auction the proceeds will be equal to the full amount of the remaining mortgage debt.

FHA insurance was organized along actuarial lines in that payments made by the agency were covered by fees charged to borrowers. Thus there was no subsidy. However, the effect on markets was enormous because of the willingness it created among lenders to write long-term mortgages with low down payment requirements.

The existence of the FHA also increased the availability of mortgage financing by stimulating the formation of private mortgage insurance companies. These insure the top portion of conventional mortgages and work in the following manner. For a fee paid by the borrower the mortgage insurance company will insure a portion of the mortgage, say, 20 percent. This means that if the borrower fails to make the payments, the insurance company will pay the lender a specifed sum. If the insurance is for, say, 20 percent of the purchase price of the property the risk for the bank on a 95 percent mortgage is the same as it would have been for a 75 percent mortgage in the absence of insurance. The existence of mortgage insurance thus expands the demand for owner-occupied housing by bringing into the market buyers who have sufficient income to carry the mortgage but insufficient liquidity for a large down payment.

Although the FHA declined in relative importance in the 1960s and 1970s its effect on home finance has been massive. From 1935 to 1979 it insured some 13 million home loans as well as mortgages covering over 2 million apartments.[13]

Another Depression-era innovation was the Federal National Mortgage Association (FNMA), generally referred to as Fannie Mae. Its original function was to buy FHA-insured mortgages, thus rendering the mortgage a "liquid" investment and making the issuance of such mortgages much more attractive to banks. FNMA is no longer a government agency, but it is still under federal regulation. It is now empowered to issue mortgage-backed securities (MBS) for other than VA and FHA mortgages. These are bonds whose interest payments and principle are paid from payments made by mortgage holders. The issuance of such securities gives the issuers of mortgages access to sources of financing not normally connected with mortgage lending. For example, mortgage-backed securities enable savings and loan associations to compete for the same funds that might have gone into stocks, corporate bonds, or government securities.

[13] For statistics on federal housing programs see Department of Housing and Urban Development, *Yearbook*, annual.

At the end of World War II the Veterans Administration (VA) began to insure home mortgages. Unlike the FHA mortgages the insurance was not issued on actuarial principles, and the lending requirements were somewhat less strict. In some cases 100 percent financing was provided so that buyers could purchase homes with almost no cash up front, again greatly increasing the numbers of potential buyers. FNMA made VA mortgages more attractive to banks by its willingness to purchase them. By 1979 over 10 million home loans had been guaranteed or insured by the VA.

Another agency that provided a framework for private mortgage lending was the Federal Home Loan Bank Board (FHLBB). This organization served to expand and support savings and loan associations (S&Ls) in a variety of ways. First, it insured deposits in these banks, enabling them to compete with other types of banks for deposits and thus accumulate capital for mortgage lending. Second, the FHLBB made loans to member banks so as to relieve temporary liquidity problems. This is analogous to the loans the Federal Reserve Bank makes to member banks through the "discount window." In addition, the board performs a number of monitoring and chartering functions.

Still another agency that furnishes support to private mortgage lenders is the Government National Mortgage Association (GNMA), often referred to as Ginnie Mae. Created in 1968, GNMA is housed within HUD. Unlike FNMA, Ginnie Mae can subsidize construction for designated types of households by purchasing low-interest mortgages at more than their market price, the differential being a subsidy delivered to the lending institution to compensate it for taking a below-market interest rate.

In addition, GNMA creates a market for VA and FHA mortgages by insuring MBSs as described in connection with FNMA. GNMA oversees the process and insures the buyer against failure on the part of the seller to make the payments specified by the security. GNMA makes a small charge for its services sufficient to keep the insurance aspect of its operation on a self-sustaining basis. Mortgages are packaged in blocks of $1 million or more, so most purchasers are financial institutions rather than individuals.

The above discussion is not comprehensive but does indicate the rough extent to which mortgage-lending practices have been shaped by the federal government. Very clearly there has been an intent, dating back almost 50 years, to make mortgage money more available and on better terms than it would otherwise be. As noted, the construction and purchase of housing is highly credit-sensitive, so the net effect on home ownership and total construction volume has been quite significant. If one views the amount of capital available for all purposes as a relatively fixed sum, then the net effect nationally has been to allocate more capital to housing and therefore less capital to other uses. Whether, on balance, this has been a wise decision is arguable.

Inflation, Leverage, and Mortgage Lending

The low-interest, fixed-rate mortgage was tremendously attractive to buyers for several reasons. If buyers believe that the future will be even moderately inflationary they will expect the burden of a fixed-rate mortgage to become lighter over time as personal income rises. Alternatively, they may think of it as being a matter of paying off a debt with payments of decreasing real value. Inflation yields the homeowner a capital gain by reducing the real value of the debt on the property. The lender's loss is the buyer's gain. The more highly leveraged was the purchase the greater will be the rate of return on the initial investment (owner's down payment). The possibility of capital gains through inflation occurs when inflation is "unanticipated" by lenders. This does not mean they literally do not expect inflation, only that they take no steps to protect the value of their assets (the debt that they hold) from inflation. In that meaning, mortgage lenders behaved as if they did not anticipate inflation up until the end of the 1970s.

There is nothing mysterious about the effects of leverage combined with inflation. In fact, if one peruses the spate of books written in the 1960s and 1970s along the general theme of "How to Get Rich in Real Estate Starting with Very Little Capital," they all basically suggest use of highly leveraged investment in an inflationary environment. Nor was such advice proferred only by those on the fringes of economic respectability. One such book was written by Herbert Stein, a well-respected former head of President Nixon's Council of Economic Advisors, and his son.[14]

Let us consider a simple leveraged real estate transaction. In 1970 Ms. X bought a house for $40,000 by putting down $4000 and taking out a mortgage for $36,000. Over the next 9 years real value of the house remained constant but its cash value rose to $80,000 (the consumer price index approximately doubled between 1970 and 1979). Let us simplify matters somewhat by assuming that Ms. X made interest payments only, so the value of her mortgage debt remained $36,000.

If Ms. X sold in 1979 she received $44,000 (80,000 − 36,000). Because of inflation her initial investment of $4000 was leveraged to $44,000, leaving her a capital gain of $40,000 in 1979 dollars. If we convert the results of the transaction into 1970 dollars we see that $4000 in equity was converted to $22,000 in equity ($44,000/2), for a gain of $18,000. Where did this $18,000 come from? It has been lost by the lender, for if we deflate the mortgage debt of $36,000 in 1979 dollars to 1970 dollars we arrive at $18,000. Subtracting this from the initial $36,000 we arrive at a loss, in 1970 dollars, of $18,000. Thus to the financial incentives offered homeowners by favorable tax treatment must be added the financial incentives offered by inflation.

Can we estimate the size of the incentive offered by inflation? The two elements that enter into such an estimate are the magnitude of mortgage debt and the rate of inflation. Let us make a "back-of-the-envelope" estimate for one year, say, 1977. In that year the consumer price index rose by 6.5 percent, a figure slightly below the average annual rate for the 1970–1980 decade. Mortgage debt on one- to four-family homes was $656.4 billion. Since some of those units were in rental use rather than in owner occupancy, let us drop that figure to $500 billion. Applying the above rate of inflation to the adjusted mortgage debt figure we get $469.5 billion ($500 billion × 1/1.065) as the value of $500 billion deflated for 6.5

---

[14] Herbert Stein and Ben Stein, *Moneypower*, Harper & Row, New York, 1980.

percent inflation. Thus one year inflation destroyed roughly $30 billion in the real value of mortgage debt. The gainer was the homeowner and the loser was the lender. For 1977, it would appear that the inflation premium for home ownership was comparable to that from tax expenditures.

Direct Subsidies

We have discussed in some detail the very large indirect subsidies in the form of tax treatment and, stretching the term *subsidy* a bit, our tolerance for inflation. Let us now turn to direct subsidies for housing. These involve much smaller sums of money than tax expenditures. They are also much more subject to short-term change than tax expenditures which are built into the basic structure of the Internal Revenue Service code. We note also that they apply to far fewer units than do the tax expenditures.

There are two basic and quite different reasons for subsidizing housing: (1) we do not think we produce enough housing, or (2) there are some classes of households for whom we believe the cost of acceptable unsubsidized housing is too high.

In the most general way we can divide subsidies into two classes, supply-side and demand-side. In the former case the subsidy is delivered to the supplier in the hope of reducing the cost of the product to the consumer. In the latter case the subsidy is delivered directly to the buyer in order to increase his or her ability or willingness to purchase the product. In more formal terms the former shifts the supply curve to the right, while the latter shifts the demand curve to the right. In addition, subsidies may be either "shallow" or "deep." These terms, which do not have a precise numerical definition, refer to the percentage of the total investment or purchase that is financed by the subsidy. "Deep" implies a larger percentage than "shallow."

If we assume a fixed sum available for subsidy the two goals listed above may imply very different policy options. The first is likely to be best served by relatively shallow subsidies directed to the nonpoor and the latter by a smaller number of deep subsidies directed solely to the poor. For either case we might take the supply-side or the demand-side approach.

It is virtually impossible to confine the benefits of a subsidy solely to the intended beneficiary, the "leaky bucket" effect noted by Arthur Okun.[15] Figure 7-3 shows the price and quantity effects of both supply-side and demand-side subsidies under various conditions. Note that demand-side subsidies, in principle, always produce some increase in price and supply-side subsidies, in principle, always produce some reduction in price.

If the supply curve has zero elasticity (vertical), then there can be no quantity effect. A demand-side subsidy would elevate the market price by the full extent of the subsidy and a supply-side subsidy would decrease the supplier's costs by the full extent of the subsidy. In either case, the subsidy would be a pure windfall for the supplier. At the other extreme, if supply is infinitely elastic (horizontal), then a demand-side subsidy affects only quantity and the entire subsidy is captured by

---

[15] The image comes from Arthur Okun, *Equality and Efficiency, the Big Tradeoff*, Brookings Institution, Washington, D.C., 1975.

(a)

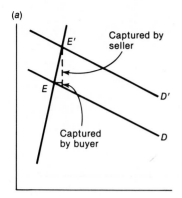

(b)

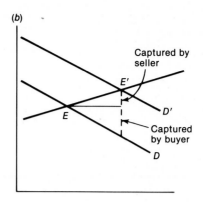

(c)

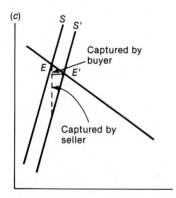

(d)

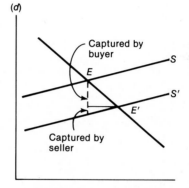

FIGURE 7-3
Price and quantity effects of subsidization. (*a*) A demand-side subsidy whose magnitude is indicated by the broken vertical line. The subsidy shifts the demand curve from *D* to *D'*, moving the equilibrium from *E* to *E'*. Note that the quantity effect is small and that most of the subsidy is captured by the seller, since price increases by almost the full extent of the subsidy. (*b*) *D* and *D'* are shown as in (*a*), but the supply curve is more elastic. In this case the quantity effect is larger and the price rise is smaller. The buyer thus captures a larger share of the subsidy than in the previous figure. (*c*) A supply side subsidy shifts supply from *S* to *S'*. Equilibrium is moved from *E* to *E'*. Note the small change in quantity and the fact that most of the subsidy is captured by the seller. (*d*) The demand curve is represented as in (*c*), but the supply curve is more elastic. Note the greater increase in quantity and the greater share of the subsidy captured by the buyer.

the buyer. A supply-side subsidy simply depresses the market price by the full extent of the subsidy and it, too, is captured in its entirety by the buyer.

Patterns of subsidization have changed as the nation's perception of the housing problem has changed, as experience has been accumulated about what works and what doesn't work and, lastly, with swings in political ideology.

Public Housing   Major public participation in the subsidization of housing began during the Great Depression with the building of public housing. There was a brief period in which the Public Works Administration built public housing directly. This approach encountered legal problems and was supplanted by the public housing law of 1937, which enables the federal government to give financial assistance to local public housing agencies. The assistance takes two forms: loans for construction and annual contributions toward the debt service of local agency bonds, which were issued to repay the federal loans. There is also a tax expenditure in that bonds issued by local agencies are tax-exempt securities. They therefore carry a lower interest rate and thus impose a lower debt service requirement upon the local agency. But that is achieved at the price of revenue loss to the federal government, as discussed earlier in connection with the tax-exempt financing of industry.

There is also a significant local subsidy behind public housing. Because public housing is owned by government or by a nonprofit agency it is exempt from local property taxation. Often, the project will make payments in lieu of taxes, but the payments are generally much smaller than property taxes paid by comparable nonexempt structures. Some of the local opposition to public housing comes from the fiscal burden it often imposes upon the community.

In the typology described above public housing is a deep supply-side subsidy. Since the inception of the program about 1 million units have been built in the United States. Thus at any time only a relatively small portion of the poor benefit from it.

Though often viewed with despair, the record of public housing is not all bad. In many cities there is a long waiting list, indicating that the poor regard it as a better value than they can get in the private market. The problems with it seem largely to have arisen because, with the passage of time and the growing affluence of the country, the population in public housing became a residual population. It thus acquired a concentration of problems that go beyond the question of housing. In the late 1930s the nation's poor included many who were not normally poor and would soon leave poverty. During and immediately after World War II the shortage of housing was so great that the population of public housing projects included a considerable mix of tenants. McFarland notes that Jimmy Carter and his family occupied public housing for a brief time after the war. He then goes on to say:

> But by 1955, a significant change had occurred. Because of sustained national prosperity and low unemployment, the Jimmy Carters of the country no longer needed public housing as a temporary way station. In addition, the massive migration of poor blacks from the rural South to the larger cities was well under way. Increasingly, public housing became the haven of the rural blacks, the culturally deprived, the broken families, the welfare recipients, the permanent poor. Social prejudice produced bitter local resistance to public housing projects and social turmoil within them. As a result, it was difficult for local housing authorities to find sites on which to build. Where sites could be found, the land was expensive. Expensive land made high-rise construction an economic necessity. Too many public housing projects became concentrations of culturally deprived families packed into large, tall structures—an environment ill suited for normal family life (what mother can supervise the play of her children from the twelfth floor?) and very conducive to the disruptive behavior encouraged by the anonymity and monotony in which the deprived families lived.[16]

[16] McFarland, op. cit., p. 131.

The ultimate failure in the field of public housing in the United States was the demolition of the Pruitt Igoe project in St. Louis, Missouri, several thousand units of public housing built adjacent to downtown in 1965. The design was generally admired and, in fact, won an American Institute of Architects award. A majority of its families were female-headed and a majority subsisted on welfare. An overwhelming majority were black, adding a dimension of racial segregation to its other problems. Crime, vandalism, and general despair and disorganization were rampant. As a community, it simply didn't work. After less than a decade HUD ordered the several thousand units of structurally sound, award-winning high-rise construction demolished and the site cleared.

Other Supply-Side Programs   In the early 1960s a series of additional supply-side subsidy programs began to appear. Most of the funds were directed to reducing the cost of supplying housing to those who were above the income limits for public housing but not prosperous enough to afford new unsubsidized housing. Implicit in this approach was the view that the filtering-down process did not work adequately. If filtering did work adequately, then measures designed solely to increase the total output of housing would be sufficient. Implicit in this approach, too, was the major political liability that those above the eligibility limits would be treated to the sight of those poorer than themselves living in new housing while they lived in used housing.

The first of these supply-side approaches was the section 221 (d) (3) program initiated in the Kennedy administration. Under this program mortgages were provided to nonprofit and limited-profit developers at effective rates of 3 percent. Banks were encouraged to make the loans because the FNMA purchased the loans at par value. (If a loan is made at below market rates, its value as a negotiable instrument is less than its face or par value because the same revenue yield can be obtained from a loan with a smaller face value at market interest rates. The subsidy involved is thus the difference between the face value and the value for which the mortgage would sell in a purely market transaction.) Mortgage insurance was provided by FHA at no cost.

In 1965 this was replaced by a program of similar intent, the Rent Supplement Program. Rather than providing the subsidy all at one time through purchasing a mortgage at its par rather than its market value, the subsidy was spread out in the form of annual payments to the builder or owner. One reason for the change was quite unrelated to the relative merits of the two programs. Congress preferred the latter because the subsidy showed up in the federal budget over a period of years rather than all at once.[17] Both programs were relatively shallow supply-side subsidies intended for a means-tested population, namely those of low and moderate income.

In 1968 still another program was introduced. This was the so-called 236 program, named for that section of the National Housing Act. The program essentially reduced the effective interest rate on mortgages for multifamily projects to 1 percent. To be eligible for the program the builder had to meet HUD guidelines regarding rentals and the income of renters. Rent supplement payments

---

[17] McFarland, op. cit., p. 137.

could be provided for up to 20 percent of the tenants in a project, so for them a very deep subsidy was provided.

Section 235 of the same 1968 act also provided subsidies for single-family home ownership by moderate-income families. Here HUD paid the difference between the actual carrying cost of the mortgage and a stated percentage of the family's income. The mortgage was insured by FHA. Thus the federal government assumed both a long-term commitment to subsidize and also the risk of having to repay the lender in event of default by the low- or moderate-income purchaser.

Both programs were successful in achieving their immediate goals in that there were a very large number of multifamily housing starts under section 236 and a large number of families became homeowners under section 235. However, dissatisfaction with the programs mounted. It was claimed that section 236 reached only a small proportion of those in need, that it furnished inordinate tax shelters to wealthy investors, and that it committed the federal government to massive housing expenditures for decades to come. There were also charges of corruption and mismanagement. The section 235 program ran into its own set of problems. Speculators bought housing in rundown areas and resold it to low-income buyers at more than market value. Banks were willing to grant mortgages under very risky conditions because of their guaranteed status. The FHA, apparently staggering under the expanded work load stemming from the program, was less than careful in appraising the properties whose mortgages it guaranteed. Many low-income familes, unused to home ownership and possessing little equity due to minimal down payment requirements, failed to make their monthly mortgage payments. The result was a large number of defaults, and HUD soon found itself in possession of a large number of relatively low quality single-family houses.

The Demand-Side Approach   In 1973, distressed at the problems with supply-side assistance, President Nixon called a moratorium on all federal housing assistance programs. After some months, a demand-side approach to housing subsidy emerged.

The underlying philosophy was to give the poor money, which they would then take into the market to use in purchasing housing. This approach appeared to promise administrative simplicity and to avoid some of the pitfalls of the section 235 and section 236 programs. In addition, it appeared to maximize consumer choice and, in this sense, was in keeping with a relatively conservative political philosophy. The centerpiece of the Nixon approach was section 8 of the Housing and Community Development Act of 1974. This program had two main components. The section 8 existing housing program provided payments to landlords, which made up the gap between the fair-market rent for the housing unit and 25 percent of the tenant's income. Though the payment was made to the landlord the intent was to provide tenants with a sum they could take into the housing market and spend on the unit of their choice. The way it worked out is somewhat more complex. For tenants who remained in their presubsidy unit the payment was simply a disguised cash transfer (see the appendix on welfare economics in Chapter 6). The other half of the section 8 program was designed to accelerate construction of new housing for low- and moderate-income families. Essentially,

HUD guaranteed builders that it would make up the difference between fair-market rents and the rents that low-income tenants could pay, subject to the rule that rental payments by tenants would not exceed 25 percent of income.

The Present Status of Housing Assistance At present, section 8 subsidizes housing for about 1.2 million families, at a cost in 1982 of about $1.6 billion.[18] Beyond that there are somewhat over 1 million families in public housing. Although the construction of public housing has ceased, both capital subsidies (payments to help local public housing authorities retire bonds) and operating subsidies will continue into the next century. Current expenditures on public housing are over $1 billion annually.

Altogether HUD subsidizes about 3.5 million housing units at a cost in the $4 billion range. Although legislation may at any time abolish an existing program or initiate a new program, the overall direction of HUD subsidy programs does not change quickly. This is because of the stability (the cynical might say "inertia") that comes from long-term contractual commitments. For example, in order to induce builders to construct section 8 new housing HUD offered 20-year commitments to make the supplementary payments described above. These commitments begin with completion of the project. Thus a building for which the contracts between builder and HUD were signed in 1979 and which was ready for occupancy in 1983 will be a cause of federal expenditures to the year 2003. Similarly, section 8 existing commitments to tenants run 20 years and are portable. The tenant takes the subsidy when he or she moves. If the household's income rises past the upper limit, it may lose the subsidy, but if not, the commitment is binding on HUD for the next 20 years. One might note the work-disincentive effect mentioned in Chapter 6.

At present the section 8 program is in process of being modified. The current initiative would end the making of commitments under the present program and initiate a related program referred to as the modified section 8 certificate program. The program would move section 8 further in the direction of a pure income transfer and would also be more tightly targeted than the current programs. Under this program recipient income could not be more than one-half the median income in that market area. For most of the country this would be equivalent to confining the program to families at or below the poverty line. Essentially, the program would give the family in question a voucher payable to any landlord redeemable in cash from HUD. Unlike the present situation there would be no stipulations regarding how much of the recipient's own income would be spent on housing.

In principle it is difficult to differentiate this program from a pure transfer program. Theoretically it would differ only in the rare instance in which the amount of the voucher was larger than the total sum the recipient would otherwise spend on housing. Presumably it is ideologically more in keeping with the position of the Reagan administration. Obviously, the economic freedom of the recipient is maximized and federal interaction minimized by assistance in as untied a form as possible. The omission of any program component specifically designed to

---

[18] For statistics on federal housing expenditures, number of units or households assisted, etc., see Department of Housing and Urban Development, *Yearbook*, annual.

stimulate new construction for the poor is, according to HUD personnel, a response to the very high cost of providing new housing for the poor. Section 8 new-housing subsidies now cost about twice as much per unit as section 8 existing-housing subsidies.

Housing Assistance Payments: Theory and Evidence

In principle, unless there are quite restrictive stipulations attached to how an allowance is to be spent we should expect that the payment will be handled as a pure income transfer. The percentage increase in expenditures on housing will depend on the recipient's income elasticity of demand for housing and the percentage by which the transfer increases his or her income. The absolute increase in expenditure on housing will be that percentage increase multiplied by the amount being spent—pretransfer—on housing. Consider the following example.

The X household has an income of $600 per month and spends $200 a month on rent. Assume that its income elasticity of demand for housing is .7 and that it will receive a voucher for $100 a month. The family's income rises by 100/600 × 100 = 16.7 percent. Applying the presumed elasticity of demand for housing to that figure we have 16.7 percent × .70 = 11.7 percent. Housing expenditures now rise by 11.7 percent of $200 or $23.40. Thus to the nearest whole percent, 23 percent of the subsidy has gone into the consumption of housing and 77 percent into the consumption of other things.

There are some assumptions in the above. Housing is a somewhat "lumpy" good in that a person cannot buy it in finely calibrated amounts but can choose between this unit and that unit. We also note that market transactions are not costless in that house-hunting and moving take time and money. Therefore the smoothly flowing adjustment pictured above is not quite realistic. It should be taken as a paradigm for how a group of households might adjust over the passage of several years.

One point stands out. It is very difficult to make any set of plausible assumptions that do not show the major share of the housing allowance being spent on nonhousing items.

By contrast consider a supply-side approach. Assume that the price elasticity of demand for the household in question is −.7. Again, assume the same level of expenditure on rent. Further, assume a supply-side subsidy equal to 20 percent of price (rent), which thus lowers rents by 20 percent. The amount of additional housing consumed will increase by 20 × .7 × 100 = 14 percent. The amount of housing consumed will thus rise to $228. The cost of the subsidy will be .20 × $228 = $45.60. The amount of the subsidy going into housing will be $28/$45.60 × 100 = 61 percent. Again, the numbers are arbitrary but plausible. They illustrate that a supply-side (cost-reducing) approach is likely to direct a much larger percentage of the subsidy into the designated activity.

The above is not to say that supply-side programs are better than demand-side programs. In fact, if the goal is simply to increase the general welfare of the poor the demand-side program, which more nearly approximates a pure transfer system, may be better. It allows the recipient to use the funds in the manner that he or she deems best, and it probably involves fewer leakages and windfalls to the nonpoor. The writer's impression is that the majority of economists would prefer the voucher approach.[19] The only question one must confront is why not simply adopt a "truth-in-packaging" position and call it a transfer program?

However, if one's view is that the goal of the program is specifically and solely to improve the quality of the housing, then a voucher system will not appear to be efficient. A supply-side program, with all its potential for leakages and windfalls, may still be preferable. The real question, then, is not so much one of mechanics but of fundamental goals.

When the voucher system was submitted to a rather elaborate test (see Box 7-1)

BOX 7-1

A TEST OF THE VOUCHER SYSTEM

To test the effects of a voucher system the Experimental Housing Allowance Program (EHAP) was authorized by Congress in 1970. It ran for several years, cost approximately $160 million, and involved 30,000 households. In dollar terms it may well have been the largest social science or social policy experiment ever conducted in the United States.[20]

Randomly selected poor families in a number of test areas were offered vouchers if they would agree to a variety of reporting and inspection requirements. In some cases the amount of the voucher was based on the difference between expert estimate of the cost of adequate housing in that area and some fraction of the family's income. In other cases the size of the voucher was determined by taking a percentage of the rent the family was paying at the start of the experiment. In order to receive the voucher the family was required to live in a unit meeting certain physical standards set by the experimenters. If the unit in which the family lived at the start of the experiment did not meet such standards, then either it had to be brought up to standard or the would-be recipient had to find alternative quarters.

The term *voucher* is arguable here because of its use in regard to this experiment. In its ordinary meaning a voucher is an authorization that the recipient can give to a vendor as payment or partial payment for some good or service. In this experiment, however, the payments went from HUD directly to the household and were not transmitted as such to the landlord. For the household that lived in standard housing at the start of the program the payment was simply a cash transfer by another name. For the household living in substandard housing at the start of the experiment the payment was not quite a pure transfer, in that in order to receive it the recipient had to perform certain actions. Specifically, the recipient had to either get his or her own unit up to code or move to another unit that is up to code. On the basis of this lack of complete freedom the experimenters termed the grants vouchers.

A number of results were obtained from the experiment. One central finding was that among renter households the income elasticity of demand for housing was quite low—generally in the .3 to .4 range. Thus a very small percentage of the total sum transferred to renters was actually spent on rent. The elasticities found in the experiment were about half those that recent literature on elasticities suggested they ought to be. However, the findings in this study were supported by an analysis of data from the SIME and DIME experiments discussed in connection with income transfer in Chapter 6.

In some communities the experiments tried to achieve high enough participation rates to assess the effect of a national subsidy program upon rents. One argument against demand-side subsidies has been that they may elevate housing prices, with the result that those of the poor who do not receive aid are actually hurt by them (see Figure 7-3). No elevation in prices attributable to the vouchers was detected.

---

[19] See the conclusion of John C. Weicher, "Urban Housing Policy," in Mieskowski and Straszheim (eds.), op. cit.

[20] For a detailed description of the experiment see Raymond J. Struyk and Marc Bendick, Jr., *Housing Vouchers for the Poor*, Urban Institute, Washington, D.C., 1981.

several interesting results emerged. One was that the income elasticity of demand for housing among the subjects of the experiment was quite low, generally in the range of .3 or .4. Why this is so is not known with certainty. One possibility is that at very low income levels, where people are more pressed to provide for other necessities, the income elasticity of demand for housing is actually very low. Another possibility is that because participants in the experiment knew that the allowances would not continue indefinitely they responded more cautiously. The Friedman permanent-income hypothesis would support this interpretation.[21] Essentially, Friedman suggests that consumption patterns are not so much a function of income in a given short-term period but rather a function of both past earnings and expectations of future earnings. Still another possibility is that housing expenditures by households are "sticky" for some reason and adjust to income changes more slowly than do other types of expenditures. Perhaps the duration of leases and the time and money costs of moving contribute to this stickiness.

Another finding of the study was that the vouchers produced no discernible elevating effect upon rents. This can be considered a point in favor of the demand-side approach. However, a plausible interpretation is that such a small share of the total subsidy actually went into housing that the effect upon rents was necessarily small. Two other points could also be made. One is that housing markets may adjust sluggishly for reasons noted above. Another is one made by Anthony Downs. Much of the rental housing stock is in the hands of entrepreneurs who own very few—sometimes only one—unit. These owners may be, in his terms, "turnover minimizers" rather than "rent maximizers." If you own only one unit and it is empty you have a 100 percent vacancy rate regardless of the general state of the market.[22] This is another reason for believing that changes in demand manifest their effects very slowly. For these reasons the experiment may not have registered the full effect of increases in demand upon prices.

Clearly, there is room for some speculation about the precise meaning of all the experiment's results. However, on balance, the results of the experiment strongly suggest that a national housing voucher system would deliver relatively little of its total effect to the housing market.

Subsidies, Tax Expenditures, and the Rental-Housing "Crisis"

Looking back at the situation up to, say, 1980 we see the following. For those who had sufficient capital and income to become owners there were very powerful indirect subsidies available. These took the form of favorable tax treatment on interest and local taxes, failure to tax imputed rent, and, lastly, the capital gains to be afforded by the combination of inflation and long-term, low-interest, fixed-rate mortgages. As noted, the tax benefits were skewed to the upper-income owner because of the progressivity of the federal income tax. By the end of the 1970s the annual sum of all the items mentioned above may have been, very roughly, in the $100 billion range.

---

[21] Milton Friedman, *A Theory of the Consumption Function*, Princeton University Press, Princeton, N.J., 1957.
[22] See comments by Anthony Downs in John C. Weicher, Kevin E. Villani, and Elizabeth A. Roistacher (eds.), *Rental Housing: Is There a Crisis?* Urban Institute, Washington, D.C., 1981.

At the other end of the spectrum was a much smaller sum of direct subsidy that was generally targeted quite tightly to lower-income individuals. This included federal expenditures on public housing, both supply-side and demand-side subsidies connected with the 236 program, rental-assistance programs, the section 8 programs, and a number of smaller federal programs not mentioned in text. In rough terms direct federal subsidies aided somewhat under 4 million households. A number of state programs also assisted the poor or near-poor. The class of households not aided are nonpoor renters.

If we bear in mind the preceding discussion of housing finance many of the trends of the 1970s make a good deal of sense. Tax policy and inflation created very powerful incentives to own. Alternatively, we can state that the opportunity costs of renting became extremely high for many households, particularly upper-income households. One fact we observed, particularly in the latter part of the decade was that house prices increased more rapidly than either personal income or the consumer price index. This was true of used as well as new units. One way to explain this is that the expectation of further inflation shifted the demand curve for housing out to the right because of the inflation-leverage effect discussed earlier. Housing was attractive not only because of the possibility of capital gain but also because it appeared as one of the few ways in which the ordinary middle or upper-middle-income person could protect the real value of his or her capital. Interest is taxed as income but the accumulating equity in real property is not taxed until sale. At that point it is taxed at the lower rate for capital gains. (Currently, long term capital gains are taxed at 40 percent of the rate for earned income.)

The fact that the increase in rents probably lagged behind both the rise in the consumer price index and the rise in personal income may be explained by the leftward shift in the demand curve for rental units accruing from the very large opportunity costs of renting. The paradox that rents lagged behind the increase in personal income and yet rent/income ratios rose begins to make sense. If the advantages of owning versus renting pulled renters into owner status, it presumably did so selectively. Thus renters as a class become poorer, not because they lost income as individuals but because the wealthier members of the group left. The commonsense arguments regarding the relative attractiveness of owning versus renting are supported by some evidence on income elasticity of demand. In the early 1970s DeLeuw estimated the income elasticity for owner-occupied housing at between 1.25 and 1.46, while he placed that for renter-occupied housing at .80—a very large difference.[23] The rapid increase in the price of owner-occupied housing during the 1970s strongly suggests that the disparities in elasticities may have increased during the 1970s.

The marked slowdown in rental construction as the decade wore on is a natural outcome of weakening demand. Ownership of rental property clearly became less profitable as the decade progressed. Anthony Downs states:

> my overwhelming impression in talking to housing developers is that, in most parts of the country, they cannot get rents high enough to pay for the cost of building and

---

[23]Frank de Leuw, "The Demand for Housing: A Review of Cross-Sectional Evidence," *Review of Economics and Statistics*, February 1971. Vol. LIII, pp. 1–10.

operating new rental units. That may be true in part because cost elements such as interest, energy and property taxes have gone up much faster than consumer prices generally, and therefore faster than rents. However, a more important reason is the lure of homeownership.[24]

Another writer on the subject, Ira Lowry, states:

> The level of discontent among landlords also rose during the decade. They complain that the cost of supplying rental housing rose faster than did rental revenue. I estimate that rental property operating cost rose by 9.2 percent annually, 1970–1980, a rate that compounds to an increase of 141 percent for a decade in which rental revenue rose by 87 percent. The net operating return—income available for depreciation, debt service, and equity returns—increased by 34 percent in current dollars.
>
> The 34 percent increase in net operating return can be assessed from several perspectives, all yielding gloomy conclusions for rental property investors. Considered as income to the property owner, the purchasing power of net operating return decreased by 37 percent because of general price inflation. . . . Finally, considering the 34 percent increase in net operating return as an average value reminds us that many properties must have yielded less. In those cases, refinancing at current interest rates would create a severe cash flow problem for the owner, impeding property sale or major capital improvement.[25]

A phenomenon that is consistent with both the profit squeeze on rental housing and the tax and speculative advantages of owning—two interdependent phenomena—has been the conversion of rental housing to condominium or cooperative status. Though they differ in legal detail, both forms of ownership make property taxes and mortgage interest deductible from federal and state income taxes, and both, in general, permit the individual owner to capture the capital gains accruing from inflation or increase in the real value of the property. When property owners convert and sell their buildings to individual owners they are, in effect, selling something that is not theirs—namely, the right to benefit from tax expenditures provided by the IRS code. This is one reason that the combined value of the units as cooperative or condominium units often far exceeds their combined value as rental units. Quoting Lowry again:

> The remarkable feature of these conversions is that the change in tenure sometimes doubles or triples the market value of a property. Under those circumstances, conversion generates enough cash to retire the former owner's mortgage, reimburse displaced tenants, and brighten the lives of any number of middlemen. Not uncommonly, the purchasers of these dwellings face annual costs that are twice the preconversion rents. Why are consumers willing to pay so much more as owners than they would have to pay for equivalent rental quarters? The answer seems to lie in a magical combination of income tax advantages and the expectation of highly leveraged capital gains.[26]

The conversion process is selective in that it tends to be those who are in relatively high tax brackets who find it financially advantageous. Then, too, as Lowry notes, purchase may involve a trade-off between higher immediate costs and the prospect of a long-term capital gain. It is the more prosperous tenant to whom that trade-off will be attractive. For the poor person, perhaps subsisting

---

[24] Weicher, et al., p. 87.
[25] Weicher, et al., p. 28.
[26] Weicher, et al., Ibid., p. 29.

BOX 7-2

CRISIS IS IN THE EYE OF THE BEHOLDER

Lowry quotes a report by the U.S. General Accounting Office as follows:

> Millions of Americans cannot afford home ownership and cannot find affordable rental housing. Immediate national attention is necessary if an adequate supply of rental housing is to be available. The Department of Housing and Urban Development is the principal federal agency responsible for providing assistance for rental housing. The Congress and the administration should take steps to mitigate this nationwide crisis.[27]

The report cited as evidence such points as:

1 A March 1979 rental vacancy rate of 4.8 percent, the lowest on record
2 Large numbers of units lost to abandonment and conversion
3 Falling unsubsidized rental construction
4 Rising rent/income ratios
5 Falling profit margins on rental housing
6 Aging of the rental housing stock (essentially owing to low rates of construction)

Many of the same facts can, however, be viewed in a very different light. Lowry quotes from the "Report of the Pollyanna Institute," as follows:

> The past two decades have seen steady improvement in the housing circumstances of renters, especially those with low incomes. Rents in constant dollars have dropped, per capita housing consumption by renters has increased, and the incidence of both overcrowding and major housing defects has decreased sharply. Millions of single adults, formerly constrained to live with relatives, have been able to afford separate homes—either living alone or with friends. The supply of suburban rental dwellings has increased, widening the locational options of those who prefer renting to owning. And for renters who prefer owning, the opportunities have seldom been better[28]

The Pollyanna report cites the following in support of its rosy view.

1 From 1960 to 1980 consumer prices rose by 179 percent, but rents rose by only 108 percent.
2 In rental housing the rooms to person ratio rose from 1.32 in 1960 to 1.73 in 1978.
3 From 1960 to 1978 the number of rental units occupied by single individuals more than doubled.
4 The increases in rental stock in the last two decades have largely been in the suburbs, thus broadening locational choice for those who will not or cannot be owners.
5 Each year from 1960 to 1978 an average of 375,000 "obsolete or inappropriately located" rental units were removed from the housing inventory. In spite of this, the number of rental units in the nation rose by 6.4 million.

---

partly on transfers, capital gains and tax expenditures do not mean very much. As indicated in Table 7-3 the median family income of condominium owners is more than twice that of renters and more than that of owners generally. In some areas rent control has given the conversion process a further push by depressing the

---

[27] U.S. General Accounting Office, *Rental Housing: A National Problem That Needs Immediate Action*, Report to Congress by the Comptroller General, CED-80-11, November, 1979, quoted in Weicher, op. cit., p. 23.

[28] Weicher et al. p. 25.

earnings on rental property and making owners pessimistic about the long-term income prospects of their properties. In fact, the writer has heard condominium conversion referred to under this circumstance as "the most sophisticated form of abandonment." For owners taking a cash flow loss on a controlled building the prospect of walking away with a postconversion capital gain in their pocket, rather than facing a long-term slide into bankruptcy or abandonment, is most attractive.

The status of rental housing created serious concern in the late 1970s and some went so far as to describe it as a crisis (see Box 7-2). Those who cried "crisis" point to low construction rates, losses through abandonment at the low of end of the spectrum and conversion at the high end of the spectrum, low vacancy rates, and rising rent income ratios. Those who took a more sanguine view pointed to long-term increases in quality, decreases in crowding, and rent levels that rose more slowly than prices in general. In the short term the movement of large numbers of relatively prosperous renters into owner-occupied units opens up good rental housing for low-income tenants at moderate rents. The worrisome question in the longer term is whether that housing will remain good. If rents lag behind operating costs the only way property owners can show a positive cash flow is to disinvest—to spend less on maintenance than is necessary to keep the real value of the structure constant. In effect, they convert capital into income and shift their present problem into the future. There was thus serious concern over the long-term future of much of the nation's rental stock.

If rental housing is unable to generate the cash flow for adequate maintenance its future is dim. It is not a uniquely urban problem, but rental housing tends to be proportionately more imporant in the housing stock of central cities than suburbs or nonmetropolitan areas. It is also a larger part of the housing stock of older, preautomobile cities than of newer, lower-density, postautomobile cities. Thus the problem, though not confined to cities, does have something of an urban bias. To some extent it has been created by all of the centrifugal, suburbanizing, antiurban forces resulting from technological change and rising real income that have been discussed earlier. But, at least in recent years, it has been exacerbated by public policy—tax policy, housing finance policy, and in the loosest sense of the word "policy," the implicit willingness of society to tolerate inflation.

HOUSING FINANCE SINCE 1980

At the end of the 1970s the financial underpinnings of the housing market began to change. The rate of inflation accelerated, and with it went interest rates. The interest rate on new conventional mortgages almost doubled from 1970 to 1981. The immediate effect of the climb in interest rates was a sharp drop in the rate of construction. Rental construction was hit extremely hard by the combined effect of higher interest rates, increasing operating costs, and the diminished rent-paying capacity discussed earlier.

A more long-term effect of the rise in interest rates, however, has been a restructuring of the process of housing finance. The "unanticipated" inflation of the late 1970s imposed very large losses on lenders that could not be ignored. One loss, as noted earlier, is the capital loss that occurs when a debt is repaid in depreciated currency. The second is the opportunity cost that must be borne when capital is committed at low rates for a long period of time and interest rates subsequently rise. For those lenders whose assets were composed largely of low-interest, fixed-rate mortgages the rise in interest rates threatened bankruptcy. In fact, among savings and loan institutions, banks that specialize in mortgage lending, bankruptcies and mergers to avoid bankruptcy rose to levels not seen since the Great Depression. In 1981, 85 percent of all S&Ls in the United States operated at a deficit. Total losses for the industry for that year were $3.1 billion.[29] The net outflow of deposits from these institutions was much larger still. The threat to such institutions has a very simple explanation. The key point is that the bank borrows on a short-term basis (deposits made by the public) in order to lend long-term on mortgages. Consider the bank that borrowed from its depositors at 5 percent during the 1970s and lent that money on 8 percent mortgages. The 3 percent spread covered operating costs and profits. Depositors (lenders) can withdraw their funds at any time, but borrowers cannot be compelled to repay ahead of schedule. As long as the interest rate the bank must pay to borrow new funds remains stable the spread remains and all is well. As interest rates rise the rate the bank must pay to borrow in order to cover withdrawals rises and the spread narrows. If rates rise enough the spread becomes a negative. If a large proportion of the bank's assets are composed of mortgages, as is the situation with savings and loan institutions, bankruptcy looms.

In any case lenders now take steps to protect themselves from a repetition of recent experience. If they lend at a fixed rate the figure is (as of the fall of 1983) in the 13 percent range, a figure that is prohibitive for many potential buyers or investors. (A year earlier the figure had been in the 16 percent range.) If they lend at somewhat lower rates they usually insist on contractual arrangements, which index the interest rate against some agreed-upon standard such as the rate on federal securities. The adjustable rate mortgage or ARM transfers the risk of interest rate rises to the borrower and thus makes borrowers a good deal more wary. One might observe that it also enables borrowers to take advantage of lower rates if they should occur. But to some degree they have always had that option through the process of refinancing.

Another new mortgage instrument is the shared-appreciation mortgage (SAM). This device permits the lender to claim part of the capital gain on the sale of the property, in effect protecting the lender against the loss of value that occurs from being paid back in nominal dollars of diminished real value. Other instruments presumably will continue to evolve. At this writing, a large amount of seller financing is taking place, building up an enormous amount of privately held debt, with consequences yet to be seen.

Home ownership still offers the advantages of tax treatment, though these have been weakened somewhat for upper-income households by the Reagan cuts in marginal tax brackets. However, the opportunity to make capital gains from the combination of inflation and long-term, low-interest, fixed-rate financing is severely diminished. In addition, the cost of carrying property until that gain has been realized has gone up drastically.

---

[29] *The New York Times*, April 6, 1982, p. 1.

Assuming that the era of the long-term, low-interest, fixed-rate mortgage is over, what are some consequences we might reasonably expect to see? One is that construction rates will be lower. If we are to get continued improvement in housing quality it will have to come more from renovation than replacement. The rate at which household size falls will have to diminish somewhat. The processes of suburbanization and regional population shift will have to slow somewhat, since growth in the housing stock in the receiving areas is the necessary condition for such shifts. The rate at which new housing construction draws off the more affluent renters should also slow. High rates should exert downward pressure on housing prices in the short run, making the 1970s situation in which housing prices outran the CPI relatively unlikely. However, in the long term a sustained period of low construction rates will exert upward pressure on prices, just as any force which limits supply elevates prices. Since the rate of production in year X affects prices not only in year X but also in year X + 1 and X + 2, etc., a possible sequence of events would be for high interest rates to exert downward pressure on prices in the short run but upward pressure over the long run.

For one concerned with the future of rental housing, the changes in housing finance are a mixed blessing. If owner-occupied housing loses some of its speculative lure, the demand for rental housing will increase. This will elevate rents, improve owners' cash flow, and lead to improved quality. Of course, not all tenants, particularly those with lower incomes, will be happy with all of these effects. The effect on rent/income ratios is not so clear. Rising rents would tend to raise these ratios, but slowing the movement of the more affluent renters into owner-occupied properties would tend to lower them. The diminished attractiveness of owner-occupied housing presumably would increase rental construction as a percentage of all residential construction. The increased cost of capital, however, should depress total residential construction compared to rates in the 1970s, so even if the rental share went up, the absolute number of rental units built might be lower.

To compound the uncertainty of the above let us note that the painful effects of high mortgage rates have already generated powerful political pressures upon the federal government to intervene in credit markets to provide cheap housing credit. The pressures come from a variety of points in the political and economic spectrum, including those on both the supply side and the demand side of the housing market. In fact, a bill to use federal funds to write down mortgage interest rates for buyers of new homes passed both houses of Congress in the summer of 1982 but was vetoed by President Reagan. (A number of states do have programs in which the state's ability to borrow in tax-exempt markets is used to provide below-market mortgages for buyers under some income limit.) Thus, in predicting the future of housing finance the uncertainty stemming from the difficulty of forecasting economic trends is compounded by uncertainty concerning the extent to which the federal government will intervene in housing credit markets.

CHAPTER 8

PUBLIC INTERVENTION
IN HOUSING MARKETS

In this chapter we turn to direct public intervention in urban and metropolitan housing markets. Specifically, we discuss land-use controls, rent controls, and, as the prototype of government as entrepreneur, urban renewal. All are or have been important as matters of public policy and all raise interesting theoretical questions.

LAND-USE CONTROLS

Zoning laws, subdivision regulations, and building codes constitute the primary means communities have to directly control what is built within their borders.[1] The legal basis of zoning resides in what is generally referred to as the police power of the community, a somewhat misleading term that refers to the community's right to make and enforce legislation for the general purpose of promoting the health, safety, and welfare of its populace. A series of court decisions since the early years of this century has established the right of the community to substantially regulate the use of privately owned land.

Let us examine zoning first. The two documents that express the zoning of land in a community are the zoning ordinance and the zoning map. These acquire the force of law when they are adopted by resolution of the municipality's governing body. They may be prepared by the municipality's planning department or, more

---

[1] For a brief discussion of the development of zoning and the judicial history of the public control of private property see Frank So et al. (eds.), *The Practice of Local Government Planning*, International City Managers Association, 1979, chaps. 14 and 15.

commonly, by a planning consultant. The ordinance specifies the characteristics of structures that may be built in various zones and the uses to which those structures and the properties on which they are located may be put. For example, the ordinance might specify that in a R-40 zone single-family houses are permitted on lots of at least 40,000 square feet; that the house must be set back at least so many feet from the building line, so many feet from the side lot line and so many feet from the near lot line; that the lot must have a minimum frontage of so many feet; that the building height may not exceed so many feet (or stories); that there may or may not be accessory structures on the lot; etc. If any commercial uses—such as physicians' offices—are permitted in the zone, these will also be specified. A commercial zone would specify what types of uses were permitted, setbacks, parking requirements, maximum building heights, maximum ground coverage, maximum permitted ratio of floor area to land area, or floor area to ratio (FAR), etc. Within the community there may be several dozen different zones.

The zoning map locates these various zones on a base map of the community. Thus, between the ordinance and the map it is possible to state quite specifically what is permitted on any parcel of land within the community.

Subdivision requirements are a related form of public control of land use. These are a set of requirements pertaining to the subdivision of land into separate parcels. Subdivision requirements may regulate such matters as road width and turning radii, provision of easements (rights-of-way) for public utilities, dedication of land for public purposes, etc. Most subdivision regulations apply to the subdividing of land for residential uses.

Many municipalities make legislative provisions for site plan review. For sites of over a certain size the law provides for a review procedure before development can proceed. The review may cover internal circulation, buffering, drainage provisions for storm water, adequacy of parking facilities, etc. Site plan review procedures generally apply to commercial or multifamily development.

Finally, many municipalities have an adopted master plan. The master plan, usually a combination of text and maps, provides a general statement of the desired pattern of development of the community. It does not specify land use in quite the detail of a zoning map, but by articulating a community vision of development it does provide some legal support for the zoning ordinance. For example, if a municipality's zoning ordinance is challenged in court, the fact that it is in conformity with an adopted master plan lends it support and helps defend it against charges of irrationality or capriciousness. The other function of a master plan is that it may serve to guide the pattern of public capital investment and, in this sense, helps to shape the long-term pattern of land use.

Most municipalities also having building codes. These embody construction standards such as fire resistance, insulation, structural strength, depth of foundations and footings, etc. Before beginning construction, builders must show that their plans are in conformity with the code. During construction there will generally be periodic inspections to ascertain that plumbing, wiring, etc. are being done according to the standards specified in the code. When the building is completed, a final inspection for conformity to code is generally required before a certificate of occupancy is granted.

Some Basic Properties of Zoning

Several basic points about zoning should be noted.

1 Zoning is a partial replacement for the judgment of the market. It is only partial because zoning has the ability to forbid or limit but not the capacity to cause. Buildings are not constructed because the law permits them, but some buildings may fail to be constructed because the law does not permit them.

2 Zoning implies the ability of the community to impose *uncompensated* losses upon property owners. If the forbidden uses are more profitable than any of the allowed uses, the property owner suffers a loss for which no compensation need be given, an important point to which we will return.

3 Land-use controls are not retroactive. Structures built before the passage of zoning laws or subdivision requirements need not conform to them. For this reason land-use controls are often of far more importance in growing rather than in older and stable areas. Thus in all probability zoning has had far more effect on suburban land use than on urban land use. In nonurban areas zoning is often absent or of a rudimentary nature. The low population density and the physical distance between different land uses give the municipality the impression, correct or otherwise, that there is not a pressing case for major public intervention in land markets.

4 Zoning and other land-use controls are not immutable. The ordinance can always be amended so that property may be rezoned. In addition almost any zoning ordinance will specify a set of procedures by which variances, or exceptions to the law, may be granted. Finally, the ultimate arbiter of zoning is the courts. Although communities have the power to regulate land use, this power is not unlimited, and the courts may well find that the municipality has overstepped its legal powers.

Zoning as an Economic Phenomenon

Zoning is often viewed as a legal process and, indeed, there is a large literature and a large body of legal precedent on the subject. Zoning can also be viewed as a planning or administrative process, and there is a large body of literature on this score. However, zoning can also be regarded as an economic phenomenon. On this point the literature is much less voluminous.

In the most general way we could say that zoning is an attempt by the municipality to deal with externalities. In the transaction between landowner and buyer the interests of third parties are not represented. The landowner who is approached by the builder of Go Kart racing tracks presumably will consider only the offer made for the sale or rent of his property. If he fits the model of economic man, a rational being seeking to maximize his own utility, the interests of the neighbors in peace and quiet will not weigh in his calculations. A zoning law prohibiting the building and operation of Go Kart tracks in residential areas protects the third-party interest, which would otherwise go unrepresented. In general, if the development and use of land involved no externalities it would be difficult to justify zoning and other land-use controls.

Zoning and Land Costs   One major aspect of zoning is its effect on land values. Zoning cannot make development occur where the underlying economic forces do not justify it, but it can rule out types of development and reduce the intensity of what development does occur. If land value comes from the capitalized value of the stream of income which that land can generate, then by limiting either the range or the intensity of use zoning can reduce land values. In the hypothetical situation in Figure 8-1 the supply curve represents a particular parcel in the hands of a landowner. It is therefore shown as completely inelastic.

The various demand curves represent the demand for land in that municipality. We assume that only those demand curves for use for which the site is suitable are shown. If there is no public interference, the property will be sold or rented at the price represented by the highest intersection on the figure. Assume, now, that zoning limits the permitted use to single-family houses. The property owner's loss is the distance between points E_1 and E_3. This is the uncompensated loss we noted earlier.

Just as zoning may impose losses it may also create windfall gains. The value of A's property may rise if zoning prevents B from using his property in a way that would impinge unfavorably on A's property. If community X enacts a zoning code which prohibits the building of warehouses that is likely to enhance the value of warehouses in community Y.

The effect of land-use controls on land costs is complex in part because the act of zoning in a given place may have many different price effects. Community X is one town in the suburban ring of an SMSA. Assume it zones very restrictively, that is, for a much lower level of development than would occur in the absence of zoning. Given that land prices are the capitalized value of the income stream which that land will generate and that the income stream is positively related to the density of development, the immediate effect will be a lowering of land values. However, if we assume that at the metropolitan-area level demand for residential and commercial structures will be the same, then there will be a displacement

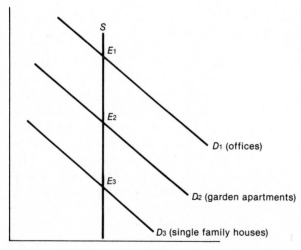

FIGURE 8-1

Zoning and land prices. We assume that a given parcel, indicated by the vertical (completely inelastic) supply curve is suitable for all the uses shown by the demand curves. The vertical distance between the topmost intersection and the intersection of the highest permitted use represents the loss imposed on the property owner by the zoning process. For example, if office use were forbidden by zoning, then the property owner's loss would be the distance from E_1 to E_2. If garden apartments are also forbidden, then the loss is the distance from E_1 to E_3.

TABLE 8-1
INCREASES IN BUILDING LOT PRICES IN SELECTED METROPOLITAN AREAS, 1975–1980

Region	Increase	Annual percentage increase
Northeast-Northcentral	67	11
South	76	12
West	148	20
Consumer price index	53	9

Source: J. Miller, "Assessing Residential Land Price Inflation," *Urban Land,* March, 1981, pp. 16–20.

effect. Demand curves will shift to the right in other municipalities and land prices in them will rise.

Zoning may have the apparently paradoxical effect of elevating land prices when they are measured by one standard but depressing them when they are measured by another. Consider the situation in which market forces would cause land to be developed at a density of four houses per acre in the absence of zoning but in which zoning limits development to one unit per acre. If we make the reasonable assumption that we will encounter the diminishing marginal utility of land before a lot size of 1 acre is reached it follows that a 1-acre lot will have a market value of less than four ¼-acre lots. But so long as we grant that the utility of additional land is not negative, it also follows that the selling price of a 1-acre lot will exceed that of a ¼-acre lot. In this case zoning depresses prices on an acreage basis but elevates them on a building lot basis. The effects on house prices will be comparable. The higher building lot prices will be directly reflected in higher house prices. This effect will be exacerbated by the fact that larger lots increase the spacing between houses, thereby pushing up per unit costs for water mains, sewer lines, streets, and the like. However, the total value of housing built is likely to be lower because of the smaller number of units.

Studies appear to indicate that the price-elevating effects hypothesized above do, in fact, occur. Sagalyn and Sternlieb studied developments in New Jersey and found that large lot zoning might elevate single-family house prices by several thousand dollars.[2] It might also be argued that zoning may elevate the average price of dwelling units by shifting the entire mix in the direction of more expensive units. Beyond these effects is the shifting supply curve, noted previously.

One phenomenon related to land-use controls, but not solely a function of them, has been the very rapid increase in residential land costs in metropolitan areas. In the 1970s the component of new-house costs that rose most rapidly was land. Table 8-1 shows the results of a study of land costs in 12 selected metropolitan areas.

Because Miller's data cover only four areas in each region it can hardly be considered conclusive. His data suggest that increases in land prices were pervasive and varied widely by region. Note that even in the northeast and north-central parts of the nation where population and employment growth were slow, land prices still increased faster than consumer prices in general. It is also not

[2] George Sternlieb and Lynne B. Sagalyn, *Zoning and Housing Costs,* Center for Urban Policy Research, Rutgers University, New Brunswick, N.J., 1972.

known how much of the increase in price was caused by land-use controls and how much by other factors. For example, a municipality can limit the land supply and thus elevate prices by failing to provide water and sewer lines to land otherwise available for development. In some urban areas land prices may increase very sharply simply because there is not much undeveloped land left. San Francisco is ringed by mountains and water that limit its growth, and there is little privately held land left in the city not built on. Thus as long as growth pressures remain strong land prices might rise quite rapidly regardless of the structure of land-use controls. But in spite of all these qualifications there is an important relationship between land-use controls, land costs, and housing costs. It behooves the planning agency charged with creating or administering land-use controls to consider not only the physical planning effects of controls but their market effects as well. While government does much to lower housing costs, it often does a good deal through land-use controls to raise them. In this case there is some truth in the words of that famous, albeit mythical, social philosopher, Pogo Possum: "We have met the enemy and he is us."

Zoning Change   Property owners who benefit from the controls applied to another's property are hardly likely to protest. However, if property owners believe they have been harmed by zoning and that a court is likely to find the zoning to be capricious, unreasonable, or otherwise unsound they may choose to bring suit. That always represents a gamble. The question is whether the value of the expectation of changed land value exceeds the probable costs of the suit. If the property owner chooses not to go to court the zoning stands. The property owner may try to get the zoning changed in some other way. She might take her arguments to the zoning board of appeals (ZBA) and hope that the reasonableness of her arguments will cause them to grant a variance. If she is unscrupulous and believes that ZBA members are likewise, she might offer a bribe. Or, she might offer some inducement to the municipality to grant a variance or rezoning.[3] She might offer to deed part of her property over to the municipality if the municipality will permit her to use the remainder as she desires. She might seek to build a political coalition that will put political pressure on the community to rezone land. For example, if she seeks to build a shopping center on the site she might assemble a coalition of construction union leaders, the local chamber of commerce, the taxpayers' association, etc., whose interests (jobs, expanded commercial activity, expanded tax base) will be served by allowing her to do as she wishes. Very often, the market value of land in its highest economic use and in its permitted use is quite different, and that difference can generate very powerful forces to change zoning. Public investment, particularly in water supply, sewers, and roads, often produce great changes in the economic value of land and hence create great pressure for zoning change.

The Use and Misuse of Zoning

Beginning in the 1960s concern began to mount over the way zoning power was being used by suburban communities. Since then suburban zoning has been the subject of much comment and, more important, much litigation. Some litigation

---

[3] A variance is permission to build in violation of the zoning law; a rezoning is a change in the law.

has been brought by landowners and developers who have an obvious pecuniary interest in more permissive zoning and more intensive land use. But much litigation has been brought by advocacy groups including the NAACP, the Urban League, and the Suburban Action Institute. The advocacy groups in general have sought to represent what they see as the legitimate interests of nonresidents—those who have an interest in the outcome of local zoning decisions but who, as nonresidents, have no say in the question.

The general brief against suburban zoning is that in the pursuit of the interests of present residents suburban communities have gone far beyond any reasonable interpretation of the terms health, safety, and public welfare and have imposed serious losses on other members of society. Essentially the opponents of suburban zoning as currently practiced have sought either to have some zoning powers transferred to higher levels of government or to change the practices of local governments by establishing legal precedents through test cases.

The Issue of "Restrictive Zoning" Suburban communities have been accused of certain specific abuses. First, they have been accused of zoning land for lower densities of development than can legitimately be defended. The community motivation for doing this is fairly plain. At essentially no cost to the majority of community residents drawbacks like crowding, congestion, loss of open space, higher ambient noise levels, that come with growth can be avoided or lessened. This makes life more pleasant for the average homeowner and also makes the house itself more valuable. It does impose a loss on the landowner, but compensation for this loss is not required. It may also impose a loss on the nonresident who might like to live in the community if housing were available. But because nonresidents don't vote in that municipality, they have no effective say in the zoning process. The residents of the metropolitan area as a whole may be affected by zoning decisions in communities other than their own because a generally restrictive pattern of zoning will decrease the supply of housing and produce a general elevation in prices. This regionwide interest in local zoning decisions goes unrepresented because there is no mechanism by which it can be represented. Whether they see it clearly or not, the population making zoning decisions is in the enviable position of being able to limit the growth of the supply of an asset they hold. From the vantage point of self-interest, the supply-limiting behavior of homeowners is quite rational.

Critics of the practice of suburban zoning have also accused suburban communities of zoning out the poor by prohibiting less expensive forms of housing: forbidding garden apartments but allowing luxury condominiums, forbidding mobile homes and row houses but allowing single-family houses on large lots, etc. Again, viewed from the vantage point of resident homeowners' self-interest this makes a good deal of sense. The mainstay of local public finance is the property tax. This tax is proportional to the assessed value of the property, which, in turn, is proportional to the market value of the property. Now assume that the cost of providing serivces to a household does not vary greatly with household income and that there are more or less constant returns to scale in the delivery of public services (marginal costs will not be greatly different than average costs). Incidentally, the labor-intensive character of many public services tends to limit the opportunity for the use of capital intensive techniques that would produce major economies of scale. Thus this assumption is quite reasonable. In this case it is in the fiscal interest of local residents to behave like a club whose policy is to admit as members only those applicants whose income is above the average of present members. Such a policy will exert downward pressure on tax rates. Housing and land-use policies that permit the building of new stock that is less expensive than the present stock will, granting the conditions assumed earlier, exert upward pressure on tax rates. Either higher rates will be needed for the same levels of service, or lower levels of service will result from holding rates constant. Readers who have any doubt about the level of concern over property taxes should refer to the discussion of proposition 13 in Chapter 10.

Nonfiscal Motives Behind Restrictive Zoning   Fiscal reasons are not the only reason communities may zone in such a manner as to exclude the poor. Residents may simply feel more comfortable with people like themselves, a trait that may not be praiseworthy but seems to be fairly common. Then, too, excluding the poor may be rational from a purely self-interested position in another sense. Assume that 99.5 percent of all poor people never commit violent crimes against strangers. Assume, also, that 99.9 percent of all nonpoor people never commit violent crimes against strangers. Then on a probabilistic basis the community is safer admitting only the nonpoor. This type of discrimination based on probabilities has been termed *statistical discrimination* and has been discussed in considerable length in regard to labor markets.[4] It explains why a slight difference in group performance (real or imagined) can lead to almost total discrimination against one group by people who in the ordinary meaning of the terms are not prejudiced or bigoted. In the housing case mentioned above it does a serious injustice to the 99.5 percent of the poor but, as noted before, one of the characteristics of zoning is that losses can be imposed without compensation.

Restrictive Zoning and the Metropolitan Pattern   Still another accusation made against suburban zoning is that it distorts the spatial pattern of the metropolitan area by distributing economic activity more diffusely than would otherwise be the case. This, in turn, reduces the possibility of having an effective public transportation system (see Chapter 9 on the collection and distribution problem), pushes up the costs of public infrastructure like roads and sewers, and increases vehicular traffic, thus degrading air quality. The argument is, again, fiscal. Because of heavy reliance on the property tax, municipalities are more likely to resist residential than commerical growth. This assertion not only makes sense on an a priori basis but can be supported empirically by examining suburban zoning ordinances and also by noting that those communities that adopt growth-control or growth-management ordinances usually apply them primarily on the residential rather than the commercial side.[5]

---

[4] See, for example, David Gordon, *Theories of Poverty and Underemployment*, D. C. Heath, Lexington Mass, 1973.

[5] For example, three widely publicized growth control ordinances—in Petaluma, California, Boca Raton, Florida, and Ramapo, New York—applied limits only on the residential side. See Robert C. Einsweiler et al., "Comparative Descriptions of Selected Municipal Growth Guidance Systems," in Randall W. Scott et al. (eds.), *Management and Control of Growth*, Urban Land Institute, Washington, D.C., 1975. See also articles on Petaluma and Ramapo in same volume for additional detail.

The ideal strategy, from a fiscal standpoint, would be to attract desirable commercial development (high assessments, low environmental and traffic impacts, visually attractive, etc.) while displacing population growth to other communities. If suburban communities were not so dependent on property taxes raised within their own boundaries they would, presumably, offer more resistance to commercial development, and thus the flight of economic activity from the central city would be slowed.

Selective Rezoning   Communities' preference for commercial over residential development and for expensive over low-cost residential development is often manifested by what we might term *selective rezoning*. Consider a suburban community in which there is a large block of land with good highway access and no serious physical impediment to development (such as steep slopes, periodic flooding, unique environmental value, etc.). At present the land is zoned for single-family houses on large lots. However, the owners and others knowledgeable about real estate understand that its economic value is too great for such a low-intensity use.

A developer of moderate-priced housing approaches the community with a development proposal that will require a rezoning. The town board or planning board considers the proposal, decides it will not yield a fiscal surplus, and informs the developer it will not rezone. They indicate that if he takes the community to court they will fight, and if he wins they will appeal. If they lose the appeal they will still obstruct and delay in every possible legal manner. The developer, knowing that time is money and that life is short, decides to go elsewhere.

Next a corporation seeking a site for a national or regional headquarters approaches the board. This looks more attractive. The proposed headquarters will not be the source of any children to burden the school system, and it will not harbor a population that makes demands for recreational facilities, social services, etc. The board indicates to the corporation that a rezoning might be considered if various specifications were met. A bargaining process ensues, and in due time agreement is reached. At this point rezoning occurs.

The fact that the town maintained an unrealistic zoning pattern gave it a bargaining position that it would not have had if the zoning had been appropriate in the first instance. This technique is commonly used and from a municipal viewpoint often works very well. For example, Westchester County, New York, is the home of numerous corporate headquarters. Most of those that are not located in the older urbanized parts of the county are built on land that was previously zoned for single-family houses. For example, the headquarters of Texaco, IBM, and Pepsico among many others are located on land that was zoned for low-density single-family development.

A somewhat analogous situation holds with regard to residential development. If land is zoned for multifamily development, then builders whose plans meet the letter of the zoning ordinance can "build by right." They simply submit the plans to the building inspector, who verifies that the plans conform to the existing zoning and, therefore, must issue a building permit. On the other hand, if the land is zoned for a less intensive use a rezoning is necessary and this permits municipal discretion. If section 8 housing is proposed the municipality can simply fail to grant a rezoning, and with any luck the proposal will go away. If a development of comparable density but intended for affluent senior citizens is proposed, then the municipality can be flexible. (Senior citizens' housing, if unsubsidized, often tends to yield a fiscal surplus, primarily because it imposes no educational expenses. It will often be permitted where other types of multifamily development will be blocked.)

In other words, the strategy permits the municipality to make distinctions that would not stand judicial scrutiny if they appeared in black and white in the zoning code. No code, for example, could state that apartments to be occupied by affluent singles and childless couples are permitted but that apartments occupied by moderate-income residents with children are forbidden. But the same effect may be achieved by refusing to rezone until a developer comes along with plans for a preponderance of small units and amenities like tennis courts and saunas.

Zoning and the Courts

In recent years a series of court decisions have established the precedent that to be valid a zoning ordinance must give some consideration to meeting regional needs as well as just those of the population resident within the jurisdiction at the time. For example, as early as 1965 in *National Land and Investment Co. v. Easttown Township Board of Adjustment* the state of Pennsylvania supreme court invalidated an ordinance that established a 4-acre minimum lot size for single-family housing. The court noted:

> It is not difficult to envision the tremendous hardship, as well as chaotic conditions, which could result if all the townships in this area decided to deny to a growing population sites for residential development within the means of at least a significant segment of the population.

In 1970, Madison County, New Jersey, rezoned much of its land to large-lot single-family status because it appeared that multifamily development cost the town more in service costs than it yielded in tax revenues. The New Jersey superior court invalidated the ordinance on the grounds that it failed to make provision for a reasonable number of the region's low-income residents.

In 1975 in the case of *Southern Burlington County NAACP v. Township of Mount Laurel* the court overturned a local ordinance on the grounds that land-use regulations must meet the needs of all income groups residing within the region.[6] In 1978 the Westchester County, New York, supreme court in the case of *Berenson v. Town of New Castle* invalidated the zoning ordinance of the town on the grounds that it failed to take into account regional housing needs. During the trial evidence was introduced by the plaintiff, a local builder, that the town's 1- and 2-acre zoning made it virtually impossible to construct new housing for less than $100,000 a unit given current land values and construction costs. The plaintiff took pains to show that zoning in surrounding municipalities was restrictive so

---

[6] For citations of a number of prominent cases see Frank So et al., op. cit., chap. 15. For an extended discussion of the legal side of the exclusionary zoning issue, see the articles in Chapter 6 of vol. 1, Randall W. Scott, op. cit.

that the town could not successfully argue that the regional need was being met by adjacent municipalities.[7]

Although the trend in court decisions has been clearly in the direction of regional considerations—forcing communities to internalize some of the externalities of their actions—judicial action has not yet forced a major change in land-use policies. In part the reason appears to be that zoning decisions do not generalize easily. Every municipality and every parcel of land is different. The weight of a mass of decisions gradually causes communities and developers to alter their expectations of trial outcomes and thus alters their behavior, but massive change from a single decision simply does not occur.

Zoning and Economic Efficiency

Academic studies of zoning have generally found it suboptimal in that it promotes lower densities of development than would maximize total welfare. The mechanics of this have been discussed previously. In economic terms a general explanation is that communities can, within what the courts or fear of the courts will permit, treat the use of the zoning power as a free good. They can do this because they do not have to compensate property owners for losses that zoning may impose. Thus, in principle the power to zone will be used to the point at which its marginal utility to the user has reached zero. But by this point the marginal disutility to others may be considerable. The net result, then, is a welfare loss. This is illustrated in Figure 8-2.

If trade were possible a better solution could be reached. For example, if a higher density were worth more to the landowner or builder than the lower density to the town residents, then a compensating payment could be made. This is analogous to the "gains of trade" argument made in the appendix on welfare economics following Chapter 6. However, such mechanisms generally do not exist, and they would be enormously complicated because of the number of parties involved. Fischel, in a perceptive article on the subject, suggests that the suboptimality resides in what he terms "an incomplete assignment of property rights."[8] Zoning gives the community some of the rights of ownership but not the right of sale. As a result certain types of bargaining that might move the situation toward a better equilibrium are not possible. He suggests that the best we can do is to make zoning more "fungible," that is, more flexible and more subject to negotiation and compromise. And, indeed, recent developments in zoning have moved in precisely this direction. Such techniques as transfer of development rights, planned unit development, density bonuses, and other devices introduce greater flexibility and the opportunity to negotiate what was formerly fixed by statute. A discussion of these techniques is not provided here, but the reader is referred to works on the subject.[9]

---

[7] Observation by author, who testified in the suit.

[8] William Fischel, "The Property Rights Approach to Zoning," *Land Economics*, vol. 54, no. 1, Feb. 1978, pp. 64–81.

[9] For a brief discussion of some new techniques along with some case history material see Robert S. Coo, *Zoning for Downtown Urban Design*, Lexington Books, Lexington, Mass., 1980. For a note on zoning techniques specifically intended to promote the building of moderate-priced housing see Barbara Taylor, "Inclusionary Zoning: A Workable Option for Affordable Housing?" *Urban Land*, March 1981, pp. 6–12.

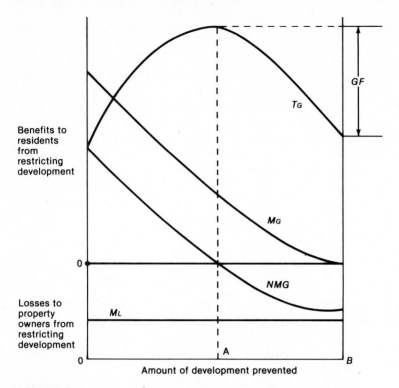

FIGURE 8-2
The net gains of making zoning fungible. Curve *MG* shows the marginal gains
to residents from restricting development. Line *ML* shows the marginal losses
to property owners from the same restriction. Curve *NMG* is the net marginal
gain and is reached by subtracting *ML* from *MG*. Curve *TG* is total gain, i.e.,
the sum of the net marginal benefits. Note that at the point where *NMG* falls to
zero, curve *TG* reaches its maximum. (This is analogous to saying that for a
firm the point at which marginal revenue minus marginal cost equals zero is
the point at which profit is maximized.) This correspondence is shown by the
broken line. If zoning is not fungible and there is no way the owners can compensate the residents, the community will restrict development out to point *B*.
However, if owners can make payments to the community, development will
be restricted out to point *A*. The net welfare gain from fungibility is the difference in the height of *TG* at points *A* and *B*. This difference, or gain from fungibility, is shown by line *GF*. (Note that we have assumed owners and residents
to be two separate groups, following the general logic of Fischel, op. cit.)

Suburban Zoning and the Central City

Part of the conventional wisdom of planning is that exclusionary zoning in the
suburbs increases the income and the racial dichotomy between city and suburb.[10]
The argument is that suburban land-use controls prevent building for the poor and
the near-poor in the suburbs and therefore confine them to the central city. The
poor, with the heavy concentration of minorities, are trapped in the city by a

[10] See, for example, William Alonso, "Urban Zero Population Growth," *Daedalus*, vol 102, no. 4,
Fall 1973, pp. 191–206.

"noose" of suburban zoning. If restrictive zoning were destroyed the central-city poor could move outward. They would benefit by better access to jobs, and their children would benefit by access to good suburban schools. The dispersion would also reduce the general degree of racial segregation in American society. Perhaps the best-known advocate of this general view is Paul Davidoff, an attorney and former town planner who for more than a decade has headed Suburban Action Institute. This is an advocacy group dedicated to promulgating this viewpoint and, more important, engaging in litigation designed to establish precedents that weaken the structure of suburban zoning.[11]

A minority view holds that even the total abolition of suburban land-use controls would still not lower real estate prices sufficiently to place housing within reach of the central-city poor or near-poor. Thus the result of knocking down the legal barriers would simply be to accelerate the building of housing, which would pull even more of the cities' middle-income population out. The exodus of the remaining middle-income population would leave the central city even poorer and, in percentage terms, more heavily minority as well. A more detailed presentation of this view can be found in an article by the author.[12] Some support for it can also be found in an article by Gruen.[13]

One can hypothesize on the effect of suburban land-use controls on the density gradients of metropolitan areas. Assume that controls reduce density of development in the suburban ring but that metropolitan population and job totals are unaffected by such controls. Then controls must either exert upward pressure on central-city densities, displace population out into exurbia beyond the suburban ring, or both. In view of the general centrifugal trends in the movement of population and industry the writer suspects the effect on peripheral movement is greater than the effect on central-city densities. One might also note that one force explaining the resurgence of nonmetropolitan-area growth might be the elevation of suburban housing prices by land-use controls. (The reader will recall that nonmetropolitan net outmigration reversed in the early 1970s.)

A Final Note on Zoning

The preceding discussion paints a clearly suboptimal picture of zoning and may thus give the impression that the institution ought to be consigned to the scrap heap. In the writer's view this is far from the case. On balance—and this is clearly a matter of opinion—the ability of zoning to help communities avoid the juxtaposition of incompatible land uses, avoid or mitigate the many negative externalities of uncontrolled land development, and advance planning goals far outweighs its faults. Development is fraught with externalities and some public control is essential. At present there is nothing on the horizon to replace zoning. It

---

[11] See, for example Paul Davidoff and Linda Davidoff, "Opening The Suburbs: Toward Inclusionary Controls," 22 *Syracuse Law Review* 510 (1971). A condensed version of the article is reprinted in Randall Scott, op. cit., vol 1, pp. 540–550.

[12] John M. Levy, "Exclusionary Zoning: After the Walls Come Down," *Planning*, August 1972, pp. 158–160.

[13] Claude Gruen, "The Economics of Petaluma: Unconstitutional Regional Socio-Economic Impacts," in Scott, op. cit.

clearly needs improvement and, in fact, improvements are being made. But, at present, we are far better off with it than without it.[14]

RENT CONTROLS

Rent controls are a major public intervention in the urban and metropolitan housing market with a long but sporadic history in the United States. Many areas implemented them briefly during World War I, but by the early 1920s they were gone from the national scene. In World War II a national system of controls was instituted. It essentially froze rents at existing levels. The rationale for it was that mobilization for was causing major movements of population, while the diversion of materials to wartime purposes severely limited residential construction. In a more formal way we might say that short-term supply is inelastic. Therefore increases in demand would simply manifest themselves as price (rent) increases, constituting a windfall to property owners. In 1947, with the war over and residential construction proceeding at a rapid pace, the federal government turned over the control of rents to the states. By 1951, New York State was the only one to retain controls, though not all jurisdictions within the state had them. Most of the controlled units (over 1 million) were in New York City and the New York suburbs. Rent control remained confined to New York State with very few exceptions until about 1970, when its political popularity began to grow. At present rents are controlled in Boston, Washington, D.C., Albany, Los Angeles, and many smaller communities. The latter include numerous towns, villages, and several cities in the New York suburbs, several communities, including Cambridge and Brookline, in the Boston suburbs, several dozen municipalities in New Jersey, Santa Monica, California, and assorted others. It appears that many factors combined to produce the upsurge in controls in the 1970s. One was inflation itself. The price of rental housing is one of the few prices that can effectively be controlled at the local level. As citizens felt the general pain of inflation and wanted to do something, local rental control was there to be done. The rising rent-income ratios discussed earlier were also a factor. Then, too, tenant activists often found that getting rent controls enacted was not difficult, partly for the elementary reason that tenants outnumber landlords.

In public debate, the procontrol side is often easier to present because it can be cast in terms of protecting the poor, preventing "unconscionable" increases and "rent gouging," etc. That is, the argument can be cast in somewhat moral terms. The case against is more pragmatic, that is, that its long-run effects are undesirable—not the sort of argument to set the pulses of headline writers jumping. The true conservative might protest that the taking of private property is indeed a moral issue. "Taking" occurs because the value of commercial property depends upon the income it can generate. By limiting that income the municipality, in effect, "takes" part of the value of the property. However, this argument has not made very many converts in the past, and the courts in both zoning and rent control cases have found such taking without compensation to be constitutional.

[14] For a much less favorable view of zoning see Bernard H. Siegan, *Land Use Without Zoning*, D.C. Heath, Lexington, Mass., 1972.

Whether the 1980s will witness a comparable expansion of controls remains to be seen. The potential rate of household formation should remain high through the 1980s, since births remained at a high level into the second half of the 1960s. This demographic pressure, combined with slow rates of residential construction of all types, could exert considerable upward pressure on rents. The changing structure of real estate financing may reduce the opportunity costs of renting for the more affluent (reversing the 1970s situation), further shifting the demand for rental units to the right and putting more upward pressure on rents. All of the above would increase the political pressure for the extension of controls. On the other hand, the somewhat more conservative political temper of the times bodes against it, for at bottom the question of rent controls bears a heavy ideological burden. It raises fundamental questions about how much government should participate in markets and, perhaps even more fundamental, how much control should government have over the private use of private property.

The Microeconomics of Rent Controls

Let us turn to the simple microeconomics of rent control and then look at how it is done and what is known about the effects. For controls to have any meaning they must hold the price (rent) of housing units below the market clearing price. This is shown in Figure 8-3(*a*). The supply curve is shown as completely inelastic, indicating that we are discussing the short-term situation. Controls hold prices at P′ rather than the market clearing price P. Line segment A indicates the shortage thus created. The shortage will be resolved one way or another. One possibility is rationing by inconvenience. The real price of an apartment is the money rent plus an extended waiting or searching time. Another possibility is the development of a

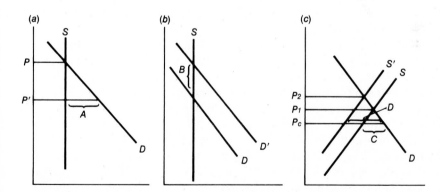

FIGURE 8-3
(*a*) The effects of control in the short run. The market would be cleared at *P* (price) but controls fix rents at *P′*. Line segment *A* indicates the shortage produced in the controlled sector. (*b*) The effects of controls on the uncontrolled sector. The shortage created in the controlled sector diverts potential renters of controlled units into the uncontrolled sector, shifting demand from *D* to *D′*. Line segment *B* shows the resulting elevation in price. (*c*) The longer-term situation. If controls reduce construction supply is shifted from *S* to *S′*. This shifts the price (rent) which would clear the market from *P₁* to *P₂*. If rents are controlled at *PC* then a shortage represented by line segment *D* is created. If controls were to have no effect on supply, the shortage would be of smaller dimensions as illustrated by line segment *C*.

black market, with bribes and illegal payments raising the true price above the legislated price.

The story does not end here, even in a purely theoretical sense. Assume that in addition to the controlled market there is also an uncontrolled market and that there is some degree of substitutability between the two. Incidentally, this is almost the inevitable case, as we shall see. The unsatisfied demand represented by line segment A appears in the uncontrolled market, where prices can rise until the market clears. As shown in Figure 8-3(b) the demand curve is shifted from D to D', with the elevation in equilibrium price shown by line segment B. How much price will rise in the uncontrolled sector will depend on several factors. A high degree of substitutability and a large controlled market relative to the uncontrolled market will predispose to more elevation in the uncontrolled markets than would the opposite conditions. Beyond that, controls which hold rents well below market clearing levels will produce a greater effect in the uncontrolled market than more permissive controls because they will produce greater shortages and thus divert more renters to the uncontrolled sector.

Controls will also affect the value of both controlled and uncontrolled properties. The value of a commercial asset is the capitalized value of the income stream it generates. Suppose that the capitalized value of apartment houses is 10 times net earnings. Then a building that yields net earnings of $100,000 will have a market value of $1 million. (We neglect such factors as the expectation of future capital gains and advantageous or disadvantageous tax treatment.) If controls cut the net income to $80,000, then that is capitalized as $800,000 and market value of the property falls by $200,000. In a similar manner, controls may elevate the capitalized value of rental properties in the uncontrolled sector. The loss of value in controlled properties is well known and much feared by property owners and has been documented in the scholarly literature. The elevation of values in the uncontrolled sector is theoretically reasonable but, to the writer's knowledge, has not been documented.

Of what importance is the loss of market value besides the sorrow it brings to property owners? One point is that it will make it harder for owners to raise capital in the future because it is the value of the building that secures credit. It may also make owners less willing to invest in the structure even if they can raise the capital. This has distinctly negative implications for the quality of the property in the long term.

The lessened income stream resulting from controls also shifts tax burdens. The tax-paying capacity of a property is a function of the income it generates. If controls hold down income, they reduce revenue capacity. If we make the reasonable assumption that controls do not lower municipal revenue needs, the burden is necessarily shifted to other revenue sources. These may be other payers of property taxes such as homeowners and the owners of commercial or industrial property or it may be the payers of user charges, sales taxes, excise taxes, etc.

In the long term, controls are likely to shift the supply curve to the left as shown in Figure 8-3(c) and thus raise the market clearing rent. This is because builders will be less willing to invest in controlled areas. Controls cannot reduce the probability of taking a loss on an investment, but they can reduce the probability of making a large profit. In fact, if not very cautiously applied, they may also reduce or eliminate the possibility of making even a normal profit.[15] Thus they reduce the value of the expectation of profit on investment in rental property. As long as other avenues for investment exist, either housing in uncontrolled areas or nonhousing assets, capital is likely to be diverted from investment in controlled areas.

The Mechanics of Controls

Having touched on theory, let us discuss briefly the manner in which controls are actually applied and then turn to what is known about the results. The goals in initiating rent control are to hold rents below market levels, generally on the presumption that if the market is allowed to clear, at least some renters will be paying "too much." Obviously there is room for an enormous amount of disagreement about what is too much. (A rent/income ratio of .25 is sometimes used as a rule-of-thumb cutoff for excessive expenditure on rent, but it is obviously arbitrary and its origins are obscure.) At the same time it is understood that rents must not be held so low that excessive disinvestment occurs and housing quality falls unduly. In addition, the ordinance should be structured so that it does not discourage new construction, for if it does, the very conditions that brought about controls will be exacerbated and the medicine will produce more of the symptoms it was meant to alleviate.

Most ordinances are structured to achieve the above combination of goals.[16] The debate about rent control is thus primarily not about goals but about results. Most ordinances contain either a rent freeze as of the date of enactment or a rollback to a point a few months before enactment (so as to nullify any last-minute increases). Virtually all have some provisions for periodic adjustment of rents to compensate landlords for increases in costs. Virtually all exempt new construction from control.

In principle each property could be judged on its own, with rent increases granted or denied on its particular situation. In practice such a procedure would be an administrative nightmare. Therefore the common approach is to adjust rents uniformly. This assumes, implicitly, that all rental structures were earning acceptable rates of return at the inception of controls, a rather questionable assumption. Thus most ordinances also contain an appeals procedure for hardship cases. Because controls are imposed when it is believed that there is a housing shortage, many ordinances also contain provisions that offer tenants some protection from loss of tenancy. At the extreme, the ordinance may make tenants "statutory," that is, the tenant may continue to occupy the unit after the expiration of the lease so long as he or she pays the controlled rent. The tenant may be evicted if the property owner shows cause in court. But the owner cannot force the tenant out simply by refusing to sign a lease. The reasoning behind this is that under conditions of very low vacancies it would be a hardship for the tenant not to be able to continue in place.

---

[15] Normal profit in this context means a return on investment comparable to that paid by other investments of comparable risk.

[16] For a general overview of rent control ordinances see Monica Lett, *Rent Control: Concepts, Realities and Mechanisms*, Rutgers University Press, New Brunswick, N.J., 1976.

Arguments Pro and Con

Those who look favorably upon rent controls argue that controls can indeed achieve the multiple goals noted above and therefore are advisable under some circumstances, notably where vacancy rates are low, rents are rising rapidly, or rent/income ratios are high.[17] They argue that when vacancy rates are low the tenant is a buyer in a seller's market and will therefore be exploited. They argue that under conditions of rapidly increasing demand property owners may earn windfall profits simply by being in the right place at the right time. Finally, they may argue that high rent/income ratios prove that rents must be restrained to prevent personal hardship among those of low and moderate income. Proponents of controls may also argue that if controls are applied with care they need not have damaging side effects on housing markets. Specifically, supporters of controls may argue that since controls do not apply to new construction, they will not diminish new construction. They may also argue that if rent ceilings are adjusted skillfully property owners will not make "excessive" profits but will earn a rate of return sufficient to maintain their properties adequately. In fact, proponents may argue that tying the rent adjustment process to adequate maintenance of the property may actually cause property owners to maintain properties more adequately than they would in the absence of controls.

Those who oppose controls generally take the position that over the long term the goals enunciated earlier have not been achieved and that there are logical reasons for believing it unlikely that they can be achieved.[18] They also argue that controls have a number of objectionable side effects, which manifest themselves over time.

They argue that though in principle rent adjustments can protect property owners from the effects of cost increases, it is unlikely that they will actually do so. Their reasoning is that if procontrol sentiment is strong enough to bring controls into being in the first instance there is likely to be a protenant bias in the adjustment process. Thus, increases will lag behind the rise in costs. If this assertion is correct then a whole Pandora's box of troubles follow in the long term. With the passage of time in an inflationary environment the difference between rent adjustments and cost increases will grow. As the cash flow on properties falls it will be more difficult for owners to make adequte expenditures on maintenance, and housing quality will decline. As owners are pushed into the red the market value of their properties will fall and their ability to obtain credit will shrink, further impairing their ability to maintain them. When the market value of the property falls below the underlying debt, bankruptcy or abandonment is at hand. In fact, if controls are imposed for a sufficient time the amount of deterioration

[17] For procontrol views see Emily P. Achtenburg, "The Social Utility of Rent Control," in John Pynoos (ed.), *Housing Urban America*, Aldine, Chicago, 1973; Chester Hartman, *Housing and Social Policy*, Prentice-Hall, Englewood Cliffs, N.J., 1975; Herbert Selesnick, *Rent Control: The Case For*, Lexington Books, Lexington, Mass., 1976; Community Research and Publications Group, *Less Rent, More Control: A Tenants Guide to Rent Control in Massachusetts*, Cambridge 1973.

[18] Claude Gruen and Nina Gruen, "The Evolution of Rent Control and a Strategy for Its Defeat," *Urban Land*, July/August 1980, pp. 5–10; Frederick A. Hayek, *Verdict on Rent Control: Essays on the Economic Consequences of Political Action to Restrict Rents in Five Countries*, Institute of Economic Affairs, London, 1972; George Sternlieb and Elizabeth Brody, "The Pitfalls of Rent Control," *Real Estate Review*, vol. 4, no. 2, Summer 1974, pp. 120–124.

may be so great that the property is doomed even if controls are ultimately removed.

In principle, exemption of new construction from controls should mean that the rate of new construction will be unaffected. In fact, proponents of controls have argued that the shifting of the demand curve in the uncontrolled sector which was discussed earlier might actually accelerate new construction. Opponents counter by pointing out that investors will fear that a jurisdiction that imposes controls once is likely to do so again. If this is so, the imposition of controls will be self-perpetuating. The reduced rate of new construction coupled with below market clearing rents will guarantee low vacancy rates, which will guarantee continuation of controls. Opponents also argue that controls cause overconsumption of housing by those who, through luck or prior tenancy, have controlled units. This imposes a burden on those who are not fortunate enough to have controlled units. In addition they argue that the existence of controls decreases tenant mobility and thus allocates resources inefficiently. The most important attribute of a unit rather than being a real entity such as size, location, or physical quality becomes its status vis-à-vis controls. When family size or income changes, the tenant in a controlled unit will be far less likely to move. Specifically, opponents allege that tenants of large controlled units are unwilling to leave when family size shrinks because a large controlled unit may be less expensive than a small uncontrolled unit.

Opponents of rent controls argue that as an income transfer mechanism controls are tremendously inefficient. To use rent controls as a means of distributing income is analogous to collecting dollar bills from random passersby in a wealthy neighborhood and giving them out to random passersby in a poor neighborhood. Some downward redistribution will occur, but the process is neither just nor efficient.

A Look at Some Evidence What is the empirical evidence on the long-term effect of controls? In the writer's view the weight of the evidence shows that over the long term, sometimes in the short term, the situation is basically as the opponents of controls describe it. Thus it would be more rational to deal with the problem of unacceptably high rent/income ratios by transfers rather than by market intervention. The writer would also argue that the case for controls is strongest where the cause of the problem is a clearly identifiable and short-term situation and weakest where there is no clear end in sight.

Let us consider some actual experience. New York City is atypical both in size and in the percent of housing stock contained in multiple-unit rental buildings. Thus one should be somewhat cautious in generalizing from its experience. However, its housing markets have been very well studied and its continuous history of controls since 1943 gives us insight into long-term effects. In studying rental housing in the city, housing economist Frank Kristoff found extremely low mobility rates in better rent-controlled housing. He states:

> The 1968 Census Survey showed that turnover in the uncontrolled sector was 1.5 times that in the controlled sector. The tendency of families to hold on to their bargain rent controlled housing is nowhere more dramatically illustrated than in post 1929 apart-

ments, most of which were constructed on vacant land in strong (middle class) market areas between 1929 and 1942. Not only was this good new housing but it was an exceptional bargain—having been caught under rent control in 1942 after more than a decade of depression rent levels. Over half of this controlled housing (51.3 percent) has been held by the same families for from 10 to over 25 years.[19]

With regard to the overconsumption fostered by controls he notes that the percentage of controlled units in which one person occupied four or more rooms was slightly more than twice the percent for uncontrolled units.

The New York City experience also furnishes support for the view that over the long term the political dynamics of controls will cause rent increases to lag behind cost increases. From 1943 (the inception of controls) to 1968 controlled rents rose by 110 percent. Rents in uncontrolled units rose by 245 percent. An operating cost index developed from NYC Housing Authority data rose by 285 percent. The disparity between uncontrolled rents and operating costs is not enormous. And if we grant that some of the owner's costs (debt service) are fixed, the owners of uncontrolled units would appear to have more or less held their own. The disparity between rent increases in controlled units and operating cost increases is huge and must inevitably lead to disinvestment.[20] A large amount of rental abandonment began to be observed in New York in the mid-1960s and persists to the present. Kristoff noted that among those familiar with the city's housing situation the disinvestment process had been recognized for years. The abandonment could not be documented until 1968 when it was possible to compare 1965 and 1968 housing census data. The decline in the size of the housing stock in spite of substantial amounts of new construction indicated abandonment of about 100,000 units in the 3-year period. The rate does not appear to have slacked off since then.

Let us look at some non-New York experience of more recent vintage. In 1975 the Province of Ontario in Canada adopted controls. The control system was built with a process by which rents would be adjusted upward to compensate for operating cost increases.[21] However, operating costs were defined rather narrowly in that many items which for tax purposes are counted as operating expenses were defined as capital expenditures and therefore not factored into the operating cost adjustment. In addition there was a maximum adjustment permitted in any given year.

As it happened the 1975–1980 period was an inflationary one in Canada. In this period the cost of living rose by 62 percent, per capita income by 63 percent, household income by 55 percent, home ownership costs by 70 percent, and apartment operating costs by 75 percent. Permitted rent increases over the period totalled 39 percent. In Toronto, the largest city in the province, the 1975 per unit price of an apartment house with six or more units was $18,903. In 1980 the figure was $17,429. Converted into 1975 dollars the 1980 figure was $11,459, a loss in real value of 39.4 percent in 5 years. The destruction of owners' equity was massive.

[19] Frank Kristoff, "Economic Facets of New York City's Problems," in Lyle C. Fitch and Annamarie H. Walsh (eds.), *Agenda for a City*, Sage, Beverly Hills, Calif., 1970, p. 317.

[20] For estimated losses imposed on property owners by controls see Joseph S. de Salvo and Barbara M. Woodfill, *Rental Housing in New York City: The Demand for Shelter*, The New York City Rand Institute, R-649-NYC, 1971.

[21] Lawrence B. Smith and Peter Tomlinson, "Rent Controls in Ontario, Roofs or Ceilings," *American Real Estate & Urban Economics Journal*, vol. 9, no. 2, Summer 1981, pp. 93–114.

Consider the hypothetical situation of an owner in 1975. Assume that he has a 70 percent mortgage and further assume, for simplicity, that from 1975 to 1980 he pays only interest. His equity in 1975 is $5671 (.30 × $18,903) and his debt is $13,232 ($18,903 − 5671). In 1980 his equity is $4197 ($17,429 − $13232). If we deflate the 1980 equity for the 52 percent increase in the CPI we get $2671 ($4197/1.52). Measured in 1975 dollars his equity has declined by 51.3 percent. A number of side effects have cropped up. Rental construction slowed drastically from 1975 to 1980 and to stimulate new construction the city began offering no-interest construction loans. Thus in order to deliver a subsidy to the tenant in a controlled building it became necessary to offer a subsidy to builders of new units. As the market value of controlled units fell some owners found it financially advantageous to demolish them and sell the sites to condominium builders. In order to block the loss of rental housing in this manner the city enacted legislation that limited the floor area ratio (FAR) of structures built on the sites of former rental units. Thus the peculiar market forces set in motion by controls precipitated the use of land-use controls in a manner unrelated to their usual purposes, namely, basing permitted densities not on site or location characteristics but on the former use of the site.

Perhaps a general principle illustrated by the Toronto experience is that one intervention in a market often produces distortions and ripple effects, which can be countered only by further interventions. Depending upon one's political and ideological position, that observation can be used to argue either that the initial intervention is a mistake and should be terminated or that more thoroughgoing intervention is needed.

GOVERNMENT AS ENTREPRENEUR: URBAN RENEWAL

Government can foster development through subsidies and tax expenditures. It can guide and shape development through laws and regulations. But government can also take a direct role as the developer. By far the largest such program was urban renewal, which began in 1949 and continued until 1973. Expenditures committed before the ending of the program continued into the early 1980s. By 1980 the federal government had expended over $13 billion on urban renewal.[22] In 1983 dollars those expenditures, which stretched over a 3-decade period, would probably be in the $25 to $30 billion range.

Over 1000 square miles of urban land were acquired, enormous numbers of housing units and commercial structures were cleared, and rebuilding on a huge scale was accomplished. Funds were expended on over 2000 projects in hundreds of communities. The program has been praised as the savior of downtowns and damned as a program that destroyed the housing of the poor in order to make room for shopping centers, office buildings, and housing for the upper middle class. Among those who saw it as racist it has been referred to not as "urban renewal" but as "Negro removal." In hundreds of communities the face of downtown has been radically changed by urban renewal, and many of the most notable examples of modern urban design—such as Boston's waterfront development and New York's Lincoln Center—were done with urban renewal funds.

[22] Department of Housing and Urban Development, *Yearbook*, various years.

BOX 8-1

THE PROS AND CONS OF RENT CONTROL

The case for is presented by Chester W. Hartman, a well-known writer on housing, and the case against by Samuel J. LeFrak, a major apartment builder in New York City. Though they come out on opposite sides of the issue there is some underlying agreement on the effects of controls. One difference is that Hartman uses those problems to argue for more public intervention, while LeFrak urges abandonment of controls.

Pro

Proponents of rent control also argue their case both philosophically and pragmatically. They hold that during periods of severe housing shortage government intervention in the housing market is desirable to protect the interest of the poor and those on fixed incomes. They concede many of the defects cited by opponents, but they argue that many of these shortcomings characterize the housing market generally and are not caused by rent control, and that alternatives such as a huge low-rent housing program appear politically unfeasible. Rent control does not encourage good maintenance, but neither does the housing system generally, and maintenance is no better in cities without rent control; indeed, rent control may be a powerful tool to ensure compliance with housing codes, because under systems such as the one in New York the city is empowered to lower rents (down to $1 per month) until serious hazards are removed. Landlord-tenant relations are inherently poor and would be poorer if rents were higher and evictions easier. Landlords' profits, it is argued, are sufficiently high, demonstrated by the fact that they continue to purchase, own, and operate property of their own free will; and many of the benefits of owning real estate are to be found, not in operating profits, but in the income tax structure.

The data from New York City indicate that rent control has not only benefited the poor, but large segments of the middle class as well—and these are the system's most vocal supporters. . . . But the New York City case also indicates that if rents are established at levels that low-income families can afford, without subsidies to increase their rent-paying abilities, one consequence can be severe undermaintenance and abandonment of buildings. (It should be noted, however, that while abandonments may be caused in part by rent control, this same problem has been experienced in many cities, such as Chicago, Detroit, and Philadelphia, that do not have rent control.)

We have regarded rent control as an emergency measure, but the housing crisis faced by the nation's poor, and the inflation that produced it, are probably not temporary phenomena but are instead indicators of a more durable structural defect in the nation's economy. The only lasting solution lies in more government intervention, not less, through a combination of subsidies, direct construction activity, and controls, to effect a massive increase in the supply of decent lower-rent housing. Without such an increase, rent control will be needed in many if not most American cities to prevent rent levels from climbing beyond the reach of low-income families.[23]

Con

I am asked the same question perhaps 100 times a week: Do you have an apartment for my son? for my daughter? mother? father? friend? business associate?

. . . Regrettably, my answer is, "No." . . . My answer usually annoys the questioner. After all, my company is one of the largest private owners of apartments in New York City. If anyone can find an apartment, it should be me.

How did we ever get into this position and how can we get out of it? . . . Suffice it to say that more housing units are abandoned every year in New York City than are built.

[23] Samual J. LeFrak, "End Rent Control," *The New York Times*, August 10, 1982. Reprinted by permission.

The rent-stabilization laws are ludicrous, to say the least. The Rent Guidelines Board meets in a setting reminiscent of Roman carnival. Ringed by police officers, tenants hurl epithets at the members of the Rent Guidelines Board and threaten physical violence. The people who set increases are only human. This year, they are allowing building owners a 4 percent rent increase for a one-year lease in a building where utilities are not included in the rent, a 3 percent increase for a one-year lease when they are included. In this inflationary period, this is sheer madness. . . .

An estimated 4,000 loans totaling $2 billion in low-interest mortgages are coming due between now and 1984. This means that apartment owners will have to refinance at today's back-breaking, usurious rates. This means the rate of abandonment will accelerate.

Rent control is really a subsidy to tenants. The presumption is that middle-class families are being subsidized, allowing them to stay in the city. I don't believe it. . . . I know of hundreds of people who keep their rent-controlled apartment as an urban *pied-à-terre* while they spend the rest of their time in warm places such as Florida, California and Arizona. Thousands have sublet their apartments and use them to make profits.

The only thing that prevents greater abandonment of apartments in New York City is their conversion to cooperative ownership. Now, new laws are making it tougher and tougher to convert.

You cannot obtain financing to build a rental apartment house in New York City. . . . The insurance companies won't accept any new mortgages on rental housing in New York City. They're not stupid. Why should they make loans on an asset that can be confiscated by the city government through rent control and rent stabilization? . . .

The best solution for a housing shortage is an end here and now of the entire rent-control and rent-administration nonsense. Let the bureaucrats earn an honest living for a change.[24]

Though now at an end, the program had a major influence on the shape of its successor, community development, funded by community development block grants (CDBGs). Those in charge of any major future effort to reshape the central city will undoubtedly look back on urban renewal both for what to do and for what not to do.

The Economics of Urban Redevelopment

Before turning to the history of urban renewal let us say a word about the economics of urban redevelopment. One problem confronting the private developer is land assembly. In downtowns land ownership tends to be fragmented. A project occupying even one block may involve individual negotiations with a dozen or more property owners. Not only may some refuse to sell at any reasonable price, but as the developer acquires parcels those owners who hold out acquire enormous leverage. The developer who has acquired 11 out of 12 necessary parcels is over quite a barrel when bargaining with the twelfth owner if that owner is knowledgeable about what has transpired.

Beyond the problem of assembly is that of what we might term *residual value*. To acquire land downtown in a normal market transaction the would-be developer must be willing to pay for the residual value of the structures on that land.

[24] Chester Hartman, *Housing and Social Policy*, Prentice-Hall, Englewood Cliffs, N.J., 1975, pp. 87–88. Reprinted by permission.

Otherwise there is no reason for the owner to sell. More precisely, we might expect the selling price of a parcel of land and the structure on it to be

$$LV + RV - CC$$

where LV = land value
RV = residual value
CC = clearance costs

The existence of buildings that may be obsolete and would never be duplicated under present market conditions, but that still yield some return to their owners, is a barrier to redevelopment.

To illustrate the residual-value problem let us consider the following situation. Assume an investor wishes to build on a ½-acre of downtown land, which would be worth $200,000 if cleared. At present the site is occupied by an old office building. The economics of the area and building costs are such that it would not be worthwhile to duplicate the building today. However, that point is not of much interest to the building's owner. The building has a rent roll of $60,000 per year. Using a rule of thumb that a commercial property is worth 10 times its rent roll the building's owner considers it worth $600,000. Presumably she would sell for an offer of $600,000 or more but reject an offer below $600,000. To obtain the site and place it in another use the investor must buy out the owner of the building and pay for the land under it. We note that the land may or may not be owned by the same party as the building. The land value is the value of the cleared site minus the cost of clearing it. If we assume a clearance cost of $50,000 the cost to the investor of acquiring this ½-acre of downtown land will be

$$\$200,000 + \$600,000 - \$50,000 = \$750,000$$

which is a rate of $1.5 million per acre. If the investor must pay all of these costs himself he may well decide to build in the suburbs, instead, where there is still virgin land available and where he does not have to absorb the residual value of obsolete structures.

Thus redevelopment may proceed far less rapidly than municipal government and its citizens may desire if the process is left to the market. Urban renewal was, to a large extent, an attempt to get around the land assembly and residual-value problems.

The Origins of Urban Renewal

The political origins of the program go back to the 1930s when the federal government began to fund public housing. The two goals were to provide decent housing at low prices and to achieve macroeconomic stimulus by creating construction and related jobs. By 1941 the Federal Housing Administration (an agency which was ultimately subsumed under HUD) was proposing to deal with slums and blight through creation of "city realty corporations," which had the power to acquire land through eminent domain and lease that land to private parties for development in conformity with the municipal master plan. They also suggested that federal financial support would be required.

In December 1941 an article by Greer and Hansen listed the two key problems of slum redevelopment as land assembly and high land acquisition costs, precisely the problems just discussed. The authors then proposed a combination of federal aid, the creation of special development authorities with the power to assemble land using eminent domain, and a master planning process to bring about the redevelopment of urban areas.[25] The war focused national attention on other matters and the question of what was then termed urban redevelopment lay dormant for the next several years.

The Housing Act of 1949 brought urban renewal into being. The act provided for the creation of local public agencies (LPAs) to acquire, clear, and prepare sites for lease at market value. It was understood that market value would generally be well below acquisition and clearance cost. The federal government was to absorb two-thirds of this loss, with the LPA absorbing the remainder. However, the LPA could make up part of its third with contributions of land, labor, or the provision of public buildings (which might have been built there or elsewhere within the municipality in any case). Thus, in reality the local cash share was considerably less than one-third. The act also contained provisions that confined renewal activity to sites that had been or would be primarily residential. In 1954 the residential requirements were weakened and urban renewal agencies were permitted to spend money on rehabilitation of sites outside of designated urban renewal areas—a recognition of the high costs of clearance and new construction. Amendments in subsequent years further weakened the residential emphasis of the program and also made more generous provisions for compensating individuals and firms displaced by urban renewal.

One unique aspect of the program was that government could take the property, albeit with compensation, of one private party and transfer it to another private party. Previously when property had been condemned under the right of eminent domain it had always been for public use. But here was a process by which government could take the home of a poor family or the site of a mom-and-pop grocery and sell or lease it to a millionaire real estate developer. Needless to say, this process incensed many who saw it as an assault on traditional concepts of property rights. Litigation followed and ultimately the case reached the Supreme Court, which found the urban renewal process to be a legitimate use of the power of eminent domain. If the decision had gone otherwise it would have been necessary to make a radical change in the mechanics of urban renewal or abandon the program.

As expressed in federal legislation and in the record of congressional debate, the program had several goals. These included the elimination of substandard housing, the construction of good housing, the revitalization of city economies, and a reduction in the de facto segregation of American society. These goals are all praiseworthy, but they can be contradictory and they can all have side effects that, if stated explicitly, would not meet with general approval. For example, economic-revitalization goals might best be met by projects that remove substandard housing and replace it in its entirety with commercial structures. But this does nothing for the housing goal. In fact it reduces the supply of housing, drives up rents, and drives down vacancy rates. It worsens the housing situation of the same people the federal government is trying to help with public housing and with

[25] Guy Greer and Alvin W. Hansen, "Urban Redevelopment and Housing," pamphlet published by the National Planning Association, 1941.

subsidies. Bringing middle- and upper-income residents into the city to live in good housing built on urban renewal land does, indeed, reduce de facto segregation. But it means demolishing the housing of the poor to build housing that they can't afford. It also means subsidizing (through the writedown of land costs) the housing of those who do not, by general agreement, need subsidization. On the other hand constructing low- and moderate-income housing meets housing needs but can damage the economic prospects of the city. Such housing is likely to impose costs that far exceed the taxes it pays. It thus exerts upward pressure on the tax rate and diminishes the municipal capacity to provide services. This makes the city less attractive as an economic location.

There can also be serious conflict between federal and local goals. If the city uses urban renewal money to demolish substandard housing and the displaced residents subsequently move to other jurisdictions, the city has solved both its housing and its poverty problem. But from the federal level that looks as if public moneys are simply being used to play a zero sum game.

Criticism and Rebuttal

After some years of operation urban renewal became subject to a barrage of criticism. Perhaps the most influential and formidable criticism was contained in a book called *The Federal Bulldozer* by Martin Anderson. Published in 1964 it portrayed urban renewal as a well-intentioned program run amok, one that did more harm than good.

The charges that Anderson made were quite serious. Perhaps the most powerful was that rather than being a housing program urban renewal was, in reality, a dehousing program. Looking at data for the first dozen years of the program he found that for every five units demolished only one new unit had been built. And often that unit was for middle- and upper-middle-income tenants and thus far beyond the reach of those displaced. Nor, he asserted, could it be argued that those displaced could easily find good housing elsewhere.

> The people are poor. A great many of them are Negroes and Puerto Ricans. Good quality, conveniently located housing is relatively scarce; good quality, conveniently located housing for $50 or $60 a month is almost impossible to find. It is difficult to picture hundreds of thousands of low-income people, many of them subject to racial discrimination, moving from low-quality housing into higher-quality housing at rents they can afford. And then, one might ask why, if all this good housing at low rents is available, didn't they move before urban renewal nudged them along?[26]

It was also argued that the displacement of slum populations might create slums in adjacent marginal areas, in effect accelerating the succession process described in Chapter 3. But even if new housing at rentals of no more than the demolished housing were to be built on the site, the long-time delay between clearance and new construction created great hardship. Anderson analyzed project schedules up to that time and asserted that a period of 5 years would be an optimistic estimate of the average time between the start of clearance and the completion of the major

---

[26] Martin Anderson, *The Federal Bulldozer*, MIT Press, 1964, p. 64. Note that Anderson was writing of events 2 decades ago so readers should not be misled by the dollar amounts cited.

portions of the new development. This, incidentally, followed an average planning and acquisition period of about 3 years.

Anderson argued that the destruction of small businesses by urban renewal was a major defect in the program. Very often, small businesses operating in renewal areas were there partly because they could not afford higher rents in better quarters. Thus even if new space were to come into being instantaneously, it would do many of these businesses no good. Furthermore, much of the value in retail and service businesses is in established patterns of trade and patronage, what is generally referred to as good will. Having to move, particularly for a retailer, obliterates much of that good will, an item for which compensation is not paid. Thus for a variety of reasons many small businesses forced to close by urban renewal would never reopen. This gets at one of the vital functions of the city—the incubation and nurturing of small businesses.

Finally, Anderson attacked the view that urban renewal would necessarily increase the municipal tax base if the matter were viewed comprehensively. First, he argued that the lengthy time lag between clearance and construction reduced the tax base for several years. That revenue loss had to be subtracted from any subsequent increase. Since $1 now is worth more than $1 in the future, the near-term loss weighs more heavily than an equivalent long-term gain. (See the appendix on the present value of future income at the end of this chapter.) Second, he pointed out that some portion of the construction that occurred in the urban renewal area would have appeared elsewhere in the city in the absence of urban renewal. For example, to pursue his argument in the light of the export-base model presented in Chapter 2 we could argue that the amount of retailing floor space and employment the city can sustain is a function of personal income. That, in turn, is determined by export-sector activity. Thus, the building of a retail complex in an urban renewal area will necessarily reduce the amount of retail business done elsewhere in the city.

This last point is of more than purely academic interest. At present a good deal of community development money is spent on the development of local retailing. Unless that retailing is physically situated so as to capture sales from other areas, or sales that would have gone to other areas, one has to wonder whether the agency spending the CDBG funds is not playing a zero sum game. If so, the funds might be better spent on stimulating export-sector activity even if the immediate job or floor space increase appears to be smaller.

Other critics of urban renewal have argued that urban renewal may have a depressed investment in areas peripheral to the project by creating uncertainty. This is not difficult to understand. Imagine that you own a 40-year-old office building in a downtown area one block outside of the proposed urban renewal area. The building has proven relatively profitable over the years, and you are considering investing some money in renovation. But you read in the newspaper that preliminary plans call for construction of a substantial amount of office space to be built in the urban renewal area. No matter how much you renovate, your 40-year-old building will still be a 40-year-old building. You thus begin to wonder how well it will compete with all that new space to be built on written-down land. Perhaps you had better wait a while and see how things will work out. If the long-term future of your building is really going to be darkened by urban renewal, perhaps it would make more sense to cut back on maintenance and increase your cash flow in the short term, that is, disinvest. Precisely the same arguements can be made with regard to housing. If new subsidized housing softens the demand for older housing, will that not reduce investment in older housing and hasten the time when good older housing becomes bad older housing?

Urban Renewal in Retrospect

Anderson's powerful indictment came out when much clearance and demolition had occurred and when much of the construction on urban renewal sites was still in the future. In 1973, very shortly before the termination of the program the Congressional Research Service (an arm of the Library of Congress) prepared a report for the Senate Committee on Banking, Housing and Urban Affairs Subcommittee on Housing and Urban Affairs. It found the following. Urban renewal agencies had demolished 600,000 housing units (housing for about 2 million people), and about 250,000 units had been built on urban renewal sites. Thus the 5 to 1 ratio Anderson had found had been cut roughly in half. Roughly 120 million square feet of public construction (schools, hospitals, civic centers, etc.) and about 224 million square feet of commercial floor space (stores, factories, offices, etc.) had been erected on urban renewal sites.[27]

To convey some indication of what the commercial space means economically, a rough estimate for employment density in a typical mix of commercial space is about one worker per 500 gross square feet. On that basis workplaces for perhaps 450,000 private-sector workers had been created on urban renewal lands.

The assessed value of taxable property on urban renewal sites was 3.6 times what it had been before renewal and tax yields were 3.5 times their prerenewal levels. If a study were done today the results would look still more favorable because the filling-in process continued for many years after the termination of the program. For example, in White Plains, New York, urban renewal planning took place in the mid-to-late 1960s. Site clearance began at the end of 1969 and was largely completed in 1970. In the early 1970s a new county court house was erected, and in the mid-1970s one "luxury" high-rise was built. But the main construction phase, which included a large department store, an enclosed shopping mall, and a massive multilevel parking structure, did not begin until 1978 and continued into the 1980s. Small amounts of land still remain to be disposed of.

What can be said about urban renewal in retrospect? Perhaps 2 million people, many of them poor, were forced to relocate—undoubtedly a hardship and expense for most. Many small businesses were destroyed, and the paralyzing effect on investment in surrounding areas seems clear. But there is another side of the coin. Even if there was a net loss of units, urban housing quality was raised by the construction of new housing and, perhaps even more, by the destruction of bad housing. Downtowns all over the United States have been transformed into areas that have some chance of holding or gaining employment. In many cities shabby, deteriorated areas have been turned into sources of civic pride. Some of the poor who may have been hurt by relocation may also have been helped by job

---

[27] Congressional Research Service, Library of Congress, *The Central City Problem and Urban Renewal Policy*, prepared for the Subcommittee on Housing and Urban Affairs, Committee on Banking, Housing and Urban Affairs, United States Senate, Washington, DC, 1973.

opportunities created on urban renewal sites. The powers that Congress and the courts gave to urban renewal agencies enabled them to plan and modernize on a major scale. While granting the problems inherent in urban renewal, Charles Abrams, a noted writer on housing and urban affairs, put the case for it as follows:

> The power of land assemblage makes possible establishment of contiguity between plots and the bringing into use of land with unmarketable titles that have held up development of whole sections; it facilitates the synchronization of public and private improvements as well as the planning of cohesive shopping centers. It allows room for more squares and parking spaces and is a useful tool for the long overdue rebuilding of cities enslaved to the 20- to 25-foot lot, the traffic-laden street, and the gridiron pattern. It provides the opportunity for enlarging the street system surrounding the new projects, the closing of streets where necessary, the diversion of traffic, the addition of streets or widening of intersections. It makes possible the creation of footways separating pedestrian traffic from the automobile, and two level or double-decked streets which have been talked about ever since Leonardo Da Vinci put forth his plan for a model city. It facilitates running the new highways into the city's shopping centers and the creation of off-street parking and enclosed parking space. In short, the renewal project supplies a multipurpose opportunity in place of the piecemeal efforts to correct traffic problems, provide playgrounds and open spaces, provide neighborhood amenities, and new housing, public and private.[28]

But Is It Efficient?

In an otherwise efficient market system subsidies promote inefficiency because they cause excessive use of the subsidized factor. In more formal terms, they cause the subsidized factor to be used past the point at which marginal cost equals marginal product. If, for example, we subsidize capital but not labor, then entrepreneurs will use too much capital and too little labor for maximum efficiency. To produce a given amount of product they will use a factor mix that is more expensive than the one they would choose if their behavior were not being distorted by a third-party payment. If the government offered you $1000 to junk your well-used but still-running car you might accept the offer and buy a new car sooner than you would otherwise have done. The waste in the process seems evident. Is this not what urban renewal did when it used federal funds to write down the residual value of old but still usable structures and have them demolished? Yes, it is. But perhaps it can be justified by a point made earlier in this chapter. The market for urban land is far removed from the economist's model of an efficient market because it is fraught with externalities. Thus it may be that the inefficiency of demolishing a building while it still has remaining value is compensated, or more than compensated, by the positive externalities flowing from better street patterns, an enhanced image of downtown, and a climate of optimism about the city.

Community Development, the Sequel to Urban Renewal

In 1973 the urban renewal program was ended, though federal funds obligated under urban renewal contracts still continue to be expended. In 1974 the Housing

---

[28] Charles Abrams "Some Blessings of Urban Renewal" in James Q. Wilson, ed., *Urban Renewal, The Record and the Controversy*, MIT Press, Cambridge, Mass., 1966, p. 560.

and Community Development Act eliminated a number of separate grant programs and replaced them with community development block grants. These grants, unlike urban renewal grants, are awarded not competitively but on the basis of a formula that counts population, poverty, and housing condition.[29] However, to receive grants a community must satisfy HUD that most of the monies will be used for activities that will aid low- and moderate-income people. It must also show HUD that the monies will actually be used for community development purposes and not simply to lighten the municipal tax burden by substituting for other funds such as sales or property tax revenues. (Here we note that money has a rather "fungible" quality and that determining whether or not substitution of funds has occurred is not always a simple matter. This point is explored in more detail in Chapter 10.)

Recipients of CDBG money must produce a housing assistance plan (HAP). This plan details the city's housing needs, particularly those of low- and moderate-income people, and indicates how those needs are to be met. In making up the HAP the city is required to consider the needs of those who can reasonably be expected to reside in the city as well as those who actually do so at present. HUD insistence on considering the "expected to reside" category parallels the recent thrust of judicial decisions requiring communities to take regional needs into account when formulating land-use control plans. In addition to the above stipulations, federal regulations also impose citizen participation requirements upon the community formulating the CDBG grant application. This, in part, is a reaction to the perception in years past that urban renewal agencies often acted in ways that had major effects upon the poor without adequately considering their interests.

How strictly HUD enforces all of these requirements has varied somewhat with presidential administrations. At present, enforcement largely takes the form of accepting municipal certification that the requirements have been met. This is hardly the most formidable of enforcement procedures. However, it is not entirely trivial either. The existence of requirements and community certification that it has adhered to them could easily furnish grounds for litigation by an advocacy group that felt that the interests it represented have been overlooked or slighted.

Community development funds can be used for a very wide range of purposes, including some which are similar to those noted in connection with urban renewal. Funds may also be used for a wide variety of economic development purposes, for the construction and rehabilitation of housing, for the provision of physical infrastructure, for the provision of public facilities, and for the provision of social services.[30]

In general, community development efforts tend to take a much gentler approach to the urban fabric than did urban renewal. There is, typically, much less emphasis on the clear-and-rebuild approach and much more emphasis on preservation. For example, efforts in regard to the commercial sector of the city are likely to take the form of street improvements, loans to businesspeople to improve their facilities, and the like—rather than efforts to clear land and attract

---

[29] For a brief account of CDBG-funded programs, see chap. 16 in Frank So, ed., op. cit.
[30] For a list of eligible activities see *The Federal Register*, March 1, 1978, part III.

new businesses. Most communities are now quite leery of actions that will displace existing economic activity. On the housing side there is an emphasis on preservation. This often takes the form of grants or loans to property owners to rehabilitate existing structures. One approach which has been the subject of much attention has been urban homesteading. In many ways it typifies the gentler post-urban renewal approach.

In this process deteriorated housing that has come into the city's possession, perhaps because it has been abandoned or because it has been foreclosed for tax reasons, is essentially given to the occupant if he or she will bring the property up to standards within a specified time. For the occupant the cost of acquiring title is, for practical purposes, the cost of rehabilitating the structure. The cost may be primarily monetary if the work is done by contractors or it can be largely sweat equity if the occupant does the work. The technique improves the physical quality of housing and frequently arrests neighborhood decline. And it does so without the physical and social disruption associated with clearance and new construction. It also sprinkles the neighborhood with residents who have made a serious commitment to it, a fact that in itself should contribute to stability.

In Baltimore, the technique has been used extensively with apparently very successful results in old row house areas. The prospect of obtaining title for the cost of repairs seems attractive enough to bring working-class and middle-class urban homesteaders into decaying neighborhoods. At the same time it has generally not proven to be so profitable as to attract speculative capital. In other words the homesteader is likely to be a long-term neighborhood resident.

The UDAG program mentioned in Chapter 5 might also be considered something of a successor to urban renewal. In that its funds have been used to assemble and clear land it does resemble urban renewal. As a practical matter it differs in scale. Urban renewal projects often involved many blocks and major displacements of population and economic activity. Typically the UDAG project is on a much smaller scale and much less disruptive.

APPENDIX: The Present Value of Future Income

Very often it is useful to convert the value of a stream of future payments into present value. For example, a firm or government agency contemplating a present expenditure that will yield future income or benefits needs to be able to weigh one against the other in order to make a go or no-go decision. To obtain the present value of a future sum one uses a discount factor to make the conversion. Assume that at present the most secure form of investment, say, a government obligation, pays interest of 10 percent per annum. How much is a firm commitment to pay $100 a year from today worth today. The figure $100/1.10 will give us the sum that would yield $100 a year from today if invested today at 10 percent. And that is the present value. If the commitment were to pay $100 two years from today, then the present value would be $100/(1.10)^2$. If the commitment were to be to pay $100 per year for the next 25 years, the present value would be the sum of all the terms from $100/(1.10) + $100/(1.10)^2$, etc., up to $100(1.10)^{25}$. Note that with any positive rate of interest value of a given sum declines with the passage of time, and the larger the rate of interest the more rapidly the decline occurs. The point Anderson was making in connection with the fact that the loss in tax revenue precedes the increase in tax revenue was that the total accounting should be done in terms of the sort of present-value calculation shown above. (Parenthetically, it should be said that choosing a discount rate is often a good deal more complicated and more of a judgment call than the illustration suggests. In cost-benefit analysis choice of the discount rate can often determine whether or not a project shows an acceptable or unacceptable cost-benefit ratio. Those who favor a project may argue for a low discount rate, and those opposed for a high discount rate.)

CHAPTER 9

URBAN TRANSPORTATION

John Dickey
College of Architecture and Urban Studies
Virginia Polytechnic Institute and State University

It has been said that the urban transportation problem is quite simple: everyone wants to go to the same place at the same time. And, of course, they would like to go there quickly and at low cost.

Obviously, all of the above is not literally true, but there is a great deal of truth in it. While all of us do not want to go to the same place, no one who has traveled to midtown Manhattan or the Chicago loop at 8 a.m. on a weekday can doubt that many of us wish to go to the same place at the same time. Clearly, travel time is important, and in fact studies of travel demand clearly indicate that people judge the quality of alternative modes of transportation more by time than by any other single quality. Given that we spend about one-eighth of our GNP on private transportation, it is clear that cost is also a significant factor.

The above statement of goals contains many contradictions. The "same place" and "same time" statements are at odds with the speed and price considerations, which are themselves contradictory. And so on. Therefore, transportation planning, policy formulation, and investment are, in part, matters of allocating limited resources among competing and contradictory goals. No matter how skillfully allocations are made, the inherent contradictions between goals guarantee that there will always be some public dissatisfaction with the choices made and the results achieved.

Economists might cast the problem in still more general terms. The urban transportation problem is one of allocating scarce resources efficiently—a matter first of deciding how much is to be allocated to urban transportation and then of deciding precisely how that sum should be allocated between different individuals, modes, etc. Microeconomic theory tells us that an efficient allocation of resources in a market system will not occur without a system of true prices, that is, prices

259

that accurately reflect the true costs of production. The provision of transportation services, private or public, is fraught with externalities, and thus the prices
we pay at the gas pump or the turnstile often are very inaccurate representations
of true costs. Thus economists might argue that to a large degree the problem of
achieving efficient resource allocation resolves itself into one of improving price
signals—not an easy matter, as we will demonstrate later.

FACTS AND RECENT TRENDS

It can be said that almost nothing stops the growth of urban travel. The energy
crisis of 1973 barely put a dent in annual mileage in urban areas and the near
doubling of petroleum costs in 1978–1979 simply stopped the increase in travel for
1 year. Urban transportation, like transportation in general, seems to be income-
elastic. From 1960 to 1979 real GNP increased by 101 percent, but vehicle mileage
in urban areas increased by 159 percent. In the last several decades the number of
automobiles in the United States has increased far more rapidly than the human
population. In fact, from 1970 to 1980 the number of passenger cars registered in
the United States increased by about 30 million and the number of people living in
the United States by about 23 million as shown in Table 9-1. From 1972 on the
number of automobiles also increased more than did the number of licensed
drivers.

As noted in earlier chapters, the post-World War II period was one of rapid
suburbanization. The growth of the nation's stock of automobiles is closely tied to
this process. The widespread ownership of automobiles facilitates suburbanization, while suburbanization increases the demand for automobiles. Thus it might
not be too farfetched to say that the automobile industry has been one of the
beneficiaries of the homeowner tax treatment described in Chapter 7.

TABLE 9-1
VEHICULAR TRAVEL IN URBAN AREAS, 1940–1979
(Figures in Billions Except where Noted)

	1940	1945	1950	1960	1970	1975	1979
Total miles of travel	150	130	218	332	578	730	859
Passenger cars	129	109	182	285	495	610	684
Trucks and combinations	20	19	34	45	81	118	172
Transit*	2.6	3.3	3.0	2.1	1.9	2.0	2.0
Transit revenue passengers	10.5	19.0	13.8	7.5	5.9	5.6	6.4
Passenger car registrations (in millions)†	27.4	25.8	40.3	61.7	89.2	106.7	120.2

* Includes trolley, subway, and commuter rail, which are about one-fourth to one-fifth of total transit, depending
upon year. Excludes school buses.
† Entire United States; separate figures for urban areas not available.
Sources: American Public Transit Association, *Transit Fact Book* (annual); Federal Highway Administration,
Highway Statistics Annual; Department of Transportation, Federal Highway Administration, releases; and Department
of Commerce, Bureau of Public Roads, releases.

TABLE 9-2
EXPENDITURES ON TRANSPORTATION, 1979
(Figures in Billions)

Gross national product	2,414
Total vehicle-related expenditures for transportation*	507.7
Passenger	305.4
Private	264.8
Private ground	258.2
Public (for hire)	40.6
Public local	12.4
Bus and transit	6.9
School bus	2.9
Taxi	2.9
Selected sources of expenditure and revenue:	
Expenditures on highways, all levels of government	37.5
Receipts from highway user taxes and fees and intergovernmental transfers	37.5
Taxes on motor fuel, all levels of government	14.7
Transit operating assistance, all levels of government	2.8

* Figure includes freight transportation. Thus figures below do not add to this total.

Sources: U.S. Bureau of the Census, *Governmental Finances in 1979–80*; Survey of Current Business, Bureau of Economic Analysis, National Income and Product Accounts of the United States, 1976–1979; Transportation Association of America, *Transportation Facts and Trends*.

Paying for Transportation

Expenditures on transportation amount to roughly one-fifth of the GNP, as shown in Table 9-2. Passenger transportation, exclusive of airline and intercity bus and rail, amounts to approximately one-eighth of GNP. Given that about three-fourths of the U.S. population resides in urbanized areas, it is clear that the major share of that eighth is spent by urban residents in urban areas.

For private ground transportation the figures in Table 9-2 clearly indicate that most costs are paid directly by consumers to suppliers of vehicles, fuel, repair services, and the like. Most of the remaining costs are carried by a variety of taxes and user charges levied directly upon travelers. Such charges include the gasoline excise tax, license fees, and tolls.

For public transportation the situation is quite different. Less than half of the cost of providing service is recovered from the fare box. The remainder is paid by subsidy. For public transportation to be self-sustaining at the present passenger volume, average fares would have to more than double. But this, of course, would substantially cut patronage. Thus it is dubious that much public transportation would survive if it were required to be self-sustaining to the same extent as is private transportation.

The Cost of Transportation

Figure 9-1 shows changes in the price index for various components of ground passenger transportation from 1970 to 1980. Note that the item that increased most in cost was fuel and the item that increased least was the cost of automobiles themselves. (From 1980 to 1984 fuel costs have declined slightly.) The increase in fuel costs would appear to have favored public transportation, which in the early 1970s required about one-third as much fuel per passenger mile as did private transportation.[1] However, this advantage was counterbalanced by the fact that labor costs mounted very rapidly. As a labor-intensive activity, public transportation was hit much harder by labor cost increases than was private transportation. Even if transit fares had remained constant in real terms, operating losses would have mounted. In point of fact, transit fares have generally lagged behind inflation

FIGURE 9-1.
Price indexes for selected transportation items. (*U.S. Department of Labor, Bureau of Labor Statistics, Monthly Consumer Price Index Reports.*)

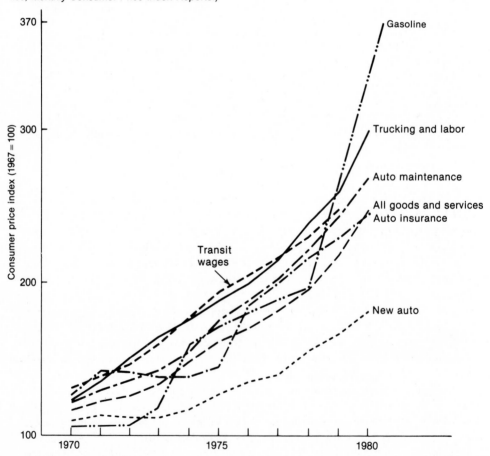

[1] J. W. Dickey et al., *Metropolitan Transportation Planning*, 2d ed., McGraw-Hill, New York, 1983.

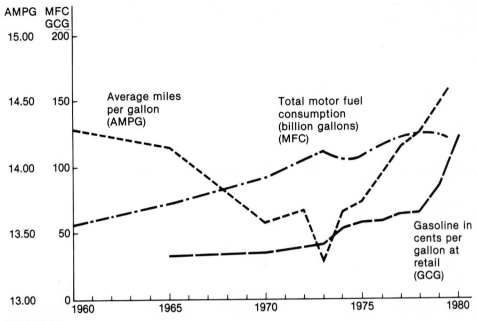

FIGURE 9-2
Motor fuel consumption and average mileage, 1960–1980. (*U.S. Federal Highway Administration, Highway Statistics, various issues.*)

in recent years, resulting in an increasing deficit, which has been made up by subsidy.

The approximate tripling of motor fuel costs between 1973 and 1980 is generally regarded as the most significant transportation-related event to occur in many years. Yet its apparent effect on travel behavior has been small. Figure 9-2 illustrates the U.S. response to increases in fuel costs. If we compare the percentage changes in fuel consumption with percentage changes in fuel prices, it becomes obvious that the short-term elasticity of demand for fuel is very low. One reason for this is that the demand for transportation itself is a derived demand. People generally do not want transportation for its own sake but because it permits them to engage in some other activity such as recreation. Because transportation is only part of the total cost of the activity, demand for transportation is likely to be less price-elastic than if transportation were an end in itself.

When we turn to the price elasticity of fuel, the argument is repeated. The demand for fuel is derived from the demand for transportation. Thus a large percentage increase in fuel costs means a much smaller percentage increase in the total cost of automotive transportation. For example, assume that automobile travel has a price elasticity of 1 and that fuel costs constitute 20 percent of total cost. Then the elasticity of demand for fuel should be .2, since a 1 percent rise in fuel prices will increase total driving costs by .2 percent.

The mileage line on the chart suggests that the main effect of fuel cost increases has been to cause an increase in the energy efficiency of the nation's automobile fleet. Note that average miles per gallon had been declining until the first round of fuel cost increases in 1974 and then began a steady rise. Because the average automobile lasts about a decade, only one-tenth of the fleet is replaced each year. Therefore the mileage line on the figure seriously understates the increase in fuel economy of newly manufactured vehicles. For example, autos manufactured in the United States in 1982 had mpg averages in the mid-20s, almost twice the 1973 fleet average, and imported vehicles showed somewhat higher averages. If the cost of fuel is adjusted for inflation, the real per mile fuel cost of operating the average newly manufactured automobile in 1982 was probably somewhat lower than that of operating the average automobile in 1973.

Table 9-3 shows estimated costs for automobile and public transportation, the former on a per vehicle mile and the latter on a per passenger trip basis. To convert the automobile costs to a passenger mile basis the vehicle figures should be divided by about 1.6 to adjust for the average number of occupants per vehicle. This yields a figure of about 16 cents per mile. Transit trips cost about 86 cents apiece, equivalent to between 5 and 6 miles of automobile travel. This should indicate why transit must be heavily subsidized if it is to survive. For the automobile owner deciding whether to drive or take public transportation the decision is likely to be made on the basis of marginal cost of driving rather than average total cost. Thus items like insurance, license fees, and perhaps repair and depreciation costs as well, which figured in the per mile cost cited earlier, will not figure in the car versus transit decision for a particular trip. This further weights the decision against transit.

Some General Characteristics of Transportation Systems

A basic characteristic of most transportation systems is the tradeoff between velocity and volume. This relationship, which has been determined by studies of traffic flows, is shown in Figure 9-3. For a modern limited-access highway maximum volume (that is, vehicles passing a given point per unit of time) is

TABLE 9-3
AUTOMOBILE AND TRANSIT COSTS, 1979
(In Cents)

Total automobile costs per vehicle mile*	24.6
Depreciation	6.3
Repair and maintenance†	5.5
Fuel and oil	5.5
Insurance	2.5
Garage and parking	3.2
Taxes and fees	1.6
Total transit costs per passenger trip‡	86
Paid from fares	38

　* Based on a standard-size vehicle purchased new and driven 100,000 miles over 10 years in the Baltimore metropolitan area.
　† Includes tire replacement and purchase of accessories.
　‡ Computed on the basis of 6.4 billion revenue passengers, $2.5 billion in fares, and operating expenses of $5.5 billion.
　Sources: U.S. Federal Highway Administration, *Cost of Operating an Automobile* (periodic); American Public Transit Association, *Transit Fact Book* (annual).

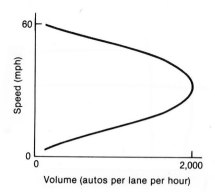

FIGURE 9-3
The speed-volume relationship. The figure shows the approximate relationship for a limited-access highway designed to Interstate standards. Note that maximum throughput occurs at moderate speed. Above this speed the greater vehicle spacing required reduces volume.

achieved at about 35 mph. Above that speed the spacing between vehicles increases so much that flow past a given point declines. Similarly, an attempt to put more vehicles onto the road causes congestion, which causes speed to fall more rapidly than the spacing between vehicles declines and again volume falls.

The Induced-Demand Phenomenon   The relationship between speed and volume explains a common phenomenon generally referred to as *induced demand*. It has been observed that when a new road is built to relieve congestion the decongesting effect is often much smaller than would be the case if the previous level of traffic were now being shared by the old and the new facility. What has happened is that as the new facility accepts traffic from existing routes, speed increases on the old routes, travel becomes more attractive, and total traffic volume rises. Thus the resulting improvement in travel speed is often much less than a naive calculation, which took total traffic volume as a given, would have suggested. If system capacity is increased, the main increase in utility may come from the fact that more travelers are now using the system at the peak hour. But travelers may justifiably wonder what was accomplished by the additional public investment because they are not much better off than before. Downs has summarized this phenomenon in what is sometimes referred to as Downs's Law of Peak-Hour Traffic Congestion: on urban commuter expressways peak-hour traffic congestion rises to meet maximum capacity.[2]

The Peaking Phenomenon   Another characteristic of travel is its peaking in time. In metropolitan areas the highest volumes are, as we would expect, found in the early morning and at the end of the workday. This is shown in Figure 9-4. Typically, the evening peak may contain somewhat more travelers than the morning peak because a certain number of people who have traveled to downtown after the end of the morning peak return home with the evening peak. Peaking is sharpest for work trips, which is again as we would expect. If we examine peaking characteristics by mode of travel we see that those modes that are most specialized in commuting to work peak most sharply. Thus in a major metropoli-

[2] Anthony Downs, *Urban Problems and Prospects*, 2d ed., Rand McNally, Chicago, 1976, chap. 9.

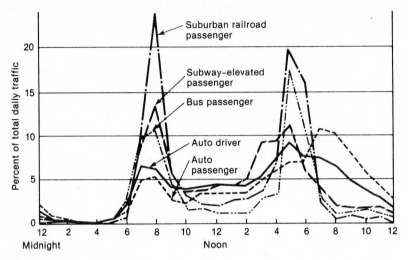

FIGURE 9-4
The peaking of travel in Chicago. (*Chicago Area Transportation Study*, Survey Findings, 1959.)

tan area, where all modes are in use, commuter rail and subways (or elevated railways) peak most sharply. Buses peak somewhat less sharply, and automobiles peak least sharply of all. The peaking characteristics of travel can be altered somewhat by the level of service offered. For example, extreme congestion in the peak hour may spread the peak somewhat as travelers seek to avoid discomfort and delay by traveling before or after the peak. Conversely, as noted in connection with Downs's Law, increasing peak-hour capacity with the intention of relieving congestion may sharpen the peak, with the result that peak-hour delays are not reduced as much as might have been expected.

Marginal Costs of Peak-Hour Capacity Almost all transportation systems have a great deal of overcapacity built into them because they are designed to handle, however badly, peak-hour loads. This statement is true of both roads and public transportation facilities. Improving the peak-hour performance of transportation systems often involves very high marginal costs because the additional capacity needed is only used for a very small portion of the weekday and may be entirely unused on weekends. Thus the answer to the question, Why don't they do something about rush-hour congestion? may well be, Because the marginal costs are too high. How satisfying this answer is to the citizen with a limited interest in marginal economics is another matter.

If fares (or tolls) are constant across the day, it can be argued that the off-peak traveler subsidizes the peak-hour traveler. This is because the off-peak user of the system uses capacity that is also used during the peak, whereas many peak-hour travelers use capacity that is idle for the rest of the day.

The Collection and Distribution Problem One obvious but sometimes overlooked point about travel is that trip time is made up of three components. These are generally referred to as collection, line haul, and distribution. The first refers to the time required to get to the main mode employed, the second refers to travel on that mode, and the third to the time between departing from the main mode and actually arriving at one's destination. For automobile trips where the vehicle is kept near the orgin and parked at or near the destination, the line haul will account for the overwhelming percentage of total trip time. For fixed-route and fixed-schedule modes or for auto trips in congested areas where the vehicle cannot be parked at the precise point of origin or destination, the collection and distribution segments of the trip may account for much of the total travel time. Thus substantial increases in line-haul speed may produce much smaller percentage improvements in total trip time.

To illustrate this point assume the following. A traveler takes 10 minutes to walk to the boarding point and wait for a vehicle that takes 30 minutes for a 10-mile trip. At the end of the trip the traveler gets off and walks 10 minutes to the actual destination. The trip covered 10 miles in 50 minutes, for an average of 12 mph, even though line-haul speed was 20 mph. Suppose line-haul speed were doubled to 40 mph. Travel time would be 35 minutes and trip speed 17 mph. Thus line-haul speed increased by 100 percent, but total trip time decreased by only 30 percent. If line-haul speed is increased to 60 mph, trip time falls to 30 minutes. In this case a 200 percent increase in line-haul speed produces a 40 percent decrease in travel time. In fact, even if line-haul speed were infinite, so that line-haul time was zero, the door-to-door speed would be only 30 mph.

Income and Price Elasticity of Travel Demand   As noted earlier the income elasticity for urban travel in general appears to be greater than 1. But this relatively high figure applies only to private transportation. For public transportation there is little doubt that the figure is much lower, and in fact the income elasticity of public transportation may actually have the "wrong" sign. That is, as income rises, the absolute amount of public transportation may fall. This is indicated by the negative sign of the last number shown in Table 9-4.

TABLE 9-4
SELECTED TRAVEL ELASTICITY DATA

	Variable	Mean elasticity
Transit ridership in 263 cities	Fare	−.33
New York City after July 1966 fare increase	Fare	
7 a.m. to 10 a.m.		−.07
7 p.m. to 11 p.m.		−.44
	Bus miles of service	.76
Transit ridership	Income	
$0–3,999		.28
$10,000 and over		−.03

Source: U.S. Department of Transportation, Office of the Secretary, *Public Transportation Fare Pricing*, NTIS, Springfield, Va., 1977

For private transportation the price elasticity is probably less than 1. This relatively low figure seems likely because the demand for transportation is generally a derived demand, a point discussed earlier.

Studies of the price elasticity of demand for public transportation generally show it to be low. A commonly quoted figure is $-.33$, as shown in Table 9-4.

The low price elasticity figure for public transportation is consistent with the economists' view of the factors that predispose to inelastic demand. Specifically, for many who use public transportation (those too young to drive, the elderly, and members of households which do not own automobiles) no close substitute is available. Then, too, the demand for public transportation is a derived demand in that few of us ride buses or subways simply for pleasure. Finally, compared with other items in the household budget, the cost of public transportation is not very large. As shown in Figure 9-4, peak-hour demand is less elastic than off-peak demand. Presumably, travel to work is more of a necessity than other types of travel.

The difference between peak-hour and off-peak elasticity suggests some policy points. One is the possible desirability of varying the fare by time of day; indeed, some systems, such as Washington, D.C.'s Metrorail, do this. The low elasticity of demand in the peak hour permits fares to be raised substantially without major loss of patronage. In the off-peak period lower fares are appropriate, since maintaining peak-hour fare levels would result in considerable patronage loss. Then, too, higher fares in periods when marginal costs are highest should move us in the direction of efficient resource allocation by narrowing the gap between price and marginal cost. Finally, it can be argued that it is just that those who impose the highest costs on the system pay the highest prices.

As a generalization, one consequence of the low elasticity of demand for public transportation is that attempting to increase ridership by means of fare cuts is a very expensive process. A large fare cut produces only a small ridership increase and thus the marginal cost of attracting a new rider is quite high. Research has shown that the quality-of-service elasticity of demand for public transportation may be twice as high as the price elasticity (e.g., for bus miles of service in Table 9.4). However, the cost of providing either faster or more frequent service can be very high.

The Problems of Public Transportation

Unlike private transportation, public transportation has followed a generally declining course in recent decades. Public transportation ridership peaked in 1945, a time when employment was high, production of automobiles for civilian use had been stopped for several years, and gasoline was rationed. Since then, ridership has dropped substantially. In the mid-1970s a gentle upturn began. The upturn corresponds to a period of rising fuel costs and increasing subsidization of public transportation. But the overall picture is one of the public treating public transportation as an inferior good in the economist's meaning of the term: a good whose consumption declines in absolute terms as incomes rise.

In general, transit (by which is meant bus, subway, trolley, commuter rail, and other scheduled public modes) is much more heavily used for work trips than for

TABLE 9-5
MEANS OF TRANSPORTATION TO WORK IN SMSAs, 1975
(In Thousands)

Total	55,146
Drive alone	36,378
Car pool	10,120
Public transportation	4,625
Bus or streetcar	2,953
Subway or elevated train	1,177
Railroad	395
Taxicab	100
Other means	734
Walked only	2,482
Worked at home	1,079

Source: U.S. Bureau of the Census, *Current Population Reports*, ser. P23, no. 99.

other types of travel. Yet as shown in Table 9-5 transit accounts for only a small percentage of all work trips. In fact, the last three categories account for almost as many trips to work as transit. Public transportation use varies considerably from one SMSA to another. For example, a 20-area sample in 1977 showed a range of 2 percent for Fort Worth to 16 percent for Boston.[3]

There appear to be several reasons behind the decline of public transportation. Perhaps the most obvious is that increasing real income has made it possible for the great majority of households to own an automobile. But this begs the question of why most people appear to prefer the automobile. Privacy and flexibility of schedule are clearly points in favor of private transportation. Then, too, the collection and distribution problem noted earlier tends to make the door-to-door speed of public transportation low. Beyond that, the line-haul speeds on public transportation tend to be low because of frequent stops. Line-haul speeds can be increased by reducing the number of stops. That, of course, complicates the collection and distribution problem.

Data collected by Vuchic for various transit systems in the 1970s show speeds in the range of 5 to 6.2 mph for buses on city streets.[4] For buses on reserved lanes the average speed was about 7 mph. Express buses were faster, but still slow. Cleveland's Clifton Boulevard express service averages 11.2 mph. Rail rapid transit did better, but average speeds were still not impressive. The figure for Chicago was 26.7 mph and for Philadelphia and Toronto, less than 19 mph. These figures are point to point from the moment of embarkation to the moment of debarkation. If average waiting time were counted, the figures would be lower.

Point-to-point speeds by automobile vary greatly by locale but, in general, are far higher than by public transportation. Table 9-6 shows speeds in the more heavily traveled direction during the peak in Maricopa County, Arizona, for a number of years. Although speeds appear to have fallen somewhat with increasing

[3] U.S. Bureau of the Census, *Current Population Reports*, ser. p 23, no. 105.
[4] V. Vuchic, *Urban Public Transportation: Systems and Technology*, Prentice-Hall, Englewood Cliffs, N.J., 1981.

TABLE 9-6
AVERAGE PEAK PERIOD (PEAK DIRECTION) SPEED BY JURISDICTION IN MARICOPA
COUNTY, ARIZONA

	Speed (mph)				Change in speed, 1966– 1979
	1966	1970	1976	1979	
Glendale					
Major streets	31.0	33.6	33.0*	32.0	1.0
Mesa					
Major streets	38.9	39.7	35.0*	33.3	−5.6
Freeway	—	—	—	49.3	—
Phoenix					
Major streets	28.4	29.0	29.0*	29.4	1.0
Freeway	58.4	58.0	49.2	48.8	−9.6
Scottsdale					
Major streets	32.1	32.1	35.0*	32.2	0.1
Tempe					
Major streets	33.8	33.1	26.0*	27.4	−6.7
Freeway	—	66.9	54.3	53.9	NA
Maricopa County					
Major streets	43.5	44.5	43.0*	41.2	−2.3
Total					
Major streets	31.5	32.2	32.0	31.2	−0.3
Freeway	58.4	58.5	49.9	49.8	−8.6

* Estimated for all streets surveyed in 1979 from a more limited number of streets surveyed in 1976.
Source: Maricopa Association of Governments, Transportation and Planning Office, *Travel Speed Study, Phoenix Metropolitan Area, 1957 through 1979*, Phoenix, December 1980.

congestion, it is apparent that they are several times higher than can be achieved by public transportation.

The slowness of public transportation appears in large measure to account for its apparent inferior-good status with a large percentage of the population. This status, in turn, would appear to go far toward explaining the inability of public transportation to be self-sustaining financially.

Transportation and Land Use   The automobile is a big consumer of space, both when it is in motion and when it is stopped. Thus the ideal environment for private automotive transportation is a relatively low density area where traffic flow will not be unduly affected by congestion and where land costs will be low enough that providing adequate parking space will not be difficult.

The ideal environment for public transportation is very much the opposite. A place like New York City, where a mass of employment is concentrated in a densely built central business district and where the densities in residential areas are also high, is close to ideal for public transportation as we have come to know it. Such a land-use pattern minimizes both the average distances from residences to the beginning of the line haul and the average distance from the end of the line to the destination. The high volume per corridor makes possible frequent service, which minimizes the waiting time in the collection phase of the trip. In point of fact, about one-third of all transit trips in the United States are made in the New York metropolitan area even though the region contains only about one-twelfth of the U.S. population. As noted in earlier chapters, the pattern of development just described is the opposite of trends in the last several decades. The lowering of commercial and residential densities militates against fixed-route transportation, and the weakening of fixed-route transportation in turn encourages automobile use, thus encouraging further low-density development.

Unit Costs and Corridor Volumes For the automobile, the unit cost of a trip is not greatly affected by volume along that particular route. For buses, unit costs fall at first but flatten out at relatively low volumes. For rail, unit costs are extremely high at low volumes but continue to fall until very high volumes are reached. Given the heavy investment in capital costs associated with rail transport this is not surprising. Estimates made by Meyer, Kain, and Wohl in the 1960s show that the crossover point between rail and auto doesn't occur until a one-way peak-hour corridor volume of close to 20,000 is reached.[5] The number of CBDs in the United States that have the potential for generating volumes of that magnitude is quite small; thus the potential for rail in all but a few metropolitan areas is limited. Again, the continuing suburbanization of employment and population further tips the scales against any mode that requires a large concentration of origins, destinations, or both.

ECONOMIC INTERVENTIONS

Why is there public intervention in the provision of transportation services? Three reasons generally advanced are the existence of public goods, the desire to meet equity goals, and the presence of externalities. Let us examine these considerations in order.

One salient characteristic of a public good, in the economist's meaning of the term, is that "exclusion" is not possible. This means that it is not possible to exclude the nonpayer from benefiting; thus there is no way to make people pay for the good in a market transaction. Therefore, the good must be provided from public revenues if it is to be provided at all. Standard examples of public goods are national defense and lighthouses to guide mariners. Roads are generally treated as public goods. In principle it would be possible to charge for their use, but as a practical matter it is not.

Another reason for market intervention may be the desire to achieve equity gains. We may subsidize a particular service because we think it is used heavily by the poor, and we wish to, in effect, increase their real income. As discussed in the section of Chapter 6 devoted to welfare economics, a general argument can be made that it is more efficient to make direct transfers than to intervene in markets, and the majority of economists probably accept this position. Nonetheless, transportation policy is influenced to some degree by equity considerations, and

[5] J. R. Meyer, J. F. Kain, and M. Wohl, *The Urban Transportation Problem*, Harvard University Press, Cambridge, 1965. Some of their data are reproduced in an extract in Munby and Denys (eds.), *Transportation*, Penguin, New York, 1968.

the public discussion of transportation policy commonly includes such. In particular, the subsidization of public transportation has been defended on equity grounds, since in general those of low and moderate incomes spend a much larger percentage of their incomes on it. We note, however, that subsidizing public transportation does not always redistribute income downward. Commuter rail is often used by a fairly affluent segment of the population. For example, a large percentage of all commuter rail passengers arriving at New York City's Grand Central Station come from either Westchester and Nassau counties in New York State or Fairfield County in Connecticut. All three are among the most affluent counties in the United States. Similarly, the average income of patrons of the Bay Area Rapid Transit (BART) system in San Francisco is about that of the region as a whole.[6] Thus, subsidizing commuter rail is likely to achieve no downward redistribution of income and may even redistribute income upward.

Finally, we may intervene in markets because of the existence of externalities. If such exist, then the price signals upon which both the suppliers and the purchasers of transportation services make their decisions are distorted and a pure market solution will not give efficient results. Thus we may intervene with taxes and subsidies to cause prices to more nearly resemble true costs. In other words, we attempt to cause the internalization of externalities. The heavy subsidization of public transportation is based partly on the view that there are major positive externalities to be realized from diverting travel from automobiles to transit. For example, diversion of riders from autos to buses or trains may reduce air pollution. Those travelers who continue to drive benefit from the diversion of other drivers to transit because congestion is reduced and therefore traffic flows more rapidly. At the national level there may be political and balance-of-payments gains achieved by shifting some travel from private to public modes.

Marginal-Cost Pricing Those concerned with achieving efficiency in the provision of transportation, both public and private, have long been interested in the concept of marginal-cost pricing as a means of achieving an efficient allocation of resources. Let us digress briefly on the theory of marginal-cost pricing and then apply it to urban transportation. In any standard introductory text on economics the competitive firm is held out as the model of efficient resource allocation. The reason for this is that under competitive conditions $P = MC$ where P is price and MC is the marginal cost of production (see Figure 9-5). The argument, in brief, is that if production stops before $P = MC$ then there is an opportunity cost loss, represented by area A. Where the supply curve lies below the price, the factors are worth less in any other use than when combined into the product in question. The reason we know they are worth less in any other use is because they can be purchased for less than P. The distance between P and MC is the difference of the value of these resources when combined in the next highest use and when combined in the product in question.

Conversely, if production continues past the point at which $P = MC$, then, by the same sort of reasoning, the factors are worth more in some other use than in

---

[6] U.S. Department of Transportation, *BART's First Five Years: Transportation and Travel Impacts,* Washington, D.C., April 1979.

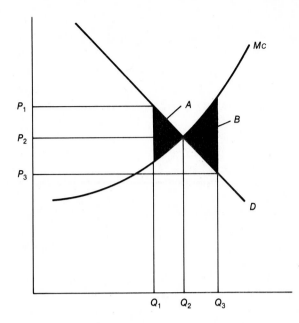

FIGURE 9-5
Marginal-cost pricing and economic efficiency. At price P_1 the quantity produced is Q_1 and the area A represents the opportunity cost loss of underproduction. At P_3 quantity Q_3 is produced and area B represents the waste of overproduction. Only at P_2Q_2 is the level of output efficient.

the product in question. We know this because they cost more to purchase individually than they are worth when combined into the product. That difference, again the distance between P and MC, is a measure of the economic waste of producing past $P = MC$.

The reader will recognize that there are a number of assumptions embedded in the argument. For example, the argument assumes implicitly that the prices of the factors of production are not distorted. It also assumes that there are no externalities present, for if there were, P would not be a correct measure of the total utility derived from consumption of the product, nor would MC accurately represent the cost to society ˙of the production of the marginal unit. Positive externalities would make prices too high and negative externalities would make prices too low.

Marginal-Cost Pricing and Time   To consider marginal-cost pricing further, we must make a distinction between *long run* and *short run*. The long run is a time period sufficient for all the factors that go into the supply of the product or service to be changed. The short run is any period shorter than that. In an extremely short period almost no costs may be variable. For example, in the case of a rapid transit line the long run would be a period sufficient to construct new routes, new terminals, etc. The short run might be a time period sufficient to hire new personnel or buy new rolling stock but not sufficient to change the fundamental dimensions of the system.

The above terms bear a relation to two other commonly used ones, *fixed cost* and *variable cost*. A variable cost is one that can be adjusted in the short term. A fixed cost is one that cannot be changed in the short term. In general, operating costs are regarded as variable and capital costs as fixed. But precisely what constitutes a fixed or a variable cost is a function of the length of the time period in question. For example, labor costs are generally considered variable. But for a very short time period, say 1 day, they are fixed. Over a period of 1 month those expenditures on labor for the basic 40-hour week may be fixed, but expenditures on overtime may be variable. Over a period of 2 or 3 years, all labor costs may be variable. For purposes of thinking about pricing decisions it is useful to keep the distinction between fixed and variable in mind.

Consider the following situation. We are contemplating construction of a bridge. The bridge is somewhat unusual in that although it involves substantial expense for construction, its maintenance and operations costs are zero. If the question is whether to build the bridge, a reasonable way to proceed would be to estimate the total value of the services the bridge will deliver over its estimated service life and compare them in one way or another with the cost of construction. If funds are unconstrained, the decision rule might be to build if benefits exceed costs. If funds are constrained (the more usual case), then the decision rule might be to compute a benefit-cost ratio for all projects, arrange them in order, begin funding with the project showing the highest benefit-cost ratio, and go as far down the queue as funds will permit.

Now assume that the bridge has, wisely or otherwise, been built. What charge should be levied for crossing? A strict marginal approach would dictate a charge of zero: since the cost of delivering a crossing is zero, the charge should be zero. But what about the capital cost? The answer is that those costs are sunk costs and should have no influence on the pricing decision. The purpose of attempting to set prices correctly is to achieve the best possible resource allocation. The resources that went into building the bridge have already been allocated. Assume that the decision to build the bridge has been, in retrospect, a very poor one. So few people use it that when we divide annual debt service by number of crossings, we get a per crossing cost of $100. Should we not recover some of this from those who use the bridge, considering how much has been spent to permit their crossing it? Again, the answer if we are to be strict marginalists is no.[7] There is no way we can recover the resources wasted in building the facility. All we can do is attempt to allocate resources efficiently from this point forward.

Marginal-Cost Pricing and Cost Recovery   Though the bridge example is a bit extreme, it does raise an important point. The original go–no go decision should be based on total costs because at that point all costs are variable. Once the decision has been made, pricing decisions should be made on the basis of costs to be incurred, not costs that have been incurred. If the pricing rule is to set $P = MC$, then the operation in question may run with a surplus ($P > ATC$), break even ($P = ATC$), or run at a loss ($P < ATC$), where P is price and ATC is average total cost.

In the first instance surplus revenues ought to be returned to general revenues, where they will presumably be allocated on the basis of sound marginal principles. In the middle case marginal-cost pricing will result in break-even operation and no transfer of funds will be necessary. In the last case subsidization will be

---

[7] This marginalist approach was set forth in an essay that appeared in 1844, about 3 decades before the marginalist revolution in economics. See J. Dupuit, "On the Measurement of the Utility of Public Works," reprinted in Munby and Denys, op. cit.

necessary. The $P = MC$ principle would dictate that in neither case should P be adjusted to deal with either surpluses or deficits. Obviously, there are many practical reasons why strict marginal-cost pricing is not always useful, so the above must be tempered with an eye to political realities, availability of funds, equity considerations, and the like.

Figure 9-6 shows examples of the three cases discussed above. Note that in the case of a declining cost industry a marginal-cost pricing policy will necessarily mean deficit operation because marginal cost will always be less than average variable cost.

Peak-Hour Pricing   A concept closely related to marginal-cost pricing is that of peak-hour pricing. The $P = MC$ ideal would suggest that the use of facilities should be priced so that during the day the price charged corresponds to the cost of delivering the service. For public transportation this would mean significantly higher fares during the morning and evening rush. To accommodate the marginal passenger in the evening rush the system has to maintain capacity that is used only once a day (the evening peak is generally somewhat higher than the morning peak). Obviously, the per rider cost of such capacity will be much higher than per rider cost of capacity that is used all day long. One effect of peak-hour pricing is to flatten the morning and evening peaks. This is desirable in that it permits the same passenger volume to be carried by a system with lower capacity. It may also increase travel speed by reducing congestion. However, an economic asset of the city is that it promotes interaction by collecting a large number of people in the same place at the same time. If the peak is spread too much, one of the remaining strengths of the city comes under attack. Staggered work hours have also been suggested and sometimes tried in order to reduce peak-hour congestion. But they, too, exact a cost in terms of decreased opportunity for interaction.

Some transportation agencies—for example, the Washington Metropolitan

FIGURE 9-6
Marginal-cost pricing and cost recovery. In all three cases, both P and Q are determined by the intersection of the marginal-cost curve MC and the demand curve D. AFC is average fixed cost, AVC is average variable cost, and ATC is average total cost. (a) Area I is revenue, areas I and II represent cost, and therefore area II is loss. (b) Areas I and II represent revenue, while area I represents cost, and area II is surplus or profit. (c) A decreasing-cost industry. Area I is revenue, areas I and II are cost, and therefore area II is loss.

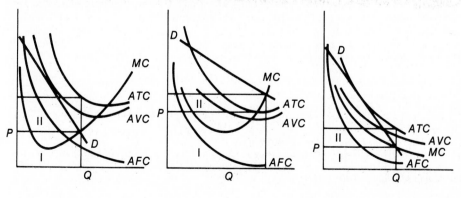

Area Transportation Authority—have adopted peak-hour pricing for their rail systems. The system also adjusts its fares for trip length. A recently built system, the Washington Metrorail system, uses a computerized fare collection system that facilitates such flexible pricing. For an old system, like that in New York City, which uses coin-operated turnstiles, implementing a complex fare system might pose very serious technical problems.

Adjusting Prices for Positive and Negative Externalities   Another aspect of the idea of marginal-cost pricing is that of adjusting the price of travel for externalities. When one decides to travel, one is implicitly making a decision to impose certain costs on others. Driving downtown, for instance, imposes time costs on other travelers because of the volume-velocity relationship noted earlier. Any use of a vehicle will impose some pollution costs upon those in the same airshed. Because one is not charged for imposing these costs (externalities), one does not normally take them into account in making decisions about whether or how to travel. Microeconomic theory would suggest that the situation would be made more efficient if we moved in the direction of truer prices by incorporating congestion and pollution costs in the cost of travel. More than 2 decades ago the economist Vickrey suggested using a metering scheme to charge motorists for driving in congested areas.[8] Essentially his scheme involved a meter mounted on the car that would be tripped electronically when the car was driven into certain designated areas. Periodically, the owner of the car would be billed for the sum accumulated on the meter. A variant of this scheme is now being tried in Singapore and another one is being considered for Hong Kong.[9]

BOX 9-1

MODELING THE EFFECTS OF TAXES AND SUBSIDIES

The idea of intervening in transportation markets with subsidies and taxes has been mentioned many times. For example, levying an excise tax on automobile use to divert drivers to transit has been suggested in order to save fuel and reduce air pollution. One way to evaluate such an idea is with a model that predicts the probable effects of such a tax or subsidy, as in the following example. The locale is Fairfax County, Virginia, and the model is one developed by Dickey and based somewhat on the work of Zahavi.[10] Zahavi originally showed vehicle miles of travel (VMT) to be a function of household income and the distance from the CBD of the concentric ring in which the household is located. Once VMT is predicted, we can predict fuel consumption and air pollution by applying empirically derived constants to the VMT figures. For example, for a household with an income of $20,000 to $25,000 located in the farthest ring the Zahavi model predicts 1811 trips per year and a VMT of 20,464. At an average mileage of 14.92 (a prevailing figure when the model was built but too low at present) annual fuel consumption is 1372 gallons. Carbon monoxide emissions are 1622 pounds based on a similar type of calculation.

---

[8] See, for example, William Vickrey, "Economic Efficiency and Pricing," in Selma. Mushkin, (ed.), *Public Prices for Public Products,* Urban Institute, 1972.

[9] *Relieving Traffic Congestion: The Singapore Area Income Scheme,* World Bank Staff Working Paper No. 281, Washington, D.C., 1978. See also, "Hong Kong to Put Electronic Toll Takers in Streets," *The New York Times,* April 7, 1983, p. A7.

[10] J. W. Dickey, "Methodology for Assessing the Impact of Various Transportation Taxes," Center for Urban and Regional Studies, Virginia Tech, Blacksburg, Va., March 1975. Y. Zahavi *Traveltime Budgets and Mobility in Urban Areas.*

The results of nine different interventions are shown in Table 9-7. If there are no additional taxes levied, VMT for the region is 2.47 billion, fuel consumption is 165 million gallons, and carbon monoxide emissions are 98,000 tons. If a tax of 1.33 cents per mile (20 cents per gallon) is levied, VMT and the related fuel and pollution figures drop by only 6.5 percent.

One point on which the straight gallonage tax of scenario 2 can be criticized is regressivity. Since VMT rises less rapidly than personal income, it will take a higher percentage from the less affluent than from the more affluent. This problem can be remedied by granting an exemption on some base level of mileage (neglecting the mechanical difficulties involved). If this is done, the regressivity does not show up until a fairly high level of income is reached. This option is shown as scenario 3. We have solved the equity problem but in order to do that we have lost about half of the VMT reduction of scenario 2. In scenario 4 we see the effects of raising the tax to 2.0 cents while leaving the 7500 mile exemption. The equity effects are similar to scenario 3 but the mileage and revenue effects are considerably larger. If we raise the exemption to 15,000 miles (scenario 5), the revenue and VMT effects shrink so much that the tax hardly seems worthwhile.

Scenario 6 presents a tax based on marginal-cost pricing. We have estimated the marginal costs of motor vehicle use as $MC = .02\ VMT + 0.0015\ VMT^{4.43}$. The tax is thus set to vary with the number of miles driven. With VMT at the scenario 1 figure of 2.47 billion miles, the tax would be set at the extremely high figure of 57 cents per mile. Of course this would immediately produce a drastic lowering of mileage with lower marginal costs and therefore a lower tax. After several iterations we are at the figures shown under scenario 7. The tax rate is still quite high and the reduction in vehicle miles is moderate. The tax would generate quite large revenues, which might be used to effect a general reduction in other tax rates. In spite of this, one would suspect that the attempt to impose such a large tax would meet with formidable and probably overwhelming public opposition.

The last two scenarios involve subsidies. Scenario 8 involves general income supplementation, and scenario 9 the direct subsidization of transportation. The conclusions we reach here are rather similar to those reached in Chapter 7 on the subsidization of housing. The direct subsidization of transportation is far more effective in increasing the amount of travel by low- and moderate-income households than is the untied transfer. The reasons for this are very much the same as those disucssed in Chapter 7.

Perhaps the most salient point brought out by this illustration is the difficulty of achieving a significant change in travel behavior with any pattern of taxation or subsidy whose magnitude is politically acceptable. One point the model does not address, however, is the long-term effects that taxation or subsidy might have on the technology of transportation. At the national level an excise tax might have little effect on the number of miles driven but a considerable effect on the types of vehicles purchased and hence on fuel consumption.

The Practical Limitations of Marginal-Cost Pricing   In general, any municipal administration would be well advised to think long and hard before applying microeconomic theory unquestioningly. For example in Manhattan, where a daytime population of over 3 million is crowded onto 22 square miles, automobile use has obvious negative externalities of pollution and congestion. Thus the marginal auto entering the island, particularly during the work day, imposes significant disutilities. Since all access to the island is via a relatively small number of bridges and tunnels, it would be an easy matter to apply fairly stiff tolls from, say, 6 a.m. to 6 p.m. and force entering motorists to bear the true cost of their travel decisions. But justifiable as such an action appears on a theoretical level, it might have some unpleasant practical consequences. For example, firms that were contemplating relocating from the city to the surrounding suburban counties might decide that this was the last straw and move. The result for the city would be job losses and falling tax revenues. The market for urban locations is a

TABLE 9-7
TAX AND SUBSIDY EFFECTS, FAIRFAX COUNTY, VIRGINIA
(Based on 1970 Data)

Item	1	2	3	4	5	6	7	8	9
Exemption	0	0	7,500	7,500	15,000	0	0	0	0
Tax per mile	0	1.33	1.33	2.00	2.00	58.0	23.0	0	−1.33
VMT (bil/yr)	2.47	2.31	2.39	2.35	2.45	0.64	1.16	2.56	2.65
Auto driver trips (billions/yr)	.32	.29	.31	.30	.32	.08	0.15	.34	.36
Fuel consumption (mil gal/yr)	165	155	160	157	164	43	77	172	177
Carbon monoxide (thou tons/yr)	98	92	95	93	97	25	46	102	105
Revenues* ($ mil/yr)	0	30.8	16.4	24.0	4.1	372.6	266.0	−260.1	−35.2
Mean tax burden as percent of household income*									
$10,000–12,000		1.25	.051		0				−1.60
12,000–15,000		1.20	.56		0.03				−1.40
15,000–20,000		1.08	.55		.07				−1.20
20,000–25,000		.97	.55		.19				−1.00
25,000+		.77	.43		.12				−.84
Minimum tax† burden for $15,000–$20,000 class		.84	.37		0				−1.50
Maximum tax† burden for $15,000–$20,000 class		1.33	.79		.35				−.97

* Negative number indicates subsidy.
† Minimum figure is for household in innermost ring. Maximum figure is for household in outermost ring.
Source: John W. Dickey, "Revised Analysis Methodology and Results: Selected Transportation Taxes in Fairfax County," *NSF Service Pricing and Urban Development Project,* Virginia Tech, Blacksburg, Va., June 7, 1975.

complicated one, and a clumsy intervention, even if well-justified in theory, might be the cause for regret.

The practical caveats are not meant to deride the use of microeconomic theory in the formulation of transportation policy. They are only meant to say that, like hard liquor, microeconomic theory should not always be swallowed straight.

A FRAMEWORK FOR ECONOMIC ANALYSIS

Economists and others concerned with the costs of alternative policies and actions have long worked with the "willingness to pay" concept. In this, all items of value to the potential user (demander)—that is, those for which he or she is willing to pay to gain or keep from losing—are considered. The idea of willingness to pay, then, is expressed in the demand curve, which relates quantities that would be purchased to prices. In the highway case the product offered is trips and the cost is the sum of vehicle operating cost, parking and other fees, and the time of the driver and passenger. Figure 9-7 shows a demand curve for travel between two points, as well as two different price figures. Here we follow the common textbook practice of showing demand curves as linear (straight lines). In practice, ascertaining what the demand curve actually looks like is not simple. In particular, it is difficult to know what either end looks like because travel is rarely either so expensive that almost none takes place or, conversely, so cheap that consumers can treat it as a free good. Thus what the curve looks like close to either the ordinate or the abscissa is not knowable in any practical sense.

The total benefit accruing to the consumer is the total area under the demand curve. Net benefit to the consumer (analogous to profit to the entrepreneur) is a residual obtained by subtracting total costs from total benefits. This leaves the triangle shown as net benefits to the consumer. A more formal term for net benefits is *consumers' surplus*. Note that this concept is not unique to transportation. Wherever there is a downward-sloping demand curve and the same price is charged all customers, some consumers' surplus must exist.

In order to estimate the net benefits to society as a whole it is also necessary to have cost data. In Figure 9-8 area I is the net benefit to the consumers. The small sliver-shaped area II is the producers' surplus. This is the difference between the

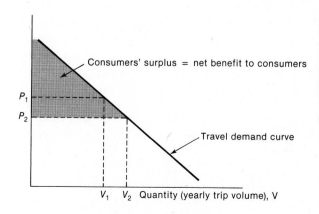

FIGURE 9-7
Consumers' surplus and the demand for transportation. When price is P_1, then volume is V_1 and consumers' surplus is indicated by the upper triangle. When price is lowered to P_2, volume increases to V_2 and consumers' surplus is measured by the larger triangle.

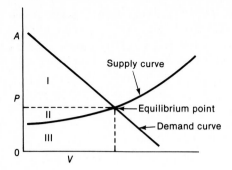

FIGURE 9-8
The supply and demand for transportation. Area I constitutes consumers' surplus, area II producers' surplus, and area III producers' costs. Net benefits are the first two items.

cost of supplying the service and the revenue obtained from it. It might be considered analogous to profit. Area III is the cost of supply. Net benefit to society is the sum of areas I and II, consumers' surplus plus producers' surplus.

EVALUATING TRANSPORTATION PROJECTS

In the above discussion we took for granted that we knew precisely what project costs and benefits were. In fact, determining what project costs and benefits are and placing them in common-denominator terms so that they can be compared can be a very complex matter. When this has been done we are then in a position to think about whether a particular project is a justifiable expenditure of funds and whether that project is relatively more or less justifiable than other projects. In order to fill in both sides of the ledger, it is necessary to make two basic types of determinations, neither of them easy. One is to determine, as accurately as possible, project costs and benefits and to express them in monetary terms. The other task is to determine how to weight future costs and benefits relative to present costs and benefits.

Converting Benefits and Costs to Monetary Terms

The conversion of as many values as possible to monetary terms is necessary because it is very difficult to think about the matter if we do not have common terms. Some items such as construction costs and savings in vehicle-operating costs are easily converted in principle, even if calculating them accurately may be difficult in practice. However, other matters are more complicated. If so many dollars in capital costs will save so much in traveler's time, how can we think about whether the investment is justifiable unless we can attach a money value to time? This is discussed at some length subsequently.

Since investment in transportation facilities affects the probability of deaths and injury to travelers or bystanders, then it is also necessary to try to assign a value to human life and health. Putting a dollar value on a human life may strike the reader as impossible or perhaps bizarre. Yet it is difficult to get away from the necessity. For example, limited-access roads have much lower accident figures per vehicle mile than do roads with unlimited access. In considering whether to replace the latter with the former, should we not count the reduction in probable death and injury as one of the benefits? But how can we count it if we are not able to put it in the same terms—namely, dollars—as the costs? A common technique is valuing life is to use estimated lifetime earnings. It may not be a good technique, but before condemning it too much, one ought to be able to suggest a better technique, something which is not easily done.

As a practical matter, when cost-benefit studies are done, three items generally emerge as the dominant magnitudes. These are construction costs, vehicle operating costs, and travel time saved. If, as is usually the case, only a limited number of possibilities are under consideration, the choice may come out the same no matter what reasonable assumptions are made about other matters such as death and injury. However, this may not always be the case. One approach may be to make an initial decision on the basis of the "big three" and then look at other questions to at least ascertain that including them would not change the decision. Apart from the matter of life and health, general matters of urban design might be considered, since the provision of access shapes land use. A project that would otherwise be selected might be ruled out if it clearly contributed to an undesirable land-use pattern.

Estimating the Value of Time

Often the most valuable benefits achieved by transportation system improvements are the saving of travelers' and shippers' time.[11] As an illustration of the estimating of benefits let us consider the valuing of time.

The monetary value of a given unit of time will, presumably, vary with the characteristics of the traveler, the trip purpose, and the amount of time saved. Four general approaches to the valuation of time include:

1 Study actual situations where a time-money tradeoff has been made by travelers and calculate value from travelers' choices.

2 Develop travel demand functions that include both time and money.

3 Estimate monetary gains in private and public employment accruing from time savings.

4 Extrapolate the value of time from housing demand functions in which travel time is a factor in determining the price of housing. Note the conceptual link here to the Alonso residential location model discussed in Chapter 3.)

Technique 1 is by far the most commonly used, even though it suffers from the limitation that it provides only minimum valuations. That is, if travelers shift from a slow, low-cost route to a fast, high-cost route, we know they value their time by *at least* the difference in costs, but we do not know how much more they would have paid to save that much time. Technique 2 is less commonly used because it requires the existence of a model specific to the particular place in question and the use of some fairly complicated mathematics. Techniques 3 and 4 are promising but still in the experimental stage.

Figure 9-9 shows 1975 data derived using technique 1 for travelers in the $12,000 to $14,000 income range. Note that the per minute value of time varies

---

[11] American Association of State Highway and Transportation Officials "Redbook" (8-2, pp. 14– Transportation Officials "Redbook" (8-2, pp. 14–19).

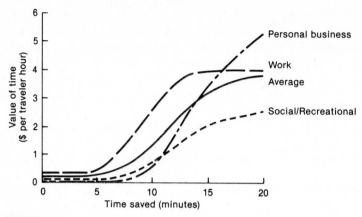

FIGURE 9-9
The value of time by trip purpose and amount of time saved. (*American Association of State Highway and Transportation Officials, A Manual on User Benefit Analysis of Highway and Bus Transit Improvements, 1977.*)

with both trip length and trip purpose. Presumably, higher-income persons value their time more highly than lower-income persons. (If the value of goods and services shows diminishing marginal utility, so too should the value of money itself.) In principle, Figure 9-9 could be used to obtain total travel time value for a particular transit improvement once the total number of trips was estimated. However, since many improvements are part of a larger program rather than isolated events, it becomes a needless refinement to select a particular point on the curve. Rather, the common practice is to either use cumulative time savings for all improvements on the route in estimating time value or establish several average time values for several general categories of travel (work, personal business, etc.).

For transit improvements it is advisable to specify different values for the time spent in and out of the vehicle, either walking or waiting. In general the latter has a higher value than the former. That is, another minute spent waiting is generally more onerous to the transit patron than another minute spent in motion. For average conditions, waiting and walking time is valued at about 1.5 times in-vehicle travel time. If the out-of-vehicle time is below average in comfort or safety, this ratio may be adjusted upward to 2 or more. Unlike travel time in the vehicle, small reductions in waiting or walking time are perceived as important by travelers.

A final point on the value of time is that data from recent studies show that total travel time in urban areas has been quite stable at about 1.1 hours per capita per day. This means that in the long term—and sometimes the short term as well—results of improved personal transportation usually show up in two ways: (1) longer trips—the tendency in large urban areas to increase spatial opportunities and decrease residential density—and (2) more frequent trips—such as increases in trips for cultural and social purposes.

Travel time savings might thus be regarded as a surrogate for other values that travelers seek.

Selecting the Discount Rate

Time also enters into the project evaluation in a sense quite different from the one discussed above. It is generally agreed that either costs or benefits accruing in the future should be weighted less heavily than equivalent costs accruing now. (See the appendix at the end of Chapter 8.)

The same kind of reasoning holds for benefits. Those that occur in the far distant future are worth less to "investors" than those that occur right away. Thus there must be a rate, otherwise known as a *discount rate*, applied to future benefits to equate these to present ones. The discounted benefits from a proposed transportation intervention should then exceed the discounted costs in order for it to be a worthwhile investment.

What discount rate to use in a given situation is a matter of some debate. If funds are being borrowed, the actual interest rate can be employed. If not, then some other means must be found for making such a determination. For further discussion on this point see Wohl and Martin and Winfrey.[12]

It must be noted that the choice of discount rate can drastically affect the present value of benefits or costs accruing in the future. Specifically, the higher the discount rate the smaller the present value of future benefits or costs. In a typical investment the bulk of the costs appear in the near term but the benefits stretch out for many years, as is shown in Figure 9-10. Thus the higher the discount rate the lower the calculated ratio of benefits to costs. In fact, the selection of the discount rate may determine whether the project's computed net benefits are positive or negative. Therefore the choice of discount rate may, to a considerable degree, predetermine the results that subsequent cost-benefit analysis will yield. This point is illustrated in Figure 9-11.

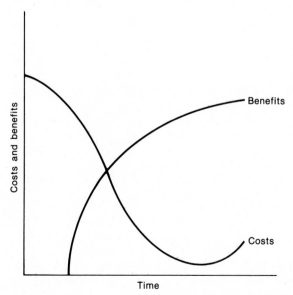

FIGURE 9-10
Hypothetical costs and benefits from a new highway project. Note that costs begin some time before benefits. The cost curve, which includes both maintenance and fixed costs, turns upward toward the end of the project's service life owing to the increased cost of maintaining an aging facility.

---

[12] M. Wohl and B. V. Martin, *Traffic Systems Analysis for Engineers and Planners*, McGraw-Hill, New York, 1967. R. Winfrey, *Economic Analysis for Highways*, International, Scranton, Pa., 1969.

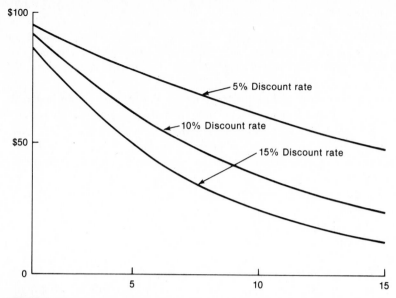

FIGURE 9-11
The present value of future payments (or benefits) discounted at different rates.
The figure shows that present value of a stream of $100 payments beginning 1
year hence and continuing to 15 years. The values are calculated from $S = \$100$
$(1/1+d)^n$ where S = present value, d = discount rate and n = number of years
from the present. NPV is the sum of all the S's and graphically can be considered
as the area under the curve out to n years. Thus, choice of the discount rate can
have a major effect on the magnitude of NPV and thus on the apparent advisability or inadvisability of the proposed project.

Cost-Benefit Analysis

Cost-benefit analysis refers to the process of accumulating and comparing a
project's benefits and costs so as to make some judgment on the advisability or
inadvisability of the project or to compare the project to other projects. In general,
all costs and all benefits are cast in terms of present value so that a direct benefit-
to-cost comparison can be made. Costs and benefits are converted to present
value, as shown in the appendix to Chapter 8. In the material that follows we
discuss three different and commonly used ways of assessing benefits and costs:
(1) net present value, (2) cost-benefit ratio, and (3) internal rate of return. The
hypothetical data used in illustrating all three methods is presented in Table 9-8.
We assume that all four alternatives are expressed in terms of comparison to the
null, or do nothing, alternative. To simplify the arithmetic we have also assumed
that all costs and benefits accrue with a period of 3 years. Benefits for alternative
IV are calculated as $\$14,000/1.15 + 13,000/1.15^2 + 7,000/1.15^3$. Other benefits and
costs are calculated in a like manner.

Net Present Value The net present value (NPV) technique employs the
discount rate to calculate the value of a cost or benefit now versus some time in
the future. For the first alternative in Table 9-8, assuming a 15 percent discount
rate, the net present benefits would be $22,759. The net present costs would be
$23,137. The net present value would be obtained by subtraction, as follows:

TABLE 9-8
HYPOTHETICAL DATA FOR BENEFIT/COST CALCULATIONS

Intervention	Year	Change in			Change in user benefits
		Initial capital cost	Ongoing costs	Total	
I					
	1	21,000	3,000	24,000	14,000
	2		3,000	3,000	14,000
	3				
	Total	21,000	6,000	27,000	28,000
II					
	1	21,000	3,000	24,000	14,000
	2		3,000	3,000	14,000
	3		3,000	3,000	4,000
	Total	21,000	9,000	30,000	32,000
III					
	1	21,000	3,000	24,000	10,000
	2		3,000	3,000	14,000
	3		3,000	3,000	10,000
	Total	21,000	9,000	30,000	34,000
IV					
	1	21,000	3,000	24,000	14,000
	2		3,000	3,000	13,000
	3		3,000	3,000	7,000
	Total	21,000	9,000	30,000	34,000

$$NPV = 22{,}759 - 23{,}137$$
$$= -378$$

These are the four possibilities.

	Intervention			
	I	II	III	IV
NPV	−378	279	746	1,495
Ranking	4	3	2	1

Intervention IV will have the greatest excess of discounted benefits over costs. Intervention II has a greater excess than I, since the benefits last longer. Intervention IV's excess is more than III's because the benefits come earlier in time.

If the NPV of an intervention turns out negative, as for intervention I, the discounted costs exceed discounted benefits, and the project should not be undertaken unless there are some other, noneconomic benefits of great value.

Cost-Benefit Ratio   Some analysts prefer to see a ratio of benefits to costs rather than a difference (as in the NPV). In some senses a ratio is an indicator of "efficiency," showing the dollars of (discounted) benefits achievable for a given outlay of (discounted) costs. For alternative I we thus would have a cost-benefit ratio (CBR), as follows:

$$CBR = NPB/NPC$$
$$= 22,759/23,137$$
$$= 0.98$$

For the four projects:

	Intervention			
	I	**II**	**III**	**IV**
CBR ($/$)	0.98	1.01	1.03	1.06
Ranking	4	3	2	1

This leads to the same ranking of interventions as the NPV, and thus the same conclusions. But where project costs vary considerably, the NPV and CBR may not come out in the same order. For example, if intervention A had a NPC of 10,000 and a NPB of 20,000, the NPV would be 10,000 and the CBR 2.00. Yet intervention B may have an NPC of 5,000 and an NPB of 12,000, giving an NPV of only 7,000 but a CBR of 2.40. Thus one project is superior on an NPV basis and the other on a CBR basis. Note that if NPV is negative or CBR is less than 1 (if one is so then the other will necessarily be so), then the project cannot be justified unless some other benefits can be demonstrated. For example, in a period of high unemployment one might justify a project with a negative NPV on the grounds of providing jobs or general macroeconomic stimulation.

Internal Rate of Return A difficult question in both the NPV and CBR methods is the value of the discount rate. One way to avoid the issue is to compute the NPV for several discount rates to find the one at which the net present benefits just equal the net present costs (or, in other words, NPV = 0). This rate is known as the *internal rate of return* (*IRR*). The higher the IRR the more favorably the project would be viewed.

Calculation of the IRR is iterative because it cannot be done directly. Trials are made at successively lower discount rates until a negative NPV is found. The IRR is found by interpolating between that rate and the previous rate (lowest rate that gave a positive NPV). The IRR can also be found graphically, as shown in Figure 9-12. For alternative II, IRRs were computed for discount rates from 15 to 25 percent. The NPVs were found to be negative for greater than 19 percent. Graphic interpolation indicated an IRR of about 18.5 percent. Another way of doing this is to extrapolate from one side or the other. A similar result can be had by extending the line for the top two or bottom three points until it crosses the X axis.

The ranking of the four alternatives by IRR gives

	Intervention			
	I	**II**	**III**	**IV**
IRR (%)	10	19	20	31
Ranking	4	3	2	1

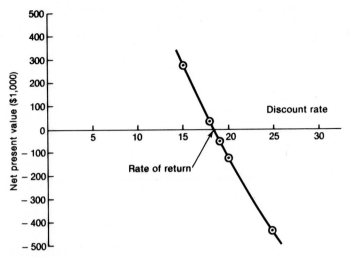

FIGURE 9-12
Graphic determination of the internal rate of return. (*John W. Dickey,*
Metropolitan Transportation Planning, *2d ed., McGraw-Hill, New York,
1983, p. 342.*)

In this case the order is the same as in the previous two situations; however, that
may not always be the case. As noted before, differences in project size may cause
rankings based on NPV to differ from rankings based on CBR. And, for reasons
too complex to explain here, there are instances in which IRR-derived and CBR-
derived rankings will not be identical.

MODELS OF DEMAND AND MODAL CHOICE

In the last section we discussed analysis of benefits and costs. In order to know
what the benefits of investment in transportation infrastructure are likely to be we
must be able to model transportation demand and behavior. For example, to know
whether investment in a new road is justified one must be able to estimate, among
other things, how many travelers will use that road, how much time they will save
using that route, and how travel times and traffic volumes in the rest of the system
will change. Otherwise, it is not possible to estimate benefits. If one cannot do
this, there is no way to say whether a given investment is justified or to decide
whether one investment is more or less desirable than another. Thus the
transportation-modeling process to be described is a necessary component of the
analysis described in the preceding section.[13]

The modeling of transportation behavior is a complex task, which is generally
broken down into four main subtasks.

1 Trip generation
2 Trip distribution

---

[13] The presentation here is necessarily a very brief one. For a more detailed and quantitative
description of the the modeling process, as well as references to the technical literature, see the
author's text on transportation planning cited in footnote 1.

3 Modal split

4 Trip assignment

The basic unit of analysis is traffic zone and the region to be studied is broken into a convenient number of these. Each zone is then taken to be a point at which trips originate and terminate.

Trip Generation

In step 1 the total number of trips originating or terminating in each zone is estimated without regard for destination or origin. A typical estimating equation for trips originating in a residential zone might be:

$$T_i - aP_i + bY_i + c$$

where T_i = number of daily trips produced in zone i
P_i = resident population of zone i
Y_i = average income of people in zone i
$a, b, c,$ = empirically derived parameters

Parameters a, b and c are developed through statistical analysis of actual travel behavior. Note that only economic and demographic variables have been used so far. No transportation system characteristics have been employed. They will, however, make their appearance in subsequent stages.

In general, trips per household are positively related to household size, household income, and number of vehicles owned. They are negatively related to the density of development. Some of these relationships are shown in Figure 9-13.

Trip Distribution

In step 2, the trip distribution process, the trips "piled up" at each zone are "dealt out" to the other zones in the region in a manner similar to the way in which individuals are known to allocate their trips to various destinations—usually on the basis of the relative attractiveness of each destination zone and its travel distance from the zone of origin.

The most commonly used trip distribution device is the *gravity model*. As its name implies it is derived by analogy from the law of gravity as advanced by Newton in 1686 to explain the force between (and consequent motion of) the planets and stars in the universe. Newton's equation for the force between the two bodies was:

$$F_{12} = G \frac{M_1 \times M_2}{d_{12}^2}$$

where F_{12} = the gravitational force between bodies 1 and 2
M_1 = mass of body 1
M_2 = mass of body 2
d_{12} = distance between bodies 1 and 2
G = a constant

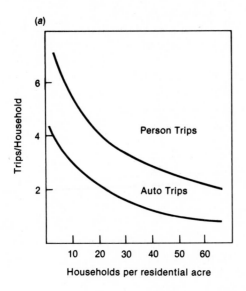

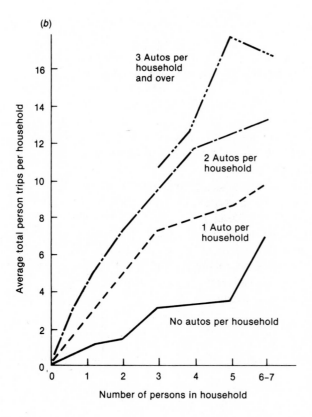

FIGURE 9-13
Two determinants of trips per household. (*U.S. Department of Transportation, Federal Highway Administration*, Guidelines for Trip Generation Analysis, 1976.)

Travel researchers noted that Newton's equation roughly described travel behavior, particularly for shopping.[14] M_1 might represent the "mass" of trips available at, say, a residential area; M_2 the "mass," or attractiveness, of a shopping area; d_{12} the distance between the two areas; and F_{12} the number of trips between the two areas. Note that trips thus vary directly with the "mass" of either the origin or destination and inversely with a power of the distance.

When the effect of several competing attraction areas (that is, multiple masses) is taken into account, the gravity trip distribution model becomes

$$T_{ij} = P_i \frac{A_j/d_{ij}^b}{(A_1/di_1^b) + (A_2/di_2^b) + \ldots + (A_n/di_n^b)}$$

where T_{ij} = number of trips produced in zone i and attracted to zone j

P_i = number of trips produced by zone i

A_j = attractiveness of zone j

d_{ij} = distance between zone i and zone j (Note that travel time rather than actual distance may be and usually is used for d)

b = an empirically determined exponent which expresses the average decrease in travel with increase in distance

What this formula states in essence is that the percentage of the trips produced in zone i (P_i) which go to zone j is dependent upon both the attractiveness (A_j) of zone j and the distance (or travel time) from zone i to zone j *relative to* the same features of all other attracting zones. Thus a new shopping center in zone j increases A_j and a road improvement between zones i and j decreases d_{ij}. Either event increases the relative pull of zone j on zone i and thus increases the share of P_i captured by zone j.

To illustrate the concept behind the gravity model consider the situation in which we are allocating trips from residential zone i to two commercial zones. We assume there are no other zones and that the relative attractiveness of the commercial zones is adequately represented by the number of square feet of commercial floor space in the zone. Zone A contains 1 million square feet of floor space and is 12 minutes from the residential zone. Zone B contains 400,000 square feet of floor space and is 7 minutes from the residential zone. There are a total of 1000 trips to be allocated between the two commercial zones. If we take the exponent b as 2 (a reasonably close figure for the average of all trips), we get the following number of trips to zone A.

$$T_{iA} = 1,000 \frac{1,000,000/12^2}{(1,000,000/12^2) + (400,000/7^2)} = 460$$

We obtain the number of trips to zone B by subtracting trips to zone A from 1000, as follows;

$$\text{Trips to zone B} = 1000 - 460 = 540$$

[14] J. W. Dickey, op. cit.

In practice, the gravity model is generally not a tool that can be used "off the shelf" but must be calibrated for the place in question using existing travel data. The actual value of b must be found and the effective distances between places must be found. In a behavioral sense 1 mile of travel on an expressway may be shorter than 1 mile of travel on city streets, and 1 mile of travel on a commuter train may effectively be shorter than 1 mile of travel by bus or subway. A barrier such as a toll gate may, in effect, lengthen a route. And so on.

Modal Choice

After zone-to-zone trips have been estimated the next step is to apportion those trips by mode. A variety of approaches are available. One approach is a disaggregative model. The model is a group of equations that estimate the probability of a randomly selected traveler or group of travelers choosing each mode. The equations are so structured that the sum of probabilities for all available modes necessarily adds to 1.

The data items that go into the probability-estimating equations include characteristics of both the mode and the trip maker. A commonly used personal characteristic is income. This variable is used because it is likely to affect the way in which the traveler evaluates the tradeoff between time and money. For example, assume that commuter rail is fast and expensive, while bus is slow and relatively inexpensive. The wealthier the traveler, the more likely he or she is to decide that the time saving outweighs the monetary difference, and the greater the probability that he or she will choose commuter rail. The modal characteristics most commonly used, as might be expected, are cost and time. Different sets of equations may be used for estimating work and nonwork trips or for estimating CBD and non-CBD trips. The equations are developed empirically from travel behavior, generally in the area for which the study is being done.

Trip Assignment

The remaining question to be settled, assuming there are modes with more than one route, is the choice of route. The variables that have been found to affect route choice measurably are (1) travel time, (2) travel cost, (3) comfort, and (4) level of service, or frequency. In practice, there are often strong correlations between these various attributes. For example, the faster route may also be more comfortable and more expensive. In practice, most models rely solely on the first variable, travel time.

To illustrate the trip assignment process consider that there are two routes from point A to point B. All travelers will not take the same route because as travel volume rises on one route, travel time on that route also increases, while simultaneously the decreased volume on the other route will reduce travel time there. If travel time were the only variable of consequence, route choice would be a marginal adjustment process, which would continue until no traveler could reduce his or her travel time by changing routes. In practice the matter is

---

[15] See J. W. Dickey, op. cit., for discussion of logit models. See also Peat, Marwick, Mitchell & Co., *Implementation of the N-Dimensional Logit Model, Final Report*, Washington, D.C., May 1972.

somewhat more complicated, in that even though speed is the predominant factor in route choice, it is not the only factor. For example, some travelers may prefer a less congested route even if it is slower. Considerations of scenery or perceived safety might also influence route choice. Finally, note that we have been treating traffic zones as points so that the time from one zone to another is the same for all travelers. In fact, of course, zone-to-zone times are not the same for all travelers, since they may have different points of origin and destination within the same zones.

CHAPTER 10

URBAN PUBLIC FINANCE

John R. Gist
College of Architecture and Urban Studies
Virginia Polytechnic Institute and State University

In the last 15 years, the urban crisis has changed focus. The 1960s crisis of social issues like racism, economic inequality, crime, and disharmony in the nation's central cities has given way to the urban fiscal crisis. Simply put, will cities be able to make ends meet? In a real sense, all other urban policy problems are subordinate to the fiscal problem because no other policies can be implemented without financial resources. In recent years, there have been fiscal crises in New York, Cleveland, Chicago, Detroit, Boston, and other large central cities. New York City was on the brink of default on its outstanding loan obligations when the then mayor, Abraham Beame, sought direct financial assistance from the state of New York and the federal government. Eventually the city was helped over its fiscal crisis by federal loan guarantees, but not before taxes were increased by several million dollars, tens of thousands of employees were terminated, numerous city programs were drastically cut and city government finances were taken over by an Emergency Financial Control Board, dominated by bankers and other members of the NYC financial community. In Cleveland, the fiscal crisis reached a head between the young populist mayor, Dennis Kucinich, and the city council over the continued public ownership of the Cleveland Municipal Light Company. Eventually, the voters chose to maintain public ownership of the light company and the city defaulted on its debt.

On top of the existing fiscal problems of cities came the taxpayer revolt of the late 1970s, epitomized by the passage of proposition 13 in California and by other tax or expenditure limitations in over half the states. This was followed by a reversal in the long-term growth in federal aid to state and local governments. Federal aid peaked and actually began to decline in the latter stages of the Carter administration. The decline has accelerated under the Reagan administration.

293

While severe fiscal problems are far from universal among American cities, they are common enough that their causes and remedies are a matter of serious national concern. In this chapter and the next, the factors influencing the finances of cities are described. The focus of the present chapter is on the causes of urban fiscal problems and the revenue sources of city governments. The next chapter will focus on fiscal federalism—the fiscal interactions of federal, state, and local governments.

THE FISCAL PROBLEMS OF MUNICIPAL GOVERNMENTS

The fiscal problem of urban governments can be stated simply enough—the inability to match service needs with financial resources—but the causes of the problem are numerous and complex. Let us begin with some general statements about causes of urban distress and then proceed to problems that afflict older and more densely developed cities, particularly in areas of slow growth or population loss. We will then turn to some recent causes and attempts to measure urban fiscal distress.

The Problem of Fiscal Disparity

In the United States a very substantial share of all funds expended by city governments must be raised within city limits. But there is no mechanism for matching a city's revenue-raising capacity to its revenue needs. One city may have several times more taxable real property per capita within its borders than another city, yet have the same or even smaller per capita revenue needs than the less fortunate city. One city may have an affluent population, which demands little in the way of social services and can easily generate a large tax yield, while another city has a poor and needy population, which has only a very limited capacity to pay taxes. One city may have absorbed enormous numbers of poor migrants from other parts of the United States or overseas, while an otherwise comparable city may have almost none.

Then, too, the fiscal responsibilities of cities may vary widely because of accidents of geography or differences in state laws. New York City, which is composed of five counties in their entirety, must provide a substantial share of public assistance for a caseload of 1 million people. The city of New Rochelle, which shares a common border with New York City, bears no such burden because it is a part of Westchester County, and in New York State the provision of public assistance is a county responsibility.

In brief, then, there is no necessary relationship between needs for revenue on the one hand and ability to raise revenue on the other hand. In this lack of correspondence lies the root of many a municipality's fiscal problem.

Another very general source of fiscal problems is the labor-intensive character of many municipal services. While many sectors of the economy, notably manufacturing, agriculture, transportation, and communications, have experienced major productivity gains in the last several decades through the introduction of more and better capital equipment, few such gains have been achieved in the provision of public services. Thus relative to other goods and services, municipal services have become more expensive to provide.[1]

The openness of the city economy can also be a source of fiscal problems in many cases. The effort to raise revenue, if it results in higher tax rates than prevail in competing areas, can lead to the loss of business activity and population, which shrinks the tax base and leads to still higher tax rates.[2] Thus the existence of intermunicipal competition may put many cities in a fiscal box from which they cannot easily extricate themselves.

The Special Problems of Older Cities

For many cities, both central cities and older urban areas within the suburban ring, the demographic and spatial trends described in earlier chapters have brought special fiscal problems. In the late nineteenth and early twentieth centuries, central cities reached their peak rates of population growth. At that time, the political boundaries of most central cities were coterminous with the economy of the metropolitan area, that is, very little urbanized population or economic activity existed outside city boundaries. But for reasons discussed in Chapters 1 and 2 this situation began to change. Between 1910 and 1920 suburban areas were already growing far faster (in percentage terms, not absolute numbers) than were central-city populations. Central cities as a class continued to grow in population during the 1930s, but the trend of far more rapid growth in suburban areas continued. In the 1950s most central cities in the industrialized northeast and midwest lost population, while their suburbs grew rapidly. The loss of population accelerated in the 1960s and spread to most central cities throughout the country, including newer cities of the sunbelt such as Atlanta, Denver, and Los Angeles.[3]

During the 1970s virtually all metropolitan population growth occurred outside of central cities, and, as noted in Chapter 5, most central cities in the east and north-central regions lost substantial numbers of residents. In the south and west there were some gains in central-city populations, but in most SMSAs central-city growth lagged far behind suburban growth. Moreover, in some SMSAs there was a net decline in population; growth in some suburbs was more than fully offset by population decline in others and in the central cities.[4]

The problems posed by population and job loss have been compounded by the fact that the outmigration of population has been an economically selective one, with the cities losing disproportionately large numbers of their more prosperous

[1] William Baumol, "The Macroeconomics of Unbalanced Growth: The Anatomy of Urban Crisis," *American Economic Review*, vol. 57, June 1967, pp. 415–426.

[2] The only time-series analysis of this hypothesis is found in Donald Shoup, "The Effect of Property Tax Rates on the Property Tax Base," paper presented at Annual Meeting of National Tax Association, 1975. For cross-sectional study see Wallace Oates, "The Effects of Property Taxes and Local Public Spending on Property Values: An Empirical Study of Tax Capitalization and the Tiebout Hypothesis," *Journal of Political Economy*, vol. 77, November/December, 1969, pp. 957–971.

[3] See sources for Tables 2-1 and 2-2.

[4] Ibid. Also see John D. Kasarda, "The Implications of Contemporary Redistribution Trends for National Urban Policy," *Social Science Quarterly*, vol. 61, December 1980, pp. 373–400.

TABLE 10-1
CENTRAL-CITY–SUBURBAN ECONOMIC AND FISCAL DISPARITIES

	East	Midwest	South	West	U.S.
Per capita income, 85 largest SMSAs, 1976					
Central City	$4,654	$4,848	$4,771	$5,322	$4,883
Suburban	5,575	5,347	4,629	5,242	5,156
Ratio	84	91	106	103	97
Ratios of per capita total expenditures					
1957	129	131	124	129	129
1970	148	139	128	127	137
1977	161	142	130	133	143
Ratios of per capita tax revenues					
1957	142	150	183	162	157
1970	130	143	158	130	140
1977	120	138	134	121	129
Ratios of per capita intergovernmental aid					
1957	108	109	79	100	101
1970	197	124	96	115	138
1977	233	155	142	113	167

Source: Advisory Commission on Intergovernmental Relations, *Central City-Suburban Fiscal Disparity and City Distress, 1977*, Washington, D.C., 1980.

residents.[5] The problem is most severe in the north-central and northeastern parts of the United States. There, local events occur in a context of regional slowdown, and the existence of established municipalities on the borders of central cities blocks the process of annexation.

The City-Suburb Dichotomy

Some of the economic and fiscal disparities between central cities and their surrounding suburbs are illustrated in Table 10-1. In 1976 the ratio of central-city income to suburban income averaged only 84 percent in the east. In no individual eastern city did central-city income exceed that of suburban areas.[6] The ratios ranged from 54 percent in Newark to 97 percent in Providence. In only 4 of the 22 midwest SMSAs—Wichita, Flint, Omaha, and Madison—did central-city per capita income exceed that outside the central city. The same is not true of the south and west, however, where per capita income in central cities generally exceeded that in the suburban areas. In these areas, cities were more easily able to annex surrounding land and internalize some of the metropolitan growth.

Per capita local government expenditures in central cities of the largest SMSAs have consistently exceeded those in suburban areas over time, and the disparities have widened. As Table 10-1 shows, the average percentage difference between

---

[5] For a detailed treatment of the selective population loss and its fiscal effects, see Thomas Muller, *Growing and Declining Urban Areas: A Fiscal Comparison*, Urban Institute, Washington, D.C., 1975.

[6] See Advisory Commission on Intergovernmental Relations, *Central City-Suburban Fiscal Disparity*.

central-city and suburban general per capita expenditures was 29 percent in 1957. This increased to 37 percent in 1970 and 43 percent in 1977. These expenditure disparities have occurred in every region but have been most evident in the eastern United States. They are largely the result of noneducational expenditures, on which central cities have consistently outspent suburban areas by 2 to 1 since 1957. Only in the area of education do suburbs spend more than central cities, but even that gap has narrowed over time. Central cities spent 80 percent as much as suburban governments on education in 1957, 86 percent in 1970, and 93 percent in 1977.

Per capita tax revenues have also been consistently higher in central cities than in suburbs. The disparities have declined from 57 percent more in central cities than in suburbs in 1957 to 40 percent in 1970 and 29 percent in 1977. This might suggest some easing of relative fiscal stress for central cities, but that is not necessarily the case. As the city-suburb income gap grows and as the city continues to lose commercial tax base to the suburbs, its relative revenue-raising capacity shrinks. The same per capita tax performance may require much more effort for a poor and economically stagnating city than for its affluent and growing suburbs.

Intergovernmental aid has been the most important factor in offsetting central-city–suburban fiscal disparities. State and federal aid to local governments has increased tremendously in the past quarter century, and during that time it has been tilted substantially to benefit central-city governments. Table 10-1 shows that on a per capita basis, cities received the same amount of aid as their suburbs in 1957, but by 1970 cities received 38 percent more, and by 1977 they received 67 percent more aid.

The problem of fiscal disparities between central cities and their surrounding suburbs is generally associated with the older, industrialized cities of the northeast and midwest. Although this description is generally correct, there are central cities in all regions of the country that experience fiscal stress. The movement of population, industry, and jobs from the frostbelt to the sunbelt has certainly had a harmful effect on the older industrialized cities and regions of the country, but it has only moderated, not reversed, the fiscal disparities that existed between central cities and suburbs in the sunbelt.

Recent Sources of Fiscal Distress

As national concern with urban fiscal problems grew during the 1970s interest in the causes of fiscal distress also grew. Several general sources of fiscal distress are discussed below. Though none of these sources originated in the 1970s, most operated with greater force than in previous decades.

Recession and Inflation   Economic cycles and inflation can affect the fiscal behavior of state and local government by affecting both the collection of revenues and the needs for expenditures. After the severe 1974–1975 recession, the Advisory Commission on Intergovernmental Relations (ACIR) undertook a study to examine these relationships.[7]

---

[7] Advisory Commission on Intergovernmental Relations, *Countercyclical Aid and Economic Stabilization*, 1978, and *State and Local Finances in Recession and Inflation*, 1979.

TABLE 10-2
THE EFFECTS OF INFLATION AND RECESSION ON LOCAL NET REVENUES
(In Billions of Dollars)

Fiscal year	Gain from inflation		Change due to recession		Loss or gain from inflation and recession	
	$	% of revenues	$	% of revenues	$	% of revenues
1973	−0.2	−0.4	+0.1	+0.1	−0.2	−0.2
1974	1.9	2.4	−0.8	−1.0	+1.1	+1.4
1975	2.8	3.4	−4.8	−5.7	−2.0	−2.4
1976	1.5	1.6	−4.9	−5.3	−3.5	−3.7

Source: Advisory Commission on Intergovernmental Relations, *State and Local Finances in Recession and Inflation*, Washington, D.C., 1979.

In general, previous studies of inflation have been concerned with its effects on expenditures, and studies of recession have generally been concerned with its effects on revenues.[8] As the ACIR report points out, inflation and recession both affect revenues and expenditures; thus the net effect of each influence must be examined before the aggregate effect can be determined.

The early 1970s was a period of substantial inflation followed by the most severe recession since the 1930s. The ACIR study found that inflation increased both revenues and expenditures during this period, but the revenue increase due to inflation generally *exceeded* the expenditure increase for local governments. Table 10-2 shows the magnitude of revenue gain and inflationary loss in purchasing power for local governments. From 1973 to 1976, local governments enjoyed a $6 billion net gain.[9] One reason that inflation may have favored local treasuries was that suggested in Chapter 7 in connection with housing: unanticipated inflation favors debtors by reducing the real value of debt and imposing a real (as opposed to nominal) loss on creditors.

Recession proved to be another matter entirely. Although the severe effects of the recession do not show up in these figures until fiscal year 1975, the magnitude of the revenue loss due to recession in 1975 and 1976 totaled nearly $10 billion for local governments. Thus, while the beneficial effects of inflation seemed to buoy these governments in 1973 and 1974, the recessionary effects swamped the inflationary effects in the latter 2 years.

Uncontrollable Expenditures   The phenomenon of budget uncontrollability has been recognized in recent years as one of the primary causes of instability in federal expenditures. In 1967, roughly 59 percent of the federal budget was considered uncontrollable (that is, could not be altered through the appropriations

---

[8] *State and Local Finances in Recession and Inflation*. The findings cited are summarized from this report.
[9] See also David Greytak, Richard Gustely, and Robert Dinkelmeyer, "The Effects of Inflation on Local Government Expenditures," *National Tax Journal*, vol. 27, 1974, pp. 583–598. David Greytak and Bernard Jump, "Inflation and Local Government Expenditures and Revenues: Methods and Case Studies," *Public Finance Quarterly*, vol. 5, July 1977, pp. 275–302.

process) under current law. By fiscal 1981 this had increased to roughly 75 percent.[10] Recently the problem has been recognized as one that also besets local governments. In the wake of New York's 1975 fiscal crisis, the comptroller general of the United States examined the long-term fiscal outlook for New York City and found that one of the main reasons for New York's fiscal problems was the large percentage of uncontrollable costs the city faced.[11] An estimate for 1976 placed uncontrollable items at $8.7 billion out of a total budget of $12.1 billion. Acknowledging that there are degrees of uncontrollability, the report cited the following categories of uncontrollable costs, in order of increasing controllability: debt service, public employee pensions, medicaid, public assistance, and public education.

Granted that the New York situation is in many ways unique because, unlike most cities, it makes contributions for public assistance out of its own budget and operates its own public school system, there are still many large central cities that experience heavy uncontrollable costs. One study estimates that the costs of debt service and pension contributions for several large cities range from 20 to 30 percent of total expenditures (see Table 10-3).[12] The magnitude of these fixed spending obligations suggests that the problem of budget uncontrollability is not only fairly widespread among central cities but is likely to be long-term as well.

Regulatory Policies   Regulatory policy is one means by which the federal government can achieve public-policy objectives without the expenditure of massive amounts of federal funds. But regulation creates cost for other governments and the private sector. The federal government has long been involved in regulation of economic activity both in the private and the public sector. But prior to the 1960s, federal activity was traditionally focused on economic issues, such

---

[10] U.S. Office of Management and Budget, *The Budget for Fiscal Year 1980*.

[11] Comptroller General of the United States, *The Long Term Fiscal Outlook for New York City*.

[12] George Peterson, "Transmitting the Municipal Fiscal Squeeze to a New Generation of Taxpayers," Urban Institute, Washington, D.C., 1979. See also Roy Bahl and Bernard Jump, "The Budgetary Implications of Rising Employee Retirement System Costs," *National Tax Journal*, vol. 27, 1974, pp. 479–490.

TABLE 10-3
DEBT SERVICE AND PENSION CONTRIBUTIONS AS A
PERCENTAGE OF TOTAL GENERAL FUND SPENDING

City	Debt service	Pension contributions	Total
Detroit	7.3	17.9	25.2
Newark	12.9	9.0	21.9
Philadelphia	10.9	9.3	20.2
Boston	10.3	8.4	18.7
Buffalo	12.8	18.0	30.8
Cleveland	19.7	11.7	31.4

Source: George Peterson, "Transmitting the Municipal Fiscal Squeeze to a New Generation of Taxpayers," mimeo, Urban Institute, Washington, D.C., March 1979.

as minimum wage legislation, collective bargaining, and antitrust policy. In the 1960s this changed dramatically with the rise of the new social regulation, in which the federal government became involved in environmental policies, consumer protection, antidiscrimination policies, and worker protection. This thrust toward social regulation spawned a series of new agencies and acronyms on the federal policy scene, including the Environmental Protection Agency (EPA), the Consumer Product Safety Commission (CPSC), the Equal Employment Opportunity Commission (EEOC), and the Occupational Safety and Health Administration (OSHA). The effects on the local treasury, though unintended, may be significant. Environmental regulations may directly affect what local governments must spend on sewage treatment and the like. Indirectly, they may affect the pattern of industrial locations by causing firms to consider differences in abatement costs. That, in turn, will affect both the revenue and the expenditure positions of local governments. OSHA regulations regarding workplace conditions may affect municipal labor costs. DOT regulations on access for the handicapped affect the vehicles-acquisition and operation costs for public transportation authorities. The list is nearly endless.

Partly as a response to the added fiscal burden that such regulations imposed on local governments, the federal government required that agency regulations that have "major economic consequences for the general economy, for individual industries, geographical regions or levels of government" be accompanied by an economic-impact analysis.[13] It was hoped that through this analytical procedure, the most economically harmful regulations might be prevented. The authority for economic-impact analysis was expanded in 1978 to cover agency programs and regulations that would have significant impacts on urban areas when President Carter required executive branch agencies to prepare "urban and community impact analyses" for major program initiatives.[14]

These "urban-impact analyses" were to examine the effects of legislative or regulatory changes on the employment, income, population, and fiscal conditions of central cities and how these changes might differentially affect the central city and its surrounding suburbs. These analyses were intended to avert federal policies that would have deleterious effects on central cities, but it is difficult to determine whether they have had any material effect on the enactment or implementation of federal policies.[15] This requirement was canceled under the Reagan administration.

Mandates   Mandates are a closely related but somewhat broader category of actions by higher levels of government that impose costs on municipal governments. They are defined as "responsibilities, procedures, or activities that are imposed by one sphere of government on another by constitutional, legislative,

---

[13] Executive Order #12044.

[14] Executive Order #12074.

[15] A volume of studies initiated in conjunction with this mandate was originated by the Department of Housing and Urban Development and published under its auspices. See Norman Glickman (ed.), *The Urban Impacts of Federal Policies*, Johns Hopkins University Press, Baltimore, 1980.

administrative, executive or judicial action."[16] Because they generally require local action of some kind, mandates impose costs on local governments, generally without any kind of offsetting financial support. Lovell and Tobin classify mandates into two major categories—requirements and constraints.[17] Requirement mandates are either *programmatic* (identifying what should be done) or *procedural* (how things should be done). The constraint category consists mostly of fiscal limits, such as revenue base constraints, revenue rate constraints, and expenditure limits. These will be discussed later in this chapter.

Some of these mandates are direct orders to do certain things where there is no local discretion involved, whereas others are imposed as conditions of receiving external aid. In their inventory of federal mandates, Lovell and Tobin found over 1200 federal mandates, over 1000 of which were conditions of receiving aid, whereas state mandates are overwhelmingly direct orders.[18] This difference is not too surprising in view of the fact that local governments are creatures of states. The latter are thus in a position to require action whereas the federal government can generally only encourage through grant incentives or threaten the loss of aid. State mandates on localities include rules governing the organization and procedures of local governments, personnel rules that set standards for public employee compensation and benefits, and rules requiring certain levels of service provision in education, health, environment, and transportation.

Although many federal mandates have existed for decades, such as the requirement under the Davis-Bacon Act that wages paid on construction projects be at the rate prevailing in the local labor market, older mandates generally involved issues of commerce or economic regulation. The bulk of recent federal mandates are the product of the new social regulation noted earlier.

A particularly noteworthy example of this regulation is the requirement under section 504 of the Rehabilitation Act of 1973, which enjoins federal grant recipients from discriminating against handicapped individuals in the provision of services. This provision requires local public school districts to provide "appropriate" educational services to all handicapped children, the cost of which has been estimated to be as much as $5 billion.[19]

The Department of Transportation's regulations implementing section 504 require that public transportation be accessible to handicapped individuals. DOT required that all new buses purchased with federal funds be equipped with wheelchair lifts and the rail transit systems also be made accessible to the handicapped.[20] According to one estimate it would cost the Washington, D.C.,

---

[16] Catherine Lovell and Charles Tobin, "The Mandate Issue," *Public Administration Review*, vol. 41, May/June 1981, pp. 318–331. See also Advisory Commission on Intergovernmental Relations, *State Mandating of Local Expenditures*, July 1978, and Catherine Lovell, Max Nieman, Robert Kneisel, Adam Rose, and Charles Tobin, *Federal and State Mandating on Local Governments*, Report to the National Science Foundation, 1979.

[17] Lovell and Tobin, op. cit.

[18] Ibid.

[19] Stephen Barro, *The Urban Impacts of Federal Policies: Fiscal Conditions*, Rand Corporation, Santa Monica, Calif., 1978.

[20] Catherine Lovell, "Federal Deregulation and State and Local Governments," in John Ellwood (ed.), *Reductions in U.S. Domestic Spending*, Transaction, New Brunswick, N.J., 1982, p. 124.

metro system $72 million to meet the Department of Transportation's mandated accessibility requirements. The mayor of New York City has argued that it would be cheaper to provide every handicapped citizen with a door-to-door taxi ride rather than retrofit city buses and provide access for the handicapped in every subway station in the city.[21] As a result of the deregulation efforts of the Reagan administration, the section 504 provisions were loosened considerably.

Infrastructure Needs and Unfunded Liabilities

In the last several years two major potential sources of municipal fiscal stress have emerged. Though both appear to be large and growing problems, neither has yet been measured or estimated with any degree of accuracy.

One problem looming over many municipalities is that of finding the funds to adequately maintain their physical infrastructure. The problem received a dramatic public introduction in the early 1970s when a truck plunged through the roadway of Manhattan's elevated West Side Highway and landed on the cobblestones of West Street below. Several miles of the West Side Highway were immediately closed to traffic, and, subsequently, the entire structure has been torn down. What became apparent at the time was that the city had been deferring maintenance on the structure for years, if not decades, until the inevitable happened. While no overall inventory of the state of America's urban infrastructure has been taken, there is indirect evidence of underfunding. One point cited by Peterson is simply that there has been a sharp decline in the percentage of state and local expenditures allocated to infrastructure maintenance and construction compared with just a decade ago.[22] The congressional budget office has estimated that annual spending for public works infrastructure under current policy would have to increase from $36 billion to $53 billion annually from 1983 through 1990.[23]

The reason that underinvestment has occurred seems fairly obvious. Structures last longer than terms of office. For the administration squeezed between rising costs and resistant taxpayers or constitutional revenue-raising limits, maintenance of infrastructure is an attractive place to cut back. Unfortunately, when the bill does come due it may be a very large one.

A comparable situation has arisen with regard to public employee pensions.[24] If one gives the municipal employees an increase in take-home pay one must immediately find the funds with which to do so. As municipal labor forces grew and the unionization within them increased, many cities found it increasingly difficult to meet growing wage demands. One way out was to offer improved pension benefits rather than immediate pay increases. If one gives municipal

---

[21] Edward Koch, "The Mandate Millstone," *The Public Interest*, vol. 61, Fall 1980, pp. 42–57. See also George E. Hale and Marion L. Palley, *The Politics of Federal Grants*, Congressional Quarterly Press, Washington, D.C., 1981, p. 72.

[22] George Peterson, op. cit., Bernard Jump, "Meeting State and Local Financing Needs in the 1980s: Can the Municipal Debt Market Do its Share?" *Public Budgeting and Finance*, vol. 2, Winter 1981, pp. 58–72; Pat Choate and Susan Walter, *America in Ruins*, Council of State Planning Agencies, Washington, D.C., 1981.

[23] Congressional Budget Office, *Public Works Infrastructure: Policy Considerations for the 1980s*, 1983.

[24] See George Peterson, op. cit.

workers improved pension benefits while simultaneously failing to put away the funds to pay for those benefits, no new expenditures are required in the short term. The long-term result has been an increase of unfunded liabilities, in this case predictable pension costs for which adequate funds have not been put away. As the presently large municipal labor forces retire in massive numbers, this obligation may be a major source of problems for a number of cities. Like the underfunding of infrastructure, incurring such unfunded liabilities is a difficult temptation to resist.

Measuring Fiscal Distress

With the increasing fiscal stress cities experienced from the 1970s on, considerable interest has developed in the question of whether and how we can measure fiscal distress. The question bears directly upon the important issue of how federal and state assistance to localities ought to be allocated. First, it should be noted that we are a long way from consensus on the matter as evidenced by the variety of terms in use, including fiscal stress, hardship, strain, decline, distress, or the more neutral fiscal conditions.

The variables used in the measurement of fiscal conditions generally fall into the categories of demographic, socioeconomic, and fiscal-managerial. Perhaps the most frequently used demographic variable in fiscal studies is that of population decline. This variable has been cited in so many fiscal studies as a "determinant" of fiscal decline that to some it has become synonymous with that process.[25] Population decline is associated with numerous other variables, such as loss of businesses and jobs, declining property values, relatively high per capita costs of local services, and increases in the proportion of poor or needy individuals in the population. Thus population decline may serve as a surrogate for many other indicators relevant to fiscal distress. Other demographic variables often used include the dependent proportion of the population (under 18 and over 65 years of age), number or percentage of poor families, and the number or percentage of minority group members in the population.

Among the most popular socioeconomic variables are unemployment, rates of inflation, loss of jobs and firms, and changes in personal income.

The fiscal and management variables used in fiscal studies have been quite diverse but include such measures as expenditures and revenues per capita, bond ratings, long- and short-term debt per capita, debt service expenditures per capita, mandatory expenditures as a percentage of total expenditures, and many others.

Developing a Combined Index of Fiscal Distress A number of studies have attempted to combine indicators of need into overall indexes of fiscal distress. Table 10-4 compares rankings of fiscally distressed cities on certain selected indexes. One of the most frequently used indexes is that of Nathan and Adams.[26]

---

[25] Two studies that make fiscal comparisons between cities growing in population and those declining are Muller, *Growing and Declining Urban Areas*, op. cit., and George Peterson, "Finance" in William Gorham and Nathan Glazer (eds.), *The Urban Predicament*, Urban Institute, Washington, D.C., 1976.

[26] Richard Nathan and Charles Adams, " Understanding Central City Hardship," *Political Science Quarterly*, vol. 91, Spring 1976, pp. 47–62.

TABLE 10-4
ORDER OF CITIES IN FISCAL STRESS

Dearborn	Stanley	Cuciti	HUD index	Nathan-Adams index
New York	New York	Washington	Washington	Newark
Baltimore	Buffalo	Boston	New York	St. Louis
Boston	Detroit	New York	Boston	Gary
Milwaukee	Newark	Newark	St. Louis	Miami
San Francisco	St. Louis	St. Louis	Newark	Birmingham
New Orleans	Boston	Philadelphia	San Francisco	Youngstown
Cincinnati	Cleveland	Baltimore	Philadelphia	Baltimore
San Antonio	Philadelphia	Jersey City	Buffalo	Cleveland
Jacksonville		Detroit	Baltimore	Detroit
Pittsburgh		Birmingham	Detroit	Buffalo

Sources: Philip Dearborn, "The Financial Health of Major U.S. Cities in Fiscal 1977," Special Report, First Boston Corporation, 1978; David Stanley, "Cities in Trouble" in Charles H. Levine (ed.), *Managing Fiscal Stress*, Chatham, Chatham, N.J., 1980; House Committee on Banking, Finance and Urban Affairs, *City Need and The Responsiveness of Federal Grant Programs* (Cuciti); Richard Nathan and Charles Adams, "Understanding Central City Hardship," *Political Science Quarterly*, vol. 91, Spring 1976, 47–62.

It comprises six variables: unemployment, dependency, education, income level, crowded housing, and poverty. They used this index both to compare central cities to their surrounding suburban areas and to make comparisons between central cities *across* metropolitan areas. The Nathan-Adams index was not originally intended to be primarily an index of *fiscal* distress but a composite measure of overall distress, having elements of economic, social, and physical need as well. In fact, it actually contains no explicitly fiscal variables at all. Nonetheless, it has been used consistently as an index of fiscal distress.

A study done for the Subcommittee on the City of the House Banking, Finance and Urban Affairs Committee has attempted to deal with the various aspects of urban distress by differentiating among social, economic, and fiscal need using three separate sets of variables to represent these three dimensions.[27] The social-need factor was represented by low income, poverty, unemployment, and crime variables. Economic need was measured by changes in population, per capita income, the employment of manufacturing establishments, and retail sales. Fiscal distress was measured by cumulative budget deficits, debt burdens, cash reserves, and tax effort. The latter term involves a comparison of locally collected revenues and some measure of tax-paying capacity such as full value of taxable real property, aggregate personal income, or the like.

The committee study found that fiscal need was most apparent in medium and large northeastern and southern cities, and in large midwestern cities. Only two cities—Newark and St. Louis—ranked among the ten most distressed cities in terms of all three sets of indicators. Cities ranking high in terms of fiscal need were

[27] U.S. House of Representatives, Committee on Banking, Finance and Urban Afairs, Subcommittee on the City, *City Need and the Responsiveness of Federal Grant Programs*, 1978.

Washington, D.C., Boston, New York, Philadelphia, Baltimore, Jersey City, Detroit, and Birmingham.[28]

Some authors have argued that determinations of fiscal need should most appropriately focus on *financial* variables, rather than socioeconomic indicators. The reasoning is that deteriorating socioeconomic conditions do not in themselves induce fiscal stress. Management practices can ameliorate the fiscal problems created by economic decline. One such study focused on financial variables such as tax, debt, and expenditure ratios.[29] Aronson and King examined trends in short- and long-term debt per capita in New York City to see if other cities were headed toward similar problems.[30] A study by Clark and associates isolated four financial variables—long-term debt per capita, short-term dept per capita, total expenditures, and tax effort—as the most important fiscal-strain indicators.[31] Dearborn uses the liquidity position of city governments to assess financial health, liquidity being measured by the overall cash position of the government (including both general-fund revenues and "restricted" funds, which can only be used for certain restricted purposes) and by unrestricted (available for any use) current assets in excess of current liabilities.[32] Others have used the operating budget surplus or deficit as a measure of distress.

The advantage that financial indicators have over socioeconomic measures is some semblance of face validity, meaning that they are obviously related to fiscal conditions. However, not all financial indicators are likely to be equally valid measures of fiscal stress, and validity is still the basic problem in establishing fiscal indicators. One of the problems in identifying or constructing valid fiscal indicators is that fiscal distress is a complex process that single indicators cannot encompass. Another problem is that the indicators thus far employed do not seem to emanate from any conceptual or theoretical understanding of the *process* that we refer to as "fiscal stress."

Yet it is important for policy reasons that we attempt to devise such indicators, because any intergovernmental aid policy should take into account differences in local fiscal capacity. This is true both for reasons of fairness—those with less need should receive less aid—and because fiscal scarcity at both federal and state levels of government means that aid will be more efficiently allocated if it is targeted toward the places having the greatest need.

The Fiscal Opportunity Schedule   One of the best *conceptual* approaches to the measurement of fiscal distress was developed by Stephen Barro.[33] Barro uses the

[28] Ibid.

[29] James Howell and Charles Stamm, *Urban Fiscal Stress*, D. C. Heath and Co., Lexington, MA, 1979.

[30] J. Richard Aronson and Arthur E. King, "Is There a Fiscal Crisis outside New York?," *National Tax Journal*, vol. 31, 1978, pp. 153–163.

[31] Terry N. Clark et al., *How Many New Yorks? The New York Fiscal Crisis in Comparative Perspective*, Comparative Study of Community Decision Making Report No. 70, University of Chicago, Chicago, 1976.

[32] Philip N. Dearborn, "The Financial Health of Major U.S. Cities in Fiscal 1977," Special Report, First Boston Corporation, Boston, 1978.

[33] Stephen Barro, op. cit.

concept of a fiscal opportunity schedule, which has the virtue of directly linking the demand, or expenditure, side of local government finance to the supply, or revenue, side. Barro defines a ratio of fiscal opportunities which is equal to

$$\frac{\text{Expenditures}}{\text{Need}} = \frac{\text{AID} + (\text{BASE} \times \text{EFF})}{\text{DEM} \times \text{COST} \times \text{RESP}}$$

where AID = per capita intergovernmental aid
       BASE = per capita revenue base
        EFF = per capita revenue effort
       DEM = demand for local government services
       COST = relative cost of local government services
       RESP = relative scope of service responsibility

The numerator of the index represents the major sources of differential ability to raise revenues and the denominator represents major sources of differential costs among municipal governments. The terms *expenditure* and *need* are developed from the variables in the above list. The lower the expenditure/need ratio, the higher the degree of fiscal distress, that is, the weaker the municipality's ability to meet its public service needs. DEM is not used in its formal sense but more in the sense of need based upon the demography of the area and the presumed service needs that such a population would be expected to have. COST refers to the cost of providing services in a given area relative to costs in other areas. Since the provision of public services is a labor-intensive activity, this item essentially comes down to an interarea comparison of labor costs. RESP refers to the relative scope of service of the government in question. Since municipalities in different states are charged with different levels of responsibility for services, it is necessary to control for these variations in order to make valid comparisons among cities in different states.

The fiscal opportunity schedule (FOS) avoids the shortcoming of looking at only single variables or at the expenditure or revenue sides in isolation. However, the FOS still has some of the same liabilities as other measures of fiscal need. While it has a strong intuitive rationale and a plausible underlying theoretical structure, it has not been applied broadly to major American cities because of the difficulties in measuring the need factors, especially DEM and COST.

TRENDS IN MUNICIPAL EXPENDITURES AND REVENUES

For the 3 decades preceding the 1974–1975 recession the local-government sector of the national economy consistently grew faster in percentage terms than did the GNP. Apparently during this period the nation's income elasticity of demand for urban public services was considerably higher than unity. From 1960 to 1980, city revenues expanded by over 500 percent in current dollars, from just under $12 billion annually to $76 billion, in contrast to a 418 percent increase in GNP in current dollars. Expenditures have undergone a similarly rapid rate of growth. During this same period, there has been a fundamental restructuring of the sources of municipal revenue, while the objects of city expenditure have remained relatively stable.

TABLE 10-5
SOURCES OF CITY REVENUES, 1960–1980
(In Millions of Dollars)

	1960		1970		1980	
	Amount	**%**	**Amount**	**%**	**Amount**	**%**
General revenue	$11,647	100.0	$26,621	100.0	$76,056	100.0
Intergovernmental revenue	2,321	19.9	7,906	29.7	28,270	37.2
Taxes	7,109	61.0	13,647	51.3	31,256	41.1
Property	5,179	44.6	9,127	34.3	16,859	22.2
Sales and gross receipts	1,217	10.4	2,422	9.1	8,208	10.8
Licenses and other	695	6.0	2.098	7.9	6,189	8.1
Charges and miscellaneous	2,217	19.0	5,068	19.0	16.530	21.7

Source: U.S. Bureau of the Census, *Statistical Abstract of the United States*, 1981, Table 500.

The Changing Municipal Revenue Base

As Table 10-5 shows, total general revenues for all city governments in 1960 consisted of approximately three-fifths (61 percent) tax revenues and two-fifths revenue from all other sources. Property taxes were 45 percent of total general revenues and 73 percent of tax revenues. By 1980, only 41 percent of total general revenues were derived from taxation; only 22 percent of total city general revenues came from the property tax. Compensating for this substantial decline in own-source revenues for city governments was a remarkable increase in the proportion of city revenues received in the form of intergovernmental aid. Total federal and state aid to cities went from $2.3 billion in 1960 to over $28 billion in 1980. Intergovernmental aid grew from 20 percent of general revenue in 1960 to 37 percent in 1980, almost accounting for the 19 percent decline in the share of city revenue coming from local taxation.

During the same period there was a small percentage increase in reliance on charges, fees, and miscellaneous revenue sources. In 1960 these totaled 19 percent of municipal revenue but increased to nearly 22 percent in 1980.

In addition to property taxes, aid, and charges, approximately 10 percent of city revenues is in the form of sales and gross receipts tax revenues, a figure that has changed little over the 20-year period from 1960 to 1980. A few cities levy an income or earnings tax (for example, New York, Philadelphia, St. Louis, Cleveland, and Cincinnati), and it is a significant revenue provider in the budgets of some cities (particularly for Ohio cities such as Cincinnati, Toledo, Dayton, and Columbus).

Revenue Sources and Municipal Size

The sources of city revenue exhibit substantial variation by city size. Table 10-6 shows that reliance on the property tax ranged from 16.7 percent for cities with populations of 300,000 to 500,000 to 29.1 percent for cities from 50,000 to 100,000. In general, cities up to 200,000 population rely more heavily on property tax revenues than larger cities, but the pattern is by no means consistent across all categories of city size.

TABLE 10-6
CITY REVENUE AND CITY SIZE, 1980

	All cities	Less than 50,000	50,000– 99,999	100,000– 199,999	200,000– 299,999	300,000– 499,999	500,000– 1,000,000	More than 1,000,000
General revenue	100	100	100	100	100	100	100	100
Intergovernmental	37.2	30.8	32.8	37.5	38.0	38.5	42.9	41.5
Taxes	41.1	40.2	43.7	40.0	39.6	37.8	38.7	43.6
Property	22.2	23.9	29.1	26.7	19.0	16.7	20.1	19.7
Sales and gross receipts	10.8	10.7	10.2	9.8	11.9	13.5	9.7	11.0
Current charges	12.7	16.7	14.0	14.0	13.2	13.2	11.4	9.5

Source: U.S. Bureau of the Census, *Statistical Abstract of the United States,* 1981, Table 501.

Two patterns of revenue collection that are related to size of city are reliance on intergovernmental aid and current charges for government services. The larger the city, the higher the percentage of revenue received in intergovernmental aid. The smallest cities average 30.8 percent of general revenues from aid, and the largest cities (over 500,000 population) average well over 40 percent. On the other hand, the smallest cities average 16.7 percent of revenues from charges, and the largest cities under 10 percent. One policy implication of these differences is that large cities, because of their substantially greater dependence on intergovernmental aid, have become extremely vulnerable to federal-budget cutbacks.[34] Under the Reagan administration, cuts in federal aid to state and local governments have been larger in percentage terms than cuts in most other areas.[35]

The Expenditure Side of the Ledger

In percentage terms the allocation of local monies has not changed dramatically over the last 20 years. Table 10-7 shows the distribution of municipal general expenditures over a 2-decade period. These figures represent operating expenditures, that is, they exclude expenditures for capital projects. Over 60 percent of local general expenditures go for certain "common functions" such as public safety (police and fire protection), roads and highways, sewage, public welfare, and health and hospitals. Although education is one of the largest categories of city expenditures, it is not usually considered a "common function" because it is generally provided by independent school districts. The largest exception to this generalization is New York City. Others include Boston, Baltimore, and Washington, D.C. The few city-operated school districts (some of which are very large) account for the relatively large percentage of municipal funds going to education. But the $9 billion spent by municipalities on education pales in comparison to

[34] Astrid Merget, "The Fiscal Dependency of American Cities," *Public Budgeting and Finance,* vol. 1, Summer, 1981, pp. 20–30; Catherine Lovell, "Evolving Local Government Dependency," *Public Administration Review,* vol. 41, Special Issue 1981, pp. 189–202.
[35] John Ellwood (ed.), *Reductions in U.S. Domestic Spending,* Transaction, New Brunswick, N.J., 1982, p. 56.

TABLE 10-7
EXPENDITURES BY CITY GOVERNMENTS, 1960–1980
(In Millions of Dollars)

	1960		1970		1980	
	Amount	**%**	**Amount**	**%**	**Amount**	**%**
General expenditures	$11,818	100.0	$27,682	100.0	$72,445	100.0
Police protection	1,275	10.8	2,994	10.8	8,200	11.3
Fire protection	885	7.5	1,762	6.4	4,535	6.3
Highways	1,573	13.3	2,499	9.0	5,977	8.3
Sewerage	1,332	11.3	2,553	9.2	7,913	10.9
Public welfare	608	5.1	2,215	8.0	3,801	5.2
Education	1,801	15.2	4,548	16.4	9,284	12.8
Libraries	185	1.6	407	1.5	883	1.2
Health and hospitals	799	6.8	1,944	7.0	4,457	6.2

Source: U.S. Bureau of the Census, *Statistical Abstract of the United States,* 1981, Table 500.

spending by school districts. In 1980, a total of $96 billion was spent by school districts in the United States for elementary and secondary education.

Variations by City Size   City government expenditures on the common functions of city government show some variation by city size. The pattern of city expenditures by size of city is shown in Table 10-8. Three categories of expenditures—highways, police and fire protection, and sewage and sanitation—comprise a substantially higher proportion of city budgets in smaller cities than they do in larger cities, which may reflect economies of scale in the provision of these services.

A substantial literature has developed over the years on economies of scale in the provision of local government services. In general, when per capita expenditure is plotted against municipal size, a U-shaped cost curve is obtained. Costs may decline to a population of perhaps 10 or 15,000. Then there is usually a long

TABLE 10-8
CITY EXPENDITURES BY CITY SIZE, 1980

	All cities	Less than 50,000	50,000– 99,999	100,000– 199,999	200,000– 299,999	300,000– 499,999	500,000– 1,000,000	More than 1,000,000
General expenditures								
Police and fire	17.6	20.2	20.1	18.8	17.0	18.4	16.2	13.8
Highways	8.3	13.4	9.8	8.4	7.5	6.8	5.9	3.3
Sewerage and sanitation	10.9	15.2	11.1	9.9	7.3	11.4	11.1	6.6
Public welfare	5.2	0.5	0.6	1.4	1.9	1.6	5.7	14.9
Education	12.8	7.3	13.7	17.7	13.9	8.1	13.3	17.6
Health and hospitals	6.2	5.3	5.3	4.9	3.3	5.3	7.4	8.1
Housing	4.8	2.6	5.2	4.6	6.0	6.4	5.5	5.9
Interest	4.2	4.5	3.7	3.4	5.0	4.8	4.4	3.8

Source: U.S. Bureau of the Census, *Statistical Abstract of the United States,* 1981, Table 501.

relatively flat section after which costs gradually begin rising. The explanation generally offered for the long relatively flat section is that many municipal services are labor intensive and not amenable to the economies of scale that characterize manufacturing or transportation. The gradual rise may occur partly because of diseconomies of scale such as increased administrative costs. But it also occurs because larger places typically must provide a larger range of services than required in a smaller place. This notion of a U-shaped cost curve has received considerable attention in the urban economics literature.[36]

The expenditures that loom larger in the budgets of large cities are those for public welfare, health and hospitals, and housing and urban renewal. These larger concentrations of social-welfare expenditures in very large cities reflect the higher concentrations of poor people in the nation's largest cities and may suggest the extent to which big cities attempt to redistribute income from the middle to the lower classes through social-welfare programs. Owing to the openness of local economies, however, there is a limit to how much cities can attempt to redistribute income without driving away middle-class residents through higher taxes.[37]

As the data above suggest, city government functions have remained relatively stable over the past 2 decades, but the sources of city revenues have undergone some very significant shifts. In the next section the sources of revenue are examined in greater detail.

SOURCES OF REVENUES FOR LOCAL GOVERNMENTS

The various levels of government rely upon quite different sources of revenue, a distinction that has become increasingly important as local governments have come to rely more heavily upon transfers from higher levels of government. The major revenue sources for the federal government are, in descending order, the personal income tax, the Social Security payroll tax, and the corporate income tax. At the state level the major sources of revenue are sales and gross-receipts taxes, intergovernmental transfers, personal income taxes, various fees and user charges, and the corporate income tax.

At the local level the situation is quite different. The largest single revenue source is transfers, either from the state or the federal government. The largest source of tax revenue is the property tax. Sales taxes provide roughly half as much revenue as the property tax. The other major sources of income are a variety of user charges and license fees, which together bring in about as much revenue as sales taxes. Personal and corporate income taxes play a relatively small role.

---

[36] For an extensive bibliography on economies of scale, see William Fox, *Size Economies in Local Government Services: A Review*, U.S. Dept. of Agriculture, Rural Development Research Report No. 22, 1980.

[37] See Wallace Oates, "The Effects of Property Taxes and Local Public Spending on Property Values: An Empirical Study of Tax Capitalization and the Tiebout Hypothesis," *Journal of Political Economy*, vol. 77, November/December 1969, pp. 957–971. It is worth noting that even if cities did not adopt explicitly redistributive policies, because there are inevitably some low-income city residents who pay little or no property tax but who still benefit from public goods and services there will always be some redistribution.

At the local level there is, in addition to government, an important quasi-governmental entity, the school district. In most regions of the United States the school district is an independent entity with some of the powers of government—most notably, the power to tax. School districts receive funds from three major sources: taxes they themselves levy, transfers from state governments, and transfers from the federal government. The first two items are of roughly comparable size, while the third item is substantially smaller. Almost all of the tax revenues raised by school districts are from a single source, the property tax.

The importance of the school district in the local public finance picture should not be underestimated. Of the roughly $67 billion in property taxes collected in the United States in 1980, $28 billion were collected by school districts.[38] In many suburban areas, where the childhood population is large and the structure of government is not as elaborate as in more densely developed areas, educational expenditures may be as large as all other local government expenditures combined. Property taxes levied by the school district may exceed those levied by local government itself.

The reliance upon different tax sources by different levels of government is partly a matter of custom, but it also has a certain inherent logic. The federal government can levy a substantial personal income tax because federal taxation is hard to escape. Emigration is a high price to pay for eluding the long arm of the IRS. States do tax incomes, but they do so at much lower rates than the federal government. Presumably they are somewhat restrained in their taxing behavior by the fear of driving residents out of state. States are also users of the corporate income tax, but again their behavior is similarly restrained. Local governments by and large are not major users of either the personal or the corporate income tax, in part for fear of encouraging outmigration of people and firms. One reason that localities rely so heavily on the property tax, aside from custom, is the relative immobility of real property in the short run. That which can neither be concealed nor moved makes a better target for the local tax collector.

Characteristics of Revenue Sources

Decisions about the revenue structure of local governments involve questions of efficiency and equity—that is, how revenue can be obtained with minimum efficiency loss and how the tax burden should be distributed—as well as the question of elasticity.

Tax Efficiency Much of the literature on tax efficiency begins with the assumption that Pareto optimality (see appendix to Chapter 6) has been attained in the pretax situation, and the analysis is carried out on the posttax efficiency effects.[39] In this view, an efficient tax would be one that does not alter the relative (pretax) allocation of resources in the private sector. Or, to put it in other words, an efficient tax would have neutral effects on prices. It would merely transfer resources to the public sector without altering the relative prices of private goods.

[38] U.S. Bureau of the Census, *Statistical Abstract of the United States*, 1981, table 256.
[39] For a typical example see John Due and Ann Friedlander, *Governmental Finance*, Richard D. Irwin, Homewood, Ill., 1977.

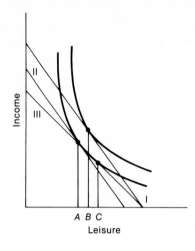

FIGURE 10-1
Taxation and the work-leisure tradeoff. Line II represents the effect upon the consumer's budget line of a lump sum tax. The line is shifted parallel to its original position by the amount of the tax. Both income and leisure are reduced, the latter by distance AB. Line III shows the effect of a proportional tax. Note that leisure is increased (work time diminished) by distance BC.

The lump-sum or poll tax (where everyone pays exactly the same amount) is the classic instance of an efficient tax because it creates only a loss of income (income effect) and does not distort economic choices by altering prices (substitution effect). It does, however, have some equity problems, which we will address shortly.

This point is illustrated in Figure 10-1, which shows the effects of a lump-sum tax and a proportional income tax on the choice between income and leisure. Note that the same illustration would also apply for good X and good Y or for good X against all other goods. In Figure 10-1 we see the effects of a lump-sum tax. It shifts what is essentially a budget line for income and leisure from position I to position II. There is an income effect, since the worker is now poorer at any given level of work effort. But there is no substitution effect because the rate at which leisure time can be exchanged for income (the after-tax wage rate) remains unchanged.

In the figure we also see the effect of a proportional tax. This changes the rate at which leisure can be exchanged for income and is represented by the rotation of the budget line from position I to position III. Thus, to the income effect is added a substitution effect very much analogous to the substitution effect that occurs when the relative prices of two goods are changed through taxation, subsidization, or any other cause.[40]

To the extent that taxation distorts the worker's choice by changing the ratio at which money and leisure are exchanged, it can be said to be inefficient. This is analogous to the argument made in Chapter 6 regarding the efficiency effects of subsidization. The figure shows the effects of a proportional tax, but the argument is essentially the same for a progressive tax. Diagrammatically, the difference would be that line III would be shown as concave to the origin rather than straight.

---

[40] For a fuller discussion of income and substitution effects than is possible here see C. E. Ferguson and S. Charles Maurice, *Economic Analysis: Theory and Application*, Richard D. Irwin, 3d ed., Homewood, Ill., 1978, pp. 143–148.

No serious student of public finance would advocate that all or most of local revenue should be raised by a lump-sum tax. The important point about the above illustration is that it shows that even a proportional tax which falls on all income will, in principle, have some distorting or "excess burden" effect—that is, it will reduce economic efficiency. Most taxes, in fact, are a good deal more distorting than the proportional tax.

Tax Equity

At least as important as the efficiency effects of taxation are the equity effects; that is, how the tax burden is distributed among taxpayers in various income classes. Two basic criteria of tax equity are commonly recognized: the benefit principle and the ability-to-pay principle.

The Benefit Principle One equity criterion might be that taxes be levied in proportion to the benefits derived from their subsequent expenditure. There is obviously an element of fairness about this approach. There is also an efficiency argument in its favor. If we could accurately determine individuals' preferences for public goods and then supply these goods in the amounts that people would purchase if the exclusion principle applied, we would have a system that mimicked the operation of an efficiently functioning market.

This principle is most applicable in those situations where the benefits of public goods are divisible and the tax is analogous to a price that reflects their consumption. An example would be the motor fuel tax. The revenues from the tax are generally earmarked (dedicated) for road and highway construction. Thus, there should be a rough correspondence between the costs borne by consumers and the benefits derived from access to roads and highways.

The Ability-to-Pay Principle This principle asserts that taxes should be levied in accordance with people's ability to pay them. Ability to pay is generally measured in terms of personal income. The ability-to-pay principle has two subsidiary principles—horizontal and vertical equity. The former holds that equals should be treated equally, the latter that those who are not equal should be treated unequally, that is, those with higher incomes should pay more than those with less income.

Clearly, the ability-to-pay principle is at odds with the benefit principle. The benefit principle appears to imply a regressive tax system. For example, if the rich have no more children on the average than the poor, then they should pay no more in absolute amounts for school taxes than the poor. That means a tax rate that decreases as income rises, that is, a regressive system. On the other hand the ability to pay criterion clearly implies that the wealthy should pay more. As a purely practical matter it would be incredibly difficult to design a tax system on the benefit principle because the exclusion principle often cannot be applied to governmentally provided goods. In such cases there is no market to reveal the value of the benefits received. Ability to pay, on the other hand, is relatively easy to ascertain if income is taken as the measure of ability.

The conflict between these principles might be reconciled by suggesting that the benefit principle apply where exclusion is more feasible and ability to pay where exclusion is not feasible, where goods are public. But where exclusion is more feasible, the market may operate more efficiently than government to allocate goods.

It is difficult to justify regressive taxation on any equity grounds other than a rigid application of the benefit principle (which, as noted above, is not feasible with most governmentally produced goods). However, many tax provisions with regressive effects, such as capital gains or home ownership provisions, are justified in terms of the creation of incentives to encourage certain behavior such as business investment or housing construction. Arguments on the basis of fairness can more easily be made for both proportional and progressive taxation. The latter is usually justified in terms of the economic principle of diminishing marginal utility, which says that the utility derived from each additional increment of any good, after some point, is smaller than the increment from the previous one. When this principle is applied to income, it suggests that downward redistribution of income should produce an increase in total utility. It should be noted, however, that because income is substitutable among many different goods, its marginal utility would not be expected to diminish nearly as quickly as the marginal utility of any individual good.

Tax Incidence—Who Really Pays

Closely related to the whole question of tax equity is that of *tax incidence*, or who actually bears the burden of the tax. If the tax falls, in the final analysis, on someone other than on whom it was levied, we refer to a *shifting* of the tax burden. Taxes can be shifted forward or backward. An example of forward shifting would be the shifting of sales tax from sellers to consumers in the form of higher prices. An example of backward shifting would be a reduction in wages or in payments to suppliers in response to the corporate income tax.

The factor that determines, for a given supply function, how much a tax can be shifted is the price elasticity of demand. The more elastic demand is with respect to price changes, the more difficult it is to shift the tax forward. This is shown in Figure 10-2. The reader may note that the reasoning behind the figures is very similar to the reasoning presented in connection with the distribution of subsidy effects in Chapter 7.

Taxes such as personal income and estate taxes are difficult or impossible to shift and thus are sometimes called direct taxes. Other taxes, such as general sales taxes, selective sales (excise) taxes, or property taxes are easier to shift and are sometimes called indirect taxes.

Revenue Elasticity

Tax elasticity refers to the responsiveness of the tax to changes in income. More specifically, the elasticity of a tax is measured by

$$\frac{\text{Percent change in tax revenue}}{\text{Percent change in national income}}$$

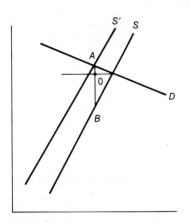 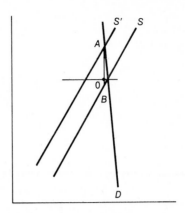

FIGURE 10-2
Tax shifting under different demand conditions. In both figures a tax of *AB* shifts supply from *S* to *S'*. The price increase *OA* is shifted forward to the buyer, while the segment *OB* is absorbed by the seller. Note that where demand is less elastic, the price increase is greater and the amount of the tax shifted forward is greater. If elasticity of demand equals zero, (demand curve vertical) then all of the tax is shifted forward.

Those taxes having values greater than 1 are termed elastic and those with values less than 1 are termed inelastic. An elasticity of 1 is referred to as "unitary." The income tax is the most elastic type of tax, a characteristic that it owes to its progressive rate structure. As personal incomes rise, not only is the tax base larger but more income appears in higher brackets so that the average rate at which income is taxed rises. It is therefore advantageous during times of economic expansion. The federal income tax is believed to have an income elasticity of about 1.7. For state income taxes the income elasticity will vary with the degree of progressivity. But elastic revenues can be a mixed blessing. During recession, elastic revenue sources decline more rapidly than income and therefore can create severe fiscal problems. The property tax is often criticized for being relatively inelastic and thus an inadequate source of revenue for local governments. But it is also less subject to decline during times of economic contraction.[41]

The Property Tax

The property tax is the principal tax on wealth in the United States.[42] Originally intended to be a general wealth tax, it is today primarily a tax on real property. It is called an ad valorem tax because it is based on *value*, rather than on the number of units sold. It is a very old tax, predating the founding of the country by many

[41] For a comparison of the revenue elasticities of different state and local taxes, see Advisory Commission on Intergovernmental Relations, *State-Local Finances in Recession and Inflation*, 1979, Table 11.
[42] For a general discussion of property taxes and a classic work on the subject see Dick Netzer, *Economics of the Property Tax*, Brookings Institution, Washington, D.C., 1966.

decades. To some degree it is a holdover from an age in which the tie between the ownership of property and the generation of income was much closer than it is today.

There are two main categories of property generally subject to taxation in most jurisdictions—real and personal property. Real property consists of land, structures, and improvements, and personal property consists of tangible property such as machinery, equipment, inventory, furniture, and motor vehicles or intangible property such as stocks, bonds, and mortgages. Since the first step in the levying of any property tax is discovery of the property, the personal property tax has been extremely difficult to implement for many types of household goods. Thus it has been virtually abandoned in some states, with the exception of taxes on motor vehicles or certain kinds of business inventory and machinery. The tax on real property, however, remains the predominant tax for substate governments and school districts.

The tax is collected in the following manner. Properties are assessed (value determined) and entered on the municipal tax roll. Sometimes the actual market value is also the assessed value, but often some fraction (an assessment ratio) is applied to the true market value to determine assessed value. This practice of fractional assessment is fairly widespread nationally. A uniform rate of $X per $100 or per $1000 of assessed value is applied to the assessed value to determine the tax levy (amount owed) and the owner of record is billed accordingly. The tax is easy to administer and hard to evade. In the case of nonpayment the property can be foreclosed by the taxing jurisdiction and sold at auction to recover past due taxes.

The property tax has historically been the most widely criticized tax in our federal system. The Advisory Commission on Intergovernmental Relations has conducted an annual opinion survey on government taxing and spending for the past several years, and until 1979 the property tax was consistently voted the worst tax—the least fair among all major types of taxes.[43]

It has been criticized on the grounds that assessment practices are inconsistent. Thus properties of comparable value, which should in theory pay comparable taxes, may actually carry substantially different tax burdens. It has been accused of contributing to urban blight because property improvements are taxed and thus repair and renovation discouraged. It has been said to be a weak revenue source because of its reputed low-income elasticity. Those who are concerned with the question of suburban land use often criticize our heavy reliance on the property tax on the grounds that it creates one of the motivations behind exclusionary zoning (see Chapter 7). Finally, and perhaps most seriously, the property tax has traditionally been viewed as regressive because housing costs constitute a larger proportion of the budgets of low-income people and because it is thought that the tax on owners is usually shifted forward to renters.

Old and New Views of Property Tax Incidence Recently, the accepted view of the property tax as regressive has been called into question and many scholars

---

[43] Advisory Commission on Intergovernmental Relations, *Changing Public Attitudes on Governments and Taxes*, 1980.

TABLE 10-9
TWO VIEWS OF PROPERTY TAX INCIDENCE

Object of tax	Old view	New view
Unimproved land	Landowner: Supply of land is inelastic; a tax on goods in fixed supply cannot be shifted	Landowner: Supply of land is inelastic; a tax on goods in fixed supply cannot be shifted
Residential structures	Owner occupant: Not shifted	Owner occupant: Not shifted, but tax not regressive if lifetime income considered, rather than annual income
	Renter: Tax shifted to renter because of long-term elasticity of housing supply. Tax burden is in proportion to consumption of housing	Renter: Tax not shifted because intrametropolitan mobility will allow renters to avoid tax

Business property	Consumers: Tax on real property shifted to consumers in proportion to their consumption of taxed goods	Differentiates between effects of tax as a nationwide tax at the national average rate, and variation in tax rates around the nationwide average (excise tax effects)
		
		1 Nationwide tax: Rests on capital
		
		2 Differential tax:
		  a Interurban effects: Raises prices in high tax areas
		  b Intraurban effects: Tax not shifted; workers, tenants, and consumers avoid tax through mobility

now take a much more favorable view of this most venerable of taxes. This shift in viewpoint comes from a relatively new analytical approach to tax incidence.[44] The basic tradeoff in tax incidence analysis is between simplicity of the tax incidence model and its realism. The simpler the model, the easier it is to apply but the more oversimplified and unrealistic its assumptions are likely to be. Conversely, tax incidence models that attempt to consider all possible influences may gain realism at the cost of being unmanageable. (See Table 10-9 for a synopsis of the differences between the old and new views.)

Traditional tax incidence analysis relied on what is known as a partial-equilibrium theory. This approach assumes that when a tax is imposed all other commodity and factor prices remain unchanged. While this simplifies the incidence analysis tremendously, it is clearly unrealistic and has therefore been discarded in some analyses in favor of a general-equilibrium model.

Let us consider the old view first. Because the property tax is really composed

[44] This "new" approach to tax incidence is known as general-equilibrium analysis and is identified with Arnold C. Harberger, developed further by Charles E. McLure and Peter M. Mieskowski, See Harberger, "The Incidence of the Corporation Income Tax," *Journal of Political Economy*, vol. 70, June 1962, 215–240; McLure, "The Theory of Tax Incidence with Imperfect Factor Mobility," *Finanzarchiv*, vol. 30, 1971, pp. 27–48; and Mieskowski, "On the Theory of Tax Incidence," *Journal of Political Economy*, vol. 75, June 1967, pp. 250–262.

of two conceptually distinct taxes, that on land and that on "improvements," it is useful to discuss the incidence of these components separately.[45] Because land is an immobile factor of production in fixed supply, that is, a perfectly inelastic supply, the tax on land is borne entirely by landowners.[46] The tax cannot be shifted because supply cannot be altered. Thus, taxes on land reduce the value of land and therefore its price. The tax becomes "capitalized" into the value of the land and the land value declines. At a prevailing interest rate of 10 percent the present value of a parcel of land that returns $1000 per year is $10,000. If a tax of $100 is imposed, the annual return from the property is reduced to $900, and the value of the property drops to $9000. Buyers do not bear the burden of a prior tax increase because they are already reflected in lower land values, but subsequent tax increases will make the buyer worse off.

The traditional view is that structures are not in fixed supply, and therefore adjustments can be made in response to taxes on structures.[47] Investment can be curtailed, causing supply to decline and prices (rents) to increase. Thus, at least some of the burden is shifted forward to consumers in the form of higher rents and house prices. Because low-income households spend a higher percentage of their incomes on housing than higher-income consumers, this portion of the tax is viewed as being regressive.

The amount of shifting is partly a function of the time frame in question. Consider, for example, the case of rental housing. In the very short term supply cannot change. If we assume, quite reasonably, that demand is not influenced by the size of the property tax, then the equilibrium rent will not change and none of the tax will be shifted forward. The entire burden of the tax will be borne by the property owner. On the other hand, assume that the supply of housing is very elastic in the long term. In that case almost the entire burden may be shifted forward to the renter. These two cases are illustrated in Figure 10-3.

The New View The new view is in agreement with the old view on the incidence of the property tax on land value but diverges sharply on its incidence on improvements. Since improvements constitute the bulk of the property tax base in urban areas, this difference is of considerable import. Those who take the new view distinguish between a conception of the property tax as a national tax that is levied at the average rate of all local jurisdictions and a view of the tax as having different rates in different parts of the country.[48] In the general-equilibrium approach, the incidence of a nationwide tax levied at the average tax rate for the country as a whole is not readily shiftable and therefore rests on capital income generally. The argument here is that the normal functioning of capital markets will equalize the after-tax return on all forms of capital. Thus the ownership of capital, in general, becomes less profitable. The property tax therefore becomes a tax on all owners of capital, regardless of whether the particular capital they own is

[45] Henry Aaron, *Who Pays the Property Tax?*, Brookings Institution, Washington, D.C., p. 19.
[46] Ibid.
[47] Ibid.
[48] George Break, "The Incidence and Economic Effects of Taxation," in Alan F. Blinder and Robert Solow (eds.), *The Economics of Public Finance*, Brookings Institution, Washington, D.C., 1974.

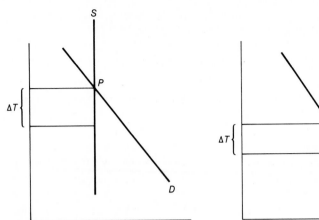
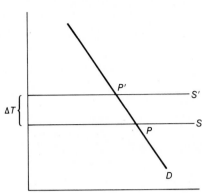

FIGURE 10-3
Incidence of the property tax on rental housing in the short and long term ("old" view). (*a*)
In the short term supply is completely inelastic and, therefore the increase in tax, ΔT, has
no effect on price. Thus the entire tax is borne by the owner. (*b*) In the very long term
housing supply is viewed as almost infinitely elastic. The tax shifts supply from *S* to *S'* and
price goes from *P* to *P'*. Almost the entire tax increase is shifted forward to renters.
(Whether viewing the long-term elasticity of housing as almost infinite is realistic is discussed in Chapter 7.)

subject to the property tax. Since the ownership of wealth is heavily concentrated
among those with higher incomes the tax would appear to be strongly progressive.[49]

Property tax rate differentials between or within regions create excise tax
effects. Prices become higher and output lower in the relatively more heavily
taxed regions and industries. To the extent that a firm has any degree of monopoly
power it will be able to shift some of the excise effect forward to the consumers of
its products or services. Similarly, if it has any degree of monopsony power, it will
be able to shift some of the burden back to its suppliers or employees. This is in
distinction to the pure competitor (price taker), who has no choice but to accept
the existing market price and absorb any unfavorable cost differentials in their
entirety. In rental housing markets, tenant mobility will make it difficult for
owners to shift much of the burden of local differentials forward to tenants. Thus
the burden will tend to be borne by the property owner.

Which View to Take?   Given the existence of two reasonable but very different
views of property tax incidence, is there any convincing reason for choosing one
view over the other? One writer on the subject of taxation and public finance,
Henry Aaron, suggests that we make the choice on the basis of the question being
posed.[50] If the issue is whether a locality should increase revenue collections by
using the property tax versus some other instrument such as a sales tax or
increased user charges, the old view is the appropriate one. No action that a single

[49] H. Aaron, op. cit.; G. Break, op. cit.
[50] H. Aaron, op. cit.

municipality takes will affect capital markets and the overall rate of return on capital. On the other hand, if the question were whether federal fiscal and tax policy ought to be altered so as to increase or decrease local reliance upon the property tax, then using the new view would make more sense because its aggregate perspective would be more appropriate than the partial-equilibrium perspective of the old view.

Sales and Excise Taxes

Whereas the property tax is a tax on wealth, the sales tax is a tax on consumption. General sales taxes are known as *ad valorem* taxes rather than per unit taxes. The tax is computed as a percentage of the total value of the sale, rather than as a fixed charge for each unit of the good sold. The latter method would be characteristic of excise taxes, such as that on cigarettes. A basic distinction between consumption taxes and other taxes is that to some extent an individual can affect the amount of tax paid by altering his or her pattern of consumption.

The general sales tax, on all retail sales, is not nearly as common among local governments as the property tax; localities in all the states levy the property tax, whereas only about one-half of the states authorize local sales taxes. However, selective sales taxes on certain commodities such as liquor and tobacco, generally known as excise taxes, are much more widespread.

A sales tax can only achieve a high level of efficiency (that is, nondistortion of prices) if it is truly a *general* tax on all sales transactions. The more general the tax, the more difficult it is to avoid the tax, the less encouragement there is to altering consumption behavior, and therefore the fewer the distortions it will introduce into the price system.

As a matter of practice, however, most states attempt to ease the burden of the tax on low-income families by exempting items that are regarded as necessities or that are believed to constitute a higher proportion of the expenditures of low-income households than of upper-income households. Localities in about one-third of the states exempt food from the tax, more than half exempt prescription drugs, and several states exempt clothing. These equity-based revisions presumably increase the progressivity of the tax and thus secure some equity gains if one accepts the ability-to-pay criterion, although there is some evidence that the clothing exemption has a regressive rather than a progressive effect.[51] However, in theory at least, they decrease the efficiency of the tax by distorting the relationship between the prices of taxed and untaxed items. The exemptions also reduce the base of the sales tax by a considerable amount. Some estimates place the exempted amounts of sales at 60 per cent of the total nationwide.[52] Nevertheless, these exemptions are generally considered critical in order to make the sales tax more acceptable on equity grounds.

Local sales taxes can either be levied on the vendor of goods and services or

---

[51] J. M. Schaefer, "Clothing Exemptions and Sales Tax Regressivity," *American Economic Review*, vol. 59, September 1969, pp. 596–599.

[52] James D. Rodgers, "Sales Taxes, Income Taxes and Other Revenues," in J. Richard Aronson and Eli Schwartz (eds.), *Management Policies in Local Government Finance*, International City Management Association, Washington, D.C., 1981.

levied on the sale and collected by the vendor. In either case they are regarded as consumer levies, and most of the burden is probably shifted forward to the consumer.

Income Taxation

The local income tax dates back to 1938, when the city of Philadelphia adopted one. The income tax has not become popular across the country as a local tax. Its use is concentrated in certain eastern and midwestern states such as Pennsylvania, Ohio, and Maryland. Generally speaking, local income taxes that have been adopted are flat-rate taxes (that is, nonprogressive) on earned income. After the original Philadelphia tax was ruled unconstitutional due to an exemption of the first $1000 of income (which made the tax slightly progressive), the law was changed to eliminate exemptions and personal deductions. Many cities have since followed suit.

The base of most local income taxes differs considerably from that of federal or state income taxes. Local income taxes generally exclude income from property (interest income, capital gains, etc.) from the tax base, and they often disallow personal exemptions and deductions. For all of the above reasons, the local income tax tends to be substantially less progressive than state or federal income taxes. If one accepts ability to pay as the prime basis for judging equity, one will not find the local income tax to be as attractive as the typical state or federal income tax.

But as a practical matter, a strongly progressive local income tax is not likely to be a good idea. The small geographic scale means that the tax is relatively easy to escape by moving. Those who would be most strongly motivated to move would be those in higher tax brackets.

For reasons discussed before, it is not in the interest of most municipalities to cause the selective outmigration of wealthier residents. In fact, even at the state level, a high degree of progressivity may not be advisable for this reason. For instance, several years ago the marginal tax rate in New York State was 15 percent, while the adjacent state of Connecticut had no personal income tax. New York State was very concerned about the movement of corporate activity out of New York and into nearby Connecticut. It was widely believed that one force behind many corporate relocations was that high-bracket individuals, those hardest hit by a steeply progressive tax, are also the people who make corporate-location decisions. In effect, a vice president in charge of corporate planning might solve his own tax problems by encouraging his firm to move. As a result of this sort of thinking, the state has cut its marginal tax rate slightly, even though the state's revenue needs have not diminished and even though a steeply progressive tax is well suited to the generally liberal political temper of the state.

User Charges and Fees   A major portion of the local revenue of city governments comes in the form of user charges and fees for governmental services provided. As noted in Table 10-5, charges and fees comprise anywhere from 10 percent of total revenue for large cities to nearly 17 percent of revenues for the smallest cities. Growth in this revenue source has been substantial in the past few years, owing to efforts to relieve what is commonly perceived to be an excessive property tax burden, and in some cities to replace shrinking tax resources lost due to property tax limitations.

The basic argument for user charges and fees as opposed to taxation is that of efficiency. To the extent that the exclusion principle operates in the provision of local government services, it may be possible for local governments to approximate the workings of the market by charging for public services and facilities. This is commonly done for utilities such as water and electricity, as well as for public transit, trash collection, and the use of recreational facilities. Aside from the efficiency advantages, certain kinds of charges such as tolls or parking fees may also serve to ration the use of roads and highways and thus reduce social costs such as congestion and pollution.

Given the advantages of user charges and fees, they might appear to be a solution to central-city fiscal problems. However, there are limits to their use for reasons already cited—the absence of the exclusion principle for many governmentally produced goods. Police and fire protection, public health, street and road construction and maintenance, and public welfare are public goods that have substantial spillover benefits, which are difficult or impossible to charge for. These constitute much of the cost of city government, and therefore the applicability of user charges and fees is limited. Furthermore, there may be equity losses with user charges (in terms of the ability-to-pay principle) if lower-income households pay a larger portion of their income for public services. These may offset the efficiency gains.

Nonetheless, there is a strong interest in user charges among local government officials today because they can alleviate fiscal pressures while promoting economic efficiency, and they are often attractive from a political point of view because they seem fairer or less noticeable than property tax increases. Whether the latter is a desirable aspect of user charges, however, is a point that may be fairly debated.

Revenue Diversification and Fiscal Illusion

In the years since the Great Depression, local governments have come to rely more and more on revenue sources other than the real estate tax. One reason for this is that a number of factors restrain the amount of revenue that the property tax can generate. The relatively low elasticity of the property tax base was mentioned earlier. Another factor is that many states and localities have constitutional provisions limiting property taxes to some fixed percentage of the full value of taxable property. Finally, taxpayer resistance to further increases in property tax increases can be formidable, if not overwhelming, as is discussed subsequently. Due in large part to the relatively greater elasticity of sales and income taxes, and the absence of restrictions on the ability to collect revenues through user fees and charges, these alternative revenue sources are often advocated as ways of easing, if not solving, the fiscal crisis of local governments.

However, there may be a negative side to the diversification of revenue structures. Public choice theorists have suggested for some time that the complexity of local revenue structures may cause citizens to misperceive the costs of government and therefore result in a public sector that is too large. This notion is referred to in the literature as *fiscal illusion*.[53]

Fiscal illusion is a concept that dates back to the late nineteenth and early twentieth centuries.[54] It suggests that the manner in which taxes are collected from citizens affects their perception of how much tax they are actually paying. For example, withholding of income by employers makes the burden of the personal income tax less apparent than it would be if income taxes had to be paid at one time. Similarly, the total burden of the general sales tax may appear smaller than it really is because it is levied in such small amounts.

Even less obvious in terms of its impact is the value added tax (VAT), in which the consumer sees only the tax imposed at the retail stage but actually pays, through a higher price, the taxes imposed at previous stages of production. In fact, when a national VAT was proposed in the United States (it is in wide use in western Europe) by Congressman Al Ullman several years ago, strong conservative opposition was raised precisely on the grounds of the relative invisibility of the tax.

Although very little empirical research has been conducted on the fiscal-illusion concept, one study has found an apparent relationship between the complexity of a city's revenue structure and the relative magnitude of the city's total expenditures.[55] The study hypothesizes that the more complex the revenue structure and the more diverse the methods of revenue extraction the greater the likelihood of fiscal illusion. It finds that revenue structure complexity (as a surrogate measure for fiscal illusion) is related to a larger public sector size, controlling for a series of other variables. The study concludes that fiscal illusion is a reality.

There is other evidence of a less systematic nature that local officials do deliberately attempt to conceal tax burdens from citizens (whether this causes the public sector to be too large is an analytically separate question). One study catalogs a series of rules of thumb followed by city officials in Oakland in raising revenues.[56] Two such rules cited were (1) "an old tax is a good tax" and (2) many small increases in taxes are better than one big increase. The use of these rules of thumb suggests that fiscal illusion may be a product of deliberate local-policy decisions.

If it is possible for local residents to misperceive the burden of taxation, however, it is also possible for them to misperceive the benefits of public expenditures. Public choice theorists have generally stressed the burden of taxation without recognizing that citizens' preferences for public services and therefore their willingness to pay may be greater than is commonly thought,

---

[53] James Buchanan, *Public Finance in Democratic Process*, University of North Carolina Press, Chapel Hill, 1967; Richard Wagner, "Revenue Structure, Fiscal Illusion and Budgetary Choice," *Public Choice*. vol. 25, Spring 1976, pp. 45–62

[54] The late-nineteenth-century Italian economist Puviani is credited by Buchanan with the idea.

[55] R. Wagner, op. cit.

[56] Arnold Meltsner, *The Politics of City Revenue*, University of California, Press, Berkeley, Calif., 1971.

because they are likely to undervalue the benefits they receive from public goods and services.[57] In some ways it seems more likely that benefits will be undervalued because they can often go unnoticed unless there is a sudden breakdown in delivery, whereas taxes, even if not perceived completely accurately, do not go unnoticed.

[57] Anthony Downs, "Why the Government Budget Is Too Small in a Democracy," *World Politics*, vol. 12, July 1960, pp. 541–563.

CHAPTER 11

INTERGOVERNMENTAL FISCAL RELATIONS

John R. Gist
College of Architecture and Urban Studies
Virginia Polytechnic Institute and State University

When one hears the term government without any modifier one tends to think of the federal government. After all, the federal government is the largest collector of taxes; it dominates the evening news and deals with the most important issues, like peace and war. But viewed in some other ways, state and local governments loom much larger than the federal government. In 1980, federal civilian employment was roughly 3 million, while state and local government employment (including school and other districts) was over 13 million.[1] Total federal outlays in 1980 were about $580 billion. But if we subtract transfers to individuals and to lower levels of government, that figure shrinks to $217 billion. By contrast, state and local spending (including school and special districts) was $367 billion. Thus, in terms of the purchase of goods and services the state and local sector was half again as large as the federal sector.

Although state and local governments exceed the federal government in direct expenditures, they have far less revenue-raising capacity, in part because of the mobility of population and economic activity. Thus there has developed a system of intergovernmental transfers summarized in Table 11-1. Note that local government is the big net recipient and the federal government is the big net donor. Given the large flow of funds and the massive role of the federal government as donor, the matter of fiscal federalism is of considerable theoretical and practical interest.

---

[1] The source for these and the following figures is U.S. Department of Commerce, Bureau of the Census, *Statistical Abstract of the United States 1982–83*.

TABLE 11-1
INTERGOVERNMENTAL FLOW OF FUNDS, 1960 and 1980
(Figures in Billions)

Level of government	1980		
	Originating	Final recipient	Net flow
Federal	83.0	—	−83.0
State	169.3	152.3	−17.0
Local*	130.0	230.0	+100.0
	1960		
Federal	7.0	—	−7.0
State	20.6	18.1	−2.5
Local	22.9	32.4	+9.5

* Local figures include school and other districts.
Source: U.S. Bureau of the Census, *Governmental Finances in 1979–80*
and previous years.

AN ECONOMIC THEORY OF FEDERALISM

Since the publication of Richard Musgrave's classic *Theory of Public Finance* in 1959,[2] his categorization of the fundamental functions of the public budget—allocation, distribution, and stabilization—has become widely accepted in public finance. *Allocation* refers to the choice regarding the amount and type of public goods that the economy will produce. *Distribution* refers to decisions that alter the distribution of wealth and income within society. *Stabilization* refers to the use of taxes and expenditures to stabilize the economy—to minimize inflation and unemployment and maximize economic growth.

The separation between the three functions is clearer in theory than practice. For example, a public works program may be initiated to provide macroeconomic stimulus (a stabilization goal), but it also has the effect of allocating resources to public works as distinct from other activities. In addition, it has distributional effects because it produces a different pattern of wage and factor payments than would other expenditures. Nonetheless, the Musgrave typology is still a very useful one.

The allocation function can be adequately performed by both national and local governments, but it is difficult for local government to carry out redistribution or stabilization. The reasons are the scale and the openness of the local economy. If a local government attempts to use its limited taxing power to redistribute wealth and income, it will impose a greater tax burden on its prosperous citizens relative to the burden in neighboring jurisdictions. It thereby creates an incentive for taxpayers to emigrate to lower-tax jurisdictions and for low-income individuals to immigrate to receive the higher benefits provided. If these effects occur, the tax base eventually shrinks as tax increases become capitalized into property values, and tax rates will have to increase to compensate.[3] This process may in time

[2] Richard Musgrave, *The Theory of Public Finance*, McGraw-Hill, New York, 1959.
[3] Wallace Oates, "The Effects of Property Taxes and Local Public Spending in Property Values: An Empirical Study of Tax Capitalization and the Tiebout Hypothesis," *Journal of Political Economy*, vol. 77 November/December 1969, pp. 957–971.

become unsustainable. In fact, the longstanding north-south differences in tax rates and willingness to provide transfer income may have helped produce such effects at the state and regional level.

For similar reasons local governments cannot stabilize the economy. Their tax bases are too limited for them to have a significant impact on the national economic conditions individually and the problem of coordinating the actions of thousands of separate governments would be overwhelming.

Federal and State Participation in Local Allocation Decisions

In a system in which local governments carry out only allocation activities and the national government handles distribution and stabilization, differences would most certainly exist among localities in the extent of service provision, some providing high levels and quality of services and other doing the bare minimum. Assuming there are many local governments and assuming a relatively high degree of geographic mobility, variations in service provisions could lead to an economically efficient situation, where citizens could choose to live in that jurisdiction which provided the level of services that most closely matched their preferences for public goods. This argument is generally referred to as the Tiebout Hypothesis, after its originator, Charles Tiebout.[4] In this situation, there would be no role for federal or state governments in providing fiscal assistance to local governments. Interjurisdictional differences in provision of public goods would presumably reflect voter preferences.

Note, however, that the Tiebout argument is critically dependent upon the assumption of easy mobility. The reader might rightly question how realistic this assumption is. A still more serious objection to the Tiebout economic efficiency hypothesis is the existence of externalities. As long as local public goods benefit only local residents and do not spill over, economic efficiency may result. But we know that the costs and benefits of local government actions such as education, waste management, environmental protection, zoning, and numerous others do spill over to neighboring jurisdictions and their residents. If the city government of Gary, Indiana, acts to reduce the level of pollutants released into the atmosphere by its steel manufacturers, residents of neighboring jurisdictions receive benefits for which they would, in principle, be willing to pay. But because no mechanism for the making of such payments exists, too little of this activity will be undertaken. The result is an inefficient allocation of resources.

In theory, an efficient allocation of goods can be attained if a higher level (usually federal) government were to subsidize the desired local activity by means of a conditional grant-in-aid, that is, a grant for the sole purpose of undertaking the activity yielding the positive externalities. Grants to encourage specific government action should also be matching, requiring local commitment of some magnitude as a condition of receiving the aid.

To achieve marginal efficiency, the ratio of external benefit to total benefit ought to be reflected in the structure of the matching provision. For example, if 90 percent of the total benefit of a pollution control program will accrue to

---

[4] Charles Tiebout, "A Pure Theory of Local Expenditures," *Journal of Political Economy*, vol. 64, October 1956, pp. 416–424.

nonresidents, then a ratio which provided 9 federal dollars for each local dollar would, presumably, encourage the municipality to spend to the point at which the marginal expenditure equaled the marginal benefit.[5]

Beyond the matter of externalities, there is another, and very powerful, reason to favor federal grants to localities. This is the existence of large inequalities in wealth between localities. If there is not some revenue transfer to the less affluent jurisdictions, some of them may not be able to provide what is generally agreed upon as a minimum acceptable level of public services. Disparities in the services provided local citizens due to differences in wealth may also encourage low-income individuals to migrate to areas that provide superior services and wealthier individuals to emigrate as tax burdens get too high. Thus, even in the absence of any externalities, we might favor intergovernmental transfers to achieve equity goals.

However, if the purpose of the grant is to equalize the interjurisdictional distribution of income, lump-sum grants, which have no matching provision and are not limited to a specific purpose, are the most appropriate grant design because they increase the income of the jurisdiction without influencing the relative prices of goods to the community and thus not distorting economic allocation. Conceptually, this argument is the same as that advanced in Chapter 6 for the superiority, in principle, of direct transfers to assistance in kind.

The Theory of Grants

Since the late 1960s, an extensive theoretical and empirical literature has developed regarding the design of grants and the effects of different grant designs on the fiscal behavior of recipient governments.[6] The theoretical literature on grant design generally divides grants into conditional and unconditional and matching and nonmatching grants.

Conditional or restricted grants are grants that must be used for a specific purpose. These are often referred to as categorical grants. Unconditional or unrestricted grants are not limited with respect to use. Matching grants require a local contribution or match as a condition of obtaining the aid, whereas with nonmatching or lump-sum grants, the recipient government receives a fixed amount regardless of its own actions. Generally, the matching ratio of donor dollars to recipient dollars is fixed. Thus the amount of aid received depends upon how much the locality itself is willing to spend, up to the point at which the federal funds are exhausted.

---

[5] Wallace Oates, *Fiscal Federalism*, Harcourt Brace Jovanovich, New York, 1972.

[6] The literature is too voluminous to give detailed citations. Good summaries of the theoretical literature are Lester Thurow, "The Theory of Grants-in-Aid," *National Tax Journal*, vol. 19, 1966, pp. 373–377. James Wilde, "Grant-in-Aid: The Analytics of Design and Response," *National Tax Journal*, vol. 24, 1971, pp. 143–156; David Bradford and Wallace Oates, "Towards a Predictive Theory of Intergovernmental Grants," *American Economic Review*, vol. 61, 1971, pp. 440–448. A good review of the empirical literature through the early 1970s is found in Edward Gramlich, "Intergovernmental Grants: A Review of the Empirical Literature," in Wallace Oates (ed.), *The Political Economy of Fiscal Federalism*, D.C. Heath, Lexington, Mass., 1977, and perhaps the best single analysis of grant impacts is Edward Gramlich and Harvey Galper, "State and Local Fiscal Behavior and Federal Grant Policy," *Brookings Papers on Economic Activity*, vol. 1, 1973, pp. 15–65.

TABLE 11-2
EXAMPLES OF FEDERAL GRANT TYPES

Type of grant	Example	Federal $ amount in fiscal year 1980
Unrestricted lump sum	General revenue sharing	$6.8 billion
Restricted lump sum	Community development block grants	$3.9 billion
Open-ended matching	Aid to families with dependent children	$6.8 billion
Closed-ended matching	Grants to states for historic preservation; hazardous waste management	——

Matching grants are generally of the closed-ended kind, meaning that beyond a fixed point the federal grant is exhausted. But in a few cases, in the public welfare area, grants are open-ended, meaning that there is no ceiling on the amount obtainable from the donor government, as long as the local government is willing to provide the match. The major open-ended matching grants are AFDC and Medicaid. Matching-grant programs still constitute by far the largest number of federal grants, but nonmatching or lump-sum grant programs, such as general revenue sharing, have become a very large proportion of total federal aid since 1972. Table 11-2 provides some examples of federal grants that fall into the various categories discussed above.

The Effects of Grants on Municipal Expenditures   The effects of grants are usually discussed using indifference curve analysis and a utility maximization framework.[7] The indifference curves are taken to represent the preferences of the local governing body for goods and services, both public and private. The indifference map is not intended to represent aggregate social preferences or a social-welfare function but is a simplified way of viewing the local resource allocation process.

The geometric representation is essentially that discussed in Chapter 6. In Figure 11-1 the X and Y axes can each represent individual public goods, or X may represent one good while Y represents all other goods. AA' represents the original budget line for a given community prior to receiving any external aid, and point E represents the initial equilibrium point of consumption of goods X and Y. At this equilibrium point, this community purchases OC of good X and OD of good Y.

Now let us consider the case of a lump-sum unrestricted grant of amount AB, shown in Figure 11-1. Because it is unrestricted, the amount AB can be spent for either X or Y. In the case shown, Y may represent either public goods or tax relief because an increase in income to the local government is analogous to an increase in income to the community, only part of which would normally be spent on public

[7] James Wilde, op. cit.

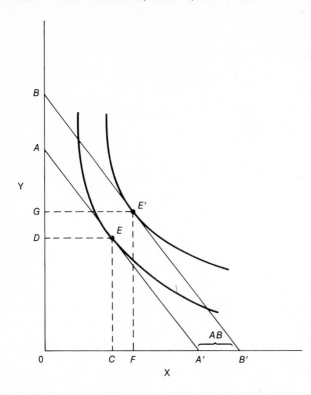

FIGURE 11-1
The effect of an unrestricted lump-sum grant on local government expenditures. A grant of size *AB* shifts the budget line to the right but parallel to its initial position. Expenditures on *Y* increase by *GD* and expenditures on *X* increase by *CF*.

goods. In other words, an increase in income to a community is conceptually the same as an increase in unrestricted aid, and theory says that the same percentage of each should be spent on public goods. This situation in Figure 11-1 is analogous to the unrestricted transfer discussed in Chapter 6. There is no effect on relative prices, so the budget line simply shifts out parallel to *BB'*. The new equilibrium point is *E'*, and the community now is able to purchase amount OF of good *X* and OG of good *Y* (or of tax relief).

Figure 11-2 describes the situation in which a lump-sum grant of *AB* is given, but the grant is restricted to the purchase of good *X*. In this case, the budget line again shifts out by the amount *AB*, but since the grant can be used only for good *X* and not for other goods *Y*, the new budget line becomes horizontal from *A* to *B*. Thus the new budget line is *ABB'*. But notice that the equilibrium point in Figure 11-2 is exactly the same as in Figure 11-1. Thus a lump-sum grant of *AB*, whether restricted or unrestricted, may have identical effects on the community's purchase of goods and services.

The case of matching grants is explored in Figures 11-3 and 11-4. Figure 11-3 represents the effect of an open-ended matching grant. Such a grant not only increases the total revenue available to a community—income effect—but alters the relative prices of goods and services—substitution effect. Because the grant is restricted to the purchase of *X*, the budget line shifts outward on the *X* axis, but its intersection with the *Y* axis remains fixed at point *A*. Because the grant is open-ended, there is no upper limit on the donor government's contribution—the new budget line obtains for the entire range of possible purchases of *X*.

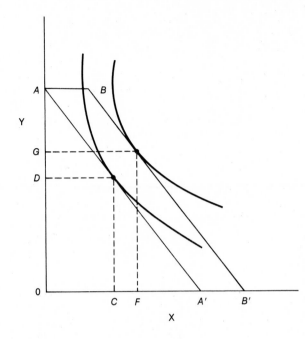

FIGURE 11-2
A lump-sum restricted grant. The grant shifts the municipal budget line from *AA'* to *ABB'*. Note, however, that the effect upon municipal expenditures is exactly the same as for the unrestricted lump-sum grant shown in Figure 11-1.

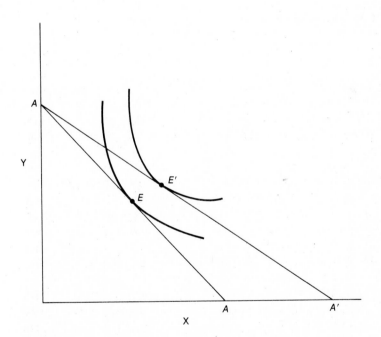

FIGURE 11-3
The effects of an open-ended matching grant. If the grant is restricted to good *X*, the budget line shifts to the right along the *X* axis but intersects the *Y* axis at the original position. The increased expenditure on *X* includes both an income effect and, because the cost of *X* has been lowered relative to *Y*, a substitution effect.

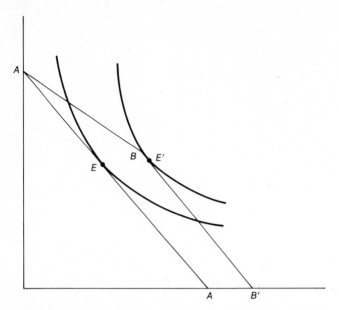

FIGURE 11-4.
The effects of a closed-ended matching grant. The original budget
line is *AA*. The matching grant changes its slope out to point *B*
where the grant is exhausted. From *B* to *B'* the new budget line is
parallel to the old budget line. Whether the fact of being closed
causes the outcome to be different than it would if the grant were
open-ended depends on whether *E'* occurs above or below the
kink.

Figure 11-4 shows the effect of a closed-ended matching grant. From *A* to *B* the
new budget line has a different slope than the old line because the grant alters the
price of *X*. At point *B* the grant is exhausted and the price to the community of *X*
reverts to its old value. Thus from this point on, the slope of the new budget line is
the same as that of the old budget line. Whether the fact of closed-endedness
affects the community's allocation of funds depends on whether the new equilibrium point *E'* occurs before or after the kink in the new budget line. Whether the
community exhausts the grant depends on its elasticity of demand for *X* and the
amount it would have spent on *X* in the absence of the grant.

The Substitution Phenomenon   Note that even in cases such as Figs. 11-3 and
11-4 where the grant is restricted in its use for good *X* only, the increased income
the grant generates may permit the municipality to increase its consumption of
other goods and services as well. This substitution phenomenon is one of the
central issues in the design of grants.[8] The greater the degree of fiscal substitution,
the more difficult it will be for a donor government to achieve its objective of
increasing spending for specific functions. Note the parallelism here with the

[8] Most of the empirical literature starting in the late 1960s was concerned with estimating the
magnitude of this substitution effect. See, for example, Gramlich and Galper, op. cit.

earlier discussion of housing vouchers, food stamps, and other types of in-kind aid. If we visualize an indifference curve with public goods on one axis and private consumption on the other axis, then it is reasonable to believe that as intergovernmental aid increases, expenditures from local sources will fall, that is, that local tax effort will decrease. The grant will permit the locality to consume more of both categories of goods, public and private.

The terms *substitutive* and *stimulative* are sometimes used to describe the effects of grants. If a grant had a completely substitutive effect, locally funded spending would fall by the full amount of the grant and total spending would remain constant. If local spending increases in response to the grant, then the grant has a stimulative effect on spending. This theoretical structure underlying the design of grants allows us to make certain predictions regarding the relative stimulative or substitutive effects on local spending. Take first the case of unrestricted lump-sum transfers. This kind of grant, of which general revenue sharing is the purest case, has effects comparable in theory to any net increase in the private aggregate income of the community (as noted earlier). Their expenditure effect depends, therefore, on the local government's propensity to spend increased revenues, as opposed to using them to reduce taxes. Since this type of grant has only an income effect and no price effect we would expect a considerable amount of substitution.

Theory would predict that open-ended matching grants should be more stimulative than lump-sum grants because the effective price of the aided good is reduced and there is no limitation on the availability of the grant. How much stimulation occurs will depend upon the price elasticity of demand for the good being subsidized through the grant. If demand is elastic with respect to price, spending by the recipient government will be more than the amount of the grant (stimulative). It will be less than the grant amount (substitutive) if demand is inelastic. In this case, there will be a reduction of local expenditures on the aided function and a "leakage" of funds into either tax relief or expenditures on some nonaided function. With unitary elasticity, spending will increase only by the amount of the grant.

The spending effects of closed-ended matching grants are potentially more complex than the other types because of the limitation placed on the grant amount. The price effect should result in higher spending than with lump-sum transfers, but the limitation on funds suggests that the degree of substitution or stimulation will depend not only on demand elasticity (as it does also with open-ended grants) but also on how much a jurisdiction would spend on the aided function in the absence of the grant. If in the pregrant situation the jurisdiction already spent enough to exhaust the full grant amount, then the grant has no price effect at all, only an income effect, and the spending impact is similar to that of a lump-sum transfer. The jurisdiction cannot obtain any further aid by increasing local spending. But if local spending in the pregrant situation is not enough to totally exhaust the grant, then there is both a price and income effect. In this case the closed-ended grant actually functions as an open-ended matching grant, and local spending may be stimulated, particularly if the elasticity of demand exceeds 1. If the elasticity of demand is less than 1, then the grant will lead to an increase in spending less than the grant amount.

In general, the empirical research on the effects of grants is broadly consistent with these theoretical predictions, but there are anomalies as well.[9] Research has confirmed that matching grants stimulate more spending per grant dollar than do nonmatching lump-sum transfers. However, the empirical literature has failed to demonstrate that the effects of nonmatching revenue-sharing grants are comparable to increases in private income, as conventional theory would suggest. Most of the empirical evidence suggests that nonmatching grants stimulate several times more local spending per grant dollar than do increases in private income. Gramlich and Galper estimate the spending effects to be four times greater for lump-sum grants than for income increases. This phenomenon has been termed the fly-paper effect (that is, money sticks where it hits) by Courant, Gramlich, and Rubinfeld.[10]

The most obvious explanation for the fly-paper effect is that government decision makers, both bureaucrats and legislators, find it easier to avoid cutting taxes when funds from external sources increase than to increase taxes when community income increases. This interpretation is also consistent with other theories of government growth, such as those of Tullock, Niskanen, and Migue and Belanger.[11] But it is also consistent with the notion that bureaucrats and legislators act merely to reduce uncertainty about future availability of revenue.

In general, some degree of substitution appears to occur with most grants. If nothing else, local officials are likely to become highly skilled in rendering grants more flexible or "fungible" than their designers intended them to be. If a grant can be obtained for an expenditure that would have been made in any case (a condition which need not be revealed to the grantor), the locality will rationally regard it as a pure lump-sum transfer regardless of how the donor views it.

The Growth of Federal Grants

The growth in federal and state aid to local governments was one of the most remarkable aspects of state and local finance in the period from 1960 to 1980. During this time federal grants grew from $7 billion to over $80 billion annually. Most of this growth occurred during the decade of the 1970s, when grants grew from $24 billion to over $80 billion. In terms of the impact of combined federal and state aid on local government budgets, the trend has been dramatic. In 1960, combined federal and state aid comprised 20 percent of municipal and local government budgets. By 1980, nearly 40 percent of municipal general revenue came from intergovernmental aid.[12]

---

[9] These theoretical expectations are nicely detailed in Ray D. Whitman and Robert J. Cline, *Fiscal Impact of Revenue Sharing in Comparison with Other Federal Aid: An Evaluation of Recent Empirical Findings,* Urban Institute, Washington, D.C., 1978, and E. Gramlich, op. cit.

[10] Paul Courant, Edward Gramlich, and Daniel Rubinfeld, "The Stimulative Effects of Intergovernmental Grants: or Why Money Sticks Where It Hits" in Peter Mieskowski and William Oakland (eds.), *Fiscal Federalism and Grants-in-Aid,* Urban Institute, Washington, D.C., 1979. Actually Gramlich credits Arthur Okun with the coining of the term.

[11] Gordon Tullock, *The Politics of Bureaucracy,* Public Affairs Press, Washington, D.C., 1965; William Niskanen, *Bureaucracy and Representative Government,* Aldine Atherton, Chicago, 1971; Jean-Luc Migue and Gerard Belanger, "Toward a General Theory of Managerial Discretion," *Public Choice,* vol. 29, Spring 1977, pp. 37–51.

[12] Advisory Commission on Intergovernmental Relations, *Significant Features of Fiscal Federalism.*

The theoretical literature on grants-in-aid in some respects developed more rapidly than federal grant practice. Differences in the effects of lump-sum and matching grants were recognized even before the former existed in the federal grant structure. Prior to the enactment of general revenue sharing in 1972, virtually all federal aid was of the categorical, matching variety. This changed dramatically with the advent of the Nixon administration's New Federalism proposals to introduce broad-purpose formula-based grants.

Nixon proposed a general revenue-sharing program and six special revenue-sharing programs in the areas of education, employment and training, urban development, rural development, transportation, and law enforcement. These proposals were intended to consolidate existing categorical grant programs into larger, broader-purpose grants with a minimum of federal reporting requirements, no matching requirements and noncompetitive, formula-based allocation mechanisms. The ostensible purpose was to reduce the complexity of the federal grant structure, reduce the paperwork burden on state and local government officials and reduce the advantage in grant application writing that larger (wealthier) cities seemed to have over smaller ones. The new programs were advertised as add-ons to existing grant programs, not replacements for them.

The general revenue sharing program was enacted in October 1972 with the support of the "intergovernmental lobby," including the Council of State Governments, the National Governors Association, the National Association of Counties, the National League of Cities, and the United States Conference of Mayors. After Nixon's reelection, he pushed harder for the special revenue-sharing programs, but he offered them at the price of reduction in funding for categorical programs, contrary to earlier commitments. Many cutbacks in grants were achieved by the impoundment of funds, which led to a bitter confrontation with the Congress in 1973 and a series of lawsuits, which generally overturned the presidential impoundments.[13]

Eventually, three of the special revenue-sharing proposals were modified and enacted by Congress as block-grant programs. The Comprehensive Employment and Training Act (CETA) was enacted in 1973 and the Community Development Block Grant program and Social Services block grants (Title XX of the Social Security Act) were enacted in late 1974, after Gerald Ford had replaced Nixon as president. By 1980 general-purpose grants—primarily revenue-sharing—and block grants comprised $19 billion out of $91.5 billion total federal aid to state and local governments. But categorical grant programs continued to be the most numerous type of federal grant assistance, with approximately 500 federal grants of this type.[14]

The Case for Federalizing Public Assistance   Because a number of the federal transfer programs are constructed on a matching basis there are large disparities from state to state. As noted in Chapter 6, for example, average AFDC payments in California are roughly four times as large as in Mississippi. Both for reasons of equity and because such disparities are believed to encourage interregional migration, there has been constant pressure for years by state and local

[13] Louis A. Fisher, *Presidential Spending Power,* Princeton University Press, Princeton, N.J., 1975.
[14] Office of Management and Budget, *The President's Budget for Fiscal Year 1980.*

governments for the federal government to assume full responsibility for all welfare programs. This would mean a national set of standards for eligibility and a national benefit schedule, as there is with the food stamp program. A partial federal assumption of means-tested welfare programs took place in 1974. Old age assistance, aid to the blind, and aid to the permanently and totally disabled, which prior to 1974 had been part of public assistance, were broken out and given a separate identity as the Supplemental Security Income (SSI) program. This is now completely funded by the federal government. Despite periodic pressure to do the same with AFDC, no serious legislative proposal to bring this about has come close to enactment. The problems inherent in a negative income tax and the results of the income maintenance experiments done in the early 1970s were discussed in some detail in Chapter 6.

Reagan Administration Proposals With the advent of the Reagan administration, numerous proposals were made (and some enacted) to continue and extend the consolidation of grant programs begun during the Nixon era. Reagan's fiscal year 1982 budget contained proposals for six block grants, consolidating 83 programs in such areas as elementary and secondary education, health and social services, and special education.[15] In the Omnibus Budget Reconciliation Act of 1981 Congress ultimately modified this proposal and enacted nine block grants, consolidating 54 grant programs in the areas of social services, home energy assistance, small city community development, elementary and secondary education, alcohol, drug abuse, and mental health, maternal and child health, community services, primary health care, and preventive health services.[16] But there were major differences between the Reagan block grants and those enacted in the Nixon-Ford era. The Reagan block grants were to be allocated to states, which would then distribute funds to local governments. The earlier block grants had gone directly to localities on the basis of legislative formulae. Second, there were no federal restrictions as to the use of funds. This was left totally to the states. Finally, funding was cut by about 25 percent from the previous level of categorical grants.[17]

This was followed in April of 1982 by a plan for a massive reorganization of federal-state welfare responsibilities, the centerpiece of which was a "swap" involving AFDC, Medicaid, and food stamps. Under the terms of the proposal, the federal government would assume full responsibility for the costs of Medicaid (which it had shared with the states) and place full responsibility for AFDC and food stamps with state governments. The federal government now has full responsibility for food stamps and shares responsibility for AFDC with the states. The proposal was later modified so that food stamps would remain a federal responsibility. At the same time, the federal government would "turn back" to the states responsibility for 44 other grant programs to be financed at first by a

---

[15] Office of Management and Budget, *Fiscal Year 1982 Budget Revisions*.

[16] John Ellwood (ed.), *Reductions in U.S. Domestic Spending: How They Affect State and Local Governments*, Transaction, New Brunswick, N.J., 1982.

[17] John Palmer and Isabel Sawhill (eds.), *The Reagan Experiment*, Urban Institute, Washington, D.C., 1982.

federal trust fund comprised of revenue sources such as alcohol, tobacco, and telephone excise taxes and a portion of the federal gasoline tax and windfall profits tax, which would enable them to carry out these additional responsibilities. Because some states (those with more generous eligibility requirements and benefit schedules) would have been at a disadvantage under the proposed arrangement, a federal trust fund would have been established to hold those states harmless for a limited time period. By 1991, the trust fund would cease to exist and the states would have permanent and sole responsibility for these programs.[18] By 1991, federal spending for intergovernmental aid would be reduced, on a percentage basis, to the percentage of the budget it had claimed in the 1930s. This dramatic change in federal, state, and local fiscal relations has been deferred by the Congress, and it is unlikely that it will surface again in its previous form.

REVENUE LIMITATIONS AND THE TAXPAYER REVOLT

One of the newest concerns in the local fiscal situation is the taxpayer revolt of the late 1970s and the ensuing series of constitutional and legislative tax and expenditure limitations enacted across the nation. Proposition 13 in California is the best known of these limitations because it was the forerunner of many other attempts, because of its severity and its repercussions, and because of its initiative format. Although the taxpayer revolt, especially citizen-initiated tax provisions, is a somewhat new concern, tax limitations are far from a new phenomenon. Nearly all states impose some form of tax or expenditure limitation on their constituent local governments. But historically tax limits have been in the form of limits on the rate of taxation localities could impose.[19] The newer kind of tax limitation spawned by proposition 13 is aimed much more directly at limiting local revenue, local expenditures, or both.

Types of Tax Limitations

In a study published in 1973, the ACIR identified five basic types of fiscal limits—rate limits, levy limits, full-disclosure laws, expenditure limits, and assessment ratios.[20] Rate limits are the most common type of fiscal limits, with at least 36 states limiting tax rates for either counties or municipalities. With rate limits, either a constitutional or a legislative limit is placed on the maximum tax rate that can be levied without a vote of the electorate. The limit is generally expressed either in mills per dollar (a mill is one-tenth of a cent) or dollars per hundred of assessed property value. Rate limits are the oldest type of tax limit, but they do not always succeed in holding down government expenditures and revenues. As long as property values continue to increase, the revenues generated with a fixed tax rate will still increase because the tax base is increasing. Only when the tax

---

[18] Edward Gramlich and Deborah S. Laren, "The New Federalism" in Joseph E. Pechman (ed.), *Setting National Priorities: The 1983 Budget*, Brookings Institution, Washington, D.C., 1982.

[19] John Mikesell, "The Season of Tax Revolt" in John Blair and David Nachmias (eds.), *Fiscal Retrenchment and Urban Policy*, Sage Publications, Beverly Hills, CA, 1979.

[20] Advisory Commission on Intergovernmental Relations, *State Limitations on Local Taxes and Expenditures*, 1977.

base is stagnant or declining, as it often is in central cities, will tax rate limits effectively limit tax revenues.

Tax levy limits, in contrast to rate limits, specify the maximum amount of revenue that can be generated by a local government via the property tax, usually expressing it as an annual percentage increase in the property tax levy. For example, a levy limit might limit total property tax revenues to a 5 percent increase over the revenues generated the previous year. If property values are rising rapidly, such a limit may actually compel a reduction in property tax rates.

Full-disclosure laws provide that before a local government can increase the total levy, it must inform its citizens of the tax rate that would be required to yield the same revenue as the previous year (usually a slightly lower rate), and then must hold public hearings if it proposes to raise more revenue than it did the prior year. After public hearings, the governing body must formally vote to approve the new levy. Otherwise, property tax rates are automatically reduced to a level that will yield revenue equal to the previous year's. It is possible that both the proposed tax rate and the tax rate required to maintain the previous year's revenue collections will be lower than the current tax rate. The purpose of full-disclosure laws is to focus the responsibility for levy increases on the governing body and thus presumably bring downward pressure on local expenditures.

Expenditure limits are generally expressed as a maximum percentage increase in annual expenditures or revenues. This type of limit differs from the levy limit in that it puts a cap on all expenditures and revenues, whereas levy limits restrict the amount of growth in property tax revenues.

Assessment ratio limits place a limit on the percent of market value at which property can be assessed. While not really intended to be fiscal limits they can serve to reduce revenue-raising ability by restricting the growth of the taxable property base.

Proposition 13 and the Taxpayer Revolt

Not surprisingly, there has been tremendous interest in the causes and consequences of the recent spate of fiscal limitation proposals and enactments.[21] Many explanations of the recent fiscal limitations posit some sort of rational voter model and see fiscal limitations as a decision by the voters to cease increasing public consumption at the expense of private consumption.[22] Yet at least one study has found that support for fiscal limitations provisions such as proposition 13 is associated more strongly with general political cynicism and disaffection than with attitudes toward taxation or government waste.[23] On a purely speculative basis we might argue that the slowing of real income growth in the 1970s made voters less willing to countenance increasing public sector expenditures than they were

---

[21] The volume of material is too lengthy to cite in detail. A conference on tax limitations was held at the University of California, Santa Barbara, in 1978. A symposium on tax and expenditure limitations was published as a supplementary issue of the *National Tax Journal*.

[22] Helen Ladd and Nicholas Tideman (eds.), *Tax and Expenditure Limitations*, Urban Institute, Washington, D.C., 1981.

[23] David Lowery and Lee Sigelman, "Understanding the Tax Revolt: Eight Explanations," *American Political Science Review*, vol. 75, December 1981, pp. 963–974.

in earlier years. It is also possible that inflation in the 1970s gave voters a strong impetus to cut back somewhere and state and local budgets were more accessible to them than the federal budget.

Proposition 13   California's proposition 13 came to symbolize the entire fiscal-limitation movement. Its extreme character cautions against generalizations to other cases, but it is still worth examining. Proposition 13 was a 400-word initiative on the California ballot that passed with a 64.7 percent majority on June 6, 1978.[24] No provision was made in the proposition itself for its implementation. This was done through separate legislation passed by the California General Assembly. The combined initiative and implementing legislation did the following:

1 Reduced property taxes from an estimated $12.5 billion to $5.4 billion.

2 Set property assessments back to their 1975 level and limited their growth to 2 percent annually or the annual increase in the state consumer price index, whichever was less. The only exceptions are new houses or houses exchanged after 1975, which are reassessed at their sale price.

3 Limited property tax rates to 4 percent of assessed value or 1 percent of fair market value, and required a two-thirds majority for new and increased state and local taxes.

4 Provided that only *counties* would levy and collect the property tax. This reduced the number of local governments levying the property tax from 6300 to 58. Counties were to distribute property tax revenues to their constituent units of government in proportion to the average share of property tax revenues these governments had received in the previous 3 years.

The immediate and short-term effects of proposition 13 are demonstrable. Property tax revenues declined by 60 percent. The biggest revenue losers were school districts because they relied most heavily on the property tax. But the loss in property tax revenues was offset in many communities by increased reliance on service charges and fees. Even more important was the availability of a more than $7 billion surplus in the state treasury, over $4 billion of which was set aside to offset the revenue loss to local governments. By 1982, however, due to the protracted recession and the use of the California treasury for the local government bailout, the surplus in the state treasury had been thoroughly depleted.

Other consequences of proposition 13 were less obvious but real nevertheless. For example, although public opinion surveys prior to the vote on proposition 13 indicated that the greatest citizen dissatisfaction was with city taxes and city government performance, the diversity of the city revenue base meant that cities suffered the smallest revenue losses in percentage terms from proposition 13. School districts suffered the greatest losses, with counties the next most severely hurt.

Although the obvious intention of proposition 13 (or any tax limitation, for that matter) was to benefit individual taxpayers by reducing their tax burden, another

---

[24] The descriptive material that follows is taken from Jerry McCaffrey and John Bowman, "Participatory Democracy and Budgeting: The Effects of Proposition 13," *Public Administration Review*, vol. 38, November/December 1978, pp. 530–538.

beneficiary is the federal government. Because property taxes are deductible from federal adjusted gross income, property tax payments reduce federal income tax liability. Conversely, reductions in property tax liability increase federal (and state) income tax liability. Thus, while individual local tax burdens may be reduced, the reduction is offset to a degree by increased federal tax liability. The amount of the offset in any given case depends on whether an individual itemizes deductions on the federal tax return, on the marginal income tax bracket in which an individual falls, and on the magnitude of the property tax reduction. In California about 35 percent of the total tax reduction ($2.5 billion) would go to owner-occupied residences, and even if the average marginal tax rate was only 20 percent, it would mean an increase in federal taxes of $500 million.

Another effect of proposition 13 is a loss in general revenue-sharing money from the federal government. The GRS allocation formula includes a tax effort factor, which is related directly to GRS allocations—the higher the effort the higher the allocation, other things being equal. Proposition 13 reduced per capita local tax revenues and therefore reduced local tax effort, thus altering this factor in the GRS formula.

Finally, the fiscal restrictions imposed by proposition 13 reduced the fiscal autonomy of local governments in California, and the bailout program of state aid to localities had the effect of centralizing government in the state, putting relatively more power in the hands of the state administration.

The effect of the assessment provisions of proposition 13 is that there is a penalty on the transfer of property. Since exchanged properties are reassessed at market value, while other properties increase in value by 2 percent or less annually, there is no doubt that exchanged or new properties of real value similar to those not exchanged will pay higher taxes. The effect is obviously to discourage mobility.

Another effect has to do with the tax-sharing provisions of the implementing legislation. The legislation provided that property tax revenues would be allocated to each noncounty government in proportion to its average share of within-county property tax receipts for the 3-year period preceding the year of allocation. Thus increases in the property values in a given jurisdiction will be shared by all jurisdictions within the county, since only counties now collect property taxes. The allocation mechanism means that there is not as much incentive for individual jurisdictions to increase the value of property within their boundaries, and therefore there may be less competition between localities for taxable properties. Proposition 13's implementing legislation has unintentionally devised a tax-base sharing program such as that enacted in Minneapolis-St. Paul. Presumably much of the motivation for fiscal zoning (see Chapter 8) has been eliminated in California. Most planners, regardless of their opinion on proposition 13 as a whole, should view this aspect of it as highly desirable.

The Effects of Tax Limits on Local Spending   Although the severity of proposition 13 in California suggests that it has already had a significant effect on reducing the size of local governments there, the verdict is not yet in as to the effects of tax limitations in other parts of the country.

One early study of the effects of tax limits that preceded the taxpayer revolt of the late 1970s was conducted by the ACIR.[25] This study first divided the 50 states into those having some type of fiscal limit (in fiscal 1974 there were 38 such states) and those having none, and then divided the former states into those having rate limits (26) and those having levy limits (12). The study attempted to determine whether the presence of tax limits, or the presence of certain types of limits (that is, rate versus levy) was associated with a lower level of *local* per capita own-source expenditures. Because numerous other factors also influence the level of local per capita expenditures, several variables were controlled for, including income, state and federal aid, urbanization, and expenditure centralization within the state (that is, what percentage of combined state-local spending was accounted for by the state government). The study found that, even controlling for these factors, spending was 6 to 8 percent *lower* in those states having tax limits. It was also found that there was a "more significant tendency for lower per capita local expenditures" in the states with rate limits compared to those with levy limits.

Proposition 13 and other tax limits have spawned another series of spending impact studies.[26] Generally these studies have tended to find no significant statistical evidence of expenditure reduction immediately after the enactment.

STRATEGIES FOR COPING WITH FISCAL STRESS

Given the grim fiscal realities that have been laid out in the preceding pages, are there any solutions to the problems of fiscal stress or, at least, strategies for coping with shrinking resources? In the past, local governments turned to the federal government for fiscal assistance in hard times and frequently obtained it, as the growth in federal aid until 1980 demonstrates. But economic and political conditions have essentially eliminated this option for the present. The recession of the early 1980s coupled with the 1981 Economic Recovery Tax Act, which reduced federal personal income tax rates substantially, have created high deficits in the federal budget, and one of the Reagan administration's primary targets for budget cuts has been intergovernmental grants. The 1981–1982 recession also seriously depleted state treasuries, leaving little likelihood of increased state aid to offset federal cutbacks, at least in the short run. Even if treasuries are replenished during economic recovery, the recent volatility of the economy will make states wary of carrying out extensive programs of local aid. It is likely, therefore, that local governments will have to look internally for the resources or means to deal with fiscal austerity.

User Fees

One way in which local governments have responded to the increasingly heavy fiscal burden is by increasing the use of fees and charges to finance government

[25] ACIR, *State Limitations on Local Taxes and Expenditures*, 1977.
[26] See, for example, Jerome Rothenberg and Paul Smoke, "Early Impacts of Proposition 2½," *Public Budgeting and Finance*, vol. 2, Winter 1982, pp. 90–110; Richard Eribes and John S. Hall, "Revolt of the Affluent: Fiscal Controls in Three States," *Public Administration Review*, vol. 41, Special Issue 1981, pp. 107–121; and McCaffrey and Bowman, op. cit.

services.[27] Their use is limited to those cases where the exclusion principle applies, such as public utilities (gas, electric, water), parks, and recreational facilities. Where user charges are practical they can offer the efficiency advantage that comes from simulating the market and the equity advantage of charging the actual beneficiary. On the other hand, they may offer what some see as equity disadvantages too—for example, pricing the use of some public facilities beyond the reach of the poor. From the viewpoint of the local economy as a single entity, they have the disadvantage that there is no federal tax offset, that is, fees and charges paid by individuals cannot be deducted from income for federal tax purposes.

Privatization

We have generally come to expect government to be the provider of public goods, but public goods and services can be provided by local government in a variety of ways. These alternative delivery arrangements have been discussed under the general rubric of *privatization*.[28] In discussing alternative service arrangements, Savas distinguishes among the service consumer, the service producer, and the service arranger. The service consumer directly obtains or receives the service. The producer is the agent who actually performs the work or delivers the service to the community. The arranger is the agent who assigns the producer to the consumer, or vice versa, or selects the producer who will serve the consumer. In the traditional case, where the government finances and produces the good, it acts as both producer and arranger. But there are many instances where it is feasible to introduce a third party, who acts as producer, presumably because it will result in greater efficiency of delivery. Savas identifies nine possible arrangements for public services provision: (1) government service; (2) intergovernmental agreement; (3) contract, or purchase of service; (4) franchise; (5) grant; (6) voucher; (7) free market; (8) voluntary service; and (9) self service.[29] These nine different structural arrangements for delivering public services can be categorized according to who is the arranger, who the producer, and who pays the producer of the service. Table 11-3 summarizes these characteristics for each type of arrangement.

Annexation and Consolidation

Annexation of surrounding land by municipal governments represents one way for localities not only to increase their fiscal base but also literally to internalize the externalities created by the provision of goods having significant spillover effects. Unfortunately for most central cities, the surrounding land area is generally incorporated as legal entities under the laws of the state, making annexation a difficult if not impossible alternative. Consolidation is an alternative that has been

---

[27] For an early compilation of the types of fees and charges used in different localities throughout the country see Selma Mushkin and Charles Vehorn, *Governmental Finance*, November 1977, pp. 42–48.

[28] I am not certain where this unfortunate term originated, but there is no doubt that the work of E. S. Savas has contributed as much as anything to its popular use. See his *Privatizing The Public Sector*, Chatham House, Chatham, N.J., 1982.

[29] Ibid.

TABLE 11-3
INSTITUTIONAL ARRANGEMENTS FOR PROVIDING PUBLIC SERVICES

Service arrangement	Arranges service	Produces service	Pays producer
Government service	Government	Government	Not applicable
Intergovermental agreement or contract	Government 1	Government 2	Government 1
Contract	Government	Private firm	Government
Franchise	Government	Private firm	Consumer
Grant	Government and consumer	Private firm	Government and consumer
Voucher	Consumer	Private firm	Government and consumer
Market	Consumer	Private firm	Consumer
Voluntary	Voluntary association	Voluntary association or private firm	Voluntary association
Self-service	Consumer	Consumer	Not applicable

Source: E. S. Savas, *Privatizing the Public Sector*, Chatham House, Chatham, N.J., 1982, p. 73.

achieved in a number of highly visible cases, such as Toronto Metro, Nashville, Tennessee, Indianapolis-Marion County, Indiana, and Miami-Dade County, Florida. This option is seldom a viable one in that it requires the approval of voters of both jurisdictions, and the inherent political difficulties of gaining consensus are usually decisive.

Regional Tax-Base Sharing

In view of the legal difficulties that make annexation and consolidation impracticable options for reducing fiscal stress, one alternative that has been proposed is metropolitan or regional tax-base sharing. Under tax-base sharing schemes, revenues from increases in the metropolitan property tax base are shared, according to some allocation formula, on an areawide basis. Such a system was established in Minneapolis and St. Paul, Minnesota.[30] The alleged benefits of tax-base sharing are a reduction in externalities, reduction in fiscal disparities, and reduction in central-city fiscal distress.

Despite these alleged advantages of tax-base sharing, some skepticism has been expressed regarding the likelihood that such benefits would be realized. One study has suggested that the fiscal relief provided by arrangements similar to those in the Twin Cities would be marginal, averaging less than 4 percent of total general revenues for the most fiscally distressed central cities.[31] However, 4 percent of

[30] D. A. Gilbert, "Property Tax Base Sharing: An Answer to Central City Fiscal Problems?," *Social Science Quarterly*, vol. 59, March 1979, pp. 681–689. Also see Roy Bahl and David Puryear, "Regional Tax Base Sharing: Possibilities and Implications," *National Tax Journal*, vol. 29, September 1976, pp. 328–335 and Andrew Reschovsky, "An Evaluation of Metropolitan Area Tax Base Sharing," *National Tax Journal*, vol. 33, 1980, pp. 55–66.
[31] Gilbert, op. cit.

total revenue might mean the difference between solvency and bankruptcy for some cities.

The largest problem with tax-base sharing is that it is likely to encounter extremely powerful political opposition. If the effects of sharing can be estimated in advance, which presumably they can, what would motivate the potential losers to agree to the change?

A Look Ahead

All of the above suggestions may help cities deal with their fiscal programs but, individually or collectively, they are no more than minor palliatives. As we noted, the fiscal problems of cities stem from a myriad of economic and demographic trends that show little if any sign of abating. And the capacity of any city to deal with its own revenue problems is limited by the mobility of the persons and the organizations it seeks to tax. Even the real property tax base is movable in a sense. Decisions about where to build, how much to invest in existing structures, and whether, in the extreme, to abandon are all in part conditioned by the local tax structure.

Thus unless the conditions underlying the fiscal plight of many cities change, the prognosis for the foreseeable future is a continuation of intergovernmental aid on a massive, if somewhat reduced, scale. The only real alternative to that would appear to be the reduction of urban public services to a level that many of us might regard as unacceptable.

The Musgravian typology of public expenditures offered earlier suggests the desirability of the federal assumption of many redistributive activities now handled at the local level. Such a shift would, indeed, ease the fiscal plight of many municipalities. As of this writing such a shift is not likely. In fact, the Reagan administration, as noted earlier, attempted to move in the other direction. But the political winds are always subject to change. A look back over the last 30 or 40 years would suggest that the trend has been toward greater and greater federal assumption of redistributive activities. It is certainly possible that with a shift in the political climate this trend will resume.

CHAPTER 12

THE ECONOMICS OF URBAN ENVIRONMENTAL QUALITY

W. David Conn
College of Architecture and Urban Studies
Virginia Polytechnic Institute and State University

The average urban dweller in the United States consumes about 4 pounds of food per day and uses about 150 gallons of water and 19 pounds of fossil fuel. At the same time he or she generates about 5 pounds of solid waste, 120 gallons of sewage, and 1.9 pounds of air pollutants.[1] Some of the discarded substances and pollutants are entirely new to the natural world and thus no natural pathways may exist for their assimilation and decay. In other cases the substances are naturally occurring, but we discard them in a form, place, or quantity that overwhelms the ability of the natural environment to cope with them. The result is environmental pollution.

In the past 2 decades our consciousness of the problems of pollution has greatly increased. With this new consciousness have come greatly increased public expenditures on pollution control and greatly increased private expenditures resulting from the necessity of complying with federal, state, and local environmental controls.

In 1980 the Council on Environmental Quality (CEQ) estimated that the nation had spent $55.9 billion on environmental programs during the previous year. Of that figure, $36.9 billion, or roughly 1.5 percent of GNP, had been spent complying with federal environmental protection legislation and regulations. The remainder had been spent voluntarily or in response to state and local controls. Projecting recent trends, the CEQ estimated that in 1988, environmental expenditures would total $92.9 billion in 1979 dollars.[2] That figure might be scaled back

---

[1] These figures come from Abel Wolman, "The Metabolism of Cities," *Scientific American*, March 1965, pp. 179–190. Although rather old, the figures give an order-of-magnitude sense of the daily per capita flows through a household. They do not take into account flows associated with the industrial, agricultural, commercial, and other activities necessary to support the household's continued existence.

[2] Council on Environmental Quality, *Environmental Quality in 1980*, Eleventh Annual Report, December 1980, pp. 393–396.

somewhat if the projection were being made today, given the relaxation of some standards under the Reagan administration, but it would still be several percent of GNP.

From these expenditures we have obtained tangible results. For example, combined data obtained by CEQ from 25 of the major metropolitan areas suggest that from 1974 to 1977 the number of "unhealthful" days due to air pollution declined by 15 percent, while the number of "very unhealthful" days declined by 32 percent.[3] These absolute declines may actually understate the gains from pollution control expenditures, for in the absence of pollution control efforts, continued economic and population growth would presumably have led to higher ambient levels of pollution. Thus CEQ was able to claim as a "victory for the nation's water pollution control efforts" the fact that surface water quality was "at least not getting worse" during the 1970s.[4]

For reasons to be discussed later in this chapter, pollution problems are often more serious in urban than in nonurban areas. However, the economic treatment of environmental issues tends to be the same, at least in principle, regardless of where they occur; there is little that can be said on this topic which is truly unique to urban areas. A few points that have particular relevance to urban and suburban areas are noted toward the end of the discussion.

We can all agree that a cleaner environment is desirable, but once that simple statement is made, the issue becomes tremendously complex and agreement can be very hard to reach. At the factual level there are many physical processes and risks which are simply not fully understood. Beyond that, there are tremendous problems in assigning costs to environmental pollution. For example, if we are not clear about the path a pollutant takes through the ecosystem or what its short- and long-term effects are on living organisms, it is very difficult to say how much it should be worth to us to eliminate it or at least reduce its concentration. Beyond the literal uncertainty about what actually happens there are serious questions about values and equity that make environmental policy a highly political topic. In general, the more we make American industry spend on pollution control equipment, the cleaner our air and water will be. But each time we shift the domestic manufacturer's cost curve to the left, the harder it becomes for that firm to compete with firms in Japan or Taiwan or West Germany. Thus it is not stretching matters too far to say that one person's clean air may be another person's unemployment. The potential for controversy is clear. People who make their living producing lectures and textbooks, let us say, are likely to have a different view of industrial pollution standards than people who earn their living producing pig iron or automobiles.

If a city decides to improve central business district air quality by restricting automobile traffic, those who have to breathe downtown air may be happier and healthier. But if downtown economic activity begins relocating in the suburbs where automobile access is unrestricted, those who own downtown property and downtown businesses will not be pleased. Nor will the poor inner-city resident who gets to work by bus but cannot afford a car to get to a suburban job. In brief,

---

[3] Ibid., p. 17.
[4] Ibid., pp. 75–76.

every major environmental decision is likely to create both winners and losers and to raise a variety of equity issues that may not be easy to resolve. Like all political issues, environmental questions are likely to bring together strange bedfellows from time to time. For example, industrial capital and industrial labor may be at odds on a host of other issues yet be entirely of one mind on the subject of regulatory standards, for on that point their pecuniary interests may seem to be very much the same.

A Note on Semantics Before going further, a note on semantics is appropriate. We will subsequently use the terms *polluter* and *sufferer*. These terms, as used here, are purely descriptive of actions or effects and have no moral connotations. In the language of the social sciences, they are positive, not normative. One is a *polluter* whether dumping toxic wastes at midnight or driving to a Sierra Club meeting. One is a *sufferer* when breathing or drinking in pollutants, regardless of whether one is a saint or a sinner.

THE ECONOMIST'S VIEW OF THE ENVIRONMENTAL PROBLEM

Many economists, viewing their subject as one which deals with the allocation of scarce resources in the face of essentially infinite wants, simply extend this view to environmental issues. Clear air, uncontaminated water, and unpolluted land are not free. They are obtained only at the cost of giving up something else, and the key question is to find the most satisfactory set of tradeoffs.

In the United States the primary means of allocating resources is the market. A competitive market that satisfies a variety of special conditions will allocate resources efficiently. That is to say, these resources cannot be reallocated without making at least one party worse off than previously. Another way to phrase this is to say that a free market will produce a situation in which no further gains from trade are possible. In the appendix to Chapter 6 this condition of Pareto efficiency was illustrated by means of the Edgeworth Box. When the distribution of goods falls on the contract curve, no more gains from trade are possible and Pareto efficiency has been achieved. As we shall see, it is easy to show convincing reasons why the market place, operating on its own, will not produce anything resembling a Pareto optimal outcome so far as environmental effects are considered. This is because environmental phenomena involve major externalities and because environmental quality has at least some of the properties of a public good. Let us discuss these two points in order.

The Problem of Externalities

For a market to operate efficiently it is essential that all effects of the transaction—both good and bad—be taken into account by those who undertake the transaction. If there are costs that are not taken into account then we cannot be sure that there really are net benefits from the transaction. Thus for the market to function efficiently there must be no externalities and there must be perfect knowledge. Very obviously, these conditions do not prevail in the market for goods and services whose production or consumption has serious environmental consequences. It thus can be argued that one important function of public environmental policy might be to alter market conditions in such a manner as to move toward the "ideal" of the perfect market.

Whether all benefits and costs (to the extent they are known at all) are taken into account by buyers and sellers depends largely on how the law defines property rights. If the law defines exclusive rights of ownership, then the legal system can be used to exact compensation when these rights are violated. This, in turn, causes the cost of violating these rights to be incorporated in the cost calculations of the violator. For example, someone whose front yard is flattened by an errant motorist can normally exact compensation because the law has granted the owner exclusive rights over his or her land. On the other hand, owners cannot exact compensation from motorists whose exhaust fumes waft across their property and damage their plants and shrubbery or, perhaps, their lungs as well. This is because the law does not grant owners property rights over the air above their property. Thus motorists are not required to take into account the costs imposed by their exhaust fumes and, unless they are extraordinarily altruistic, are not likely to do so. The true costs of driving are thereby underestimated, and to that extent the market for automotive transportation functions imperfectly.

The costs that exhaust fumes impose on all parties other than the motorist are generally termed *externalities* (because insofar as buyer and seller are concerned, they are external to the transaction) or *spillovers*. In older literature they are sometimes referred to as *external diseconomies*. Much of the problem of environmental quality can be discussed in terms of negative and positive externalities. The regulation of private actions that have environmental effects is, by and large, an attempt to deal with negative externalities. Alternatively, we might consider the attempt to improve environmental quality an attempt to capture positive externalities.

Environmental Quality as a Public Good Public intervention is necessary because to a large degree environmental quality possesses one of the attributes generally considered characteristic of a public good; the exclusion principle does not apply.[5] We cannot exclude the nonpayer from benefiting and therefore we cannot directly create a market for the product. If we ask the individual his or her willingness to pay for a public good, the answer will be none at all. This is not because the individual does not value the good, but because he or she hopes to be a free rider and enjoy the benefits for which others pay.

The Tragedy of the Commons The destruction of the value of a public good because of overuse resulting from the inability to exclude users has been described by Garrett Hardin as "the tragedy of the commons."[6] Consider a

---

[5] Different authors define public goods somewhat differently. According to some writers, the essential characteristic of a pure public good is that use by one party must not reduce the value of the good to another party. For example, a view of the Grand Canyon can be said to be a pure public good if it is true that my enjoyment of the view does not in any way diminish your enjoyment of the same view. In many cases, using this criterion, a good will be a pure public good up to some level of consumption, when congestion and interference effects begin to destroy the property. See, for example, D. Winch, *Analytical Welfare Economics*, Penguin, Harmondsworth, 1971.

[6] Garrett Hardin, "The Tragedy of the Commons," *Science*, vol. 162, December 1968, pp. 1243–1248.

common area on which all farmers are free to graze their animals. At first, the commons is a true public good and no harm is done by allowing its unrestricted use. At some point, however, each additional animal grazed on the commons imposes a cost on every farmer other than the one who owns the animal. Because there is no way in which any one farmer can be made to take into account the costs he imposes on other farmers, the commons is overgrazed and destroyed. Individual rationality has thus led to collective irrationality. To a large degree the goal of environmental policy is to avert the tragedy of the commons. This may be done by regulation, by taxation, by creating a market for environmental rights, or by other devices that in one way or another, introduce some of the rationality and efficiency of a properly functioning marketplace.

Cost-Benefit Analysis of Pollution Control

Economists use cost-benefit analysis to determine whether a given action yields a net benefit. As discussed in Chapter 8, the economist or policy analyst may also use the absolute net benefit, cost-benefit ratio, or internal rate of return, all of which come out of cost-benefit analysis, to rank or establish priorities for projects based on efficiency criteria. The cost-benefit analysis differs from the profit and loss calculation made by a private firm in that it attempts to take into account a much wider range of benefits and costs than does the analysis performed by the firm. The cost-benefit analysis internalizes a great many considerations that are externalities to the firm or to the consumers of the firm's products.

Consider Figure 12-1. Along the horizontal axis is plotted an increasing level of pollution, say, increasing contamination of a river by the discharges of an industrial plant. On the vertical axis is plotted the total cost of the damage done by this pollution. This cost might reflect damage to human health, damage to fish and wildlife, loss of recreational value, the cost of downstream water purification, and many other factors. Also included in the figure is the cost of eliminating pollution plotted against the number of units of pollution eliminated. A third curve, the total

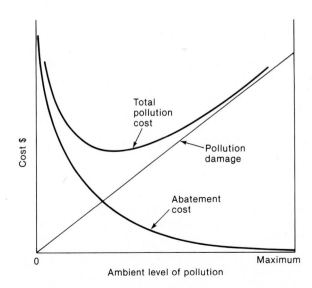

FIGURE 12-1
Pollution damage and abatement costs. Pollution costs are shown as linear, while abatement costs rise exponentially (diminishing returns). The total cost curve is obtained by the vertical addition of the other two curves. The efficient level of abatement is at the low point of the total cost curve. In this figure the low point in the total pollution cost curve is shown as being directly over the intersection of the other two curves. However, this is not necessarily the case.

pollution cost, is obtained by the vertical addition of the other two curves. In this figure the damage done by pollutants is shown as more or less linearly related to the amount of pollution discharged, although in actuality pollution effects may not always be linear. We also note that the damage is shown as extending all the way to the origin, indicating that there is no threshhold level. In reality, in many regulatory situations it is considered that a threshhold does exist and that below this level the pollutant can be regarded as harmless. The question of whether a threshhold exists is sometimes the subject of considerable debate.

The abatement cost is shown as having a more or less exponential shape. This latter shape reflects the existence of diminishing returns in pollution control. To digress briefly, this condition of sharply rising marginal costs as we approach complete elimination of pollutants is quite common. In some cases, this is because the elimination of a pollutant is a probabilistic process. For example, if a set of electrostatic plates in a smoke stack will trap 90 percent of the particles passing between them, then it takes twice as many plates to remove 99 percent of the pollutants as it does to remove 90 percent. In other cases, marginal costs may rise steeply because removing the last few units of a pollutant may require a different technology than that used for the first units.

The most efficient level of pollution abatement is the low point on the total cost curve, as shown in Figure 12-1. The total cost includes both the damage done by the unabated pollution and the cost of abatement. To pursue the theme of marginal adjustment, which recurs throughout this text, it can be shown that the point of minimum total cost corresponds to the point at which the marginal cost of abatement equals the marginal cost of pollution: the point at which the cost of abating a unit of pollution is equal to the cost of the damage that unit will do if not abated. This point is illustrated in Figure 12-2.

In principle it would actually pay those who suffer the damage caused by pollution to pay or "bribe" the polluters to abate. The sufferers might offer an amount up to the marginal cost of the damage prevented. The polluters might accept payments as long as the "bribe" exceeded the cost of abatement. Point Q, the point in Figure 12-2 where the marginal-abatement cost and marginal-damage curves intersect, is the Pareto efficient point. On either side of that point, movement toward the point will make both parties better off. At the point itself, movement in either direction will make at least one party worse off. It is important to note that *the efficient level of pollution is not zero pollution* except in the special case that the marginal cost of pollution exceeds the marginal cost of abatement over the entire range (as it might, for example, when the pollutant is extremely hazardous).

Equity and Efficiency   It is also evident that the achievement of efficiency does not necessarily imply an equitable distribution of the costs of control or damages. As has been noted elsewhere in this text, the goals of equity and efficiency are not always served by the same sets of actions. At many times, we will find ourselves moving away from one of these goals in order to move closer to the other.

Depending upon the starting point in Figure 12-1 or 12-2, it might make sense for the sufferers to bribe the polluters not to pollute, or vice versa. If we start in a high-pollution condition, the former will be the case. On the other hand if we start

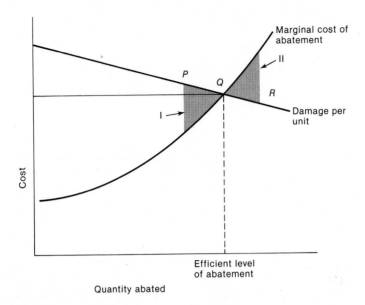

FIGURE 12-2
The efficient level of abatement. If abatement stops at point *P*, society sustains an opportunity-cost loss, indicated by area I. If abatement continues to point *R*, costs exceed benefits as indicated by area II. Only by abating out to point *Q* can both types of loss be avoided.

from a very low pollution condition in which the marginal cost of abatement far exceeds the marginal benefit of abatement, then the polluters might offer the sufferers a payment or bribe to accept a slightly lower level of environmental quality.

The problem is that the efficiency criterion does not *and cannot* say what is equitable and, indeed, there is frequently little agreement on what is fair or unfair. Some might argue that polluters should always compensate those who suffer damage, but it is easy to suggest a situation in which this position becomes quite arguable. Suppose a firm has been discharging the same effluent for many years without doing anyone any harm. The sufferers are parties who have only recently purchased property downstream with full knowledge of the discharges and *at a price reflecting those discharges*. Are they entitled to compensation? Consider a case that has troubled more than one community. If you knowingly buy a house near the end of the runway, should your complaints about aircraft noise be taken seriously?

The distributional or equity question is typically resolved by reference to the law. If the law is generally permissive regarding pollution (fails to grant property rights that may be invoked by those harmed by pollution), then pollution will tend to be above the efficient level unless a mechanism exists whereby the sufferers can bribe the polluters. But regardless of whether the compensating payment, or bribe is actually made, there is a transfer of wealth from sufferer to polluter. On the other hand, if the law is nonpermissive, then polluters may have to bribe the sufferers in order to pollute (or perhaps to operate at all), and the transfer of wealth will go in the other direction.

CONSIDERATIONS IN CHOOSING POLLUTION CONTROL MEASURES

As noted earlier, efficiency is not the only criterion for setting standards or choosing pollution control technologies. In fact, there may be instances in which equity considerations should take precedence over efficiency considerations. There is nothing illogical or incorrect about people disagreeing over matters of equity. If we consider only efficiency, we are making the tacit assumption that the initial or present distribution of rights (determined, at least in part, by present law and precedent) is acceptable. Those of a conservative persuasion may be quite satisfied with this assumption, while those of a radical persuasion may be quite dissatisfied. But even though we regard equity considerations as both important and subject to rational disagreement, most people would still agree that there are reasons for public officials to pay serious attention to efficiency. A given level of environmental improvement can be achieved at a lower cost to society as a whole using efficient rather than inefficient strategies. Alternatively, a higher level of quality can be achieved for a given expenditure. It should also be noted that it is usually easier to agree about what constitutes efficiency than about what constitutes equity. Some would argue that there is an advantage to emphasizing the side of the problem that we can deal with from a position of relatively greater certainty and agreement.

In considering the matter of efficiency realistically it must be admitted that the possibility of constructing the sorts of curves shown in Figures 12-1 and 12-2 with any degree of precision is small. In fact, it may be somewhat misleading to think of them as smooth, continuous curves at all. It is more likely that there will be a limited number of available pollution control technologies, and thus there will be several discrete levels of control. Even in the very unlikely event that perfect information were available, it might be possible only to approximate the efficient level of abatement.

The Information Problem

In reality, available information is likely to be far from perfect. Beyond the lack of fundamental knowledge is the fact that most pollution control technologies are process- and site-specific. Because of the understandable reluctance of firms to disclose information that might be used against them in the regulatory process, government agencies often have particularly poor access to reliable cost data.

Information on damage costs is likely to be even worse. In most cases, the physical nature and extent of the damage caused by particular levels of pollution are very poorly understood, so that it is virtually impossible to place a dollar value on the damage. For example, air pollution is harmful to human health. But it is very difficult to establish quantitative relationships between the amounts of pollutants emitted and ambient concentrations in the atmosphere, that is, the relationships between emissions and human exposure. Beyond this, the relationships between exposure and specific health effects are not clear. The effects of pollution may take years to show up and, for the researcher, the waters are muddied by the effects of many other variables besides the one in question.

Even if perfect data on all of the above matters were available, we would still not be entirely out of the woods. Mishan notes that in principle the correct approach to monetizing the damage to health, based on the efficiency criterion, is to examine people's willingness to pay (or willingness to accept compensation) for a change in the risk of death or illness due to exposure to pollution.[7] This is the willingness-to-pay criterion discussed in some detail in the chapter on transportation. Unfortunately, obtaining good information regarding peoples' evaluations of small, uncertain changes in small and uncertain risks is extremely problematical.

How Important Is the Future?

Another problem that complicates cost-benefit calculations is the matter of the discount rate, a point discussed in Chapter 8. The use of any positive discount rate effectively imposes a cutoff time in the future beyond which costs and benefits, no matter how large and enduring, count for very little in a present value calculation. For example, $1 million even at the very low discount rate of 4 percent, 100 years from now has a present value of only $20,000. If we use a discount rate of 10 percent, a project that imposes no costs at all for 50 years but then imposes a cost of $1 million a year for the rest of eternity need have a present value of only $185,000 to show a cost-benefit ratio of 1.

These observations have particular importance when environmental questions are considered. A project with major environmental consequences, such as a dam, may show a positive present value when the benefits and costs occurring over the next 20 to 30 years are discounted. However, the project may be greatly outlived by serious negative impacts, which, if they were to occur now, would overshadow all other benefits and costs. Given the mathematics of applying a discount rate, they may count for very little in the present value calculation. The larger the discount rate, the less heavily are the interests of future generations weighted.

The Importance of a Political Consensus   For all of the above reasons it is most unlikely that decision makers will be able to calculate the efficient level of pollution control with any degree of precision. General acknowledgment of this fact has produced a broad agreement that the target level of pollution control cannot be set solely by objective economic analysis, even if it were agreed that efficiency were the only goal. Rather, the target level must emerge in some other way from the political process. Once the target is set, however, the economist can make a useful contribution, based on efficiency considerations, to the debate on how to achieve it.

Realities in the Choice of Pollution Control Strategies

Let us consider some of the realities involved in the choice of pollution control strategies. First, there is a high degree of friction and inertia in our economic system or, for that matter, in any advanced economic system. Adjustments in the

[7] E. J. Mishan, *Cost-Benefit Analysis*, 3d ed., Allen and Unwin, London 1982.

allocation of resources can rarely be made without significant costs. Many pollution control technologies, for example, water treatment facilities, may take years to plan and build and involve very large expenditures. They are not readily adjusted or moved. Then, too, large expenditures may be made on the basis of current policy. Frequent changes in policy may cause needless expenditure and disruption of private and public activity. Thus there is not a great deal of room for trial and error in selecting the appropriate level and means of pollution control.

The Problem of Monitoring   In order to implement control measures of any sort, monitoring is needed. If control is to be achieved through purely private transactions, then the sufferer, or some surrogate for the sufferer, must monitor the polluter to see that what he or she has paid for is actually being done. In a system based on standards, monitoring is necessary to see that the standards are not being exceeded. In a system based on pollution charges, monitoring is needed to determine the charge or tax that must be levied.

Unfortunately, the direct monitoring of pollutant emissions is often difficult, expensive, and in some cases impossible with existing technologies. Continuous monitoring is desirable but not always practical. For example, it is not feasible to monitor automotive emissions except under special conditions. In many cases pollutant emissions must be monitored by indirect methods. For example, emissions may be estimated from materials balance calculations—examining what goes into the process, what comes out as product, and assuming that the difference has gone into the environment. In some cases pollution comes from clearly identified locations and is referred to as point-source pollution. But in other cases pollution may be generated ubiquitously (non–point-source pollution), which can greatly complicate monitoring and enforcement. Airborne lead from a smelter's smoke stack is clearly a point-source pollutant and can readily be monitored. On the other hand lead introduced into the hydrologic system by urban storm water runoff is a non–point-source pollutant, which is much harder to monitor, trace, or control.

Anticipating Responses to Pollution Control Measures   Those who make and enforce environmental policy must not only consider the pros and cons of various options in a static sense but also consider the likely strategic responses to their actions. For example, if polluters believe that standards are likely to be relaxed in the future, they may drag their feet on meeting current standards. If they believe enforcement is weak or sporadic they may rationally decide not to comply but rather to take their chances with apprehension and punishment.

Perhaps more important in the long term is the effect that regulations and standards will have on the evolution of pollution control technologies, including both abatement processes and the development of products that are inherently less polluting. It is important to avoid policy that locks in a particular technology and inhibits research and development aimed at improvement.

Considering Displacement Effects   Finally, it is important to consider the effect of pollution control policy on the economy as a whole. One aspect of this is avoiding policies that inadvertently favor the excessive production of pollution-producing goods and services—a risk that is inherent in the subsidization of pollution control investment. It is also important to consider what might be called the diversionary effects of pollution control strategies. If we shift the cost curve of one product, the market price and therefore the quantity demanded is affected. This, in turn, affects the demand for substitute goods. For example, assume that we increase the cost of nuclear-generated power by requiring more expensive safeguards against the accidental discharge of radioisotopes. Fewer nuclear plants will be built and more power will be generated by other means such as the burning of coal. This, in turn, will increase the amount of sulfur dioxide produced (a major cause of acid rain) as well as the concentration of airborne particulates. In short, it behooves us to look at the regulatory question in as comprehensive a manner as possible.

Alternative Pollution Control Techniques

In light of the above, let us examine some of the pros and cons of the various regulatory approaches listed previously.

Voluntary Transactions   In theory these offer the advantage that government does not have to estimate costs and benefits and then impose a solution. Rather than our having to impute willingness to pay, the market determines it directly and unambiguously. However, voluntary transactions are sharply limited in practice by the high transactions costs imposed by the existence of vast numbers of affected parties. Widespread reliance on voluntary transactions will also be handicapped in situations where rights are ill-defined or not defined at all. Finally, reliance on voluntary transactions will be limited because of the cost and complexity of monitoring. For all of these reasons it appears that pollution control is likely to fall largely into the public domain.

Standards   These are the most commonly used approach. In part their popularity stems from the fact that most people do not see environmental problems as economic problems. Rather, it appears that if there is too much pollution (however we determine what constitutes "too much") then polluters should be required to cut back. This is what standards are supposed to accomplish.

There are two kinds of standards: those governing ambient levels of pollution and those governing the emission of pollutants. From the perspective of setting the efficient level of the overall abatement effort, we are concerned with the former, since these determine the amount of damage caused. However, we rarely have control over ambient levels; instead we control emissions. The technical problems inherent in choosing the right ambient level and then linking that level to a particular emission level have been noted previously. They are not unique to standards, however, but plague any control approach that we choose, for the basic problem is knowledge, not control strategy.

Beyond the above, we face a problem that is peculiar to standards. If there are many emitters, we must select a level of control for each. Administratively it is easiest to impose the same standards on all emitters. Therefore, that is the route most often taken—so many parts per million, so many grams per mile, etc. But this is inefficient unless all emitters face the same marginal-cost schedule. One emitter will stop abating before the marginal cost of abatement reaches the marginal benefit of abatement, while another emitter will be spending more at the margin than the value to society of the abatement. Both situations are inefficient. It is in this Procrustean character of most standards that their inefficiency resides.

In principle we can and often do attempt to deal with this problem by fine-tuning the standards, which, in the extreme, might mean a different standard for each emitter. But the data needs and administrative complexity of such fine tuning can be enormous. It can also be argued that such an approach is tantamount to a preemption of the market as the primary allocator of resources, for in effect the government would be making allocative decisions on the firms' behalf. Finally, such fine tuning might be rejected by the courts if it appeared to have the property of treating equals unequally. The flat standard has at least the appearance of evenhandedness.

Another problem with standards, but also with other control techniques, is the matter of enforcing compliance. Where the cost to the polluter of complying is high, the motivation to disregard the standard may be high. Where those who implement the standards are given a high degree of discretion, a great deal of unpredictability can be introduced into the situation. In effect, the outcome is the result of bargaining in which both sides weigh the advantages and costs of holding out for more advantageous positions.

When setting standards it is important for the regulatory authority to consider emerging technology as well as short-run efficiency. This is because it is desirable for standards to be technology-forcing in that they encourage adoption of improved technology. The regulatory authority must tread a fine line between standards that are too permissive to force improvement and standards that are unrealistically stringent.

Charge Systems   A pollution charge system established by government is analogous to a price system. Polluters face a set of "prices" for the right to pollute just as they face a set of prices for other factors of production. The difference is that government collects the payments as a representative of society as a whole. Though the firm, in a sense, pays for environmental damage, it does so to society at large and not to the particular parties damaged.

For a system of charges to be efficient, the pollution charges should approximate those that would prevail in a free and perfect market. In other words, they should be equal to the marginal cost of the damage caused. This is shown as point P in Figure 12-2. In practice the regulatory authority is unlikely to know this. Instead it will try to estimate the optimal ambient level and then set the charges so as to achieve a discharge rate or amount that will achieve the goal. The charges approach is essentially the converse of the standards approach. In the former the level of discharge is fixed but the abatement costs are uncertain. In the latter, the level of abatement cost is more or less fixed but the amount of discharge is really in the hands of the polluter.

It is thus apparent that the charge approach suffers from a defect, which it shares with the standards approach. Both are only as good as the underlying data. Then, too, just as a standards approach may have compliance problems, so may a pollution charge approach. However, proponents of charges argue that there are ways in which charges are distinctly superior to standards. The first advantage is allocative efficiency. In principle, each polluter adjusts correctly at the margin so there is no under- or overexpenditure on control. This is illustrated in Figure 12-3. Another advantage is that if monitoring is effective, there is no incentive to delay implementation. To the contrary, there is an incentive to implement control measures as promptly as possible. There is also a continuous incentive to seek improved abatement measures. Because government has to control fewer variables, it can concentrate its efforts on the critical item of monitoring.

The most serious political problem with charges is that what is essentially an economic issue gets transformed into a moral issue and the levying of charges becomes a license to pollute. To the economist who sees the problem as one of achieving the efficient tradeoff between the output of goods and services on the one hand and environmental quality on the other hand, the matter is not a moral issue but a technical one. But fine distinctions have a way of melting in the heat of political debate. Like marginal cost pricing, a closely related idea, the advantages of pollution charges are not intuitively obvious or quickly explained.

One issue that can cause confusion in relation to pollution charges is the matter of payments. One might ask whether in counting the cost of abatement we should

FIGURE 12-3
The inherent inefficiency of flat-rate regulation. Lines MC_a and MC_b represent the marginal-abatement costs of two firms that discharge the same pollutants. Assume that a flat standard causes firm A to abate out to X and firm B to abate out to Y. Triangle I represents waste in that the cost of abatement past point U is greater than its benefit. Triangle II represents an opportunity-cost loss in that firm B stops abating while marginal costs are below marginal benefits. If we switch to a pollution charge of OA per unit both sources of waste are eliminated as the firms move to points U and V.

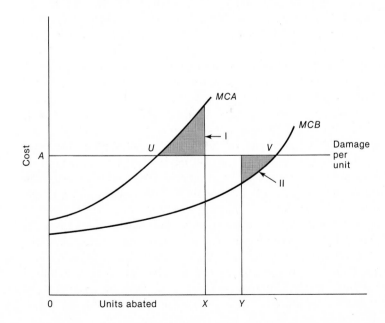

not only count what the firm spends on abatement technology but also what the firm pays in pollution charges. The answer is no. The payment of charges by the firm is not a cost to society as a whole, for it involves no use of resources. It is merely a transfer. Just as transfers like Social Security payments do not figure in the calculation of the GNP, pollution charges should not be counted as a real cost. What is to be done with revenues from pollution charges? The economist, to whom marginal thinking is second nature, is likely to argue that they should simply go into general revenues to be spent according to good marginal principles. Possible expenditures are assigned priorities on the basis of cost-benefit ratio. Spending begins at the top of the queue and proceeds until either funds or the projects with cost-benefit ratios greater than 1 are exhausted.

The argument for returning funds to general revenues is essentially the same as the argument for cash transfers rather than assistance in kind. It gives the recipient—in this case government rather than a poor household—maximum discretion so that utility can be maximized. As a practical political matter, such reasoning is not readily compressible into a few sentences or a 30-second television spot. The alternative of earmarking pollution charge revenues for a particular goal related to environmental improvement might thus have a good deal more political appeal even if it is not as defensible in marginal terms.

Pollution Rights   Assume that a particular river has the capacity to accept a certain amount of organic matter, say, wastes from food processing, before it becomes degraded. The capacity of the river to accept organic molecules and convert them into water and carbon dioxide is thus a resource just as much as a piece of capital equipment that will do the same thing. How do we put this resource, which nature has granted us, to most efficient use? One way is to create a certain number of discharge rights calibrated in physical units like biological oxidation demand (BODs) and allow them to be bought and sold. If there were initially no one using the river for organic material discharge the regulatory agency might sell them in the first instance to the highest bidders. Subsequently, they could be bought and sold in private transactions. If the river were already in use the regulatory agency might grant rights on the basis of existing use. When discharges came to equal the permitted total, any new firm coming in and wishing to discharge would have to purchase the right to do so.

The advantage of the pollution rights approach is that it places the resource, in this case the river's ability to oxidize organic wastes, in the use which people appear to value most highly (based on willingness to pay). Because the technique operates through the market, although subject to a governmentally imposed control total, it substitutes the judgment of the market for the judgment of regulators. Yet it still assures public control over the variable in which there is the greatest legitimate public interest, namely, the quality of the environment. It also leaves room for adjustment in that the number of rights available can be changed by administrative or legislative action. Finally, this approach leaves intact the motivation for technological improvement. The firm that can reduce its discharges, then, has a salable asset in the form of unused rights. The pollution rights concept is now in use in the purchase of air emission "offsets" in nonattainment areas, a practice described in a subsequent section.

BOX 12-1

CHARGES OR STANDARDS: A SIMPLE MATHEMATICAL ILLUSTRATION

Assume plant A and plant B in the absence of any abatement effort will each emit 10 units of pollutant a day. The two plants constitute the entire industry and the regulatory authority has decided to reduce emissions by 70 percent, that is, to abate 14 units. The choice is between a flat standard or pollution charges. Because the two plants use somewhat different production techniques their estimated abatement cost functions are different, as indicated below.

$$\text{Plant A: Cost} = \$100{,}000\ (6 + Q^2)$$

$$\text{Plant B: Cost} = \$100{,}000\ [3 + (Q^3)/4]$$

where Q is the number of units abated per day. The two resulting abatement cost schedules are shown below.

Units abated	Plant A Total cost	Plant A Marginal cost	Plant B Total cost	Plant B Marginal cost
0	0	0	0	0
1	700,000	700,000	325,000	325,000
2	1,000,000	300,000	500,000	175,000
3	1,500,000	500,000	975,000	475,000
4	2,200,000	700,000	1,900,000	925,000
5	3,100,000	900,000	3,425,000	1,525,000
6	4,200,000	1,100,000	5,700,000	2,275,000
7	5,500,000	1,300,000	8,875,000	3,175,000
8	7,000,000	1,500,000	13,000,000	4,225,000
9	8,700,000	1,700,000	18,525,000	5,425,000
10	10,600,000	1,900,000	25,300,000	6,775,000

If a flat standard is used, each firm will abate 7 units and total abatement cost will be $5,500,000 + $8,875,000 = $14,375,000. If the pollution charge approach is used, the regulatory agency will examine the marginal-cost data and after trying a few combinations will determine that any charge sufficient to cause plant A to abate 9 units will also be sufficient to cause plant B to abate 5 units. Accordingly the charge is set at $1,700,001. In this case total abatement costs are $8,700,000 + $3,425,000 = $12,125,000. Note that we have not counted the pollution charges themselves, but only the abatement costs, for reasons discussed in the text. The savings from using the charges approach are $14,375,000 − $12,125,000 = $2,250,000. This saving might be used to (1) effect a comparable reduction in other taxes, (2) augment government revenues, or (3) for further pollution control efforts.

One variation on the above scheme, analogous to the offsets discussed in the text, would be to require each firm to achieve 7 units of abatement but not necessarily at its own facility. In this case plant B observes that its cost for units 6 and 7 is $2,275,000 + $3,175,000 = $5,450,000, while plant A's cost for units 8 and 9 is $1,500,000 + $1,700,000 = $3,200,000. It then approaches plant A and a bargaining process ensues. For a price somewhere between $3,200,000 and $5,450,000 plant A agrees to abate units 8 and 9, thus placing plant B in compliance with the law. From the standpoint of society's interest—the efficient allocation of resources—the outcome is identical to that reached under the charge system and superior to that reached under a flat regulatory standard.

Subsidization of Pollution Control   Subsidies are used in variety of ways. For example, EPA grants have been used widely to subsidize municipal water and sewage treatment facilities. Firms can fund the purchase of pollution control equipment through the issuance of tax-exempt securities. Special tax credits may be available for various environmentally desirable types of investments. In some cases such subsidization may be justifiable on the practical grounds that if we want certain types of equipment installed or certain processes implemented, the amounts of money involved are so large that we must subsidize. (If one has an eye only to efficiency one could argue that if an industry can not bear an accurately set pollution charge and remain solvent, then it should go out of business. But such an argument may neglect both political realities and serious equity considerations.) However, in principle, there is a strong argument against subsidization. By subsidizing the acquisition of abatement equipment, we are distorting price signals to the producer in a downward direction. Thus society's combined expenditure for the production of the product and the abatement of the pollution thus entailed is too large. To put it more generally, by subsidizing abatement we may, in effect, be paying firms to create the problem we seek to alleviate.

User Charges to Finance Abatement   One way to move toward a more efficient allocation of resources is by incorporating abatement costs in user charges for publicly supplied services such as water supply and sewage treatment. By so doing we make prices "truer" in the sense that they more nearly reflect the actual cost of a particular good or service and thus the market will more accurately allocate resources among competing uses. Ideally, the charges would be set on marginal principles. Thus emitters would incorporate the true cost of treating discharges into their decisions about investment and operating procedure. Conceptually the idea is very similar to the pollution charge.

In practice, various schemes approach this idea, some much more closely than others. For instance, FWPCA regulations require that towns that receive federal aid for the construction of sewage treatment facilities must levy user charges to cover operating costs and, for industry, a portion of capital costs as well. This is far from a true marginal approach but it moves us somewhat in that direction by attempting to prevent the polluter from regarding public treatment of waste as a free good. Another approach has been a user charge based on property value under the assumption that there is some reasonably reliable relationship between property value and amount of sewerage discharge. Its theoretical defect is that it fails to establish a relationship at the margin and encourage the polluter to behave efficiently. Once one sets a fixed fee, by whatever method, one has then made marginal costs equal to zero.

Still another approach is to levy a sewage charge based on both volume of discharge and composition of discharge. A variation on this theme is to charge for volume and then add a surcharge if the concentration of pollutants exceeds a specified level. From the viewpoint of the microeconomist the last two schemes appear to most closely approach that difficult-to-achieve goal of true marginal-cost pricing.

As noted in the chapter on transportation, we have to be careful in defining marginal costs. For example, before a sewage treatment plant is built, all costs are variable and hence figure into the computation of marginal costs. The cost-benefit analysis which precedes the go-no go decision about construction should be done on this basis. But once the plant is built it is a fixed or "sunk" cost. At this point only operating costs should be considered in determining marginal costs for pricing purposes. Therefore a correct marginal-cost pricing policy might involve running at a loss when the debt service from building the facility is taken into account. On the other hand, there may be abatement situations where, because we have encountered continuously decreasing returns to scale, marginal cost is above average total cost. In this case, pricing at the margin will cause the facility to operate at a surplus. Pure marginal reasoning would suggest that in the first instance either a lump-sum charge (such as a connection fee) should be levied or the operation should be subsidized, while in the second instance the surplus should go back into general revenues. Of course, whether such policies are politically practical is another matter. As noted elsewhere in this book, one should not always swallow one's marginal economics straight.

PRESENT ENVIRONMENTAL POLICY

This chapter will not attempt the sort of detailed presentation on environmental law and policy to be found in a text on that subject. However a few words on current environmental policy and how we got here might be useful.

Concern about urban environmental quality goes back many centuries. We read of complaints about bad air in ancient Rome. There are records of a hanging in thirteenth-century London over the burning of a forbidden type of coal. The connection between contaminated water supplies and communicable disease was partially understood in the nineteenth century. The works of urban reformers like Jacob Riis contain vivid and angry descriptions of nineteenth century urban environmental pollution.[8] In the mid-twentieth century several factors combined to push society into a major effort to control or reverse the physical degradation of our environment. Economic and population growth gave humanity much more ability to damage the environment. For example, the number of automobiles in the United States increased from about 25 million at the end of World War II to well over 100 million by 1980. As noted, new industrial technologies created substances that had never before existed and for which natural degradation pathways did not necessarily exist. A petrochemicals-based chemical industry alone created literally thousands of new compounds, some harmless but others exceedingly dangerous.

On a more benign level, affluence and population growth simply reduced the realm of nature as humanity carved out more space for itself. Suburbanization ate up millions of rural acres around America's cities. Affluence and the automobile contributed to a doubling of visits to national parks between 1954 to 1962 and then another doubling from 1962 to 1971. And they have climbed considerably since then.

Coincident with our increased impact on the natural world, changes occurred in

---

[8] J. A. Riis, *How the Other Half Lives: Studies Among the Tenements of New York.* Dover, New York, 1971.

the way we viewed this impact. In 1962 Rachel Carson's book *Silent Spring* argued that pollution could enter the food chain and disrupt the life support systems upon which we depend.[9] Her work focused on the chlorinated hydrocarbons like DDT, manufactured substances for which natural degradative pathways do not exist. In the mid- and late-1960s opposition to the Vietnamese war gave rise to general antiestablishment feelings, which furnished fertile ground for the growth of the environmental movement. Books like Paul Ehrlich's *The Population Bomb*[10] and Dennis Meadow et al's *The Limits to Growth*[11] contained terrifying apocalyptic visions of the fate of humanity if we did not greatly moderate our impact upon the natural environment. Though much of this work is now taken a good deal less literally than when it first appeared, there is no doubt that it had considerable influence on building a proenvironmentalist political and intellectual climate.

Major Environmental Legislation

The National Environmental Policy Act (NEPA) was passed in 1969 and the Environmental Protection Agency (EPA) was created by executive action at about the same time. Subsequently, many states passed their own legislation patterned on NEPA, sometimes referred to as "little NEPA" acts. Major amendments to the Clean Air Act (CAA) were passed in 1970 and the Federal Water Pollution Control Act Amendments (FWPCA) in 1972. Other acts included the Marine Protection, Research and Sanctuaries Act (1972), the Safe Drinking Water Act (1974), the Resource Conservation and Recovery Act (1976), and the Toxic Substances Control Act (1976). Two of these acts, NEPA and CAA are discussed in some detail below to give the reader some of the flavor of the environmental regulatory process.

NEPA established the pursuit of environmental quality as a national objective and required that environmental objectives be weighed along with other considerations in major federal decisions that might have significant impact upon the environment. The environmental impact statement (EIS) was brought into existence as a vehicle for doing this. The NEPA guidelines state that "the weighing of the merits and drawbacks of the various alternatives need not be displayed in a monetary cost-benefit analysis and should not be when there are important qualitative considerations"; nevertheless, an EIS must have appended to it or incorporated by reference any cost-benefit analysis that is considered in the decision-making.[12] The guidelines also call for a discussion, where applicable, of the relationship between the results of a cost-benefit analysis and any analyses of unquantified environmental impacts, values, and amenities.

The CAA required the newly created Environmental Protection Agency (EPA) to set national ambient air quality standards (NAAQS) and required states to formulate state implementation plans (SIP) to show how these standards would be met. Where state plans were not submitted or approved, EPA was required to

[9] Rachel Carson, *Silent Spring*. Boston: Houghton Mifflin, 1962.
[10] Paul R. Ehrlich, *The Population Bomb*. New York: University, 1972.
[11] Dennis L. and Donella H. Meadows, *The Limits to Growth*, New York, Universe Books, 1972.
[12] 40 CFR Part 15 02.23.

develop plans. The CAA also required EPA to set emission standards for new or substantially modified stationary sources, for hazardous pollutants, and for moving sources. However, Congress was rather specific in dictating what the standards should be for automobiles.

Primary NAAQS are those "the attainment and maintenance of which in the judgment of the administrator, based on such criteria and allowing an adequate margin of safety, are requisite to protect the public health." Secondary NAAQS pertain to protection of the public welfare as it is affected by damage to plants, natural materials, and nonhuman animals. NAAQS are established without regard to cost. The economist might complain that this is irrational, for it is tantamount to assuming that the marginal-cost curve always lies below the marginal-damage curve. However, in practice EPA has considerable discretion in the interpretation of "adequate margin of safety," "public health," and even the somewhat philosophical matter of exactly who constitutes the "public."

The PSD Program   The original act was interpreted by the courts to imply that air quality should be protected in areas presently cleaner than required by the primary and secondary NAAQS, a point that has been affirmed by subsequent amendments. The so-called prevention of significant deterioration (PSD) program is intended to implement this protection. We might view the PSD approach as a fine-tuning device permitting us to adjust quality regulation for the preservation of special values in areas such as national parks. Those who favor the PSD approach argue that it improves the workings of the market by giving consumers the choice of going to an area cleaner than the NAAQS provide—a choice that would not necessarily be available otherwise. Its opponents might argue that PSD in a pristine but sparsely populated area could push a source of pollution into a more densely populated area that lacks redeeming "special values." In that case we might pay a price in human health or human life for the preservation of those special values.

National Emission Standards   The national atmospheric emission standards for stationary sources are intended to prevent industries for shopping around for areas with the weakest environmental controls; to prevent communities in search of industry from playing a negative-sum game in which they compete by lowering local standards. In general, the standards are to reflect a "degree of limitation achievable through the application of the best system of continuous emission reduction which (taking into consideration the cost of achieving such emission reduction and any non-air quality health and environmental impact and energy requirements) the Administrator determines has been adequately demonstrated." Note that the costs of control are explicitly taken into account, even if the particular decision rules to be used are not specified.

Nonattainment Areas   The above rule is modified somewhat for places whose air quality falls below the NAAQS, the so-called nonattainment areas. In such places new or substantially modified sources must use control technology with the lowest achievable emission rate. Examples of what constitutes such control technology may be drawn from anywhere in the world, and decisions are made on a case-by-case basis. Thus it may cost a firm a good deal more to open or operate a facility in a nonattainment than an attainment area, a point whose urban implications are discussed in the following section.

To overcome the problem of foot dragging in compliance, a noncompliance penalty has been introduced. When the source is not in compliance EPA has the authority to administratively levy a daily financial penalty equal to the capital and operating expenses the firm has saved by failing to comply. The penalty is in addition to any other penalties, civil or criminal, that may be imposed.

The Complexity of Regulation In connection with all of the above regulatory apparatus we note again the complexity of the task. Since regulation is generally intended to be technology-forcing, it is necessary to know not only what is now technologically feasible but also what is likely to be feasible in the future—not a trivial feat of prediction. Where the law permits costs and other considerations other than pure technical feasibility to be taken into account, complex decisions about tradeoffs may have to be made under considerations of considerable uncertainty. With regard to NAAQS we note that emissions standards are formulated essentially in isolation from ambient air quality. These two separate strands are presumably to be woven together in the state implementation plan. Because of the problems in relating emissions to air quality there is room for maneuver in demonstrating compliance.

As noted earlier, enforcement poses many problems. In particular, the difficulty of direct and continuous monitoring has caused regulatory agencies to place heavy reliance on indirect measures of compliance such as purchases of control equipment or indirect estimates based simply upon rate of production and assumed pollution-generating properties of the particular production process.

New Control Techniques

Given the high cost of abatement noted at the beginning of this chapter, the nation has moved in the direction of new and more efficient regulatory approaches, which in many ways resemble the models discussed earlier in this chapter. We illustrate this with two examples from the field of air quality. One technique now in use is the *bubble policy*. Where a plant emits a particular pollutant from more than one source it is permitted to treat the total emission as if it emerged from a single point on an imaginary bubble covering the entire plant. The firm can then achieve a plant-wide abatement goal in whatever manner is least costly rather than a fixed reduction at each point. In other words, the polluter has the motivation to achieve minimum cost by the sort of marginal-adjustment process we have discussed earlier. For example, a steel producer has achieved the required reduction in total emissions (and better) by taking steps to reduce windblown sources rather than by adopting more expensive measures to control furnace emissions.[13]

Another approach which encourages efficient marginal adjustment is the offset policy. In nonattainment areas a new firm moving in or a firm seeking to expand in

[13] R. Jeffrey Smith, "EPA and Industry Pursue Regulatory Options," *Science*, vol. 211, February 1981, pp. 796–798.

place must make a binding commitment to achieve a reduction in emissions greater than the amount of pollution it will emit from the new source. This reduction may be achieved either at the firm's other facilities in the area or by purchase from another firm. If more reduction is achieved than is required, the firm acquires credits, which it may use itself at a later date or which it may sell to other firms. In this manner a market for pollution rights is created as described earlier in the chapter. To be precise, the "right" to be traded is the right to have one's permit adjusted based on a prior or contemporaneous emission reduction certified by the regulatory agency. If the market functions efficiently, the NAAQS is met with minimum cost because the abatement is achieved at whichever point it is most economical to do so. Note that there is no auction of rights such as might be the case were we starting de novo. Rather, the rights are conferred automatically on those who are in operation on the starting date: in effect, these sources receive a windfall. New sources essentially pay for the cleanup of old sources. Some have questioned the fairness of this arrangement. One might carry the offset idea further by establishing a banking or exchange system for offsets. A few attempts have been made in this direction, but the technique is still in the preliminary stage. Finally, we might consider a system in which there is trading or offsetting between different pollutants. This would require development of a common denominator. All damages would have to be expressed either in monetary terms or in some other standard unit (sometimes referred to as a *numeraire* in economic literature).

ENVIRONMENTAL QUALITY AND URBAN AREAS

Pollution problems are often more serious in urban than in nonurban areas for two reasons. First, the greater concentration of pollution sources may produce higher levels of pollution. Second, the concentration of population may mean that there are a larger number of individuals at risk. However, in general, we tend to deal with pollution problems in much the same way in urban as in nonurban areas. For reasons discussed earlier, most emission standards are technology-based rather than based upon ambient pollution levels. Thus the same pollution abatement technology and performance might be required on a smokestack or other emitter in a densely populated urban area as in a sparsely settled exurban area. In fact, one reason that emission standards do not generally vary between urban and nonurban areas is that Congress, in enacting environmental legislation, was concerned that stricter standards in urban areas might drive economic activity out of urban areas.[14]

One significant feature of the environmental legislation passed in the 1970s was the call for full disclosure of environmental impacts. As mentioned earlier, the 1970 National Environmental Policy Act mandated the preparation of an environmental impact statement prior to the taking of any federal action likely to have a

---

[14] See for example, U.S. Congress, House Committee on Interstate and Foreign Commerce, *Clean Air Act Amendments of 1970: Report to Accompany H.R. 17255*, 91st Cong., 2d sess., H. Rept. 91-1146, 1970, pp. 9–11; and U.S. Congress, Senate Committee on Public Works, *National Air Quality Standards Act of 1970: Report to accompany S. 4358*, 91st Cong., 2d, sess., S. Rept. 91-1196, 1970, pp. 15–19.

"significant impact on the environment." Since a great many municipal actions have some element of federal participation, this means that an EIS is likely to figure prominently in the planning and implemention of any major project. Even in the absence of federal involvement, some state laws also call for environmental impact assessments to be made. The purpose of these requirements is to cause government officials to take environmental consequences into account when making decisions. They do not preempt these officials' actual decision-making powers. In other words there is nothing in the laws to stop decision makers from approving an action that would be damaging to the environment, providing that the environmental consequences have been taken into account.

One consequence of the EIS requirement is that it frequently furnishes grounds for litigation by those opposed to a particular project. For example, both the government of New York City and the state government have wanted to accept federal funding for the building of Westway. This is a highway that would run along the west shore of Manhattan and, according to its proponents, make a major contribution to reducing traffic congestion on city streets. The project has been opposed by many residents of adjacent neighborhoods and also by some who favor diversion of funds from Westway to public transportation. Opponents of the project have blocked it with an environmentally based suit, which charges that the effect of Westway upon marine life along Manhattan's Hudson shore was not adequately considered. A federal judge found that state and federal officials had "colluded" in concealing information about the effect of Westway on the river and, particularly, about its effects upon striped bass in the river. He ordered a reconsideration of the effects of Westway. Subsequently *The New York Times* reported that "the Army Corps of Engineers required at least two more years to assess the impact of the Westway on striped bass in the Hudson River before it could consider granting the project a permit." According to *The Times*, the project has "been tangled in red tape and suits for at least 12 years."[15] Whether Westway will ever be built remains to be seen. Like many other planning questions, this one may well be settled neither by the planners nor the politicians, but by the courts.

In general, some people argue that environmental impact reporting requirements act as a significant constraint on growth in that they (1) add significant transaction costs to major projects and (2) can impose long time delays by providing opponents of a project with the means to cause delays on procedural grounds. The environmentalists, on the other hand, tend to argue that all of the above is as it should be. Developers are being forced to take environmental considerations into account and are penalized if (and only if) they fail to do so. Since costs that were once external are now internal, the supply curve for development is being shifted to the left, and as a result less development is occurring. This, they argue, is the result of improving the market, and thus it leads to a more efficient allocation of society's resources.

Admittedly, environmental legislation and our raised environmental consciousness have strengthened the hand of those seeking to limit growth in many

[15] "Army's Engineers to Study Westway for 2 More Years," *The New York Times*, September 14, 1983, p. 1.

suburban and nonurban areas. Environmental legislation and concerns furnish, respectively, legal tools and rationales for opposing growth. The cynical might say that environmental considerations furnish respectable reasons for the basically self-interested defense of privilege. Rather than being antipeople, especially less affluent people, one can be protree. Freiden, who takes an extremely strong position on this, states that environmental considerations are being used by the affluent in a "powerful, ideologically driven crusade to keep the average citizen from home-ownership and the good life in the suburbs."[16] The writer disagrees. While it is indeed true that environmental provisions are occasionally used for the "wrong" reasons, in a much larger number of cases they play their intended role of seeking to correct acknowledged market failures.

BOX 12-2

CHANGING THE PRICE SIGNALS TO IMPROVE THE URBAN ENVIRONMENT

If a good is free it will be consumed down to the point at which the marginal utility of its use is zero. By that point the negative externalities associated with its use may be considerable. Putting a price on the good will thus move us to a more efficient allocation of resources. The suggestions by Professor Donald C. Shoup of the University of California at Los Angeles in "Breaking Out of the Tangle Caused by Parking Subsidies" are somewhat unusual in that he proposes several schemes by which all parties appear to benefit.

Two out of three American commuters . . . park free—at their employer's expense. Free parking at work may seem harmless or even beneficial, but it isn't: it contributes to traffic congestion, wastes gasoline and pollutes the air by encouraging commuters to drive to work alone.

In 1969 researchers at the University of Southern California surveyed two groups of government employees who parked in the downtown civic center. The federal employees paid for their spaces while the county employees did not. Only 40 percent of the federal employees drove to work alone, while 72 percent—almost twice as many—of the county employees did so.

A 1981 survey of commuters in Baltimore found that 59 percent of those who paid to park drove to work compared with 70 percent of those who could park free. Among the group with access to free parking only 10 percent commuted by bus, while more than twice as many bus riders (22 percent) were found among the group that had to pay for parking.

Subsidized parking helps only those who drive to work, and does even that unequally because it doesn't reward car poolers. If an employer provides free parking to both car poolers and solo drivers, each employee in a two-person car pool receives only one-half the parking subsidy given to the solo driver.

Employees pay no personal income tax on the cash value of parking subsidies provided as a fringe benefit. This exemption encourages employers to subsidize parking rather than pay higher salaries. For example, a couple with a taxable income of $30,000 a year face a combined state and federal income tax rate of 50 percent in California, so their employer-paid parking can be worth twice its fair market value in taxable salary. But even if an employer already subsidizes parking, he can still encourage ride-sharing without reducing anyone's subsidy. Consider the following strategies.

---

[16] B. J. Frieden, *The Environmental Protection Hustle*, MIT, Cambridge, 1979.

An employer who, say, pays $50 a month for parking spaces and gives them to employees for $15, could offer employees a salary increase of $25 as an alternative to the parking subsidy. Employees who choose the $25-a-month salary increase instead of the $35-a-month parking subsidy would be better off, after taxes, or they wouldn't voluntarily choose it. The employer would save $10 a month, less any payroll taxes on the $25-a-month salary increase. And the rest of us would benefit because fewer commuters would drive to work alone.

Employers can encourage ride-sharing by offering parking price discounts to car poolers. The same employer who pays $50 a month for parking spaces and leases them to commuters for $15 a month could allow car poolers to park free. By teaming up, drivers would save on gas and other driving costs as well as parking. The employer would provide only one subsidy of $50 a month for a single parking space instead of two subsidies of $35 for two parking spaces. Again, everyone concerned would be better off.

Employers can encourage ride-sharing by offering other fringe benefits, such as child care or improved health insurance as an alternative to free parking. Offering benefits equal in cost to parking subsidies would enhance job attractiveness without increasing employer costs, and deflate the demand for parking spaces without deterring commuters from working downtown.

If alternatives to parking subsidies existed, more commuters would do what they have long been urged to do—ride the bus, carpool or bicycle to work, or even take to their skates.[17]

An issue of concern for urban areas has been that environmental requirements might favor nonurban over urban areas and thus compound the economic plight of many cities. A reason for believing this is the likelihood that it is more difficult to attain acceptable ambient levels of pollution in areas with high concentrations of emitters. Indeed, many cities are currently in nonattainment areas for one or more air pollutants. Major new industrial sources wishing to locate in these areas must meet special requirements (relating to emission standards, offsets, and preconstruction permits), which are likely to involve greater costs than those faced in areas where the ambient standards are attained. However, this situation represents an exception to the more general rule that federal emission standards are the same regardless of location. As noted earlier, in order to avoid producing urban flight, the Congress intentionally avoided mandating different emission requirements for urban and nonurban areas. Because emissions standards are national, states are also prevented from competing by lowering environmental standards.

Evidence on the existence of significant urban-to-nonurban shifts due to pollution controls is generally lacking. It appears that where differences in abatement costs exist, the additional burden in urban areas is usually small compared to other costs that influence the choice of location. For example, in the Portland cement industry, a study by Newby suggests that, all other things being equal, attainment rather than nonattainment areas are favored for plant locations.[18] Since nonurban areas are more likely to be attainment areas this would appear to show some nonurban effect of environmental controls. However, the

[17] Excerpted from *The Los Angeles Times*, Op Ed page, March 14, 1983, by permission.
[18] Timothy W. Newby, *The Impact of Air Quality Regulations on Industrial Plant Location Decisions*, graduate paper, Virginia Polytechnic Institute and State University, September 1981.

study also suggests that the attainment status of the area is a relatively small factor compared with other considerations that weigh in the location decision. As noted earlier, labor-force and market-access issues are very often the dominant considerations in the choice of industrial and commercial location, and these appear to far outweigh differences in the cost of complying with environmental regulations. According to the National Commission on Air Quality, "studies that considered the limited data available concerning plant migrations and siting decisions indicate that environmental regulations have an insignificant effect on plant closings, migrations, or interregional siting decisions."[19]

[19] National Commission on Air Quality, *To Breathe Clean Air*, March 1981, p. 195. The Commission cited: William J. Stanley, and Associates, *Environmental and Other Factors Influencing Industrial Plant Migrations*, NTIS Document No. 79/24, Chicago Institute of Natural Resources, August 1979.

PART **THREE**

THE URBAN FUTURE

CHAPTER 13

THE URBAN FUTURE

Most futurists—those whose profession it is to think and write about the future—take great pains to inform their readers and clients that they do not predict the future. In fact, one think tank that specializes in futures studies not only makes the above point but goes a step further. In at least some of its reports, it notes in the foreword that in the state in which it is based it is illegal to claim to be able to foretell the future!

The reasons for such caution are not hard to find. In human affairs, where causes are numerous and causal relations are generally not fully understood, our understanding of how we got to our present state is generally quite imperfect. However, even if our understanding of past events and past causality were perfect, our capacity to predict the future would be limited by our uncertainty about what new forces will appear on the scene. For example, much has been made in this book about the effects of technological change. Technology forecasting is a high-risk activity, and the track record of those who have practiced it is not especially inspiring. It is difficult enough to assess the probable course of existing areas of technology. But it is, by definition, impossible to anticipate original ideas. Furthermore, it seems to be very difficult to anticipate new combinations of existing ideas and technologies.

Social movements are no easier to anticipate. The civil rights movement of the 1950s and the women's liberation and environmental movements of the 1960s both burst upon society with relatively little warning. All had their advocates for many years, and a perceptive observer might have predicted their ultimate emergence and triumph. But the speed with which, and the time at which, they transformed themselves from minor movements to major societywide forces was beyond prediction.

The reader may notice, or complain, that this chapter on the future isn't very futuristic. It is not difficult to image an urban high-tech future. We might live and work in megastructures, travel about the city on monorails, people movers, or small individually dispatched and routed vehicles moving along an electronically controlled guideway, take an occasional intercity trip by bullet train or gravity tube, and be served by utilities that are unseen and unheard. We might even live in Paolo Soleri type megastructures half a mile high, covering several hundred acres, and containing the homes and workplaces for a population of several hundred thousand people. Or we might live in a compact domed city in which rain and snow never fall and in which we have virtually total control over the climate. Most of the technology needed to implement these visions now exists and a good deal of it is now in operation in at least a few places. People movers and monorails are in use in a number of airports and cities. The technology for the electronic guideway and the automobile to go with it has been here for some years. The same is true for the individually dispatched and routed mass transportation system. Intercity trains in Japan now regularly cruise at over 100 mph and a French prototype cruises at over 200 mph.

One reason that we do not pursue the high-density, high-technology urban future further is that technology and tastes appear to be taking us in precisely the opposite direction for reasons discussed elsewhere in this book. Densities that would justify a people mover are rare and, given the continuing dispersion of population and jobs, getting rarer every year. As noted in Chapter 9, conventional rail-based modes do not achieve competitive per unit costs until very high volumes per corridor are reached. For very high speed systems, which require high-technology vehicles and very well maintained rail beds, achieving competitive per unit costs will be even more difficult.

Modern construction technology might enable us to house hundreds of families in comfort in a high-rise structure with a "footprint" of an acre. But without widespread demand for that kind of existence, such structures will remain no more than design problems for architecture students. Or, perhaps, they will be confined to one or two atypical areas of spectacularly high land values, such as Manhattan's upper east side or the area adjacent to Chicago's lakeshore.

Another reason for eschewing serious discussion of the high-density, high-technology city is the matter of urban public finance discussed in Chapter 10. For most of the nation's more densely built areas, the foreseeable fiscal future looks stringent. Slowly growing or even stagnant tax bases will be required to support the full range of municipal services and deal with the capital shortfall discussed earlier. Before major new capital-intensive initiatives can be undertaken the funds for maintenance of a prosaic but essential infrastructure must be found. Finding the funds to keep trucks from plunging through other West Side Highways is likely to take precedence over more exciting and imaginative projects.

THINKING ABOUT THE URBAN FUTURE

One way to think about urban futures is to ask two questions:

1 What can we say about the prospects for some of the underlying societywide processes discussed earlier in this book?

2 Do the main trends we observe appear to be essentially self-limiting or essentially self-perpetuating?

The material that follows is projection based on present and recent events and trends. It is not prediction and it is offered in the full knowledge that at any time new and important actors may suddenly appear on the stage and alter the plot in ways we cannot image.

Underlying Social and Economic Trends

In earlier chapters we noted the demographic force behind the growth of urban populations. The major factors in the last several decades have been the baby boom beginning after World War II and persisting into the mid-1960s, immigration, and the migration of millions of rural households to urban areas, the latter resulting from the rapid mechanization of agriculture after World War II. Among the other most general and pervasive factors reshaping urban areas we noted the long-term increase in real income and the long-term reduction in the cost of transportation and communication. Let us take up these factors in order.

Demographic Forces   From 1980 to 1981 the population of the United States increased by 0.9 percent, the combined result of natural increase (births minus deaths) and net migration (immigration minus emigration). Twenty years earlier, from 1960 to 1961 the increase was 1.7 percent. The difference is primarily due to the difference in birth rates, for 1960 and 1961 was very close to the peak of the baby boom. Thus, in the broadest sense, there is much less demographic force behind urban area population growth now than there has been in previous decades.

In the 2 decades after World War II the population pressure exerted on urban areas by national population growth was greatly augmented by rural-to-urban migration. The agricultural labor force of the country is now about one-third the size it was at the end of World War II. Thus no matter what further increases in agricultural productivity may lie ahead, another rural to urban migration on anything like the scale of the 1950s and 1960s is not possible. In fact, at present there is a small net migration from metropolitan to nonmetropolitan areas.

The demographic force behind household formation should also lessen in the next few years, further easing growth pressures on metropolitan areas. This is because of the age structure of the U.S. population. At present, people in the late teens and early 20s are those who were born in the last years of the baby boom. By the end of the 1980s those in the same age range will come from the much smaller cohorts born in the first years of the so-called baby bust.

Whether birth rates will remain near their present low levels cannot be predicted with any confidence. Although we have much experience and much data, there is no agreement among demographers on a general model for predicting future births. Some demographers view the baby boom as an aberration and the current low fertility levels as putting us back on the long-term trend line. But others forecast a rebound phenomenon well before the end of the century.

Immigration is also a wild card in the demographic deck. At present, about one-fourth of U.S. population growth each year is directly accounted for by legal immigration. How much is accounted for by illegal immigration is not known. There seems little doubt that for the foreseeable future there will be no shortage of potential immigrants. But how the U.S. will move on immigration policy, both in its admission of legal immigrants and its resistance to illegal immigration, is unknown. Pressures from a diverse anti-immigration constituency, including organized labor, environmental groups, and others, will be opposed by those who adhere to a political tradition of relative openness to immigration. On the matter of illegal immigration there is a real question of just how much we are willing to reduce the openness of society and intrude on privacy to effectively seal the nation's borders. The outcome is not easy to predict.

Perhaps the most certain statement we can make about demography is that, barring some catastrophic event or a sudden decrease in life expectancy, the retirement-age population of the U.S. will continue to rise for several decades. For the people who will make that assertion come true have already been born. The biggest increase in older population will come in the early twenty-first century as the children of the baby boom enter the foothills of old age. Life expectancy in the United States has been increasing slowly (about 3 years per decade), and there are no signs that the rate of increase is slowing. Obviously, continued increases in life span will further weight the population toward the upper end. Earlier, we noted the dispersing effects of a large and generally prosperous retirement-age population.

The Future of Real Income Growth   Previously we argued that increasing real per capita income may in itself be a very powerful decentralizing force. It permits people to spend more on housing and transportation and to allow nonpecuniary factors to weigh more heavily in their choice of residence. It has permitted us to treat older yet still usable housing stock and urban infrastructure as inferior goods, to be discarded years before their physical service lives are over. It has permitted us to make generous transfers to a retirement-age population. This further decouples the choice of place of residence from economic necessity and stimulates the growth of amenity-rich areas, which are often far from major urban concentrations. Continued growth in real income would presumably continue to be decentralizing, while reduction in real income might be a powerful centralizing force.

Until the early 1970s real capita income in the United States rose on the strength of increasing productivity, a result of more and better capital per worker, and a better-trained and educated work force. Since the early 1970s productivity per worker has remained relatively constant. Real per capita income continued to rise modestly on the strength of increased labor force participation rates. That force, however, has obvious limits.

Views on the future of productivity vary widely. Pessimists believe that further increases in productivity will be hard to achieve and that increases in resource costs may actually force real per capita income down.[1] Some have argued that as

[1] A generally pessimistic age-of-limits view can be found in the works of Dennis Meadows and publications of the Club of Rome. For example, see *The Limits to Growth*, Dennis L. and Donella H. Meadows, Universe, N.Y., 1972. For a more recent discussion of global modeling see Donella H. Meadows et. al., *Groping in the Dark, The First Decade of Global Modelling*, Wiley, N.Y., 1982. The U.S. Council on Environmental Quality, *Global 2000 Report to the President*, 1980, has taken a generally pessimistic view. More recently P. Hawkens et al., *Seven Tomorrows: Toward a Voluntary*

we shift into a service economy—fewer workers involved in manufacturing, agriculture, and materials extraction—productivity growth will slow because we are shifting away from areas in which capital is readily substituted for labor.

The optimists argue that we are in the early stages of a production revolution, comparable to that brought about by the steam engine and the mechanical technology of the early nineteenth century. This is the application of the computer to the entire range of economic activity, including those areas that are now highly labor intensive. In the service sector, where productivity growth has long lagged behind growth in manufacturing and agriculture, major increases in productivity will be forthcoming as we learn how to integrate the computer into what are now essentially manual operations.

Proponents of this view would argue that we are currently witnessing the beginnings of this revolution. Secretarial and clerical work is being facilitated by word processors and the other technologies of the electronic office. The filing cabinet is giving way to the random-access disk. Lawyers and law clerks are using electronic databases to search out precedents rather than by poring through printed volumes. Physicians are beginning to use computerized expert systems in the making of diagnoses. In general, all those service activities that involve the manipulation, storage, and retrieval of words and numbers as well as many areas that involve abstract thought will be greatly aided as we learn how to combine humans and computers in complex systems.[2] In manufacturing itself, computer-aided design and computer-aided manufacturing appear to promise substantial improvement in both products and productivity.[3]

Whether the pessimists or the optimists have the better side of the argument remains to be seen. We return to some of the implications shortly.

Transportation and Communications Costs   The effects of improved communications technology have been discussed at length earlier. There is general agreement that the computing and telecommunications revolution shows no signs of stopping. There is every reason to believe that the real cost of electronic communications will continue to fall and that new capabilities will continue to emerge.

The question of transportation costs is more arguable. So far as the automobile is concerned, the big unknown is fuel costs. Informed opinions on the future of fuel costs vary widely. It is possible that fuel costs might rise so rapidly that increases in fuel efficiency would not be able to keep up and real per mile fuel costs will rise. It is also possible that real fuel costs will rise, but at a slow enough rate that increases in fuel efficiency will cancel them out. It is also possible that real fuel costs will not rise, or even that they may fall somewhat, as has been world experience since about 1980.

History, Bantam, New York, 1982, take a resource-short future as given even though the book, as its title implies, presents a variety of scenarios for the future. For more optimistic views see the works of the late Herman Kahn, for example, *The Next 200 Years*, Wm. Morrow, N.Y., 1976. See also Julian Simon, *The Ultimate Resource*, Princeton University Press, Princeton N.J., 1983.

[2] For a discussion of the past and future effects of automation in various fields see articles by Leontieff, Guiliano, Gunn and others in the *Scientific American*, September 1982.

[3] G. Bylinsky, "The Race to the Automated Factory," *Fortune*, February 21, 1983, p. 52.

The situation with public transportation is somewhat different. Due to its generally greater energy efficiency, its cost is likely to be less influenced by fuel price increases. However, as a labor-intensive activity, its cost will be far more sensitive to wage increases than will be the cost of private transportation. In a sense the traveler who switches from public to private transportation is substituting capital for labor. If, over time, the cost of capital falls relative to the cost of labor the effect will of course be to favor private transportation.

The Momentum of Present Trends

To what extent are the major urban trends we now observe self-perpetuating, or positive-feedback, processes. Consider the question of agglomeration itself. In Chapter 1 we argued that a positive-feedback effect operated there. Each new unit of commercial activity and each new worker produced agglomeration economies that made the area still more attractive to new firms and new workers. Thus, it appears to follow that each loss of a firm or a worker reduces the agglomeration economies of the place and predisposes to further loss of economic mass. After some loss, countervailing forces that stop the process may develop. For example, falling demand for housing and commercial locations will exert downward pressure on prices and rents, making the city more attractive as a residential and commercial location. Then, too, loss of activity may reduce some diseconomies of scale such as congestion. In some cases a natural feature, such as a deep-water port, that yields a competitive advantage in some particular economic activity may place an absolute lower limit on a city's work force. Thus there may a stopping point to positive feedback or the self-perpetuating process described above. But if there is such a point, its location may be quite problematical for many cities. Particularly in the case of the largest urban places, a very large amount of decline may have to occur before these countervailing processes become manifest.

Is Regional Growth Self-Perpetuating?   It would appear that regional growth may have many self-perpetuating characteristics. Regional growth presumably creates agglomeration economies in markets, labor supplies, and infrastructure just as we argued that metropolitan-area growth does.

Whether or not we can see limiting factors appears to depend on the region. In the south-central and southeastern parts of the country it is hard to identify limiting factors of an environmental nature or limiting factors stemming from congestion. In the southwest, say, roughly from Texas to the Pacific coast there are serious problems of water supply, and these may limit growth. Falling water tables have already forced a cutback in agricultural acreage in parts of Texas. There is also a major political and social question hanging over the future of the southwest. In his book entitled *The Nine Nations of North America* Garreaux refers to the southwestern corner of the United States as well as parts of northern Mexico as Mexamerica, a way of dramatizing the very strong links across the Rio Grande River.[4] The southwestern United States is closely tied to Mexico in terms of trade, movement of population, and in less tangible ways as well. Events in Mexico—a country that has been stable so far but suffers from great degrees of

---

[4] J. Garreaux, *The Nine Nations of North America*, Avon, New York, 1982.

inequality, very high unemployment, and extremely rapid population growth—may well have powerful but difficult-to-anticipate effects upon events in the American southwest.

Given its climate, lack of energy resources, and rough topography, New England could be expected to decline. But in the last several years the region has staged something of a turnaround, largely on the basis of its ability to attract high-technology industry. Apparently people's perception of its quality of life causes it to do better than consideration of purely objective characteristics would lead one to expect.

Positive Feedback in the Level of Taxation   Another area in which positive feedback may operate is taxation and expenditures. As Muller has noted, the one thing that does not seem to decline readily in declining areas is municipal expenditure.[5] One reason for this is that even though population and employment shrink, many elements of the municipal budget such as debt service do not. Many elements of the municipal infrastructure, such as the number of miles of water mains under the streets, remain constant in size when population and jobs depart. Still another reason for Muller's observation is that the more affluent members of the population tend to be more mobile. Thus net outmigration may produce a smaller than proportional decline in the numbers of those heavily dependent on social services and a larger than proportional decline in those who yield more in taxes and other revenues than they cost the municipal treasury. If the need for public expenditures declines more slowly than the tax base shrinks, then loss of revenue leads to higher rates of taxation. The higher taxation makes the area less attractive to firms and to affluent residents, and this in turn further shrinks the tax base. It is hard to see where the limits of the process are to be found unless there is an outside source of funds whose beneficence is triggered when local tax effort passes some threshold.

Positive Feedback and Political Strength   The distribution of national political power may also be a positive-feedback situation. As population changes, representation in Congress changes and the population-losing area suffers a loss of political strength. The shift in political power is probably quite slow. Reapportionment occurs only once every decade (following the decennial census), and the shift in effective political strength may lag still more because of the importance of seniority within the Congress. Over the long term, however, the effects of demographic shifts on political power may be substantial. Given that federal policy has enormous effects on the fate of cities, this does not bode well for the future of cities. The relationship between loss of central-city political strength at the national level and the tax issue cited immediately above is clear.

The Tipping-Point Phenomenon   Another positive-feedback situation was discussed under the term *tipping point* in Chapter 3. The tendency of areas to tip concentrates poor minority populations in central areas. If this reduces the ability

---

[5] T. Muller, "The Declining and Growing Metropolis—A Fiscal Comparison," in *Post Industrial America,* Center for Urban Policy Research, Rutgers, 1975, p. 207. See also Muller's article in R. W. Burchell and D. Listokin (eds.), *Cities Under Stress: The Fiscal Crisis of Urban America,* Center for Urban Policy Research, Rutgers, 1981.

of the area to attract affluent residents and economic activity, then that area is less able to provide employment and finance public services. This inability, in turn, further impoverishes the resident population, making the area still less attractive as a location for economic activity.

Transportation Choice   Transportation choice also may be characterized by positive feedback. Automobile ownership destroys the demand for public transportation, which reduces the amount of transit service that can be provided. This, in turn, increases the demand for automobiles. Over half of the operating costs of public transportation are now carried by subsidy. It is clear that if such subsidies were not forthcoming, the amount of public transportation that would survive in the United States would be minimal. The per trip subsidy now required is quite large and the percentage of the population dependent on public transportation is relatively small (see figures in Chapter 9). Thus it is politically realistic to argue that massive increases in subsidy are unlikely to be forthcoming in the near future.

As transportation shapes land use still another loop is set up. The land-use pattern adapts to private transportation, which both increases the demand for private transportation and increases the cost of supplying any given level of public transportation. Limits to the loop may exist, but they are not discernible.

Other feedback loops might also be identified. The central point here is that we have identified a number of loops of the positive variety. This strongly suggests that there are considerable forces that will cause present trends to continue or even accelerate.

Energy Costs and Urban Form

No contingency affecting the fate of urban areas has received more attention in the last several years than rising energy costs. Thus the question appears to merit separate treatment here, even though we touched on it earlier under the heading of transportation costs. The argument that first appeared in the period after the 1973 oil embargo and the subsequent price rises was that higher energy costs would force population and employment back into urban areas where trip distances were shorter and the availability of public transportation was greater. There does not seem to be any hard evidence that this has happened. But, of course, it can be argued that costs have not been high enough for long enough to have brought about these effects. Some attempts at mathematical modeling have been attempted, but given the complexity of the problem and our relative lack of useful experience, the results are hardly definitive. Above all of this speculation, of course, looms the question of whether real energy costs will climb sharply. Here we have our choice of experts with an opinion to fit almost any taste on the subject.

It still seems reasonable to believe that very high energy costs would force some change in land-use pattern. However, there is considerable uncertainty as to precisely what that effect might be. It is now realized that a variety of different urban geometries might be more energy-efficient than the present form of most U.S. metropolitan areas. One serious possibility is the dense central city mentioned above. Such a physical arrangement reduces average trip length, makes possible an increased number of trips by foot or bicycle, and favors the use of public transportation. A very different, yet equally plausible, geometry would be a multicentric pattern with a high degree of local autonomy. A pattern of nodes in which homes, stores, offices, and other major trip origins and destinations were located in close proximity might be just as energy-efficient in terms of transportation costs as the dense central city and perhaps more attractive to many metropolitan-area residents.

Nontransportation Effects of Energy Costs   Nontransportation aspects of potential energy cost increases also leave a number of question marks. As a matter of geometry the per unit cost of heating an apartment house should be lower than that of heating a single-family house because the former exposes less surface area per dwelling unit (or unit of volume) to the outside air. That should favor denser patterns of development. But it is not clear that things will work out that way. Retrofitting old housing to achieve energy efficiency seems to be more difficult than building for energy efficiency in the first instance. A new single-family house built to modern insulation standards may, in fact, be more energy-efficient than an old apartment in spite of the geometrical argument above. Then, too, part of energy conservation is behavioral rather than structural. The division between ownership and occupancy in rental units produces a poorer set of motivations to conserve than does the situation in which the owner is also the occupant. To further muddy the waters, we might note that even if rising energy costs do promote a resurgence in multifamily construction, we do not know whether this will favor central places or if we will see a clumps of multifamily buildings in formerly single-family areas.

Technological choice also introduces uncertainty here. If we respond to higher energy costs primarily by trying to use the energy from fossil fuels or nuclear power more efficiently, that might favor higher density or clustered developments. On the other hand if our response is a major turn toward solar energy, that will favor a more scattered pattern of development, for solar technologies work best with a minimum of interference effects.[6]

The effect of higher energy costs on the location of manufacturing processes is also uncertain. On a prima facie basis, higher costs should favor sites with rail, water, or, where applicable, pipeline access, since all of these modes are substantially more energy-efficient than truck. Higher energy costs will probably also tend to favor southern and southwestern locations because of lower heating costs and the greater intensity of solar radiation (if solar energy technologies become widespread). Over the long term, higher transport costs stemming from higher energy costs might also favor more clustering of related industries. That might favor large metropolitan areas over smaller ones. Or, it might favor the sort of scattered self-sufficiency we hypothesized earlier. Whether it would favor the movement of manufacturers back to metropolitan areas to save trucking costs, just as they once moved out to save on labor, land, and tax costs, remains to be seen.

---

[6] Solar costs are still high compared to fossil fuel costs for many purposes, particularly generation of electric power. However, solar costs are falling rapidly. For a discussion of prospects for solar energy see B. Solomon, "Will Solar Sell?" *Science 82*, vol. 3, no. 3, pp. 70–76, April 1982.

URBAN PROSPECTS

The preceding material suggests that there is considerable force behind the continuance of present trends and that it is not easy to identify forces that will bring about an abrupt change in direction. Thus it seems reasonable to discuss what we might term a "continuation of present trends" future. Assume we accept the view that the outmigration of population from central areas will continue and that the central city will continue to have difficulty in holding onto employment, although this may not be true of all categories of employment.

This suggests that many cities are likely to go through a period of decline and move toward a new equilibrium at a much lower level of employment and population than is now the case. Where that equilibrium is, if it exists at all, may depend upon whether there is some irreducible core of activity that cities can hold. If such a core exists, a major part of it is likely to be in administrative and related activities where face-to-face contact is important. How strong the cities' grip on such activities is will probably depend upon the degree to which electronic communications erode the need for direct personal contact. Another component of this core might be activities that are relatively uncommon tastes. A type of entertainment that 1 person in 100 enjoys will require a larger population to generate a minimum number of customers than will a type of entertainment that 1 person out of every 10 enjoys.

After the city shrinks to a new equilibrium, the labor force of the export sector might be composed largely of high-interaction professional, technical, and managerial workers. The service sector of the labor force would be composed largely of the entrepreneurs and service workers who provide the services demanded by these relatively well-paid export sector workers.[7] The smaller labor force will mean a smaller population, permitting a less dense and more open pattern of physical development. A large, relatively low-quality housing stock may be replaced by a small, high-quality housing stock adjusted to a smaller but more prosperous population. The problem in this admittedly optimistic scenario is what happens to the urban population in the decades it takes us to get from here to there.

The Human Costs of Urban Decline

The scenario above implies a mismatch or structural-unemployment, problem with the city doing best in retaining the types of jobs that its poor residents are least capable of holding. More generally, it seems reasonable to believe that the outmigration of population will generally lag behind the outmigration of jobs. The experience of regions such as Appalachia suggests that populations may remain in place for years or even decades after the employment base that once supported them has gone. Firms, with their superior access to capital and their generally more rational decision-making processes, are likely to be a good deal more mobile than less-affluent households. If this last point is correct, the process of urban shrinkage is likely to produce decreased labor force participation rates and higher unemployment rates. That effect may be exacerbated by events in the central-city

[7] W. Baumol, "Technological Change and the New Urban Equilibrium," in R. W. Burchell and D. Listokin, op. cit.

housing market. As jobs are lost and outmigration occurs, the demand for central-city housing will weaken. Both housing costs and housing quality will fall relative to other areas. Relatively low-cost central-city housing is thus likely to become a trap for a population whose labor market ties are weak and whose subsistence comes largely from transfer payments or participation in the hidden economy discussed in Chapter 6. The potential for the creation of a permanent underclass in the above scenario seems clear.

Exceptions and Caveats

Before turning to the matter of public policy, we should note that the above is not only hypothetical but also extremely schematic. Even if the above scenario turns out to be on target in general, there is likely to be an enormous amount of variation from one city to another. One city, for example, might succeed in making the transition to a smaller but prosperous administrative and cultural center, while another might be unable to compete for those few quintessentially urban activities and decline without any endpoint in sight.

As noted elsewhere, the fate of a particular city or urban area must be considered in a regional context. Regional growth builds the markets for the city's export products, while regional decline shrinks that market. The relative size of the region's in- and outmigration streams will affect the city's migration experience. Tight regional housing markets may retard migration from the city to other parts of the region. But regional markets softened by outmigration may encourage outmigration from the city.

We must also note that many cities may follow paths that diverge quite sharply from the common experience because of peculiarities in their situations. For example, Miami has grown with remarkable vigor because events in Cuba since the rise of Fidel Castro made it a magnet for Cuban refugees. This, in turn, has made Miami the economic capital of the Caribbean. Then, too, the city's economy is partly floated on an ocean of cash generated by the drug trade. Neither of these factors could have been foreseen 25 years ago, nor is there any other city in America quite like Miami. The city of Denver is positioned to be, in Garreaux's words, the "gateway to the empty quarter" of North America.[8] If increases in energy prices cause a major expansion of extractive activity in the "empty quarter," Denver might follow a growth path very much *un*like that of most U.S. cities. The economic fate of New York City is tied to international trade and to the international movement of capital to a degree that may be true for very few other U.S. cities. The demography and economy of San Francisco is being reshaped by the fact, not predictable from any economic model, that it has become the gay capital of the western United States. It, too may follow an economic path quite different from most other U.S. cities. Just as Denver is the gateway to the "empty quarter," New Orleans may be the gateway to Gulf of Mexico oil. The facts of petroleum geology and the future of international oil markets may differentiate New Orleans' economic future from that of most other U.S. cities. Other examples of special situations with potentially atypical futures can be found.

---

[8] Garreaux, op. cit.

Dealing with Central-City Decline

Let us first consider what might be done about central-city decline generally. We pause to note that there now exists no national consensus that a major effort to preserve central cities at their present levels of population and employment is necessary.

In the most general way, the effort to stem the flow of activity of central cities would be a matter of changing the costs faced by those making locational decisions. For example, we might engage in heavy subsidization of central-city economic and residential location by grants and tax expenditures. We might attempt to assess the social costs of plant relocations from central to non-central locations and attempt to make the movers pay those costs as a way of discouraging such moves. Such a policy, we note, raises serious efficiency questions, might or might not survive court challenge, and would constitute a major change in the relationship of business and government. It is not advocated here; its possibility is simply noted.

We might also attempt to slow suburban growth by changes in tax and land-use policy. For example, we might install growth limitation policies in suburban areas and restructure the IRS code so as to cease favoring ownership over rental status. We might also begin spending less on suburban infrastructure and more on urban infrastructure. Again, we note a host of practical problems and serious objections to such policy. Why would the suburbs, which now contain more residents than central cities, agree to such policies? How do we justify attempting to overrule the demonstrated residential preferences of very large numbers of people? Would such heavyhanded policies be sustained in court? Again, to list policies is not necessarily to advocate them. One could go on in the above vein. But we would simply be listing more instruments, mostly financial, to make city locations more attractive and suburban and nonmetropolitan locations relatively less attractive. Assuming that the political force and legal consent for such policies could be found, would such policies work? Obviously, there is no certain way to tell short of trying.

Planning for Urban Shrinkage

The city planner of the past was largely preoccupied with the question of managing growth, for that was the predominant experience of most urban areas. The city planner of the future is much more likely to be preoccupied with the question of managing shrinkage. Unfortunately we have far less experience with the management of shrinkage than the management of growth. Shrinking in a manner that minimizes human costs and leaves us with a desirable end product will be, like growing old gracefully, easier said than done.

We might find ourselves confronted with difficult choices about whether to attempt to save or to write off deteriorated parts of cities that are losing population and jobs. If half of the housing units in a given area are abandoned and the area is plagued with street crime and arson, what do we do? One possibility is to try and save it with infusions of capital and social services. Another is to promote the departure of the remaining population, raze the area, and withdraw public services entirely. Arguments can be made for both courses. The merits of the case

---

BOX 13-1

MODELING URBAN POLICY EFFECTS

Bradbury, Downs, and Small tried to test a package of prourban policies on the city of Cleveland using computer simulation techniques.[9] First, taking 1975 as the base year, they projected population and employment in Cleveland to 1990 under the assumption that present trends and policies would continue. These projections showed population falling by 18 percent and employment falling by 17 percent, while suburban population climbed slightly and suburban jobs climbed considerably. They then ran a number of simulations to test a variety of policy options. These options were:

1 A job stimulus package including a development bank that finances capital investment in the city and a doubling of current CETA outlays as well as several smaller programs.
2 A housing package involving a large set of programs for both new construction and rehabilitation.
3 A transit package involving improvement of the existing system, a subway loop in the business district, and the building of exclusive busways on three existing radial routes.
4 A fiscal-equalization package. This would include government consolidation, a school financing system that equalizes school tax rates and per pupil expenditures among districts within the metropolitan area, and increased state aid to local government. The latter would bring Ohio up to the U.S. average.
5 A suburban growth control package which would reduce suburban household growth rates by 25 percent.

Each of the five policies was tested separately and then the effect of applying all five simultaneously was simulated. The all-out revitalization package showed that population loss would be reduced from 105,000 to 40,000 and the job loss would be reduced from 66,000 to 33,000. In rough terms, then, the general decline could be slowed to half of what would otherwise be the case.

The reader will recognize the very low probability of the nation being willing to commit the sorts of resources and make the institutional changes necessary to provide this sort of stimulation to large numbers of central cities. If the group's simulations are on target, they suggest that the very most public policy will be able to achieve is some slowing of the present trend. This is no reason to suggest that we either should or should not attempt to slow the tide, but only that we should not look for radical results from such an effort.

---

are likely to appear quite different to neighborhood residents and their advocates on the one hand and those who view the city on a more "macro" scale on the other. In fact, the writer observed one big-city housing commissioner shouted down and physically prevented from speaking at a public meeting when he attempted to suggest consideration of the sort of triage strategy implied by the second alternative. His career as housing commissioner ended shortly thereafter, largely over his raising of the triage question.[10] But in general the question of what

[9] Katherine L. Bradbury, Anthony Downs, and Kenneth A. Small, *Futures for a Declining City: Simulations for the Cleveland Area*, Academic, New York, 1981.
[10] The official in question was Roger Starr. The occasion was a presentation of the master plan for New York City at the Americana Hotel in Manhattan in the fall of 1969. The term *triage* comes from military medicine. In essence it implies withholding aid both from those wounded who will recover in any case and from those who will die in any case, while concentrating aid on those for whom aid will be the critical difference.

is to be saved and what is to be written off is likely to arise in various guises over the years if we are correct in our suppositions about urban shrinkage.

In the writer's view simply building new housing in areas with inadequate personal income is likely to be an unproductive strategy. Rehabilitation and selective demolition, followed by rebuilding at lesser densities, are likely to be more productive. To a large measure, the housing problem, like many central-city problems, may be one of how to shrink with a minimum human cost and in a way that does not foreclose the possibility of coming to a smaller but prosperous and desirable equilibrium.

Curiously enough, the urban renewal approach discussed in Chapter 8 might well work better under conditions of shrinkage than it did during the 1950s and 1960s. One problem that plagued urban renewal in the past was relocation. In a tight housing market the long time lag between land clearance and new residential construction works hardships on individuals and may destabilize adjacent areas. In a slack housing market, the loss of units will not be as much of a problem. Skillful use of an urban renewal-like technique to replace deteriorated and obsolete units with smaller numbers of high-quality units will, under slack market conditions, simply move the city toward its new equilibrium position without exacting the human costs experienced previously. Similar comments might be made about the commercial side of urban renewal. If the market for commercial space is relatively slack, it may be possible to demolish and rebuild with much less destruction of existing business activity than was previously experienced.

Preventing the Formation of a Permanent Urban Underclass

What policy options are open to resist the formation or enlargement of the urban underclass? One is simply to let the market take its course. If the movement of population and jobs leaves behind a stranded population, then we will meet its needs with transfers and social services but otherwise let the chips fall where they may. With the exception of the Great Depression, when we engaged in massive public job creation, we have tended to leave such matters to the marketplace. We might also note that the above approach is, to a large extent, what we do now.

The market approach has some appeal on traditional efficiency grounds. But it is worrisome in other ways. The creation of a permanent underclass holds potential for social chaos and disruption upon which it is virtually impossible to place a price. In the long run, it may not be efficient either because of the damage it does to the human capital stock of the nation. Damaged people and damaged families not only are less productive but also can and do impose all sorts of costs on society.

A second possibility, discussed in Chapter 6, is enrichment. This is the allocation of resources to core areas to provide jobs and training and prevent a generation of urban youth from falling into an underclass pattern of existence. Depending upon the ideological temper of the times, enrichment might be accomplished primarily by private capital motivated by grants and tax expenditures or by direct public job creation. The intention would not be to permanently halt the outflow of economic activity from central areas but simply to slow it down to reduce the time lag between the mobility of population and economic activity.

The other possibility, also mentioned in Chapter 6, is dispersion. This might involve a combination of job training, job placement, migration assistance, and other steps to help central-city populations go where the jobs are. Both dispersal and enrichment strategies are intended for the same problem, urban structural unemployment. Thus, in spite of their apparent oppositeness, it might well be that both strategies could be employed simultaneously.

Both enrichment and dispersal will work better in an environment of high growth and low unemployment nationally. We are likely to tolerate the short-term inefficiency of an enrichment strategy in a national condition of growing prosperity. It will be much easier for a relatively prosperous majority to give up part of a growth increment than to accept an absolute loss. The dispersal strategy will run into opposition from receiving areas in any case, as suburban resistance to subsidized housing has clearly demonstrated. However, opposition will be more determined if the receiving areas are having their own unemployment problems. This may be equally true whether the receiving area is another metropolitan area, a nonmetropolitan area, or simply the suburban ring around the distressed central city. Thus the same growth in real income that has helped pull urban areas apart and thus create the possibility of a permanent underclass may also be necessary to provide the willingness and wherewithal to take serious steps to prevent that possibility from materializing.

INDEX